power structures [writing <u>on</u> a country
vs. writing <u>from/in</u> a country

Gendering Modern German History

Class Discussion
_____

1) Gender matters
- <u>Nat'l Differences</u> (influences)
↳ diff. trajectory

• Intro, 2, 6
㊟ Translation (of concepts)
⟶ stress reading G & G intro
(arguments placed diff
+ Canning text translation

[- structure
- economic
- connection btw politics + history
- living processes

- how represented are ♀ in profession

GENDERING MODERN GERMAN HISTORY

Rewriting Historiography

Edited by
Karen Hagemann and Jean H. Quataert

Berghahn Books
New York • Oxford

First published in 2007 by

Berghahn Books
www.berghahnbooks.com

Library of Congress Cataloging-in-Publication Data
Gendering modern German history : rewriting historiography / edited by Karen Hegemann and
Jean H. Qartaert.
p. cm.
Includes bibliographical references and index.
ISBN 1-84545-207-0 (hbk. : alk. paper) -- 978-1-84545-442-5 (pbk. : alk. paper)
1. Germany—History—Historiography. 2. Feminist theory. 3. Historiography—
Germany. 4. Historiography—United States. I. Hagemann, Karen. II. Quataert,
Jean H. (Jean Helen), 1945–

DD86.G446 2007
943.087072—dc22   2006101299

British Library Cataloguing in Publication Data
A catalogue record for this book is available from the British Library

Printed in the United States on acid-free paper

ISBN-978-1-84545-207-0 hardback, 978-1-84545-442-5 paperback

Contents

PREFACE

After more than thirty years of research, it is time for a critical stocktaking of the "gendering" of the historiography on nineteenth- and twentieth-century Germany. Therefore, this book brings together experts from Germany and North America to reflect on the state of historiography and problems of theory and methodology. It grew out of a German-North American conference entitled "Gendering Modern German History: Rewritings of the Mainstream (19th-20th Centuries)" that was held at the Munk Centre for International Studies at the University of Toronto, 21–23 March, 2003. Support for the conference came not only from the University of Toronto and the Munk Center but also from two institutions that are at the forefront of encouraging and funding transatlantic cooperation and exchange among scholars and students of German history in Germany, Canada, and the United States: the German Academic Exchange Service (Deutsche Akademische Austauschdienst, DAAD) and the German Historical Institute (GHI) in Washington, DC. The DAAD is the German national agency for the support of international academic cooperation. The GHI, Washington, established in 1987, encourages precisely the types of transatlantic scholarly exchanges among German and American historians that have so directly impacted the field of German women's and gender history. Both prominent research and funding institutions are examples of the transatlantic networks making possible international scholarly cooperation between U.S. and German academics and students that lie at the heart of this volume.

The book, however, is not a proceedings volume of the conference. To be sure, it draws on many of the spirited debates and discussions that took place over the three days of meetings—questions of mainstreaming, debates over agency, tensions in the evaluation of the relationship between women's and gender methodologies in German history, among others. But the conference participants who are included in the book thoroughly rewrote their papers according to much more precise editorial guidelines; other contributors also submitted chapters. By bringing together prominent scholars engaged in historiographical inquiry, the book serves a vital educational role in today's academic climate of scholarly specialization. It combines detailed examination of historiographical trends and extensive notes on this literature with needed synthesis, conceptual clarity and thematic rubrics to keep in focus the larger interpretations and historical patterns in modern German history.

An excellent spirit of cooperation and dialogue has accompanied the final organization of the book. We, the editors, wish to thank each author for working so closely with us and for thinking about the arguments in relation to the other chapter themes in the volume. We also asked a number of well-known scholars on women's and gender history on both sides of the Atlantic to read our specific introduction to this volume. We received very useful comments and suggestions for revisions from Ann Taylor Allen, Volker Berghahn, Jane Caplan, Karin Hausen, Birthe Kundrus, Robert Moeller, Karen Offen, and Hanna Schissler. We thought carefully about all of the points raised by the readers and we are grateful for the time and attention they gave to our work. In the end, of course, we are responsible for the decisions about interpretations and lines of analysis in each chapter. We also would like to thank Laurence Hare, who assisted in the final steps of the production of this volume. Finally, the editors acknowledge the intellectual stimulation of collaborating together on this project. It has been personally and professionally rewarding to work together so closely to examine the complex history of the transatlantic flows of influences that have significantly shaped the field of German women's and gender history.

Karen Hagemann
Chapel Hill, NC

Jean H. Quataert
Vestal, NY

GENDERING MODERN GERMAN HISTORY

Comparing Historiographies and Academic Cultures in Germany and the United States through the Lens of Gender

Karen Hagemann and Jean H. Quataert

Gendering Modern German History assesses the cumulative impact of the new gender research on the writing of German history. The book departs from the approaches of many recent edited collections and journal volumes dedicated to gender analysis. These publications typically are organized around a common theme, which then is explored in different geographical regions and through national as well as culturally specific case studies.[1] The reader, however, has the difficult task of determining the validity of the implicit comparisons; left unanswered in this approach, too, are the impacts of the particular research findings on the larger national historiography.

Our book seeks to overcome precisely these shortcomings. Within a single national frame, it examines the many changes in the historiographies of modern Germany over the last several decades. And, by comparing the scholarship on modern Germany produced in Germany as well as in the United States, it deepens understandings of how different institutional settings, professional requirements, and historical traditions shape the writing of history. Through detailed comparisons of the receptivity of gender methodologies in important subfields of history, it captures the dynamic changes that currently are transforming the wider discipline. In our two geographical settings, this book also follows the ties and tensions between gender analysis and the methodological and research agendas of women's history.

In many ways, it is highly fitting to use Germany as a case study for a rewriting of historiographies. German history raises many issues that are important to historians of other societies in the nineteenth and twentieth centuries, the main time frame for this book. It shares with them the social disruptions in industrial development and nation-state building, the contradictions of modernity, the problems of citizenship and contested identities, and the Cold War pressures and gender tensions accompanying the transitions to the post–Cold War era. Given the particular extremes of German history, German women's and gender historians have grappled more openly with problems of war—victims and perpetrators, collective memory debates, including guilt and redress, which make the historiography especially rich and instructive for other national histories. Alternatively, the focus on Germany opens unique opportunities to explore gender history under different political regimes, whether limited representative government under monarchy, democracy, fascism, or communism. These insights, too, have resonance for historians, social scientists, and political and cultural theorists outside German history. In addition to scholarly interest, there also is a large lay readership on Nazism and comparative fascisms, the Second World War, and the tragedies of the Holocaust. We note here only a few examples as illustrations, but they speak to widespread interest by contemporary readers in Germany's past.

German historiography also has played an important role in the development of the historical profession. Academic history owes its origins in good measure to the German post-Enlightenment traditions of researching and writing history. The best-known example is Leopold von Ranke, who, from his base in the University of Berlin in the mid 1820s, set a normative model for academic history in the West, with its emphasis on archival research and primary source reading, meticulous training in the graduate seminar and, importantly, the elevation of the new nation-state as the primary subject of historical inquiry. In short, Ranke helped establish professional history as the narrative of the emerging nation-state. In her contribution to this collection, Angelika Schaser shows that historiography and the nation-state "developed parallel to each other"; in Germany, this intersection led to the "Prussianization of the German image of history," which continues to this day to shape a powerful tradition of national history in Germany with a focus on the *kleindeutsche* territories and the exclusion of Austria from German history even for the nineteenth century.[2] More generally, this linkage gave rise to dominant assumptions about what constituted the proper subject matter of history, which was defined originally as the study of high politics and diplomacy, the national economy, and military developments, as well as warfare. This focus, in turn, produced a set of relevant although limited conceptual and analytical tools to use in writing historical narratives, including notions of significance and methods of designating historical periods and turning points. Needless to say, *gender = tool*

the whole project was about men's public worlds, although not acknowledged
as such. This highly gendered narrative was presented as general history.

These developments in the field of academic history mark the shared starting point for each of the contributors to this book. We acknowledge, however, an unresolved paradox in our project. On the one hand, the book is about
rewriting the history of Germany—a space that of course has been defined in
many different ways over the last two centuries. In that sense, our book reaf-
firms the traditional emphasis on the nation in history. On the other, gender
analysis, our prime tool in writing and reading this history, erodes these very
borders as it pushes toward cross-disciplinary and transnational dialogues.
As we show below, it has transformed—in some instances quite considerably—the content of many of the standard subfields of the discipline, while
maintaining these divisions at the same time. It also challenges mainstream
interpretations, even as some practitioners argue for the importance of writing new metanarratives, which have the power to frame a people's identity.[3]
Through the German case, we hope to capture some of the complexities and
contradictions of modern historiography in the early twenty-first century.

metanarratives —> frame identity

Comparing Gendered Historiographies and Academic Cultures

This book brings together eleven American and German scholars in the field
of German women's and gender history. It is a product of what have been
very energetic transatlantic crossings of historians and their ideas, methods,
and practices back and forth over the past thirty years primarily between the
United States and Germany. Without fully neglecting other sites, we focus
on German women's and gender history written in these two countries.[4] As
editors, we proceed from our respective knowledge-base in the American and
German university systems to illuminate the many phases of intellectual and
institutional interactions that have shaped this work in German history.

Out of our separate histories and recent experiences of collaboration, we
have developed a comparative analytic framework, which we bring to this
study of historiographies and academic cultures. Our arguments will be
spelled out more fully in the sections of our introduction that follow. Here we
note only briefly the seven variables of our comparative analysis:

First, we recognize that gender is both a subject of historical investigation
and a method of doing historical research. "Women" and "men" constitute
identifiable classes of historical subjects; gender also is used as a theoretical
and methodological framework. In addition to maintaining a focus on women,
gender makes men and masculinity too objects of historical research. Gender
is not only a constitutive element of social relationships based on perceived differences between the sexes, it also is a primary way of signifying relationships

gender = relational

of power. It is of crucial importance for the creation of meaning in social and political life far beyond gender itself.]— political — they

Second, work in gender maintains the deep connections of women's history to feminist agendas, although in complicated ways. Like the pioneers of women's history, gender historians are committed to the social projects of equality and justice. But this project is practiced in complex ways, not at least because in a global dialogue gender sheds light on both the class, cultural, and racial limitations of early "second wave" Western feminism and its historians and critiques the hegemonic claims of Western civilization as normative, somehow, for all peoples around the world.[5]

Third, we argue that the traditions and political agendas of the national feminist movements have far-reaching consequences for feminist academic politics and thereby for the integration of women's and gender history into the universities. The comparison between the United States and Germany shows that it makes a difference if feminists aim for change inside established institutions or if they want to create their own institutions outside the academy.

Fourth, institutions matter. We recognize that history is much more than an intellectual discipline, continuously reshaped by the rigors of research and intertextual analysis. It also is a profession, rooted in university life and training and, thus, subject to bureaucratic power and struggles over resources. The opportunities for university positions and the number of departments and research options are diverse in the United States and Germany, with a profound impact on the fate of the intellectual work and that of the historians as well. Institutional practices also solidify cultural assumptions about motherhood and child-rearing responsibilities.

Furthermore, institutional authority speaks also to the staying power of historiographical traditions, our fifth variable. The profession's openness to new methods, ideas and cross-disciplinary dialogues—to the possibilities, for example, of a paradigm shift through gender—reflects the institutional context of teaching and research. The large, decentralized, demand-driven university setting in the United States is one context; the state-financed federative German university system with developed state control and hierarchical university structures is another one.

Sixth, we draw attention to language itself. The fact that in German the term *Geschlecht* means both sex and gender while English separates the two words is vital for conceptualizing and writing about the field. But, also, words and the grammatical structure of a language form our thinking and perception of the world. The difference between languages is therefore an important variable for creative research and debates across national borders. But language differences also can be barriers, which constrain the international communication between scholars as well as the perception of scholarly work in foreign languages. "Translation" is necessary for a successful international discussion—not only translation of words and meanings, but also of different traditions in academic cultures.

Seventh, and finally, as in every other field of research, international communication in the field of women's and gender history is not devoid of tensions, however much the scholarship owes to mutual debts. The difficulty is exacerbated in part by the increasing use of English as the *lingua franca* of the field, which seems to make it less necessary for the Anglophone scholars to read the research written in other languages or quote it in their own studies. This situation creates imbalances in the recognition of research and also intellectual hierarchies.

These seven variables frame the comparative argumentation in our introduction and also help to organize this book. In our book, we have worked actively to incorporate a vast amount of scholarship produced on both sides of the Atlantic. We asked the authors to assess to what extent the scholars in their field saw their own projects in relation to their understanding of the research agendas, methods, and questions being produced abroad, in particular on the other side of the Atlantic. In retrospect, these currents crossing the Atlantic occasioned ongoing reflections on the wider historiography. This is an important factor because the main question of the book is the extent to which women's and gender history in Germany and the United States has been able to influence and shape mainstream historical narratives. The discussion indeed hinges on the question: what is the meaning of mainstream?

Mainstream and the Politics of History

The notion of a mainstream history is widely used yet analytically imprecise. Structurally, mainstream partially is a function of the institutional and historiographical frameworks of power noted above, shaped and measured among other criteria by access to academic positions inside the university system and thereby to school and university curricula, to research funds, to journals and publication series, professional meetings and conferences, and last but not least, public history. Yet, our authors show that even in one national setting there is not simply one "mainstream" or national paradigm, but rather the coexistence of different competing interpretations, methods, and approaches. Moreover, the subdisciplines of history have dominant, if shifting, schools of interpretation. Our task is to explore to what extent gender has entered these "mainstreams" since 1980 and assess the debates among women's and gender historians about doing so.

The mainstreams in history are very much influenced by and, in turn, affect the politics of doing history. The writing of German history not only in Germany itself but also in the United States is a very political enterprise. But there are obvious differences. Importantly, it matters if an historian writes about the history of his or her own country or another country. In the case of Germany, much of the West German historiography after 1945 involved "coming to grips" with the Nazi era and Holocaust in an effort to write a "serviceable" past to guide (West) German democratic developments and subsequent integration into Europe. No wonder that these interpretations often became powerful master narratives. Following their own political dictates, many American historians, in turn, who worked on German history after 1945 often chose Germany as a subject of their research because they had German ancestors who were forced to leave Germany during the Third Reich. Therefore, for them too one main field of interest was the history of Weimar and Nazi Germany—but from a very different perspective.

This political (and personal) preoccupation helps explain the intensity that historians have brought to matters of interpretation. This is true of the Fischer controversy in the early 1960s[6]; the challenges launched by David Blackbourn and Geoff Eley, then both in England, in the *Peculiarities of German History* (1984), which took on the *Sonderweg* thesis of structural continuity between Imperial Germany and the Nazi era[7]; and also, more recently, the interpretive controversies around Daniel Goldhagen's book *Hitler's Willing Executioners: Ordinary Germans and the Holocaust* (1996).[8] Women's voices were not absent from these wider controversies, at times generating their own *Historikerinnenstreit* ("women historians quarrel"), most notably between the American historian Claudia Koonz and the German historian Gisela Bock, over whether German women, oppressed in Hitler's racial state, could be perpetrators in the horrors of National Socialism.[9] These *Historikerinnenstreit* reflected very different conceptions of feminism in the two countries (our third variable). Many of the authors in our collection examine the importance of these debates for their time and place.

Moreover, the mainstreams are produced by historical fashions. Here again we see an important difference between academic cultures in Germany and the United States. Because the German academic system is more traditional and less market driven, these historical "fashions" for a long time were less important. There was competition between different "schools" of history writing. Scholars differed about the leading factors that influenced history, but at the same time they often shared deep suspicion about quick changes of fashions in writing history. From a German perspective, it appears that the market-driven system of the U.S. academic culture forces young scholars, who want to get public recognition and positioning in the American academic system, to follow these fashions more readily than in Germany.

Questions and Structures of the Arguments and Their Uses

To provide coherence to this volume, as noted, we asked each contributor to respond to a set of questions about historiographical developments in his or her respective thematic field. We wanted to know what contributions women's and gender history have made to the literature; the developments and current state of research; the main research desiderata; and the theoretical and methodological problems. We also asked to what extent the work on women's and gender history has changed the mainstream in the field and what future research questions should be. Above all, we encouraged the authors to think about differences in the writing of this history in Germany and the United States. We also asked: how far have American and German historiographies on gender influenced each other? We show that the shared concerns of our authors—testing the rigors of gender analysis for many subfields in history, analyzing the contexts of women's agency, exploring the complicated relationships between women's *and* gender history—play out differently in the two distinct national contexts. For comparability, we also asked our authors to organize their chapters in similar ways.

Our introduction sets the stage for this gendered reading of German historiography. In what follows, we examine, briefly, the emergence of women's history in the United States and West Germany, explore differences in the timing and extent of professionalization in the two countries, and analyze the emergence of gender as an analytic research category. Then we offer a critical stocktaking from the chapters in this book and note the themes that have not been addressed. We conclude with an analysis of the annual 2004 meetings of historians in Germany and the United States to assess the nature and extent of gender integration into the historiography of modern Germany in our two countries.

Overall, the broad nature of the inquiry is matched by the detailed attention to the changing nature of German historiography in our chosen themes. The book is a valuable resource for academics and students. Extensive footnotes plumb the depths of the historiographical terrain while the shared emphasis on useful rubrics, subtitles, and thematic categories draws immediate attention to the broader meanings of the historiographical shifts. The book offers a detailed description of the scholarly debates in the literature while maintaining a sharp focus on the big themes and problems at the heart of German history.

Women's History—Herstories

As is by now well known, women's history (known originally as herstory[10]) emerged in tandem with the second wave of feminism in the West beginning in the late 1960s in the United States and in the 1970s in West Germany.[11]

Ann Taylor Allen points out that this historiography often is explained in terms of two different feminist strategies: a liberal model of integration (in the United States) and a radical, separatist model outside the academy (in Germany). Historical developments actually were less polarized, she says. In both countries, the two strategies were discussed together at the outset. Certainly by the 1980s, women scholars on both sides of the Atlantic demanded an equal integration of women and women's studies into the academia. As Allen puts it aptly, the "march through institutions" had commenced.[12] Nevertheless, differences emerged that had long-term consequences. In Germany, the skepticism about the full integration into "male-dominated " institutions remained even for the second and third generation of women's studies scholars into the 1990s. Unlike in the United States, furthermore, women's historians in Germany never sought to become a working group inside the Association of German Historians, the professional organization of German historians. They preferred to work in their own networks outside this male-dominated organization. Even in the 1980s and 1990s, the number of tenured female professors—in contrast to the United States—was so small that it seemed most important to strengthen the relations among female historians who worked on this field and develop "outside" strategies for empowerment "inside" academic organizations and institutions.

Despite its disciplinary home, practitioners in the field maintained their commitments to social advocacy outside the academy, whether for gender equality, social justice or, more recently, for women's global human rights gains. The field has been involved from the start also in interdisciplinary dialogues, exchanging theories and insights with other feminists in the social and human sciences; it also is a part of what now is called transnational and global debates. These broad connections are particularly characteristic of the pioneer generation of women's historians in the United States and Germany, whose approaches self-evidently contained strong feminist commitments. These ranged from making women's diverse experiences the *center* of inquiry to rethinking matters of agency and identity to affirming that history itself matters—to seeing women's history as a form of empowerment for women in the present as well as the future.

In the United States, and also in Germany, the "integrationist" women's historians, who were also the moving spirit behind professionalization, assumed that the rich research findings derived from the rigorous analytic methods and high quality of women's history would (automatically) be incorporated into the "mainstream" and would change the master narratives of historiography.[13] They expected this outcome despite their awareness that the mainstream was a "malestream." The goal of rewriting master narratives remains an important component of women's history. It is also on the agenda of the subsequent generations of historians, many of whom are committed to

♀'s history vs. gender history

gender analysis. In 1998, the cultural historian Lynn Hunt offered a strong plea for this aim. She argued that "refusing metanarratives only ensures the marginalization of women's and gender history within the historical discipline. . . . The power to reshape general history depends on active engagement with its premises. The power to act politically depends on the narratives that link past to present and future. Gender historians therefore need to construct their own metanarratives. But to do this most convincingly, they also need to examine the working of current metanarratives and endeavor to avoid their pitfalls."[14]

The project of rewriting historical metanarratives often is discussed in terms of "mainstreaming," a process complicated by the fact that over the same time frame that has given rise to women's and gender history, mainstream canons have been eroding. What constitutes "mainstream" history is a complicated question and there is decreasing agreement among historians over its definitions and sets of criteria. Writing about the history of sexuality in early modern Germany, for example, Merry Wiesner shows clearly that the empirical work of women's historians and also feminist theory constitute the main foundation of the field—"other than Foucault," as she puts it.[15] In some ways, then, they are the mainstream. Despite the lack of a uniform definition, each author in this collection confronts the question of the mainstream, either head-on or less explicitly. Each assesses the impact of the new scholarship on a particular thematic sub-branch of history over the last thirty years. While our primary emphasis tends to be on gender analysis and, thus, on recent scholarship, neither in terms of its origins nor, indeed, its methods of inquiry can research on gender as a system be easily dissociated from the sophisticated parameters of women's history. ✱ *need ♀'s hist.*

From their first entrée in the field in the early 1970s, women's historians have been raising disquieting questions about the organizational and conceptual schemes of academic history and its working paradigms. That is hardly surprising because the whole conceptual apparatus of the discipline, as we just noted, originated essentially with no regard to women's life experiences, diverse worlds, and substantive contributions to major areas of political, economic, and cultural life. The stated aim of women's history remains to write women, who are situated differently in terms of class, ethnicity, religion, nationality, and culture, into history. Defined originally (in English) as *herstory*[16] in contrast, literally, with *his-story*, the task has proved to be challenging, not the least because it entails, ultimately, rethinking the very basis of history as a discipline. With its ties to the new emerging field of social history, the first-generation women's historians grappled with the intellectual and conceptual infrastructure of the discipline. They questioned the validity of standard ways of dividing time in history (historical periods typically reflected the dates of wars or political regimes and governments), of many traditional interpretations

periodization

(of progress and modernity, for example) of causality as well as understandings of historical significance.

In an academic discipline located squarely in the empirical landscape and ambivalent about theory, many early women's historians, by contrast, were receptive to a feminist search for theoretical explanations. Seeking to make sense of women's and men's complex historical worlds, these early pioneers benefited from and contributed to new feminist theorizing. They took on and transformed Marxist theories, contributing a large literature on the uneasy relationship between socialism and feminism; tested equality assumptions of liberal ideology; and developed new strands of feminist analysis (radical feminism) of men's power over women's bodies.[17] They explored, among others, the usefulness of such concepts as androcentricity and patriarchy, examined the relationship between production and reproduction, and questioned the workings of sexual identity. Often tied to the New Left and Marxist politics, they took on the reigning conceptual tools of social and labor history, not the least class itself, examining new arenas of class consciousness (family, neighborhoods, and consumption patterns) that were not solely rooted at the points of production.

Cumulatively, this inquiry began to erode fundamental assumptions that long had underpinned historical interpretations of the modern era: the separation of public and private spheres, the division between family life and the state, biologically-determined definitions of sexual identity and difference as well as the material bases of consciousness. As early as 1976, the early modern French historian Natalie Davis called on historians "to understand the significance of the sexes and of gender groups in historical terms."[18] It is no wonder that Kathleen Canning in 1994, looking back on this early corpus of scholarship, recognizes the formative role of women's history and feminist theory in the big epistemological debates that hit the historical profession in the early 1980s. Writing in *Signs: Journal of Women in Culture and Society*, an innovative interdisciplinary journal of women's studies that was at the forefront of new thinking about historical knowledge, she makes the case that women's history set the stage for the "reception of various strains of poststructuralism, including French feminism." Canning writes, "if not always hand-in-hand, feminist and poststructuralist critiques of historical 'master-narratives' interrogated, dissembled, and recast historical paradigms in light of new histories of women and gender and of race, ethnicity and sexuality."[19]

The point is slightly ahead of our chronological argument, but it describes well the central role of women's history in the genealogies of change that are reflected in the chapters of this book. Important for our arguments, writing German women's history in the United States preceded similar undertakings in Germany by five to ten years. American scholars of German women, therefore, were at the forefront of the field and their research served as model and inspiration for a younger cohort of German women students. One example is the research on women in the Weimar Republic and the Third Reich. When scholars such as Renate Bridenthal, Atina Grossmann, Marion Kaplan, Claudia Koonz, and others came to Germany in the 1970s and early 1980s to start their research for their dissertations and other books, they met with several younger female academics and even students in Germany working on similar subjects; as feminists and professional historians they were important role models for younger German scholars. They also established close working ties with the first generation of German women's historians, among them most influentially Gisela Bock, Karin Hausen, and Heide Wunder. As early as 1974 already as an Assistant Professor at the Free University of Berlin, Karin Hausen started the first research colloquium on women's history in Germany. From the beginning she invited several American scholars to participate in this colloquium as speakers. During the 1980s several reports about progress in the development of women's studies in the United States were published in Germany and inspired new discussions about feminist academic politics.[20]

Professionalization: Integration and Marginalization

A second phase in women's history involved the professionalization of the field as it became part of the academy. Starting around the mid 1970s in the United States, women's history entered the university curricula and women's historians joined history departments and helped found women's studies programs. Attention increasingly turned to hiring new faculty, to developing graduate training and their own placement in academic jobs, and to establishing journals devoted to publicizing and legitimizing scholarly research in women's history and women's studies. This step was controversial from the start; many early faculty in the fields had deep ties to local feminist communities and feared the new criteria for academic posts would shift the commitments away from feminist practice into more abstract theories and methods of research. Indeed, many of the influential journals evolved out of underground, makeshift publications. Our selected bibliography reflects the role of these journals in publishing innovative, challenging, and controversial research—such as the introduction in 1976 of French feminist theory in *Signs*[21] (an interdisciplinary journal started in 1975); the special 1988 issue of *Feminist Studies* (published first in 1972)[22] devoted to deconstruction; and the 2003 volumes of *The Journal of Women's History* (established in 1989)[23] focused on the concept of "public and private" as part of wider global dialogues among women's and gender historians.

The earliest and most important feminist German journals that vitally enhanced the theoretical and methodological debates in Germany were *Beiträge zur feministischen theorie und praxis*, founded in 1978[24], and *Feministische Studien*, founded in 1982.[25] From the beginning, both journals were edited by inter-disciplinary groups of female historians and also political and social scientists. Both editorial collectives understood their journal not only as an academic but also a political endeavor. In their founding statement in 1982, the editors of *Feministische Studien* wrote programmatically: "The journal *Feministische Studien* provides a public forum for interdisciplinary research into women's studies. This research is not narrowly conceived because it involves half of humanity. It posits and analyzes the gender relations that structure all areas of life, thought and scientific knowledge. Women's and gender research can only realize feminist goals when it transcends the traditional academic fields and achieves a disciplined interdisciplinarity."[26]

This emphasis on interdisciplinary thinking for a long time was a charac-teristic of feminist studies. But in the process of professionalization, it became more difficult to practice it. For professional advancement, the intellectual exchanges among the peer group of male and female scholars in the disci-plines became important. Nonetheless, women's and gender studies today are more interdisciplinary than most other fields of research.

Aiding professionalization, academic conferences for women's histori-ans were organized first in the United States and later in Germany as well. Most notably in the American context is the revival in the early 1970s of the Berkshire Conference of Women's Historians (which had met originally in the 1930s). The first renewed Berkshire Conference took place at Douglass College (of Rutgers University) in 1973. Expecting only one hundred or so participants, the Douglass gathering drew instead three times that number, prompting calls for another conference. The next year, the so-called "Big Berks Conference" met at Radcliffe College and attracted over a thousand participants. By 1996 the Big Berks (now held every three years) had begun to draw several thousand participants from all over the world.[27] The Thirteenth Berkshire Conference held at Scripps College, Claremont, California, in May 2005 had over thirteen hundred advance registrations.

In Germany, too, beginning in the 1970s, women's historians were orga-nizing workshops and conferences. Most important were a series of so-called *Historikerinnentreffen* ("meetings of female historians") that took place be-tween 1978 and 1986. The first gathering was organized by a group of femi-nist historians in Berlin and attracted nearly forty participants; the subject matter was "Women in the Weimar Republic and the Third Reich." At the next meeting in Bremen in 1980, which focused on "motherhood and ma-ternal ideology in bourgeois society," more than 150 female historians par-ticipated.[28] In the following years, with every conference—1981 in Bielefeld, 1983 in Berlin, 1984 in Vienna, 1985 in Bonn, and 1986 in Amsterdam—the number of participants increased as did an international presence.[29] Only women participated—not only professional historians and students but increasingly also nonacademic feminist activists. Whether the *Historikerinnentreffen* should be open to men became an important point of debate, which culminated in 1981 during and after the Bielefelder *Historikerinnentreffen*, when male scholars who wanted to participate were excluded.[30] The growing numbers of women-only participants, however, spelled the conference's demise; in Amsterdam, seventy workshops were organized with 160 lectures and hundreds of participants. Without greater institutional infrastructure and financial support, meetings of this size could no longer be organized by young scholars in the German context. No one was willing and able to continue to organize the *Historikerinnentreffen*. Starting in the mid 1980s, the small number of professional female historians in Germany needed to concentrate their energy more on their own professional qualifications and organized instead an increasing number of research colloquia, workshops, and smaller conferences. Since the mid 1980s, there also has been at least one women's studies section at the biennial *Historikertag* (German historians' meeting). The first of these sections was organized in 1984, 1986, and 1990 by Karin Hausen, Heide Wunder, and Gisela Bock.[31] Moreover, at the beginning of the 1990s a series of national workshops for doctoral students were set up by Karin Hausen.

As these developments show, the professionalization of women's history not only happened in Germany later, it also took on different forms, reflecting the different academic settings on either side of the Atlantic. At the outset in the United States, the broad receptivity to women's history in part was a response to student demand; deans saw that women's history and women's studies generally meant large enrollments and financial benefits. In this decentralized structure, dominant interpretations could not easily establish monopolies; these structures indeed allowed for diversity in training and multiplicity of views.[32] A very important additional factor helped to develop women's studies in the United States: the tradition of women's colleges. Many female professors of these colleges wholeheartedly supported the professionalization of women's studies. The innovative book on gender and the German research university by Patricia M. Mazón shows that a similar model of colleges was never even considered in Germany.[33] Because of all-women's colleges, in the 1960s the United States already has a sizeable number of women professors: in the decade, 19 percent of all college and university faculty in the United States was female, working mostly in these all-women's colleges. The comparable figures in Germany stood at only 6 percent.[34] Only a small number of these female professors was willing to support women's and gender studies, however. The majority in Germany worked in other fields.

The relatively few universities in Germany with their limited number of history departments (seventy-one in total) and the decreasing importance of the humanities in the academic system have meant the perpetuation of powerful paradigms and the dominance of a small number of interpretive schools of thought. Furthermore, in a university system that is regimented by the states, change can only come about slowly, not the least because the federative states control the development of the curriculum. In contrast to the United States, German students do not pay for their education so student demand is not a powerful vehicle of change. In the late 1970s, female students had to organize "sit-ins" and other forms of political protest to secure the first women's history courses in the German academy. In addition, centralized sources of funding like the *Deutsche Forschungsgemeinschaft* (German Research Foundation) for a long time essentially supported "mainstream" research, because in peer assessments by mainly male reviewers this research seemed to be of higher quality and scientific standards. Ironically, the generous German system of *Forschungsförderung* (funding of research) helped to maintain the existing power and paradigm structures.

The hierarchical organization of West German academic life had far-reaching consequences for the field of women's and gender history. This structure, aided by the long training for professorships under the tutelage of mentors, insulated many male historians from the intellectual challenges of feminist research. Resistance—not absent across the Atlantic—remained powerful. The situation in East German universities differed further since the ruling authorities did not allow autonomous and challenging feminist research until 1989.[35] Nevertheless, since the 1980s more and more younger, mainly female historians have been working in the field of women's and gender history. In 1990, they founded the *Arbeitskreis Historische Frauen- und Geschlechterforschung* (AKHFG, Working Group on Women's and Gender History).[36] The AKHFG is a member of the "International Federation of Research in Women's History" (IFRWH), founded in 1987 and affiliated with the International Committee of Historical Sciences.[37] The aims of the nationwide branch network in Germany, which from the very beginning integrated scholars from the former GDR, are to support a lively exchange of research and ideas among all scholars working on women's and gender studies and to insure that their historical work on women's and gender history becomes more prominent in the scientific communities of West Germany, in and outside the academy.

Reflecting widespread interest, nearly three hundred mainly female historians became members of the AKHFG in the first year.[38] Collectively, they have produced an increasing number of high-quality publications, even though their research has often not received recognition by their male colleagues. In the first volume of the series *Geschichte und Geschlechter* (History and Gender), published in 1992 under the title *Frauengeschichte—Geschlechtergeschichte* (Women's History—Gender History), the editors Karin Hausen and Heide Wunder pessimistically described the state in Germany at the beginning of the 1990s: "Next to lack of institutional support, there existed and still exists a consensus, not really limited to the arena of history, that women's history, if it is relevant at all, is not a central but a marginal field, a decorative accessory (*schmückende Arabeske*).[39] This "double marginalization" of both the female historians and feminist history even today characterizes the field of history in Germany. Statistics capture part of the story. First, in 2005 there still are not more than five tenured professorships explicitly dedicated to women's and gender history.[40] Second, comparing history with other disciplines and Germany with other countries, there has been only a relatively small increase in the percentage of tenured female professors overall in history. Third is the small number of articles that include gender dimension published in so-called general historical journals in Germany like the leading *Geschichte und Gesellschaft* or *Historische Zeitschrift*. Whole journal volumes have come out in the last fifteen years without any article on women's and gender history; articles by female authors, which focus on women and gender history, are still rare.[41] Because of these constraints, female historians in the German-speaking regions have started their own distinct journals. The most important of these are *L'Homme*, founded in 1990 in Vienna[42] and *Metis*, founded in 1992 in Bonn.[43]

The rhetorical strategy underpinning this marginalization was the presumptuous assertion that there were not enough qualified female historians who could be hired in university positions. In addition, drawing on longstanding assumptions of academic history as gender-neutral and nonpolitical, opposition strategies in West Germany charged feminist female scholars with doing "ideological" and "special interest" work, which was neither "rational" nor "neutral."[44] In practice, these arguments served to uphold a male-dominated academic power structure. These purposes became evident when, in the 1990s, the number of formally qualified female historians who had finished their dissertation or their habilitation grew rapidly. Despite the increasing percentage of highly qualified women, the numbers of female academics increased only slightly. Even laws and regulations favoring the promotion of women "with equal qualifications" in the German university system did not dent the preexisting patterns.[45]

Of course, similar debates about the "political" character of women's history also took place in the U.S. context. Therefore, we must be clear about the major structural differences that have helped to integrate more women into the universities in United States than in Germany. It is due, we believe, to the demand-driven character of the American academic system. Course enrollments count. In practice, nowadays in Germany, despite—and in the face of—all demand for change, it does not matter what students prefer, because they are not consumers driving the market. Moreover, teaching has never counted much in advancing the university career of an historian. Other statistics on the integration of female scholars into the fields of history in our two university settings bear out the larger argument.

In comparative perspective, the statistics for the United States show the most gains for women's history faculty, reflecting and encouraging the work in women's and gender history and the growth of women's studies programs and departments in American colleges and universities. According to the data collected by the American Historical Association (AHA), the organization of history professionals in the United States, women made up 38 percent of new history Ph.D.s in 2002 while ethnic and racial minorities comprised 12 percent of U.S. citizens receiving history doctorates.[46] By 2005, minorities were just under 14 percent and women made up 28 percent of all history faculty. These data are telling, because academic and literary women of color in the United States first began to complicate feminist theory and push to disaggregate the presumed unified category of "woman" to include racial and ethnic differences as well as class. Their analytic lens helped set the stage for the move to gender in the U.S. context.

These gains for women and minorities are relatively recent and they contain disquieting patterns. Women are underrepresented at the full professor rank. In U.S. history departments in 1979–1980, women were 13 percent of the faculty, mostly as lecturers (40 percent) and only 6 percent at the full professor level. In 1988, the proportion of women in history faculties had risen to 17 percent, slightly less than the figure for completed Ph.D.s; however, they still made up only 8 percent of the full professor rank. The real gains for women have been at the assistant professor level; in 2005, women comprised 55 percent of that rank in history departments, well above their representation among new Ph.D.s in history, but there also is a shift to the use of (female) adjuncts and temporary faculty. As labor historians show, a feminization of the workforce often spells a decline in professional status. Indeed, the German professor has a much higher status than most of the professors in the United States—an important factor in the continued resistance to feminization in Germany. Finally, in the United States, disparities between the upper and lower ranks of the profession still remain. Of history full professors in 2005, 82 percent are men and 91 percent are white.

Numbers tell only part of the story, however. Linda K. Kerber, president-elect of the AHA in 2005, catalogues the social context of scholarly production in U.S. institutions of higher learning: the long hours, lack of coherent family leave policies, insufficient support for pregnancy as well as infant and child care. Across the humanities, she notes, men who have infants in their families within five years of obtaining the Ph.D. are 38 percent more likely than women to be given tenure. Combining career and motherhood is still a formidable task for women academics—even more so for single mothers. "It is time," Kerber writes, "to turn our attention to creating equitable workplaces," more attuned to the many needs of women and men as they balance careers and the shifting demands of caregiving.[47]

The German figures for women faculty provided by the *Statistisches Bundesamt* (Federal Department for Statistics) are more static. In fact, the gap between the number of female history students and female faculty members in the history departments has deepened over the last forty years. On the one hand, the number of women students has increased significantly in West German universities; their numbers rose from 22 percent of the student body in 1960 to 38 percent in 1980, rising to 48 percent in 1990 and dropping to 44 percent in 2003. On the other, women in history departments comprised only 6 percent of the teaching faculty and 2 percent of the tenured faculty in 1960; in 1980, their share of teaching faculty has risen to 13 percent and they made up 5 percent of tenured professors; by 1990, their numbers in the overall faculty had risen to 18 percent but, despite federal affirmative action efforts and the growth of women's studies, women still were only 6 percent of tenured faculty. In 2003, the overall number of female faculty in history departments reached 30 percent, but only 12 percent were tenured faculty and not more than 10 percent were full professors at the highest level (C4/W3).[48] Furthermore, in contrast to the United States, the majority of the twenty-five interdisciplinary women's and gender studies centers that were founded since 1980 are not part of the teaching program in German universities.[49] They do not have their own curriculum or degree-granting authority. One exception is the "transdisciplinary curriculum for gender studies" established in 1997 at the Humboldt University of Berlin.[50]

While the figures for women as tenured faculty at history departments in East Germany in 1989 were essentially the same as in the West (5 percent), given the official ideological commitment to women's economic integration and generous family leave policies, they comprised 35 percent of the instructors and 13 percent of assistant professors (*Dozenten*). With the takeover of East German universities by the West, the numbers of women faculty in the former Deutsche Demokratische Republik has in fact declined.[51]

In postunification Germany, furthermore, the common concept of the professional historian remains both gendered and highly traditional. From their strong institutional base, many German male professors still seem to believe that motherhood and a professorship do not belong together. As a consequence, in 2005, 49 percent of all female academics over 35 never become mothers. Even at the beginning of the twenty-first century, the German half-day child care and education systems require the mother to be at home.[52] For different reasons, a family-friendly workplace is not part of the German academic university system, either.

The professionalization of the field on both sides of the Atlantic was marked by new curricula and degrees, the founding of scholarly journals, and

is that really a consequence?

the holding of regular academic conferences and forums. Although neither university setting has accommodated adequately the many pressures of career and family—affecting the quality of the workplace overall but falling most heavily on women academics and researchers—women's historians have a larger presence in history departments in the United States than in Germany. A rise in the number of female historians, however, does not necessarily mean more work in gender history, although, of course, more women are in the field than men. However, the big methodological and conceptual debates generated by historians in women's history set important preconditions for the transition to gender research.

The Transition to Gender

"challenge of difference" (handwritten annotation)

As concept and method, gender has become so much part of global intellectual discourse in the early twenty-first century that its own historical origins easily are overlooked. Most German history scholars on both sides of the Atlantic agree that the move to define relationships of sexual difference as gender goes back to the mid 1970s[53] and the many debates in feminist theory, including the pioneering works of Natalie Z. Davis and Joan Kelly.[54] Already at the second Berkshire Conference in 1975, Natalie Davis pointed out the shortcoming of a history that focused exclusively on women: "It seems to me that we should be interested in the history of both women and men, that we should not be working only on the subjected sex any more than an historian of class can focus entirely on peasants. Our goal is to understand the significance of the sexes, of gender groups in the historical past."[55]

Others too, like Gerda Lerner in 1977, voiced her opinion that women's history as *herstory* would necessarily be only the first step in a more comprehensive research agenda.[56] Nevertheless, until the 1980s, the focus of research was mainly on women, but with an increasing awareness of the multiple differences between women: social, racial and ethnic, political and confessional, sexual and generational. The "challenges of difference" were quickly launched by women of color in the United States. Parallel sensitivities were also part of the early work examining the intersections of sexist and racist politics under National Socialism. Lesbian worlds, too, became a critical site for the differentiation of women's history.

In the mid 1980s, the linguistic turn in the social sciences and the reception of French poststructuralist theories coincided in the United States and elsewhere with the growing concerns with the development of women's studies, an uneasiness that also was expressed in women's history.[57] One of the leading spokespersons for this preoccupation was Joan W. Scott. Thus in 1986, in her conceptually powerful and by now widely cited article in the *American*

Historical Review, the major journal of the AHA, she argued that "gender" must become a key category of historical analysis.[58] In the first half of the 1980s, the term "gender" was finding its way into research. Initially, however, it was used either as an alternative to biological sex and an acknowledgement of the many ways the identities of woman or man were culturally constructed, or was taken to be a substitute for "women"–not at least because as a seemingly political neutral term it did not conjure up visions of radical feminism and thus helped female historians to win broader acceptance in the academia.

Joan Scott proposed a new usage of the category "gender." For her, "gender" has the power to alter the very foundations of historical knowledge. Coming out of the field of French labor and women's history, she begins her article with the observation that, for all its insights and innovations, women's history as practiced has as yet not been able to alter the powerful (male-centered) narratives of history. Tied to social history, it remained too wedded to the dominant materialist thinking in the discipline and failed to subject its own fundamental categories—in particular, "woman," "feminism," "female consciousness," "the sexed body"—to critical analysis. Women's history was paralleling history, Scott claimed, and, therefore, it continued to be seen as a particular case of the universal patterns that history claimed to uncover.

Timing is all-important, for with this analysis Joan Scott tapped into a growing apprehension among women's historians that their work, indeed, was not having the expected impact on historical writing. It also coincided with what later became known as an "epistemological crisis" affecting history due to the increasing currency of poststructural and cultural theories. Denying any context-free knowledge or human agency outside of the discourses that shape meanings, theorists such as Jacques Derrida, Michel Foucault, and Louis Althusser (among others) effectively destabilized the foundational assumptions of the field, notably the linear narrative structures of history writing and faith in individual experience, identity, and agency.[59]

For Scott—and many who followed her—poststructuralist theory in fact seemed to offer a way out of the apparent dead end. Poststructuralism, thus, first came to the discipline of history through gender. As theorized and formulated, gender derives from the classification system of grammar; as an historical category, it denotes the dynamics of sexual differences, which take multiple forms in time and becomes a lens through which to read the past. As Scott originally put it, gender differences lie at the heart of all social organization; they draw on putatively natural (biological) yet historically constructed categories to mark the differences between men and women, masculinity and femininity. Although these demarcating boundaries are in fact porous and fragile, their assumed solidity works to establish and reinforce rigid social hierarchies and inequalities. The gender perspective thus offers unique insights into the nature of power and resistance. In addition, it challenges the seemingly unified categories in history, particularly the assumptions about the self-evident nature of sexual identity—the very category of man, woman, or heterosexual, homosexual, for example.

In effect, Scott offers gender as a key to writing a thoroughly "new history," a history that once and for all eliminates the tensions between the hegemonic tropes of the "particular" and the "universal." Importantly, she sought to maintain and broaden the connections of this innovative approach to "feminist political strategies," arguing that "gender must be redefined and restructured in conjunction with a vision of political and social equality that includes not only sex but class and race."[60] This language was soon so influential that in 1989 a journal with the programmatic title *Gender & History* was launched, run by a large international editorial collective of women and men. It publishes new scholarship on the gender system as well as on masculinity.[61]

  Wide receptivity, however, does not constitute consensus. Many U.S.-based feminist historians were critical of this new "linguistic turn," precisely because, by virtue of its dissolution of "women," it seemed to undermine the basis of feminist politics, rooted firmly in assumptions about shared experiences and identity across class, ethnic, or racial backgrounds. As Karen Offen, a major historian of European feminism, notes, such a step could be lethal to reestablishing the history of women's protests and achievements undertaken in the name of sisterhood.[62] Indeed, many first-generation feminist historians feared gender research would dilute the feminist politics of women's studies. They resisted efforts to rename women's studies programs "gender studies." Despite the early critics and skeptics, most women's studies programs see women's history and gender research as complementary. Indeed, a listing of U.S. women's studies programs, departments, and research centers for the period 1994–2003 shows a clear preponderance of programs titled "women's studies."[63] In addition, partly because of the development of gay studies and interests by male faculty, gender and masculinity have become an increasing part of the research and teaching agendas of these interdisciplinary programs. As our contributors show, however, there is slippage in the use of the term gender in German history; sometimes, in fact, U.S.-based authors use the term gender even if their work is solely about women's lives and experiences.

The development in Germany during the 1990s was quite different. Despite all the pressures to marginalize women's and gender studies, the first half of the 1990s was a period of optimism. Feminist scholars did expect an integration of women's and gender studies into the university system. They hoped that with a move from "women" to "gender" they could demonstrate the analytical rigor of its potential for reformulating academic disciplines and their paradigms. Being a "latecomer" became an important precondition for the openness to new approaches, which the naming of the German centers reflects. The first two centers at the University of Bielefeld (in 1980) and at the Free University of Berlin (in 1981) began as Centers for Interdisciplinary Women's Studies. The next four centers founded between 1984 and 1993 followed this example. The first center to be explicitly dedicated to women's and gender studies was founded in 1995 at the Technical University of Berlin. Since then, this double dedication has become more usual. Today, there are twenty-five interdisciplinary centers conducting research on women and gender. Only four (16 percent) are women's studies centers, ten (40 percent) are centers for women's and gender studies and eleven (or 44 percent) are centers for gender studies. Bruising debates about the naming of a center have not taken place since the mid 1990s.

On both sides of the Atlantic, the 1990s was the period when "gender" as an analytical category became a leading paradigm. First, work in gender studies increasingly began to address men, masculinities, and male bodies.[64] In particular in Germany, leading gender historians, such as Ute Frevert, Karen Hagemann, Thomas Kühne, or Anne-Charlott Trepp, early on further developed the "history of masculinities."[65] On the American side, George L. Mosse was most influential.[66] Second, intensive debates opened up about theory and methodology, raising again questions of "agency" and "experience." Importantly, historians working on German women's history played an important role in these methodological debates and began to modify what they saw as Scott's overreliance on discursive practices to the point of losing sight of specific historical human beings. Through new attention to theory and experience, historians such as Kathleen Canning, Lynn Abrams, and Elizabeth Harvey sought to return "experience" to history, reaffirming the role of woman as agent, able to negotiate her place within the constraints of discourse and, in turn, to modify and transform the discursive field. In effect, they claimed gender for women's history.[67] Other historians, among them Ulinke Rublack, Barbara Duden, and Sabine Kienitz, began to stress the importance of the human body as a corporeal, material entity and not something simply discursively constructed. They turned attention to women's "feelings" of their own pregnant bodies and of birthing practices in the past and to state and medical responses to the individual woman needing to obtain an abortion.[68]

In the context of these new and exciting epistemological and political debates, attention for a while centered on an apparent "Atlantic divide," a term referenced by a number of our contributors. One of the first to use the term was Kathleen Canning. In her widely discussed 1993 article "German Particularities in Women's/Gender History," she credits the remarkable expansion and change in the writing of modern German women's and gender history since the late 1960s. But she noted differences between the work done in the United States and Germany. As she described it at the time, one was the reluctance of feminist scholars in Germany to follow a shift from women to gender. The other concerned the unwillingness of German scholars in the field to adopt poststructuralist approaches and questions. On the whole, critical feminist historiography appeared to her far better established in the United States than in the Federal Republic of Germany.[69] The field of German women's and gender history, indeed, has evolved in reference to perceptions of scholarship across the Atlantic. Ten years later, the situation has changed. In fact, the practice of naming the centers indicates that nowadays gender studies seem to be more accepted in feminist scholarship in Germany than in the United States. Furthermore, as our contributors show, poststructuralist approaches also are evident in gender history in Germany since the mid 1990s, which in turn contributed to the increasing acceptance of cultural historical approaches as well as discourse analysis in German historiography.[70]

But differences remain, particularly in the way German scholars *do* gender history. Partly the result of distinct historiographical traditions and the generally more hierarchical and conservative structures of the German academia, the themes of gender studies tend more frequently to follow the trends of mainstream research, while at the same time approaching this research from very different angles. This context explains, for example, why interest in a theme such as the military, war, and masculinity was relatively strong early on in Germany, as Karen Hagemann's separate chapter to our volume testifies.[71] However, gender historians in both settings continue to cherish the vision of reciprocity and integration among and between gender history and economic, social, and political history. Thus, they do not want to write only for the community of feminist scholars but seek instead to develop a dialogue with the "malestream." As part of this dialogue, they challenge this mainstream by questioning its theories and methods, its usage of historical periods as well as values and notions of significance. Their critique focuses on the widespread but highly problematic concepts of the "universal" and the "particular" in history, since what the mainstream defines as universal or particular is not objective but, rather, a particular male-centered decision about relevance and significance. Choices about relevance measure the so-called universal in history by the male yardstick of the decision makers who dominate politics, the military, and the economy, as well as by the mental universe of the opinion makers who shape scholarship and the media. Simultaneously, this dominant approach constructs anything that deviates from it as a "special case," even when it affects the overwhelming majority of a society. German women's historians opened a line of critique of this powerful paradigm with the idea, as Karin Hausen, one of the most influential of the first generation of German feminist historians, puts it of "unity in the diversity" of history.[72] Hausen proposes an open, undogmatic approach, which accepts the diversity of theories and methodologies in the field. This agenda for research and writing eliminates older grand narratives and insists on the importance not only of diversity, but also ambiguities and paradoxes in our historical narratives. Both the stress on diversities and ambiguities and the rejection of metanarratives create the inherent unity of this approach.

Critical Stocktaking

As the contributors show, in the last thirty years gender as analytical method and new historical subject has made significant inroads into German historiography, challenging earlier approaches to the writing of the past. This book captures these changes in the chapters that follow, which are arranged according to ten major thematic divisions of history. Our listing of selected literature in Chapter 12 provides an up-to-date compendium of the important literature in the historiography. It is divided by bibliographies, theories, and methods and also by chronology—of the "long" nineteenth century; World War I and the Weimar Republic; the Third Reich, World War II, and the Holocaust; and, finally, postwar Germany. It offers a different route into the historiography: a more expansive chronology that crosses the borders of subfields and also disciplines.

The selection of themes follows a historical logic—in our own subjective understandings. We also are well aware of important topics left out, including works in economic history,[73] intellectual history,[74] the history of sciences,[75] and gay and lesbian studies.[76] In our choices we wanted to balance the authors on each side of the Atlantic. Our sequence moves chronologically from the oldest and most traditional sub-branches of nineteenth- and twentieth-century German history itself—from nation-state building and nationalism to war and the military to politics—to themes that are themselves recent products of interdisciplinary methodologies highlighting gender, such as sexuality and the body. Our authors also examine the impact of gender research on social history, religion, and confessionalism—a promising new approach to German history capturing continuities from the early modern to the modern periods—and family history. In our chronological sequence, the chapter on imperialism is placed before politics. Imperialism is a traditional topic in European history when explored solely as a matter of great power politics and colonial conquests. A relatively new theme to German history, colonial research rewrites space and draws heavily on cultural studies. These new histories are far removed from the older studies on "the new imperialism" (1870–1914). Finally, we include a chapter on the Holocaust and the Third Reich, our most chronologically bounded theme, and on Jewish/German relations, purposefully separating the two topics since German Jews had a long history of reciprocal interactions with the dominant society that predates the tragedy of the Holocaust.

The chapters are rich, informative and well documented. Here, we offer a number of important observations. First and foremost, the traditional fields of history—the ones that had seemed the most impervious to the methodological inroads of social history or women's history—have been thoroughly reexamined through the lens of gender if not refashioned into a new accepted mainstream narrative. These changes reflect the ability of the gender framework to underscore the male perspectives of the field (as in the old adage "war is men's business") and to ask challenging new questions about the multiple meanings of men and women, masculinity and femininity, in these settings. Such changes do not take male (or female) identity for granted but explore their specific meanings in varied contexts. They provide historians with exciting new ways to read archival and other written, visual, and material evidence, even of older sources and data long known to the historical profession.

We also acknowledge that the thematic subfields themselves are fluid and porous; the chapter headings imply a neater classification than the actual empirical content. For the reader, there is, indeed, considerable overlap: religious identities are matters of politics; sexual and racial policies cannot be divorced from imperial rule; family ties are part of class formation, soldiers' identities, and statecraft. Each chapter, however, maintains a viable thematic focus that nonetheless demonstrates how the gender perspective and method erodes artificial divisions and time-honored conceptual findings. A deep empirical reach—into discourses, symbols, institutions, and subjectivities at precise historical moments in time—leads to rich and often unanticipated findings.

Angelika Schaser in Chapter 2 examines the characteristics of the new German national historiography from the 1980s. She assesses the contributions of women's and gender studies to the literature on the German nation and addresses the importance of the "cultural turn" for the development of the field. She sums up her analysis with the observation that in this field of inquiry, gender is establishing itself (despite opposition) as an important analytical category. The turn to cultural history seems to have accelerated this process. For Schaser, the main areas of gender research include the participation of women in national movements, the discursive construction of the nation, national symbols and representations, and the development of a national consciousness in the diverse territories of the German Empire. It also involves the importance of collective memory for the construction of national and regional identities. These subject areas are treated—albeit often with a considerable time lag—on both sides of the Atlantic. As in other fields, important impulses have come from the United States In one area, German women historians have come to set the standards. They now are studying men as a sex and inquiring into the dimensions of masculinity more intensely and more self-evidently than their U.S. colleagues.

This development is underscored in Chapter 3 by Karen Hagemann, who genders the history of the military and of war in nineteenth- and twentieth-century Germany. In this field major changes have occurred in the last fifteen years. Military history, for a long time one of the most traditional areas of historiography, has become a burgeoning research field and has gained growing recognition on both sides of the Atlantic, even outside the circle of military history experts. According to Hagemann, two main factors have contributed to this trend: (1) the development of world politics since the collapse of the Socialist system of states, which has strongly underscored the continued relevance of the themes of military and war and their influence on all other areas of the economy, politics, society, and culture; but, also, (2) innovations first introduced in the history of the military and war by social historians and subsequently by cultural and gender historians. The latter perspectives challenged the field both through new questions and new methods. Indeed, the wide variety of methods and questions with which scholars in the United States and Germany are currently studying the military and war in German history is remarkable. It reaches from military and operational history in the conventional sense to political, economic, and social history, the history of technology, art and cultural history, and film studies. For that reasons some scholars even speak of a "military history in extension," which incorporates all modern historiographical approaches.[77] In Germany this new history of the military and war includes the dimension of gender, particularly by focusing on the history of masculinity.

For Birthe Kundrus in Chapter 4, gender is mainly used as a category for the analysis of women as agents in the process of colonialization and constructions of colonial femininity. Kundrus draws on postcolonial theory and, for comparative purposes, a wide range of literature on British, Dutch, and other colonial experiences, to explore the many meanings of empire in German national discourses, politics, and institution building, including periods before and after the era of formal empire, 1884–1918. She demonstrates how colonial spaces created new understandings of femininity and masculinity as the colonial administrators in Berlin sought inroads into the intimate spheres of the lives of the settlers; in fact, she argues that gender became a central point of contestation between the metropole and its colonies, impacting debates about reproduction, marriage, and citizenship. From this scholarship, Kundrus offers many useful suggestions for future research. Like Belinda Davis in the following chapter, she also looks at the subjective worlds that drew aristocratic and privileged bourgeois women into imperialist ventures at home and abroad, in fact and fiction.

Belinda Davis in Chapter 5 weaves together the two related historiographies of the state and high politics on the one hand and of popular protest on the other. Both in origins and intent, she connects the challenges of this historiography to the ongoing feminist project. Yet she is careful to differentiate scholarship from the English-speaking world from its German counterparts. Thus, she explores differences in the interpretation of such contentious issues as victim/perpetrator (in the Nazi era) and the politics of difference (given the feminist commitment to equality). She relates these differences partly to the contemporary politics of the two groups of historians. Davis also shows how, collectively, this work on women's and gender history has broadened understandings of "politics," extending beyond the state and its institutions. She includes studies written in the later years of the GDR as well. Davis remains critical of the step to professionalization, however, which she sees as leading to a significant "depoliticization" of the scholarly work on politics.

In Chapter 6, Kathleen Canning offers a carefully nuanced account of the chronology of keyword development in German social history: from class to citizenship to welfare. Despite its vogue today, notions of citizenship hardly came into play in the literature of the 1960s and 1970s, despite important early study on the politics of feminism and socialism in imperial Germany, among others. She shows that feminist theoretical and empirical work on class and labor history prepared the intellectual path for the move to gender, in the process, however, dispersing labor history across a wide spectrum of thematic arenas. For Canning, the category of gender has created new linkages between class and labor in the works on the welfare state, citizenship, and empire. Canning is, however, skeptical of mainstreaming projects, because, as inherently disciplinary undertakings, they appear to foreclose ongoing intellectual experimentation and interdisciplinary inquiry.

The Nazi era is a topic that long has engaged German women's historians for deeply personal and political reasons. Over the years, research of the period has produced many "quarrels" among women's historians across the Atlantic. Claudia Koonz in Chapter 7 analyzes the development of research on the Third Reich and the Holocaust. She observes that without innovation on a lively periphery (women's and gender history), conventional history on National Socialism would have stagnated. At the same time, however, she admits that without at least some mainstream recognition, a new approach cannot flourish. In her chapter she is asking what blinded conventional scholars to the significance of women as historical subjects, what conceptual changes have created an opening for the inclusion of women and gender and at what points women's history and gender-based interpretations have flowed smoothly into the sluggish mainstream. For her, the answers lie partly in the internal transformations of academic history and its subdisciplines and partly in the shifts in popular culture and public commemoration. From her standpoint, women's history and, to a lesser extent, gender as an analytical category now constitute in the American academic culture one significant current in mainstream scholarship on Nazi Germany, although not on the Holocaust.

Do we need the mainstream?

The same is not true for Germany, however. Here, despite a developed research agenda by women's and gender historians, most of the heated public debates did not integrate female historians' perspectives. The only exception was the so called "*Historikerinnenstreit*," but this quarrel never reached the feature pages of the German newspapers.[78]

In Chapter 8, Ben Baader draws a useful and complicated map of the different historical traditions that come together in German Jewish history. With attention to detail, he interrelates the different historiographies that shape the field: German Jewish history, written originally from a religious perspective, studies on Jewish women's lives and roles in the community, the interrelationship of German and Jewish history, and the ties and tensions between German women and German Jewish women in politics and the public sphere. Baader pays particular attention to the different settings for this work, examining the studies produced by women's historians of German Jewish backgrounds in the United States and the microstudies of German/Jewish community relations prior to the Holocaust written by non-Jewish German historians in Germany. Unlike Canning, Baader is more optimistic about the project of mainstreaming, in particular in the field of social history.

Chapter 9, written by Ann Taylor Allen, explores the scholarly work on religion. Never absent from the feminist inquiry—indeed "new wave" feminist scholars early on acknowledged the emergence of Germany's first women's movements out of the Protestant milieu of church and charity in the 1840s—religion has become a challenging topic now embracing the construction of subjectivities and identities. For Allen, one of the most important, yet at the same time neglected questions in the historical research of this field is the role of religion in the twentieth century. How far does religion continue to shape the gender identities of both men and women in the modern era? For her the feminization of religion has entered a new stage as women throughout the Western world—in particular in the post-1945 period—have directly challenged male hierarchies as they aspire to leadership positions as priests, ministers, theologians, and administrators. Indeed, women sensitive to gender equity are needed to reform the churches in the future.

Chapter 10 by Atina Grossmann addresses the history of sexuality. Grossmann argues that this history, like any other field of German historiography, cannot be understood outside of the shadow and echo of National Socialism. For her, "questions of continuity and rupture, singularity and comparability," are central to research irrespective if it is directed to the time period before or after the Third Reich. The history of sexuality is tied to the history of population policy, race hygiene, and eugenics and, also, to the history of women and gender. Moreover, it also should be read with reference to German colonialism and the imperial racist legacy. Grossmann's contribution focuses on population policy, racial hygiene and sex reform in twentieth-century Germany, in

particular on discourses and politics in the 1920s and 1960s and on their consequences for sexual behavior in everyday life. In her sophisticated analysis of this
research, Grossmann shows the possibilities, limits, and problems of sexuality
as a focus of historical inquiry. She suggests that for the field the common
concepts of race, class, gender, and sexual orientation might not be developed
adequately in terms of theory and methods. Women and gender historians
probably will need to borrow more from queer theory, psychoanalysis, and sexology. Moreover, in this field as in other fields of women's and gender history,
more comparative and transnational studies could be useful.

Chapter 11 by Robert Moeller fittingly argues for reinserting family into
the main themes of twentieth-century German history. Demonstrating the
relevance of family, he states that women's and gender historians for too long
have neglected the family as a subject of inquiry. "Family" as theme has not
fully disappeared; rather, it has migrated into several other keywords of wom-
en's and gender history. For him, these key concepts are "social policy, welfare
state, and labor law," "politics," "nationalism and citizenship," "consumption"
and "sexuality." He convincingly shows the importance of the family to the
research in the context of these rubrics but, he underlines, only if the family
is explored on multiple levels. As he puts it, the family is "an ideological and
legal construct; a metaphor used to organize our thoughts about social, political, and even economic interactions; a space where generation, gender, [sex,]
and relations of power play themselves out; a bundle of emotional, physical,
and sexual relationships that can be the source of pleasure and pain; and a
structure that is thought to mediate between individuals and the state." With
this open, multilevel understanding, the family indeed occupies a key place in
German history, far beyond the immediate field of family history.

Conclusion: From Margin to Mainstream?

In our early twenty-first century, gender analysis has become part of historical
research as an independent theory and method in its own right (women's and
gender studies) and as an analytical complement to many other approaches to
the past. A regular component of the way many historians who work on German history do research, its place in university settings, curricula reform, and
publishing practices is by no means settled, however. Yet, precisely what this
means in the two national contexts of this study is different.

A quick glance at the 2004 annual meeting of the AHA in Washington,
DC. reveals a significant presence of women, women's history, and gender
themes on the panels, as innovative and comparative in their reach as is
demonstrated in the chapters of this book. At the conference, there were
176 panels, 1,300 presenters and 49 specialized societies, including the

prominent Conference Group for Central European History, the main affiliation for U.S.-based central European and German historians. The Conference Group sponsored 17 panels in Central European (the wider geographical reach for the premodern era) and German history (in the modern period). About 25 percent were on women and gender; some involved comparative approaches (examining Germany, for example, within the context of certain themes, including naval blockades, war crimes, and comparative memories of World War II) and a number focused on the interplay of German national and regional identities. Other German history panels also took up issues of race and colonialism, the East German political economy, and new approaches in cultural studies. The AHA encourages gender balance on all panels. Affirming the point made by Angelika Schaser, it favors the national framework but it also included sessions on the Atlantic World, comparative history, and global history, incorporating a growing interest in transnational themes and connections in the past and new analytical frameworks for their study. Overall, of the twenty separate women and gender panels identified as such in the AHA program index, the tendency remains still to place panels appreciably about women alone in the gender rubric. The AHA annual meeting is a receptive forum for ongoing experimentation with the analytical capacity of gender and with its ties to other innovative themes and methods in a variety of nation-state and comparative histories.[79]

Nevertheless, the new social and cultural histories and transnational approaches, including the prominence of women's and gender themes in American academic discourses, have produced a backlash under the misleading rubric of "culture wars." Underway by the late 1990s, "cultural wars" are less about culture per se than about the politics and uses of knowledge at a time when American society indeed seems to be overwhelmed by a wealth of complicated and contradictory information. The debates are reminiscent of the tensions over a "serviceable past" in West Germany starting in the early 1960s. Academic and intellectual critics on the right of the political spectrum (aided at times by conservative former heads of funding agencies such as the National Endowment for the Humanities)[80] hurl the charge of "PC" (politically correct) at the promulgation of such new knowledge. They claim that attention to race, gender, class differences, or transnational perspectives is only about the pressure to be "politically correct," as if somehow acknowledging these realities of life's chances and opportunities or exploring different causal connections are politically motivated and suspect. The divisions speak to new fault lines that have opened up in American politics, appreciably as a product of the challenges of economic globalization and its perceived threats to the sovereign independence of the nation-state. The divisions are fundamentally about different perspectives on the world, between exclusively nationalist calculations and broader transnational and international visions, between a national and a cosmopolitan education—and everything in between. It is hardly surprising, then, that the writing of history has emerged as a central terrain in the debates. There are some indications, too, that the student "demand" driving university curricula is less hospitable to exploring themes of gender and sexuality than was the case in the expansion of women's history and women's studies in the 1970s and 1980s.

For women's and gender historians the situation in Germany is no less complicated, captured by a resolution, which was sent in May 2005 by the "Working Group on Women's and Gender History in Germany" to the board of the German Historical Association. The resolution protested the continued discrimination against women and gender research. What precipitated the letter was the decision of the German Historical Association the previous year to hold its conference in Kiel without any session on women's and gender history, despite submission of several panel proposals. In marked contrast to the American practice, the number of female paper presenters had been small. The board of the German Historical Association, consisting of four men and one woman, proudly proclaimed that it had received so many proposals before the congress and had rejected 50 percent. However, the selection seems to have been biased as the officials eliminated the proposals by feminist historians. This scandalous situation was brought to public attention in February 2005 in a review of the congress in the most important electronic forum for German historians, H-Soz-u-Kult—yet nothing happened.[81] The only reaction was the Working Group resolution, which captures a sense of setback in the movement to integrate women's and gender research into German professional meetings since the mid 1990s.[82] At the last congress of the German Historical Association in Konstanz in September 2006 at least five of 52 sessions integrated the gender perspective systematically.[83]

As our comparative approach shows, the extent of women's and gender integration into the national academies and research agendas is not solely a matter of the quality and innovations of the research designs. It reflects as well the extent and nature of institutional support, cultural assumptions, ties to feminist and other social movements, and the strength of historiographical traditions, all of which shape and limit the integration despite the persuasive claims to equity opened up by the very work in gender history. Our collection highlights a vibrant exchange on the personal and professional levels that has produced innovative scholarship. The field, indeed, is enlivened by the many debates, as well as interpretive disagreements, that crisscross the Atlantic. The book demonstrates the substantive impact of gender inquiry into distinct historical topics, approaches, and methods; it also records the roadblocks that impede full realization of gender's analytical challenges. Undeniably, German historiography is being rewritten

substantially by the gender perspective. It remains to be seen if this scholarship will fashion new powerful historical narratives. It is a worthy project
since peoples' perspectives on the past shape how they think about and
work toward the future.

Notes

The authors would like to thank the following colleagues warmly for their
comments and critiques on earlier versions of this paper: Jane Caplan, Ann
Taylor Allen, Karin Hausen, Birthe Kundrus, Bob Moeller, Karen Offen, and
Hanna Schissler.

1. Important international introductions in the state of research of women's and gender history are: Karen Offen et al., eds., *Writing Women's History: International Perspectives* (Bloomington, 1991); Joy Parr, "Gender History and Historical Practice," *The Canadian Historical
   Review* 76, no. 1 (1995): 354–376; "Gender and History: Retrospect and Prospect," ed.
   Leonora Davidoff et al., special issue, *Gender & History* 11, no. 3 (1999); Bonnie G. Smith,
   ed., *Women's History in a Global Perspective*, vols. 1–2 (Urbana, 2004–2005). As examples
   of this kind of international anthology in the field of political history see among others:
   "Citizenships and Subjectivities," ed. Kathleen Canning and Sonya O. Rose, special issue,
   Gender & History 13, no. 3 (2001); Ida Blom et al., eds., *Gendered Nations: Nationalisms and
   Gender Order in the Long Nineteenth Century* (Oxford, 2002); Anne McClintock et al., eds.,
   Dangerous Liaisons: Gender, Nation, and Postcolonial Perspectives (Minneapolis, 1997); Ruth
   Roach Pierson and Nupur Chaudury, eds., *Nation, Empire, Colony: Historicizing Gender and
   Race* (Bloomington, 1998).
2. Helmut Walser Smith, "For a Differently Centered Central European History: Reflections
   on Jürgen Osterhammel, Geschichtswissenschaft jenseits des Nationalstaats," *Central European History* 37, no. 1 (2004): 122–123; Philipp Ther, "Beyond the Nation: The Relational
   Basis of a Comparative History of Germany and Europe," *Central European History* 36, no.
   1 (2003): 45–73.
3. Lynn Hunt, "The Challenge of Gender: Deconstruction of Categories and Reconstruction of Narratives in Gender History," in *Geschlechtergeschichte und Allgemeine Geschichte.
   Herausforderungen und Perspektiven*, ed. Hans Medick and Anne-Charlott Trepp (Göttingen,
   1998), 57–97.
4. This is a choice of intellectual focus; we acknowledge the significant role, for example, of
   the British historians Richard J. Evans and Jill Stephenson in writing German women's history in the 1970s and also the importance of academic migrations. Thus, the British-trained
   historians Geoff Eley and Jane Caplan, among others, moved to U.S. universities and influenced decisively the many discussions about German women's and gender history and related
   methodological questions. As our gender perspective shows, the national categories are not
   neat and tidy. Among his many publications, see Richard J. Evans, *The Feminist Movement
   in Germany, 1894–1933* (London, 1976) and *Comrades and Sisters: Feminism, Socialism and*

Pacifism in Europe, 1870–1945 (New York, 1987). For Jill Stephenson, see, among others, her *Women in Nazi Society* (New York, 1975); and *The Nazi Organization of Women* (London, 1981). Publications of the German/American forerunner conferences that integrated gender include: Geoff Eley, ed., *Society, Culture, and the State in Germany, 1870–1930* (Ann Arbor, 1996); "Gender and Rationalization in Comparative Historical Perspective—Germany and the United States," ed. Karen Hagemann and Molly Ladd-Taylor, special issue, *Social Politics* 4, no. 1 (1997). For similar comparisons from a women's studies perspective, see Ann Taylor Allen, "The March through the Institutions: Women's Studies in the United States and West and East Germany, 1980–1995," *Signs: Journal of Women in Culture and Society* 22, no. 1 (1996): 152–180; see as well Myra Marx Ferree, "Equality and Autonomy: Feminist Politics in the U.S. and West Germany," in *The Women's Movement of the United States and Western Europe: Consciousness, Political Opportunity and Public Policy*, ed. Mary Faid Katzenstein and Carol McClure Miller (Philadelphia, 1987), 172–195.

5. Leslie Adelson, "The Price of Feminism: Of Women and Turks," in *Gender and German-ness: Cultural Productions of Nation*, ed. Patricia Herminghouse and Magda Mueller (Providence, 1997), 305–319.

6. Fritz Fischer, *Griff nach der Weltmacht: Die Kriegszielpolitik des kaiserlichen Deutschlands, 1914–1918* (Düsseldorf, 1961); idem., *From Kaiserreich to Third Reich: Elements of Continuity in German History 1871–1945* (London, 1986).

7. Hans Ulrich Wehler, *Das deutsche Kaiserreich, 1871–1918* (Göttingen, 1973); David Blackbourn and Geoff Eley, *The Peculiarities of German History: Bourgeois Society and Politics in Nineteenth-Century Germany* (Oxford, 1984).

8. Daniel Jonah Goldhagen, *Hitler's Willing Executioners: Ordinary Germans and the Holocaust* (New York, 1996); Robert R. Shandley, ed., *Unwilling Germans? The Goldhagen Debate* (Minneapolis, 1998).

9. Gisela Bock, "Die Frauen und der Nationalsozialismus: Bemerkungen zu einem Buch von Claudia Koonz," *Geschichte und Gesellschaft* 15 (1989): 563–579; Claudia Koonz, "Erwiderung auf Gisela Bocks Rezension von Mothers in the Fatherland," *Geschichte und Gesellschaft* 18 (1992): 394–399; Gisela Bock, "Ein Historikerinnenstreit?" Geschichte und *Gesellschaft* 18 (1992): 400–404; Dagmar Reese and Carola Sachse, "Frauenforschung und Nationalsozialismus: Eine Bilanz," in *Töchter-Fragen: NS-Frauen-Geschichte*, ed. Lerke Gravenhorst and Carmen Tatschmurat (Freiburg i. Br., 1990), 73–106; Atina Grossmann, "Feminist Debates about Women and National Socialism," *Gender & History* 3, no. 3 (1991): 350–358; Birthe Kundrus, "Frauen und Nationalsozialismus: Überlegungen zum Stand der Forschung," *Archiv für Sozialgeschichte* 36 (1996): 481–499; Adelheid von Saldern, "Victims or Perpetrators? Controversies about the Role of Women in the Nazi State," in *Nazism and German Society 1933–1945*, ed. David Crew (London, 1994), 141–166; see also Kirsten Heinsohn et al., "Einleitung," in *Zwischen Karriere und Verfolgung. Handlungsräume von Frauen im national-sozialistischen Deutschland*, ed. Heinsohn et al. (Frankfurt/M., 1997), 7–24.

10. See Sheila Ryan Johansson, "'Herstory' as History: A New Field or Another Fad?" in *Liberating Women's History: Theoretical and Critical Essays*, ed. Berenice A. Carroll (Urbana, 1976), 400–430.

11. Overviews of the development and the state of women's and gender studies in Germany are found in: Allen, "The March"; Gisela Bock, "Women's History and Gender History: Aspects of an International Debate," *Gender & History* (1989): 7–30; Gunilla-Friederike Budde, "Das Geschlecht der Geschichte," in *Geschichte zwischen Kultur und Gesellschaft*, ed. Thomas Mergel and Thomas Welskopp (Munich, 1997), 125–150; Kathleen Canning, "German Particularities in Women's History/Gender History," *Journal of Women's History* 5 (1993): 102–114; Ute Frevert, "Bewegung und Disziplin in der Frauengeschichte: Ein Forschungsbericht," *Geschichte und Gesellschaft* 14 (1988): 240–262; Ute Frevert,

"Frauengeschichte—Männergeschichte—Geschlechtergeschichte," in *Feministische Perspektiven in der Wissenschaft*, ed. Lynn Blattmann (Zurich, 1993), 23–40; Ute Frevert, "Geschichte als Geschlechtergeschichte? Zur Bedeutung des 'weiblichen Blicks' für die Wahrnehmung von Geschichte," *Saeculum* 43 (1992): 108–123; Johanna Gehmacher and Maria Mesner, ed., *Frauen- und Geschlechtergeschichte: Positionen/Perspektiven* (Innsbruck, 2003); Rebekka Habermas, "Geschlechtergeschichte und 'anthropology of gender': Geschichte einer Begegnung," *Historische Anthropologie* 2, no. 1 (1993): 463–487; Karin Hausen and Heide Wunder, eds, *Frauengeschichte—Geschlechtergeschichte* (Frankfurt/M., 1992); Isabel V. Hull, "Feminist and Gender History through the Literary Looking Glass: German Historiography in Postmodern Times," *Central European History* 22 (1989): 279–300; Hans Medick and Anne-Charlott Trepp, eds., *Geschlechtergeschichte und allgemeine Geschichte. Herausforderungen und Perspektiven* (Göttingen, 1998).

12. Allen, "The March"; also Ursula Nienhaus, „Wir fordern Beides: Autonomie und Geld," in *Autonomie oder Institution. Über die Leidenschaft und Macht von Frauen*, Dokumentationsgruppe der Sommeruniversität der Frauen (Berlin, 1981), 118–124.

13. On master narratives, see Konrad Jarausch and Martin Sabrow, eds., *Die Historische Meistererzählung: Deutungslinien der deutschen Nationalgeschichte nach 1945* (Göttingen, 2002); Konrad Jarausch and Michael Geyer, eds., *Shattered Past: Reconstructing German Histories* (Princeton, 2003).

14. Hunt, "The Challenge of Gender." Her plea is of a different order than the poststructuralist critiques of historical metanarratives.

15. Merry E. Wiesner, "Disembodied Theory?: Discourses of Sex in Early Modern Germany," in *Gender in Early Modern German History*, ed. Ulinka Rublack (Cambridge, 2002), 161.

16. Johansson, "Herstory"; see also Karin Hausen, ed., *Frauen suchen ihre Geschichte: Historische Studien zum 19. und 20. Jahrhundert* (Munich, 1982).

17. For early historical studies reflecting these feminist debates: Jean H. Quataert, *Reluctant Feminists in German Social Democracy, 1885–1917* (Princeton, 1979); Werner Thönnensen, *Frauenemanzipation: Politik und Literatur der deutschen Sozialdemokratie zur Frauenbewegung 1863–1933* (Frankfurt/M., 1969); Heinz Niggemann, *Emanzipation zwischen Sozialismus und Feminismus: Die sozialdemokratische Frauenbewegung im Kaiserreich* (Wuppertal, 1981); Barbara Greven-Aschoff, *Die bürgerliche Frauenbewegung in Deutschland 1894–1933* (Göttingen, 1981); Herrad-Ulrike Bussemer, *Frauenemanzipation und Bildungsbürgertum: Sozialgeschichte der Frauenbewegung in der Reichsgründungszeit* (Weinheim, 1985). In its early phases, women's historians were at the forefront of feminist theorizing; recently the influences have come largely from literary and cultural theorists.

18. Natalie Zemon Davis, "Women's History in Transition: The European Case," *Feminist Studies* 3 (1976): 90.

19. Kathleen Canning, "Feminist History after the Linguistic Turn: Historicizing Discourse and Experience," *Signs* 19, no. 2 (1994): 370–371.

20. See, for example, Hanne-Beate Schoepf-Schilling, "Frauenstudien, Frauenforschung, und Frauenforschungszentren in den USA: Neuere Entwicklungen," in *Neue Sammlung* (1978): 156–173; Ruth-Ellen Joeres Boetcher, "Vom Frauenstudium zur Frauenforschung: Neuere Trends im akademischen Feminismus in den USA," *Feministische Studien* 6 (1988): 129–135.

21. For more see http://www.journals.uchicago.edu/Signs/home.html. An overview of the history of the international journals on women's history is provided by Dagmar Feist, "Zeitschriften zur Historischen Frauenforschung," *Geschichte und Gesellschaft* 22 (1996): 97–117; also Patrice McDermott, *Politics and Scholarship: Feminist Academic Journals and the Production of Knowledge* (Urbana, 1994).

22. For more see http://www.feministstudies.org/aboutfs/history.html.

23. See articles by Leonore Davidoff, Sandra Lauderdale Graham, Carole Turbin, and Elizabeth Thompson in "Women's History in the New Millennium: Rethinking Public and Private," ed. Leila J. Rupp, special issue, *Journal of Women's History* 15, no. 1 (2003); see also articles by Mary P. Ryan and Joan B. Landes in "Women's History in the New Millennium: Rethinking Public and Private—Continuing the Conversation," ed. Leila J. Rupp, special issue, *Journal of Women's History* 15, no. 2 (2003). Importantly, the journal now subscribes to work that blends women's and gender history together. The editors note that the issues, which divided women's history and gender history can be "bridged by work on women that is sensitive to the particular historical constructions of gender that shape and are shaped by women's experiences." For more on this journal, which was the first publication devoted exclusively to the international field of women's history, see http://iupjournals.org/jwh/.

24. For more see http://www.beitraege-redaktion.de/.

25. For more see http://www.feministische-studien.de/.

26. Ibid.

27. For more on the history of the Berkshire Conference see http://www.humanities.uci.edu/history/berkshire/history.htm.

28. See "Muttersein und Mutterideologie in der bürgerlichen Gesellschaft," *Frauenarbeitstreffen vom 18.–20. January 1980 in Bremen* (Bremen, 1980).

29. See "Dokumentation des 3. Historikerinnentreffens in Bielefeld, April 1981," *Beiträge zur feministschen Theorie und Praxis* 5 (1981); *Dokumentation des 4. Historikerinnentreffens, März 1983 an der Technischen Universität Berlin, zusammengestellt von der Vorbereitungsgruppe* (Berlin, 1983); *Dokumentation des 5. Historikerinnentreffens im April 1984 in Wien, zusammengestellt von der Vorbereitungsgruppe* (Vienna, 1984); *Die ungeschriebene Geschichte: Historische Frauenforschung. Dokumentation des 5. Historikerinnentreffens Wien 16.–18. April 1984*, Vienna, 1985; Jutta Dalhof et al., eds., *Frauenmacht in der Geschichte: Beiträge des Historikerinnentreffens 1985 zur Frauengeschichtsforschung* (Düsseldorf, 1986).

30. See *Dokumentation des 3. Historikerinnentreffens in Bielefeld, April 1981.*

31. The titles of these sessions in 1984 were "Frauenräume" (Female Spaces), in 1986 "Privatheit und Öffentlichkeit" (Public and Private), and in 1990 "Geschlechtsidentitäten" (Gender Identities). See Karin Hausen and Heide Wunder, „Einleitung," in: *Frauengeschichte—Geschlechtergeschichte*, ed. Karin Hausen and Heide Wunder (Frankfurt/M., 1992), 9–20. This volume presents the papers of the three sessions. See also Gisela Bock, "Geschichte, Frauengeschichte, Geschlechtergeschichte," *Geschichte und Gesellschaft* 14 (1988): 364–391.

32. For an overview of these changes through the perspective of women's studies, see Marilyn J. Boxer, *When Women Ask the Questions: Creating Women's Studies in America* (Baltimore, 1998).

33. Patricia M. Mazón, *Gender and the Modern Research University: The Admission of Women to German Higher Education, 1865–1914* (Stanford, 2003).

34. Allen, "The March," 154–156.

35. For the situation in the former German Democratic Republic (GDR), see Irene Dölling, "Situation und Perspektive von Frauenforschung in der DDR," *ZIF Bulletin* 1, no. 1 (1990): 1–23.

36. For more on the AKHFG see http://www.uni-flensburg.de/akhfg/.

37. For more on the IFRWH, see http://www.historians.ie/women/; and one of its major publications, Karen Offen et al., eds., *Writing Women's History: International Perspectives* (Houndmill, NY, 1991). The German historians Gisela Bock and Karin Hausen played an important role in the foundation of the IFRWH in 1987. Its first president was the Norwegian historian Ida Blom.

38. On the start of the AKHFG see Karen Hagemann, "Der Arbeitskreis historische Frauenforschung," *Metis* 2, no. 1 (1993): 87–92.

39. Hausen and Wunder, "Einleitung." For more on the Campus series, which by 2005 published forty-six volumes, see: http://www.campus.de/sgr/54M.
40. The number was higher in the mid 1990s. Because of the retirement of Karin Hausen (Technical University of Berlin) and Heide Wunder (University of Kassel), the first two feminist historians who obtained a professorship, women's history lost two positions. Both had not yet been replaced as of February 2007.
41. For a critical reflection of the early publication politics of *Geschichte und Gesellschaft* (*GG*) see Ute Frevert, "Bewegung und Disziplin in der Frauengeschichte: Ein Forschungsbericht," *GG* 14 (1988), 240–262. Special issues after 1988 included "Familie, Haushalt, Wohnen," *GG* 14, no. 1 (1988); "Lebenswege von Frauen im Ancient Regime," *GG* 18, no. 4 (1992); "Rassenpolitik und Geschlechterpolitik im Nationalsozialismus," *GG* 19, no. 3 (1993); "Körpergeschichte" in *GG* 26, no. 4 (2000).
42. For more see http://www.univie.ac.at/Geschichte/LHOMME/lhomme.html. On feminist journals in general see Feist, "Zeitschriften," 108–117.
43. For more see http://www.edition-ebersbach.de/seiten/metis.htm; see also Feist, "Zeitschriften," 110–117.
44. This powerful self-identity is already embedded in the programmatic statement of *Historische Zeitschrift*, the original journal of the German historical profession, founded in 1859. See "Preface," in *The Varieties of History: From Voltaire to the Present*, ed. Fritz Stern (New York, 1973), 170–174.
45. More information on the politics of the Bundesministerium für Bildung und Forschung and the federative states is available at http://www.bmbf.de/de/474.php. For the practical applications of these measures in the early period see Erika Beck-Rosenthal, ed., *Frauenförderung in der Praxis: Frauenbeauftragte Berichten* (Frankfurt/M., 1990).
46. Retrieved 7 March 2005 from http://www.historians.org/info/AHA_Data.htm. We want to thank Robert Townsend, assistant director for research and publications at the AHA, for access to statistical materials.
47. Linda Kerber, "We Must Make the Academic Workplace More Humane and Equitable," *The Chronicle of Higher Education* (18 March 2005).
48. The statistics were kindly provided by the Statistische Bundesamt. We want to thank Katja Stender for helping us to compile all the German figures.
49. The first exception was the Centre for Interdisciplinary Studies on Women and Gender at the TU in Berlin founded by Karin Hausen and Karen Hagemann. For more information, see http://www.tu-berlin.de/zifg/.
50. For more information, see http://www.gender.hu-berlin.de/eng/center/
51. Allen, "The March," 159–164.
52. The background for this is that only 40 percent of German child-care institutions for preschool kids are all-day institutions and only 5 percent of all elementary schools are all-day schools. Only 5 percent of all kids of elementary school age who go to the usual half-day school have the possibility to go to an after-school program. See Karen Hagemann, "Between Ideology and Economy: The 'Time Politics' of Child care and Public Education in Two Germanies," *Social Politics* 13, no. 1 (2006): 217–260.
53. See for example Canning, "Feminist History," 370; Bock, "Geschichte," 367–371.
54. Joan Kelly, "The Social Relation of the Sexes: Methodological Implications of Women's History," in *Women, History, and Theory: The Essays of Joan Kelly* (Chicago, 1986), 1–18; Davis, "Women's History in Transition"; Manuela Thurner, "Subject to Change: Theories and Paradigms of U.S. Feminist History," *Journal of Women's History* 9, no. 2 (1997): 122–146.
55. Natalie Zemon Davis, "Women's History in Transition," 90.
56. Gerda Lerner, *The Majority Finds its Past; Placing Women in History* (New York, 1979), 168–180.
57. Thurner, "Subject to Change."

58. Joan Wallach Scott, "Gender: A Useful Category of Historical Analysis," reprinted in *Gender and the Politics of History*, ed. Joan Wallach Scott (New York, 1988), 28–50.

59. For introductions into the wider debates, see Keith Jenkins, ed., *The Postmodern History Reader* (New York, 1996); Quentin Skinner, ed. *The Return of Grand Theory in the Human Sciences* (Cambridge, 1985).

60. Scott, "Gender," 50.

61. See for example Martina Kessel, "The 'Whole Man': The Longing for a Masculine World in Nineteenth-Century Germany," *Gender & History* 15, no. 1 (2003): 1–31.

62. See Karen Offen, *European Feminisms: A Political History, 1700–1950* (Stanford, 2000); see also Boxer, *When Women Ask the Questions*, 144.

63. Of 507 listings, 404 (or 79 percent) were centers for women's studies (the title does not mean an absence of gender research, of course); 54 (a little over 10 percent) had the title women's and gender studies, and 49 (a little under 10 percent) were officially gender studies programs. Women's studies programs, departments, and research centers retrieved November 2004 from http://research.umbc.edu/~korenman/wmst/programs.html. At the site, there also is a listing of 11 German interdisciplinary feminist research centers.

64. For the theoretical and methodological approach to the history of masculinities, Ute Frevert, "Frauengeschichte—Männergeschichte—Geschlechtergeschichte," in *Feministische Perspektiven in der Wissenschaft*, ed. Lynn Blattmann (Zurich, 1993), 23–40; Frevert, "Männergeschichte," in *Was ist Gesellschaftsgeschichte?: Positionen, Themen, Analysen*, ed. Manfred Hettling et al. (Munich, 1991), 31–43; Thomas Kühne, "Männergeschichte als Geschlechtergeschichte," in *Männergeschichte—Geschlechtergeschichte. Männlichkeit im Wandel der Moderne*, ed. Thomas Kühne (Frankfurt/M., 1996), 7–30. On the recent state of international research see John Tosh, "Hegemonic, Masculinity and the History of Gender," in *Masculinities in Politics and War: Gendering Modern History*, ed. Stefan Dudink et al. (Manchester, 2004), 41–60; John Tosh, "The Making of Manhood and the Uses of History," in *Manliness: Essays on Gender, Family, and Empire*, ed. John Tosh (Harlow, 2004), 13–28; John Tosh, "What Should Historians Do with Masculinity? Reflections on Nineteenth-Century Britain," ibid., 29–60.

65. See Ute Frevert, *Men of Honour: A Social and Cultural History of the Duel* (Cambridge, 1995); Karen Hagemann, *"Mannlicher Muth und Teutsche Ehre": Nation, Militär und Geschlecht zur Zeit der Antinapoleonischen Kriege Preussens* (Paderborn, 2002); Kühne, *Männergeschichte—Geschlechtergeschichte*; Anne-Charlotte Trepp, *Sanfte Männlichkeit und selbständige Weiblichkeit* (Göttingen, 1996).

66. See George L. Mosse, *The Image of Man: The Creation of Modern Masculinity* (New York, 1996); John Fout, ed., *Forbidden History: The State, Society and the Regulation of Sexuality in Modern Europe: Essays from the Journal of the History of Sexuality* (Chicago,1992).

67. Canning, "Feminist History"; Lynn Abrams and Elizabeth Harvey, eds., *Gender Relations in German History: Power, Agency and Experience from the Sixteenth to the Twentieth Century* (Durham, 1997), 12, 27.

68. Ulinka Rublack, "The Public Body: Policing Abortion in Early Modern Germany," *Gender Relations* 58; Barbara Duden et al., eds., *Geschichte des Ungeborenen: Zur Erfahrungs-und Wissenschaftsgeschichte der Schwangerschaft, 17.–20. Jahrhundert* (Göttingen, 2002); See also Sabine Kienitz, "Body Damage: War Disability and Constructions of Masculinity in Weimar Germany," in *Home/Front: The Military, War and Gender in Twentieth-Century Germany*, ed. Karen Hagemann and Stefanie Schüler-Springorum (Oxford, 2002), 181–203.

69. Canning, "German Pecularities," 281.

70. See Dorothee Wierling, "Alltagsgeschichte und Geschichte der Geschlechterbeziehungen: Über historische und historiographische Verhältnisse," in *Alltagsgeschichte: Zur Rekonstruktion historischer Erfahrungen und Lebensweisen*, ed. Alf Lüdtke, (Frankfurt/M., 1989), 169–190.

71. For an overview, see Karen Hagemann, "Von Männern, Frauen und der Militärgeschichte," *L'Homme* 12 (2001): 144–154.

72. Karin Hausen, "Die Nicht-Einheit der Geschichte als historiographische Herausforderung: Zur historischen Relevanz und Anstößigkeit der Geschlechtergeschichte," in Medick and Trepp, *Geschlechtergeschichte*, 15–55.

73. Once an esteemed field of history, economic history has fallen on hard times, despite the pressures of globalization and structural adjustments programs that figure in feminist transnational politics and human rights advocacy. For studies on German regions as part of the European industrializing terrain, see Jordan Goodman and Katrina Honeyman, *Gainful Pursuits: The Making of Industrial Europe, 1600–1914* (London, 1988); Sidney Pollard, *Peaceful Conquest: The Industrialization of Europe 1760–1970* (Oxford, 1981). For more recent studies with sensitivity to gender, Saskia Sassen, *Globalization and Its Discontents: Essays on the New Mobility of People and Money* (New York, 1998); Marianne A. Ferber and Julie A. Nelson, *Beyond Economic Man: Feminist Theory and Economics* (Chicago, 1993).

74. For feminism as intellectual tradition, Tjitske Akkerman and Siep Sturrman, eds., *Perspectives on Feminist Political Thought in European History: From the Middle Ages to the Present* (London, 1998); on new readings of ideas, Judith Butler, "Variations on Sex and Gender: Beauvoir, Wittig and Foucault," in *Feminism and Critique*, ed. Seyla Benhabib and Drucilla Cornell (Minneapolis, 1987); See also Jean Bethke Elshtain, *Public Man, Private Woman: Women in Social and Political Thought*, 2nd ed. (Princeton, 1993).

75. For a general overview, Sandra Harding, *The Science Question in Feminism* (Ithaca, 1986); Sandra Harding, *Whose Science? Whose Knowledge?: Thinking from Women's Lives* (Ithaca, 1991); Ludmilla Jordanova, *Sexual Visions: Images of Gender in Science and Medicine between the Eighteenth and Twentieth Century* (Madison, 1989); Londa Schiebinger, *The Mind Has No Sex? Women in the Origins of Modern Science*, (Cambridge, 1989); Londa Schiebinger, *Nature's Body: Gender in the Making of Modern Science* (New Brunswick, 2004); Londa Schiebinger, *Has Feminism Changed Science?* (Cambridge, 1999); Maryanne Cline Horowitz, "The 'Science' of Embryology Before the Discovery of the Ovum," in *Connecting Spheres: European Women in a Globalizing World, 1500 to the Present*, 2nd ed., ed. Marilyn J. Boxer and Jean H. Quataert (New York, 2000); Simon Richter, "Wet-Nursing, Onanism, and the Breast in Eighteenth-Century Germany," *Journal of the History of Sexuality* 7, no. 1 (1996): 1–22.

76. For important new work on these themes: Glenn B. Ramsey, "Erotic Friendship: Gender Inversion and Human Rights in the German Movement for Sexual Reform, 1897–1913," Ph.D. diss., Binghamton University, 2004: Emily M. Boyd, "Transexuals' Embodiment of Womanhood," *Gender and Society* 19, no. 3 (2005); 317–335; Linda Garber, ed., *Tilting the Tower: Lesbians, Teaching, Queer Subjects* (New York, 1994); Susanne zur Nieden, ed. *Homosexualität und Staatsräson: Männlichkeit, Homophobie wund Politik in Deutschland, 1900–1945*, (Frankfurt/M., 2005). For a catalogue of an exhibition with scholarly articles, Verein der Freunde eines Schwulen Museums in Berlin, ed., *Eldorado: Homosexuelle Frauen und Männer in Berlin, 1850–1950: Geschichte, Alltag und Kultur* (Berlin, 1992); see also Marita Keilson-Lauritz, *Die Geschichte der eigenen Geschichte: Literatur und Literaturkritik in den Anfängen der Schwulenbewegung* (Berlin, 1997); Marita Keilson-Lauritz and Rolf F. Land, eds., *ellung vom 7. Oktober bis 17. November 2000 in Berlin Friedrichshagen* (Berlin-Friedrichshagen, 2000).

77. See Thomas Kühne and Benjamin Ziemann, "Militärgeschichte in der Erweiterung. Konjunkturen, Interpretationen, Konzepte," in *Was ist Militärgeschichte?* ed. Thomas Kühne and Benjamin Ziemann (Paderborn, 2000), 9–48.

78. For a recent discussion of this debate see: Ralph M. Leck, "Conservative Empowerment and the Gender of Nazism: Paradigms of Power and Complicity in German Women's History," *Journal of Women's History* 12 (2002): 147–169.

79. American Historical Association, *Program of the 118th Annual Meeting*, Washington, DC, 2004.

80. Gertrud Himmelfarb, *The Roads to Modernity: The British, French and American Enlighten-ment* (New York, 2004); idem, *The New History and the Old: Critical Essays and Reappraisals* (Cambridge, Mass., 2004); Allan Bloom, *The Closing of the American Mind: How Higher Education Has Failed Democracy and Impoverished the Souls of Today's Students* (New York, 1987); Lynne V. Cheney, *Telling the Truth: Why Our Culture and Our Country Have Stopped Making Sense—and What We Can Do about It* (New York, 1995). Alternatively, Lawrence W. Levine, *The Opening of the American Mind: Canons, Culture, and History* (Boston, 1996); Joyce Appleby et al., *Telling the Truth about History* (New York, 1994). For a more tempered view of Bloom, see Jim Sleeper, "Allan Bloom and the Conservative Mind," *The New York Times Book Review* (4 September 2005): 27.

81. See Wiebke Kolbe, "Historikertag 2004: Geschlechtergeschichte," H-Soz-u-Kult, (2 November 2004), http://hsozkult.geschichte.hu-berlin.de/forum/type=diskussionen&id=540.

82. We would like to thank Bea Lund, who currently directs the "Working Group on Women's and Gender History in Germany" for providing us with this resolution.

83. See the program: http://www.uni-konstanz.de/historikertag/index2.php?menu=startseite.

2

The Challenge of Gender

National Historiography, Nationalism, and National Identities

Angelika Schaser

In a review of the literature entitled "The End of Research on Nationalism?" Árpád von Klimó notes categorically, "The self-reflexive turn, as I would like to call the tendencies towards the culture and politics of history, the culture of memory, etc., since all of them are concerned with the production and reproduction of historical knowledge and thus engage in second-order historical writing, has unsettled the discipline as a whole. In the long run, it is dissatisfying for a discipline to become overly self-involved."[1]

Reflections about our own discipline as "*second*-order historical writing"? The notion is rather astonishing. Should it not be the *first* duty of a critical discipline to examine, test, and if necessary, correct or supplement its own premises and methods and the development of the field? The boom in the new German national historiography offers a good opportunity to pose such questions. Because of the influential position of their authors and the broad reception of their books, these syntheses on German history, written by well-known German historians, will be presented here as the mainstream of German national historiography.

Even today, history continues to be written within the framework of national historiography. In many cases, texts on the nation can be found even in books and essays without the word "nation" in the title. In the United States, it was mainly women historians and historians of color who unmasked this form of allegedly objective, universal, gender-neutral and "value-free" historiography as "partisan, white male historiography." In the past fifteen years or so, inspired by U.S. scholarship and the "linguistic turn" in history, German historians, too, have increasingly come to reflect on the premises, traditions, and mechanisms of inclusion and exclusion that mark national historiography. Despite these new approaches, in many cases national historiography continues to be accepted quite self-evidently in Germany (and in the United States) as "general" history, that is, history as such.

Research on the nation tends to intensify in periods of upheaval and crisis. The functions and tasks of national historiography may be summarized in terms of the creation of meaning, a search for identity, and the manufacture of collective memory. Thus it is not surprising that national history treats many subjects and encompasses various approaches and geographical spaces. One characteristic of national historiography, whether implicitly or explicitly, is its tendency to distance itself from "others": other nations, other cultures, other values, other religions, other languages, other regions. Only by distinguishing itself from others can it work out what is "German," what constitutes "German identity" and what "German collective memories" are.

In what follows, I will begin by examining some characteristics of the new German national historiography and the lines of interpretation it has developed. The second part of my remarks will focus on the contributions of women's and gender studies to national historiography—to its gendering. In the third section I will address women's and gender history as well as national historiography in the context of the "cultural turn." In the fourth and final section of my essay I will ask whether the polyphonic critique of current national historiography might offer an opportunity to anchor women's and gender history in a transformed national narrative.

A New German National History?

Contrary to the international trend to overcome the limits of national historiography, Germany since the 1990s has seen a striking concentration of new national histories. The best-known authors of these surveys are Thomas Nipperdey, Hans-Ulrich Wehler, and Heinrich August Winkler.[2] These substantial recent general histories are not the only sign of the current significance of national historiography. At the end of the twentieth century, Lutz Raphael also noted in *Geschichte und Gesellschaft*, the flagship journal of German social history, that the writings of the so-called Bielefeld School, despite all ambitions to the contrary, simply represented "nation-centered social history."[3] Even in the next century, historical writing in Germany remains primarily national historiography.

As many studies have shown, the nation and national history were a political project from the late eighteenth century onward. In the course of the nineteenth century the nation-state and historiography developed parallel to each other and thus mutually shaped the structural preconditions for the formation of the German Empire and the traditions of a historiography rooted in the nation. The "Prussification of the German image of history" that began after 1848 set the initial course for this development, in which the Prussian-centered *kleindeutsch* position won out over visions of a greater Germany including Austria.[4] Although a few historians, such as Karl Dietrich Erdmann, Heinrich Lutz, and James J. Sheehan, have objected to this one-sided view, which relegates Austrian history to an insignificant prelude, the most recent accounts by Thomas Nipperdey, Hans-Ulrich Wehler, Heinrich August Winkler, and Wolfram Siemann continue to be oriented towards this so-called "Prussification of German history."[5] The view that national historiography is the valid and generally recognized framework to which all other studies must be subordinated continues to go largely unchallenged. In national historiography, the "big" and "universal" themes are treated from the perspectives of political and social history, according to a broad, if not universal, consensus, while regional and local histories and biographies merely investigate segments of this general (national) history. Until quite recently, such works could justify their existence only by explicitly stressing the typical and exemplary quality of their subjects, and thus their importance for "general" (national) history.

What exactly is considered German national historiography, though? On the one hand, we have as yet no satisfactory definitions for the terms "nation" and "nationalism" or for national historiography. Even the geographical territory to which German national history refers appears uncertain. The problem here is not just the complex German history of numerous small states (*Kleinstaaterei*) and the many shifts of frontiers from the Wars of Liberation in the early nineteenth century to German reunification in 1990, but also the lack of congruence between state and linguistic borders, the "overseas Germans" (*Auslandsdeutsche*), the German colonies and the still unanswered question of the existence of an Austrian nation.[6] Also, the terms nation, nationalism, and national historiography appear so "natural" to many authors that they do not even bother to attempt to define them.

National historiography—that much is generally acknowledged—plays a key role first in the construction and legitimization of the nation, which, as a "secularized religion," comprises the frame of reference in which individuals locate themselves and within which history continues to be written and interpreted at the time when the religiously oriented order of meaning and worldview based on the Christian history of salvation were being supplanted.[7] This particular interpretation emerged with renewed clarity after the upheavals of

1989 and led recently to funding for a large-scale European research project on the meaning of national historiographies in the process of reshaping Europe.[8]

Second, national historiography is closely associated with national identities, and the question of national identity gained in urgency also after 1989, and not only in Germany. An examination of the public discussion of this topic shows that the study and interpretation of the past was, and is, by no means the sole province of professional historians. In light of the competition from authors, journalists, politicians, and artists, the determined efforts by which German academic history has managed from the beginning to isolate itself from competing historiographies and traditions are rather surprising. To say that it has predominated would be a misnomer, since ideas about history among the broader population have doubtless been influenced far more by literature, historical novels, popular histories, films, and stories passed down in the family than by scholarly works. The development of historical scholarship in tension with competing representations of history can thus, thirdly, be considered a virtual characteristic of German national historiography. Numerous principles of inclusion and exclusion dominated the field.

Initially, academic historiography developed disassociated from literature, as Daniel Fulda has impressively described.[9] In a second step, German historians sought to disqualify as unscholarly and amateurish the works of nonacademic authors who wrote about German history. These strict divisions came at a price, however. Scarcely had university chairs in history been established, extensive collections of sources published, and historical journals founded in Wilhelmine Germany—signaling the acceptance of academic historiography as a scholarly discipline—when German historians in the unstable Weimar years began to lament their meager public influence. The best-known dispute was probably that between academic and popular history carried out in the pages of the *Historische Zeitschrift* and other media of the Weimar Republic.[10]

Even this crisis did not lead to a more intense discussion within the historical profession about questions of form, aesthetics, and the expectations of the nonacademic reading public. The chasm between academic historiography and the public interest in history persisted. Since little serious effort was made to bridge this gap, in the 1980s local historical associations, sometimes organized in the form of so-called history workshops,[11] took up the needs and expectations of broad segments of the population. Nowadays it is mainly filmmakers, political journalists, and freelance historians who are meeting the growing interests of the population in a more visual and tactile history. Successful films on the history of National Socialism; exhibition projects, public readings, and books on regional and urban history; municipal festivities on the anniversaries of various historical events; and the like appeal to broad segments of the population, since they make use of familiar locales and people's own experiences or create such connections. In many places, such initiatives have encouraged "amateur" historians to research family history and "dig where you stand."

The nation itself is a construct, as we learned from the work of Benedict Anderson and Ernest Gellner. Since the beginnings of the nation are hard to pinpoint because of their many-sided and ambiguous nature, national historiography has moved from the indeterminate depths of the premodern period towards the foundation of the nation-state, the German *Sonderweg* and the "German catastrophe" (Friedrich Meinecke) to the overcoming of class society or the German reunification of 1990. In these accounts, the nation often appears "natural," timeless, and ahistorical. But recent research agrees that the period between the Austro-Prussian and Napoleonic Wars up to the 1820s is one of the most important periods for German nation building. Ute Planert describes it therefore "as an epoch in its own right . . . in which the national concepts that would become influential in the further course of the nineteenth century were formulated on the basis of older notions."[12] After first focusing on the inception and the authors of the German nation and German nationalism, since the 1980s scholars have turned to its political and social functions as well as the process of nation-state building.[13] They have described the typologies of nations and nationalisms and the patterns of nation-state building. Typical of these older German studies is that they did not distinguish systematically between the nation, nationalism, "national awakening," and nation-state building and that they described more than they analyzed these phenomena and processes. Nationalism, designed by the German educated middle class for its own political ends, became highly attractive for various segments of the population, since it could appear in a myriad of guises, from a liberal-democratic model for the future to "imperialistic *Reich* nationalism."[14] Other groups in the population, in contrast, feared being left out of or actively excluded from the projected nation-state. This process of excluding Poles, Jews, and women has been illustrated clearly for the example of citizenship.[15] Although the problem of nation and nation-state building in general and the specific issues of German developments are well known, these issues had little effect on the conceptualization of German national historiography. The most recent representations of German history published by individual authors between the late 1980s and 2003 all concentrate on the modern period.[16]

Gendering the History of the German Nation

Only in the last few years have historians, inspired by interdisciplinary dialogue and international criticism, begun to reflect on the premises and implications of recent surveys of German national history. Thus Paul Nolte has noted that by writing surveys of German history, historians at the end of their academic careers have rediscovered German national historiography as the best way to ensure their reputations, "despite the internationalization of research."[17] The critique of the "master narratives" of historicism by the generation of German historians recently or soon to be retired has clearly not led them to abandon this form of historiography. The recognition of this old pattern meant that the reflections on the status of narrativity in historiographical accounts that can be observed since the 1980s were also applied to the "master narratives" of well-known German historians. Until now it appeared that the oft-discussed connections between nation building and historiography have been quite influential, but as yet have had little effect on surveys of German history, which were deemed to be above such issues.

This impression becomes especially clear, as John Breuilly and Paul Nolte have shown in their comparison of the histories of Germany by Thomas Nipperdey and Hans-Ulrich Wehler, if one does not restrict the analysis to methodological and theoretical concepts, which the authors generally present in their introductions and separate publications, but rather studies the narrative structures of the text itself.[18] Upon closer analysis of the text, Roger Chickering's assessment of Wehler's third volume—that the author's mode of presentation is about as far from historicism as can be imagined, that he dissects rather than narrates the history of Imperial Germany, and that his method neglects the actions of individuals and groups[19]—proves untenable. Nolte concludes that one can speak "of a pressure to conventionalize the portrayal, which in historiographical practice causes 'more radical' narrative experiments to melt away."[20]

Nolte points here to the problem of the implicit master narrative, which in Wehler's case can be made out behind the explicit master narrative. In his essay on "The End of the Master Narratives," Gabriel Motzkin recalls that even in historiography, knowledge and power are not independent of one another but closely linked. One of the consequences is the need for the master narrative "to assert itself constantly against new models and react to attacks with corresponding flexibility."[21]

These power relations within the German historical profession mean that many historical studies dealing both with new subjects and new methods receive at most passing mention in surveys of German history. Although master narratives always produce counternarratives, which address such topics as minorities, discriminated groups, or colonized regions, until now such accounts have by no means inspired the complete deconstruction of master narratives that their authors hoped for. These narratives, developed for groups and minorities previously "condemned to 'historylessness,'"[22] are either consistently ignored by master narrators or partially integrated, leaving the core of the traditional master narrative largely untouched. In order to better understand the structure and functions of these master narratives we need to study these texts still more carefully in the future. Which narratological principles do the texts follow? How do the authors make their case, what is deemed plausible, and which lines of argumentation emerge? Which actors, events, and structural frameworks are mentioned? What well-founded or unfounded selection is made? Where does the narrative begin and end, and what does it emphasize or leave out? Which linguistic inventory and structuring concepts are used? Which symbolic codings and gender-historical connotations are visible behind purportedly "gender-neutral" representations?

What the authors of surveys of German history present as "general history" is men's history, for historiography that explicitly or implicitly aims for the highest degree of objectivity is less objective than one-sidedly male. Put another way, historiography has a gender, even if generations of historians have sought to hide it behind alleged impartiality, the supposedly universal. What is deemed to be a scholarly text, which sources scholarly studies can draw upon, which narrative forms are considered unscholarly and which sources insignificant or uninteresting—none of these decisions are gender neutral.

As Bonnie G. Smith shows in "The Gender of History," for the period from the late eighteenth to the mid twentieth century, the signal importance of "facts," archival work, and the history of political elites that continues to dominate historiography today have not merely set standards but also marginalized competing historiographical models. The strict separation and hierarchy between scholarly and "amateur" history has done more than just consistently exclude a part of potential historical writing, making it difficult for innovative approaches to gain recognition.[23] As Angelika Epple demonstrates in her gender history of historiography between the Enlightenment and historicism, it was in this period not only that history developed as a discipline, but also that a form of historical writing she refers to as "sentimental historiography" (and Bonnie G. Smith dubs "amateurish"[24]) was resolutely marginalized.[25] This type of historical writing offered a different interpretation of the past: "sentimental historiography," which was strongly influenced by oral communication, sought to apply a morality developed within personal friendships to social life. This form of historiography, in whose development women such as Sophie Mereau and Johanna Schopenhauer participated, was soon to be labeled naive, dilettantish, and amateurish, which meant the exclusion not just of women from professional historical writing, but also of these types of questions from academic history. The distinction between professional, academic and trivial, amateurish historical writing also led to the banishing of "sentimental" issues "from the self-reflections of professional historians both male and female."[26]

As Billie Melman reveals in her study of 782 English-language historical works by sixty-six female historians, however, the exclusion of women historians occurred not just on the methodological terrain. Melman points to the paradox that late nineteenth-century research on women's history did not simply lead to an increasing integration of women's history into "general history": "the recapitulation of women's past was double-edged and served two purposes. Memory could mean membership: in the citizen-state, in the national empire. But the recapitulation of a female experience could also precipitate the dis-remembrance of the history of the wider group and the dismembering of its past."[27]

Recent scholarship has moved beyond simply querying the premises of national historiography. Historians now also question the constructions of nation, nationalism, national culture, and national identity by comparing and deconstructing these constructs, and what was apparently "typically German," across national boundaries.[28] In this context, questions about the gender of history are increasingly being posed by historians in the United States and Germany engaged in issues of women's and gender studies from the early modern period to the twentieth century. On the one hand, scholars are still concerned with making women visible in German history in the first place. Proceeding from the conviction that the category of gender provides an important key for analyzing the past,[29] scholars also have fought for and promoted the conceptualization of national historiography as gender history. Women historians on both sides of the Atlantic developed networks early on, and a number of essay collections have appeared with contributions by both American and German historians. U.S. scholarship has often provided the key here. Thus American historians were the first to place historiography and women's history in an international historical perspective.[30]

The mainstream of German national historiography has taken scant notice of the many areas treated by women's and gender history over the past thirty years. At most, it has incorporated those findings of women's and gender studies conceived within the framework of political and social history that can be integrated into the research fields of modern national historiography without challenging traditional concepts: works on the middle classes, on political parties and associations are generally cited in order to point out that women existed in all of these social formations. The results of such research rarely find their way into the new political history, however. Women's and gender history has probably made the greatest impact on younger scholars of military history. Essay collections on violence and war from the early modern period to the era of the world wars now incorporate contributions on gender history,[31] and it appears to be the liveliest exchange between gender and mainstream scholarship at the moment.

It was not until the 1980s that German research on nationalism discovered "gender" as a category, and the first essay collections on women and the nation appeared in the late 1990s.[32] In her 1995 afterword to a history of women

in the twentieth century, Gisela Bock pointed out that this subject remained
"insufficiently studied."[33] Up until then, established mainstream scholarship
had addressed neither the discursive relationship between gender and the nation nor women as individuals. Earlier works of women's history had instead
postulated women's exclusion from the nation ("women have no fatherland")
and concentrated on the organizations of the old women's movement and its
individual protagonists, often emphasizing their affinity for National Socialism.[34] The chronological focus of these organizational histories and biographies of the various women's movements was on Imperial Germany. All of
these works emphasize that women cited the nation when taking action in
times of internal or external threat. The subject of the nation and women
becomes the focus of gender history particularly at historical moments when
the nation needs to bolster its confidence, during wars, revolutions, and political upheavals. The Napoleonic occupation, the Revolution of 1848–1849,
the wars of the nineteenth and twentieth centuries, and changes of political
system constitute the main emphases of scholarship on national history written from a gender history perspective. These events, however, merely represented the eruptions of a "female nationalism" that also manifested itself in
calmer times and played its part in German society's search for its national
self. Beyond the question of women's involvement in and specific contributions to national uprisings, the analysis of the obvious gender imagery passed
down in the image of the nation as an "extended family" and the question of
its significance for constituting the German nation is still in the early stages.
All that has been studied thus far is the early phase of modern nationalism,
the period of the anti-Napoleonic wars.[35]

Older works on the many patriotic (*vaterländisch*) charitable associations
that emerged during and after the wars against Napoleon have provided important impulses for the study of national history.[36] These works inspired
discussions of the extent to which these women's associations, which considerably expanded women's scope of action in the public sphere, contributed (perhaps unintentionally) to their political emancipation. Ute Daniel
pointed out early on that patriotic women's associations cannot be treated as
women's associations if their leadership was in the hands of men. The question of women's scope of action, influence, and responsibility plays a large
part in these studies. A number of contributions published on the occasion of
the sesquicentennial in 1998 also studied the Revolution of 1848–1849 from
this perspective.[37] The topics of "right-wing women" and nationalism have
experienced a minor boom in recent years.[38] Conceived in part as longitudi-
nal studies, these works on conservative and nationalist women's associations
show that these women succeeded up until 1933 in considerably expanding
their scope of public action and influence and thus contributed to changing
women's roles, although some of them did not fundamentally question the

gender hierarchy. "Emancipation through opposition to emancipation?" asks Ute Planert in her work on the mixed gender antifeminist organizations of Imperial Germany.[39] Lora Wildenthal has studied women's associations that supported the call for German colonies beginning in the 1880s: the women's league of the German Colonial Society, the German Women's Association for Nursing in the Colonies, the German Women's Association of the Red Cross for Germans Overseas, and the like.[40]

Andrea Süchting-Hänger characterizes the conservative women's associations, which chose Prussia's Queen Luise as their role model and icon, as a female partial culture. References to the nation united these women, who were primarily beholden to their milieu of origin. They protested against the National Socialist view of women, which Süchting-Hänger considers evidence "that they were unwilling to give up voluntarily bastions they had already conquered."[41] No matter how the activities of the different women's associations were accentuated, and whatever their extent, women's arenas and radius of action clearly expanded beyond the domestic sphere. In other words, even women who opposed emancipation were busy emancipating themselves. This led to the absurd situation after 1918 of women who opposed the suffrage being elected to the National Assembly as deputies of the conservative *Deutschnationale Volkspartei*.[42]

At the beginning of the First World War it became apparent that, in this extreme situation, broad segments of the population were quite willing to accept women's informal and largely unpaid performance of "national tasks." As soon as women demanded concrete participation in the state that went beyond the vague sentiments of national community, however, "female national tasks" were quickly restricted to volunteer and charitable activities. This finding substantiates Ute Planert's thesis that the restrictive national conception of femininity as a complement to masculinity already inherently contained the seeds of change, without ever truly being able to overcome its intrinsic limitations and embrace gender-political equality.[43]

Underlying the division of humanity into two groups was the powerful concept of a gender hierarchy in a constant balancing act, which accorded or denied significance and the ability to act and participate in politics to particular individuals, groups, and nations. The lecture series, "What Are Women? What Are Men?" held at Berlin's Free University in 1993–1994 drew attention to the persistent dominance of this gender hierarchy through changing times.[44] The cementing of this gender order has been particularly well studied for the "long nineteenth century." Karen Hagemann has demonstrated this for the period of the anti-Napoleonic wars in several studies.[45] In these, she not only focuses scholarly attention on the issue of women's role and scope of action,[46] but also asks about the competing models of masculinity in times of war and crisis. Femininity and masculinity

[handwritten: How do you reconcile masc. w/ femininity? → how stable is gender hierarchy + g. roles?]

were constantly being renegotiated. For the period of the Napoleonic wars, an important caesura for both gender studies and German national history, she has pinpointed two central traits of the hegemonic model of German masculinity: first, men's readiness to defend family, "home" (*Heimat*), and "fatherland" by force of arms and to die a "hero's death" on the "altar of the fatherland"; and second, with the introduction of universal conscription, the linking of masculine "valor" and political citizenship rights. Only a "valiant" man was considered a truly German man.[47]

[handwritten: a) b)]

Since these characteristics constituted important preconditions for the state citizen capable of bearing arms, women found themselves from that period on in the position of having to present themselves as loyal citizens and responsible members of a nation without risking the loss of their femininity. The objective of the detailed ascriptions and descriptions of masculinity and femininity in the bourgeois era lay in the preservation of gender differences and the gender hierarchy. As Martina Kessel has underlined in her cultural historical works on boredom and the work ethic in the long nineteenth century, the emphasis on gender difference was not only problematic for women. At the end of the nineteenth century, men too began to feel constrained by dichotomous gender attributes and tried to present themselves as "whole men" by incorporating qualities defined as feminine such as artistic talent, empathy, and the capacity to enjoy life and entertain others.[48]

How unstable gender relations were in wartime and how men and women in extreme situations sought or were forced to conquer new terrain and/or to live up to their assigned roles is revealed by several works that study both the "home front" and the military front and address the stabilization of gender relations after wars.[49] The research project "Gender History in Politics" under the direction of Barbara Vogel studied the various incarnations of the "category of gender" and its effects on the history of politics and parties as well as the social and cultural historical constellations and configurations of political action[50] for the period from the late nineteenth century to the end of the Second World War.

At the beginning of the modern age, middle-class models of masculinity and femininity helped define what was deemed political, public, and significant on the national stage, and what would be considered unpolitical, private, and trivial. The ascription of masculinity and fatherliness to the Prussian *Landräte* (administrative heads of districts) of the nineteenth century has been impressively demonstrated by Christiane Eifert, whose monograph studied this local political elite for the first time from the perspective of gender history.[51] Thus national historiography reveals the gender hierarchy on several levels, among them the characterization of the nation's internal and external enemies, whose activities and conventions it frequently feminizes.[52]

[handwritten: middle-class masc + fem. = normative!]

Nation, Culture, and Gender

Since the linguistic turn, no new master narrative of German national history has succeeded in establishing itself. Master narratives of all kinds have attracted increasing criticism as a questionable effort at hegemony in history. At the same time, postmodern approaches have revealed possibilities of conceptualizing national history in different ways. A national historiography inspired by cultural history only developed in Germany in the late 1980s. To be sure, the American historian George L. Mosse began much earlier to study German performances of the national in the nineteenth and twentieth century, analyzing ceremonial culture and the commemoration of heroes, and writing the history of nationalism as the history of a cultural historical movement.[53] However, German historians were slow to read and discuss his work. The hesitant reception of recent cultural historical approaches certainly contributed to the skepticism of well-known representatives of German political and social history towards this new cultural history.[54]

Despite the impressive contributions that the postmodern plurality of historical approaches has made to German historiography, and despite their partial integration, the effects on national historiography with its strong orientation towards state actions in the fields of politics, the economy and society, have been minimal. This also applies to the gender hierarchy implicit in this historiography, which even borrowings from cultural history have not changed. I will elucidate this point using the example of a project whose development is closely associated with the spread of "culturalist approaches." In Berlin, Etienne François and Hagen Schulze conceived the idea of *Deutsche Erinnerungsorte* (German Sites of Memory), which was published in three volumes by Beck Verlag in 2001. The inspiration and model for this publication was *Les lieux de mémoires*, which the French historian Pierre Nora brought out in France in the 1980s and early 1990s. There, Nora presented 130 places, symbols, persons, and events, "which particularly condensed, embodied or crystalized the memory of the French nation."[55]

In the "German sites of memory," François and Schulze sought to take account of the three German "mnemo-historical consequences" of National Socialism, the Holocaust, and German reunification in the context of European unification by—in contrast to the French prototype—making the nineteenth and twentieth centuries their chronological focus, embedding German history in a European perspective, and refusing any hierarchy between "important" and "trivial" topics.[56] Interestingly enough, however, the editors emphasize from the outset in their introduction that they intend for this publication to draw a connection between two different lines of historiography, both of which they deem important, but between which they set up a clear hierarchy: "However, even if we are inclined to regard history and memory as two equally legitimate approaches to the past, they are ultimately neither identical nor interchangeable. History as a scholarly discipline is a matter for experts. We encounter it as a critical and distanced application of fixed rules for the interpretation and analysis of sources and relics of the past, with a claim to the verifiability and objective validity of its findings. . . . Memory, in contrast, serves the existential needs of communities 'for whom the presence of the past represents a decisive element of their collective nature.'"[57]

This serves to cement the hierarchy between conventional political historiography and a tradition based on individuality, subjectivity, and "unverifiable memories" that promotes the emotional cohesion of communities. This second strand of tradition is thus used to supplement and bolster old-style scholarly accounts. Only on this condition are the new cultural historical accounts integrated into national historiography—and not just in the case of the sites of memory mentioned here. The notion that nations represent collective communities of memory has become broadly accepted. With the growing influence of cultural studies, myths, symbols, and ceremonies in which ideas about the nation found and still find expression have become objects of analysis in literary studies, political science, sociology, and history. An initial focus in German historiography was on the study of national monuments.[58] Ceremonial and commemorative culture[59] represent further emphases in scholarship on the nation, whether cultural historical or inspired by cultural history —in the United States as well as Germany.[60] The functions of emotions, music, political poetry, and gymnastics in the nationalization process have also been studied in this context.[61]

Against the background of current developments in this area of research, the following questions seem particularly interesting: What made people of different ages, religions, educational levels, and economic positions in the towns and villages of the various German-speaking regions feel that they belonged to a German nation? How was this national feeling manufactured, preserved, passed down, and altered, and to what ends was it instrumentalized, and by whom? What was typical and unique in the development of German national sentiment and what was representative of the nationalization of Europe in the modern era?

Studies that approach these themes from a regional perspective offer some impressive responses to these questions. Celia Applegate was the first scholar to focus on the relationship between regional and national identities. Using the example of the Palatinate, she sketches a remarkable picture of how local associations of the most various types from the early nineteenth century to the Nazi period expressed *Heimat* and a sense of belonging to a *Heimat*, and thus how a "universal sense of *Heimat*" could assume a pivotal function for the emergence of German national consciousness.[62] In a study of Württemberg, Alon Confino demonstrated the significant role that conveying a sense of *Heimat*, "the invention of Heimat and Home," played for the creation of national identity in times of increased mobility. Confino also sees an important link in the development of national identities in the idea of *Heimat*, which, in emotionally charged and unspecific images of nature, the village, and its inhabitants, connected the past with the present and the future. *Heimat* conveyed the feeling of always having been there.[63] Literature and visual representations clearly assigned this abstract image of *Heimat* (which was thus identical for all regions) to the female sphere. "While fatherland and nation represented Germany as one and indivisible, Heimat represented Germany as the one and the many."[64]

Charlotte Tacke compares the German myth of Arminius with the myth surrounding the French hero Vercingetorix using the monuments erected in the tiny German state of Lippe and in the French Auvergne in the nineteenth century. She studies the associations, subscription drives, festivals, and erection of the monument to Arminius in Detmold and those to Vercingetorix in Clermont-Ferrand. She rightly criticizes the fact that most studies of national monuments declare particular national versions to be ideal types of *the* national monument (and as a consequence of nation building, etc.), and questions "whether national peculiarities can be used to explain a European phenomenon."[65] National symbols, Tacke also demonstrates, are always tied to regions: "In both countries, regional society played a key role in the monument movements. In symbolic practice, the nation was not represented as an abstract 'imagined community.' The representation of the nation in and from the region made it appear in an everyday social arena, in which concrete groups represented themselves. . . . Thus while the [monument] movements projected a harmonious image of regional and national society, at the same time they also represented the social hierarchy and the class and gender differences in the social arenas in which they were active."[66]

Jean Quataert turned to the nation in a study that skillfully combines "a gendered analysis of patriotism and power"[67] from a different perspective: She studied the patriotic women's associations in Baden that had been founded during the Wars of Liberation and generally merged with the German Red Cross after 1871.[68] Quataert succeeds with this example in showing that in these only apparently apolitical associations, a national-patriotic milieu emerged that mobilized women across class barriers for national causes. Much as in the *Bund Deutscher Frauenvereine* (BDF, League of German Women's Associations), women working in charitable organizations successfully used nationalism to increase their radius of action.[69] In Baden, as in other German lands, the patriotic women's associations identified strongly in their work with the wife of the monarch, who generally served as patroness of the women's associations and their activities. Patriotic and national sentiments were thus tied to the ruling dynasty. Like Applegate, Confino, and Tacke, Quataert stresses that identification with the desired, imagined, and ultimately manufactured German nation-state required local and regional catalysts. It is in the combination and complex interplay of local, regional, and national elements that Abigail Green locates the peculiarity of German national consciousness, which, logically enough, is viewed as the source of the federal German system of government.[70]

These and other studies assume, implicitly or explicitly, that memory and remembrance produce "common knowledge" of what should be considered typical of a nation and its national tradition. "The relationship between the nation and individual and collective identities" represents one of the "thorniest theoretical problems" here.[71] National consciousness and national identity were and are solidified by cultivating national myths and symbols, creating and observing national holidays, and regularly holding festivals, commemorative ceremonies, and jubilees. The relationship between memory and identity in particular has become the subject of intense interdisciplinary and international investigation. The works of Maurice Halbwachs and Jan and Aleida Assmann have proved particularly inspiring for historical scholarship. Aleida Assmann, whose work is cited by many historians, distinguishes between individual and generational memory, and separates both of these forms from collective and cultural memory.[72] Historians are especially interested in the question of how something like national memory can arise with the aid of signs, symbols, texts, images, rituals, sites of memory, and commemorative events. Numerous works on the national discourse, national commitment, and political action of various organizations and groups have made it clear that the development of a collective, national memory carries gender historical implications.

Through its choice of subjects and methods, the research on the culture of memory in "general" history has also discreetly contributed to stabilizing the gender order in the field of national memory. Tracing the transition from individual to collective memory shows that the memories of women are repressed in this process of transfer, frequently disappearing altogether.[73] Even if well-known women politicians had similar opportunities for action as their male colleagues, their memories are marginalized. For in the old tradition of German national historiography, many historians persist in viewing autobiographical sources by women as unreliable and irrelevant sources, while similar texts penned by male politicians are often cited as central to national history. Although we have as yet no systematic comparative studies for the national culture of memory and remembrance, it does not seem far-fetched to posit that the gender order of traditional historiography is likely to correspond to that of the new research on the culture of memory and remembrance.

Conclusion: Gendering the "Mainstream"?

The political upheaval of 1989–1990 in Europe underlined the continuing power of the idea of the nation-state and heightened an already existing tendency in the United States and the two German states to confront the subject of the nation more intensively. Older works on nation building were reexamined. *Imagined Communities*, published in 1983 by the American political scientist and Southeast Asia specialist Benedict Anderson, provided an important impetus for the new research on nationalism. The beginnings of German nationalism, its (male) protagonists and organizational forms and the role of the nation in the political discourse of the various German states were studied in great detail. Scholars continued to ask how national identity had been created given the fragmentation of Germany into many small states, how local and regional identities were combined, and which collective memories construct(ed) the nation and keep it alive. In the United States and Germany alike, the trend in the specialist studies of nationalism research is towards a growing pluralism of themes and methods. Violence and the nation, and war and the nation, are key shared subject areas for nationalism and gender research; their importance is likely to grow given the violent excesses of the contemporary age. Scholars in both fields pursue questions about the definition of the nation, and about the participation and exclusion of various groups, although they more frequently work alongside than with each other. Particularly striking in recent years is the return of an older theme—the sacralization of the nation, already discussed by George L. Mosse and Thomas Nipperdey—viewed from a new perspective. Inspired by the provocative thesis of a "second confessionalization" (Olaf Blaschke) in the nineteenth century, the meaning of denomination and religion has moved to the center of research on nationalism. More recent studies no longer proceed from the assumption that nationalism as a political religion alone shaped the secularized world of the nineteenth century. Instead, scholars have begun to ask how traditional religiosity and nationalism became linked and mutually influenced each other.[74] The first essay collections on this topic lack contributions from the viewpoint of gender history, although the history of religion has played a major role in more recent women's and gender history.[75] In the future, the findings of this gender history of religion should be examined for their implications for national history.

Lynn Hunt, whose essay "The Challenge of Gender" provided part of my title, has called for a complete reconstruction of history in order to escape the gender order of historiography, which is constantly stabilizing itself and trying to reestablish equilibrium. In her view, gender history offers the best preconditions for this, since it has consistently historicized the category of "gender." In so doing, it has not only clearly emancipated itself from the older women's history, but also created the prerequisites for a new form of master narrative. Historicizing the category of gender could also provide the model for overcoming "men's history," which in Germany still goes under the name of "general history." Lynn Hunt believes that gender history should not stop at deconstructing categories, but must create new master narratives, new metanarratives.

Karin Hausen has also offered a pointed summary of the questionable "general" of general history.[76] She reminds us that the reconceptualization of history as the history of (hu)mankind at the end of the ancien régime deployed two novel hierarchies with fateful consequences. First, with the help of the metaphor of education, the successful development of the bourgeois subject was described and cemented in the line from boy to youth to man. Second, and alongside it, the elaboration of a separate anthropology of woman began. In this way, the general or universal in humanity could be viewed as embodied in the male sex,[77] stabilizing the gender order through reference to nature.

In order to dismantle these powerful premises, Hausen recommends the non-unity of history as a program and calls for a critical discussion of what the fiction of a unitary history has accomplished and what it has distorted. In the future, the unity proposed until now should be replaced by the multiplicity of history as an historiographic program, and for that reason historiography must bid farewell to the master narrative once and for all.[78] Hausen is not very optimistic about the prospects for such a shift of paradigm, however.[79]

In 2000 Ida Blom presented some important studies for the theme of the nation and gender in international comparison, and concluded "that international comparison of the gendering of nationalisms and nation states is well under way."[80] This assessment certainly holds true for many individual fields. What both mainstream and gender research on the nation lack, however, are systematic, comparative studies on different nations. As Geoff Eley recommended in 2000,[81] the literature in the field has concentrated up until now on revolutions, upheavals, and armed conflict in order to study the relationship between gender and the nation. Mainstream and gender research alike, however, continue to study the manifestations of different nationalisms quite separately. We still lack systematic, international comparisons of the different nationalisms that would enable us to assess what these nationalisms share, and what the peculiarities in individual cases might be. Hans Kohn already pointed to this gap in the literature in 1944. An examination of the gender historical conception of the nations would allow for a systematic comparison of nationalisms with this end in mind.

At the moment, "European history," "global history," and "transnational historiography" are popular series titles and slogans in German historical scholarship, which are better suited to expressing uneasiness with traditional national historiography than promoting new forms of historical writing.

Current attempts to overcome Eurocentric or Western perspectives have not simply proved difficult, but underline the persistent power of national historiography, which explicitly or implicitly sets the conditions for historical writing of all kinds. Differing national scholarly traditions, fields, and research interests render even assertions that cross national boundaries difficult. A "European" or "global history" worthy of the name, which could treat European countries or different continents with anything approaching balance, does not appear to be on the horizon in the near future. When making the envisaged leap from national historiography to a European or global historiography, we should try to avoid taking the structural failings of national historiography along with us. Whether attempts to write "transnational history" will do more to stabilize national historiography than to diversify it remains to be seen. When we study "relationships and constellations that transcend national boundaries"[82] under the "transnational" rubric, it doubtless expands our perspective and knowledge beyond our own nation-states. This shift of viewpoint might help us to discover new transborder developments and relationships and to seek out international interconnections, but the relocation of the national undertaken here could also lead to the firmer establishment of national history with a transnational dimension. Before laying out the basic outlines of a new European history or transnational history, we need first to devote careful study to the preconditions for, emphases, and gaps in national historiography in order to take the appropriate measures for reconceptualizing historiography. Scholars of women's and gender history have long called for us to analyze the "effects of the process of inclusion and exclusion"[83] instead of simply continuing them unthinkingly. Has the time come to integrate at least the findings of gender studies on an equal footing into a reconceptualized national history? Given the longevity of traditions, we should not be too optimistic about the chances.

To summarize, in German national historiography, gender is in the process of establishing itself as an analytical category. The culturalist turn seems to be accelerating this process. Even if traditional social history now integrates questions and approaches from cultural history, this does not mean that it is deconstructing the master narrative. The Anglo-American scholarship on nationalism in German history has taken a more critical view of this master narrative. The focal points of a nationalism research that takes gender aspects into account include the participation of women in national movements, the discursive construction of the nation, national symbols and representations, and the development of a national consciousness in the diverse lands of the German Empire as well as the question of the relationship between individual and collective memory. Inspired by Anglo-American scholarship, in which class, race, and gender have been used as categories of analysis far longer and more emphatically, German women historians have also investigated the connections between German colonialism, nationalism, and gender.[84] Proceeding from the findings of modern research on national history, scholars have examined national discourses, social groupings, and organizations for their positions and functions in the nation. The subject areas are treated—albeit often with a considerable time lag—on both sides of the Atlantic, frequently based on the same sources, with American scholars more intrepidly undertaking studies of long periods, although they appear even more than German historians to view the nineteenth century from the perspective of National Socialism. In one area, though, German women historians have come to set standards: they are now studying men as a sex and inquiring into the dimensions of masculinity more intensely and more self-evidently than their U.S. colleagues in women's and gender history.

Translated by Pamela Selwyn.

Notes

1. Árpád von Klimó, "Das Ende der Nationalismusforschung? Bemerkungen zu einigen Neuerscheinungen über 'Politische Religion,' 'Feste' und 'Erinnerung,'" *Neue politische Literatur* 48 (2003): 285.
2. Thomas Nipperdey, *Deutsche Geschichte*, vols. 1–3 (Munich, 1983–1992); Hans-Ulrich Wehler, *Deutsche Gesellschaftsgeschichte* (Munich, 1982–2003); Heinrich August Winkler, *Der lange Weg nach Westen*, 2 vols. (Munich, 2000).
3. Lutz Raphael, "Nationalzentrierte Sozialgeschichte in programmatischer Absicht: Die Zeitschrift 'Geschichte und Gesellschaft: Zeitschrift für Historische Sozialwissenschaft,'" in den ersten 25 Jahren ihres Bestehens," *Geschichte und Gesellschaft* 25 (1999): 5–37.
4. Dieter Langewiesche, "Reich, Nation und Staat in der jüngeren Geschichte," *Historische Zeitschrift* 254 (1992): 361.
5. Ibid., 362–364.
6. Ernst Bruckmüller, *Nation Österreich: Kulturelles Bewußtsein und gesellschaftlich-politische Prozesse* (Vienna, 1996).
7. Georg G. Iggers, "Nationalism and Historiography, 1789–1996: The German Example in Historical Perspective," in *Writing National History in Western Europe since 1800*, ed. Stefan Berger et al. (London, 1999), 20; Rudolf Speth, *Nation und Revolution. Politische Mythen im 19. Jahrhundert* (Opladen, 2000), 152.
8. The project "The Writing of National Histories in Europe" is being funded by the European Science Foundation. See http://www.esf.org/fileadmin/be_user/publications/The_Writing_of_National_Histories_in_Nineteenth_and_Twentieth-Century_Europe_NHIST_.pdf

9. Daniel Fulda, *Wissenschaft aus Kunst. Die Entstehung der modernen deutschen Geschicht-schreibung 1760–1860* (Berlin, 1996).

10. For details, see Eberhard Kolb, "'Die Historiker sind ernstlich böse': Der Streit um die 'Historische Belletristik' in Weimar-Deutschland," in *Liberalitas: Festschrift für Erich Anger-mann,* ed. Norbert Finzsch and Hermann Wellenreuther (Stuttgart, 1992), 67–86; Chris-toph Gradmann, *Historische Belletristik: Populäre historische Biographien in der Weimarer Re-publik* (Frankfurt/M., 1993).

11. On the aims and program of the German history workshops (*Geschichtswerkstätten*), Hubert C. Ehalt, ed., *Geschichtswerkstatt, Stadtteilarbeit, Aktionsforschung* (Vienna, 1984). With the journal *Geschichtswerkstatt* (known since 1992 as *WerkstattGeschichte*), which was founded in 1983, a younger generation of historians responded to expectations of historical scholarship that were becoming evident outside the university.

12. Ute Planert, "Wann beginnt der 'moderne' deutsche Nationalismus? Plädoyer für eine nationale Sattelzeit," in *Die Politik der deutschen Nation: Nationalismus in Krieg und Krisen, 1760–1960,* ed. Jörg Echternkamp and Sven O. Müller (Munich, 2002), 59.

13. Peter Alter, *Nationalismus* (Frankfurt/M., 1985); Otto Dann, *Nation und Nationalismus in Deutschland, 1770–1990* (Munich, 1993); Heinrich August Winkler, ed., *Nationalismus,* 2nd ed. (Königstein i. Taunus, 1985).

14. Dieter Langewiesche, "Reich, Nation und Staat," 346.

15. Dieter Gosewinkel, *Einbürgern und Ausschließen: Die Nationalisierung der Staatsangehörig-keit vom Deutschen Bund bis zur Bundesrepublik Deutschland,* 2nd ed. (Göttingen, 2004). On women and citizenship, see also Erna Appelt, *Geschlecht, Staatsbürgerschaft, Nation: Politische Konstruktionen des Geschlechterverhältnisses in Europa* (Frankfurt/M., 1999).

16. Rudolf Speth, *Nation und Revolution: Politische Mythen im 19. Jahrhundert* (Opladen, 2000), 152.

17. Paul Nolte, "Darstellungsweisen deutscher Geschichte. Erzählstrukturen und 'master nar-ratives' bei Nipperdey und Wehler," in *Die Nation schreiben: Geschichtswissenschaft im inter-nationalen Vergleich,* ed. Christoph Conrad and Sebastian Conrad (Göttingen, 2002), 239.

18. John Breuilly, "Auf dem Weg zur deutschen Gesellschaft?: Der dritte Band von Wehlers 'Gesellschaftsgeschichte,'" *Geschichte und Gesellschaft* 24 (1981): 137–168; Paul Nolte, "Darstellungsweisen."

19. Roger Chickering, "Drei Gesichter des Kaiserreiches: Zu den großen Synthesen von Wolf-gang J. Mommsen, Hans-Ulrich Wehler und Thomas Nipperdey," *Neue Politische Literatur* 41 (1996): 364–375.

20. Paul Nolte, "Darstellungsweisen," 251.

21. Gabriel Motzkin, "Das Ende der Meistererzählungen," in *Kompass der Geschichtswissenschaft,* ed. Joachim Eibach and Günther Lottes (Göttingen, 2002), 383. On the relationship be-tween national history and power, see also Dieter Langewiesche, "'Was heißt 'Erfindung der Nation?' Nationalgeschichte als Artefakt—oder Geschichtsdeutung als Machtkampf,'" *Historische Zeitschrift* 277 (2003): 593–617.

22. Hanna Schissler, "Hält die Geschlechtergeschichte, was sie versprochen hat?: Feminist-ische Geschichtswissenschaft und 'Meistererzählungen,'" in *Die historische Meistererzählung. Deutungslinien der deutschen Nationalgeschichte nach 1945,* ed. Konrad H. Jarausch and Mar-tin Sabrow (Göttingen, 2002), 200.

23. Bonnie G. Smith, *The Gender of History: Men, Women, and Historical Practice* (Cambridge, Mass., 2000), 12–13.

24. Ibid., 6–7.

25. Angelika Epple, *Empfindsame Geschichtsschreibung Eine Geschlechtergeschichte der Historiogra-phie zwischen Aufklärung und Historismus* (Cologne, 2003).

26. Ibid., 416.

chapters: 1, 2, 3, 6, 10

<u>Gendering Modern Germ. Hist</u>
1) 5? 8?

1) Normative gender roles
   — is "gender" normative?
   (does it exclude or only include?)

Am vs.
Germ.

2) Sources → who do authors in here use?

3) If we read Schasser → how does a gendered historigraphy of Germany compare to Eley's historiography (that generally is on Germany?)

4) Translation - gender vs. Geschlecht

5) Author's ⟨Eley's⟩ Questions:
   ① continuations of f's + gender?
   ② has f's/g d'ed mainstream?
   ③ diff in writing b/w Am + Ger.
   ④ how have Am/Ger on gender influenced each other?

6) Mainstreams?

7) Seven variables

8) what is "gender"?

9) what are limits of gender? usefulness of it?

10) How can gender, as J.S. suggest, ensure that we have a history of both women + "women"? (1427)

11) Issues of publishing in "Trans-Atlantic perspective

27. Billie Melman, "Gender, History and Memory: The Invention of Women's Past in the Nineteenth and Early Twentieth Centuries," *History and Memory* 5 (1993): 5–41, quotation 41.

28. Dieter Langewiesche, "Staatsbildung und Nationsbildung in Deutschland- ein Sonderweg?: Die deutsche Nation im europäischen Vergleich," in *Nationalismen in Europa. West- und Osteuropa im Vergleich*, ed. Ulrike von Hirschhausen and Jörn Leonhard (Göttingen, 2001), 49–67.

29. Joan W. Scott, "Gender: A Useful Category of Historical Analysis," *American Historical Review* 91 (1985): 1053–1075.

30. Karen Offen et al., eds., *Writing Women's History: International Perspectives* (Bloomington, 1991); Leila J. Rupp, *Worlds of Women: The Making of an International Women's Movement* (Princeton, 1997); Marilyn J. Boxer and Jean H. Quataert, *Connecting Spheres: European Women in a Globalizing World, 1500 to the Present*, 2nd ed. (New York, 2000);Karen Offen, *European Feminisms, 1700–1950: A Political History* (Stanford, 2000).

31. On this, see the contribution by Karen Hagemann in this volume.

32. Frauen und Geschichte Baden-Württemberg, ed., *Frauen und Nation* (Tübingen, 1996); Patricia Herminghouse, ed., *Gender and Germanness: Cultural Productions of Nation* (Providence, 1997); Ute Planert, ed., *Nation, Politik und Geschlecht: Frauenbewegungen und Nationalismus in der Moderne* (Frankfurt/M., 2000); Ida Blom et al., eds., *Gendered Nations: Nationalism and Gender Order in the Long Nineteenth Century* (Oxford, 2000).

33. Gisela Bock, "Nachwort," in *Geschichte der Frauen*, ed. Georges Duby and Michele Perrot, vol. 5; *20. Jahrhundert*, ed. Françoise Thébaud, (Frankfurt/M., 1995), 641.

34. On women's and gender history research on National Socialism and the Holocaust, see the contribution by Claudia Koonz in this volume.

35. The main work thus far is Karen Hagemann, "A Valorous *Volk* Family: The Nation, the Military, and the Gender Order in Prussia in the Time of the Anti-Napoleonic Wars, 1806–15," in Blom et al., *Gendered Nations*, 179–205; and *"Mannlicher Muth und Teutsche Ehre": Nation, Militär und Geschlecht zur Zeit der Antinapoleonischen Kriege Preußens* (Paderborn, 2002), 350–393.

36. Ute Daniel, "Die Vaterländischen Frauenvereine in Westfalen," *Westfälische Forschungen* 39 (1989): 158–179; Dirk Reder, *Frauenbewegung und Nation: Patriotische Frauenvereine in Deutschland im frühen 19. Jahrhundert (1813–1830)* (Cologne, 1998).

37. The classics on the subject are Carola Lipp, ed., *Schimpfende Weiber und patriotische Jungfrauen: Frauen im Vormärz und in der Revolution 1848/49* (Moos, 1986); Dagmar Herzog, *Intimacy and Exclusion: Religious Politics in Pre-Revolutionary Baden* (Princeton, 1996); Sylvia Paletschek, *Frauen und Dissens: Frauen im Deutschkatholizismus und in den freien Gemeinden 1841–1852* (Göttingen, 1990); for one of several contributions that appeared in essay collections on the Revolution of 1848 during the sesquicentennial in 1998, see Gabriella Hauch, "Frauen-Räume in der Männer-Revolution 1848," in *Europa 1848: Revolution und Nation*, ed. Dieter Dowe et al. (Bonn, 1998), 841–900.

38. In this case it was an American historian who drew our attention early on to this spectrum of women's associations: Roger Chickering, "'Casting Their Gaze More Broadly': Women's Patriotic Activism in Imperial Germany," *Past and Present* 32 (1988): 156–185.

39. Ute Planert, *Antifeminismus im Kaiserreich: Diskurs, soziale Formation und politische Mentalität* (Göttingen, 1996).

40. Lora Wildenthal, *German Women for Empire, 1884–1945* (Durham, 2001). For more see the article by Birthe Kundrus in this volume.

41. Andrea Süchting-Hänger, *Das "Gewissen der Nation": Nationales Engagement und politisches Handeln konservativer Frauenorganisationen 1900 bis 1937* (Düsseldorf, 2002), 399.

42. Heide-Marie Lauterer, *Parlamentarierinnen in Deutschland 1918/19–1949* (Königstein i. Taunus, 2002); Raffael Scheck, *Mothers of the Nation: Right-Wing Women in Weimar Germany* (Oxford, 2004).

43. Ute Planert quoted by Angelika Schaser in "Women in a Nation of Men: The Politics of the League of German Women's Associations (BDF) in Imperial Germany, 1894–1914," in Blom et al., *Gendered Nations*, 262–263.

44. Christiane Eifert et al., *Was sind Frauen? Was sind Männer?: Geschlechterkonstruktionen im historischen Wandel* (Frankfurt/M., 1996).

45. Karen Hagemann, *Mannlicher Muth*; and German Heroes: The Cult of the Death for the Fatherland in Nineteenth-Century Germany," in *Masculinities in Politics and War: Gendering Modern History*, ed. Stefan Dudink et al. (Manchester, 2004), 116–134.

46. Karen Hagemann, "Female Patriots: Women, War and the Nation in the Period of the Prussian-German Anti-Napoleonic Wars," *Gender and History* 16, no. 3 (2004): 396–424.

47. Karen Hagemann, "Tod für das Vaterland: der patriotisch-nationale Heldenkult zur Zeit der Freiheitskriege," *Militärgeschichtliche Zeitschrift* 60, no. 2 (2001): 307–342.

48. Martina Kessel, "The 'Whole Man': The Longing for a Masculine World in Nineteenth-Century Germany," *Gender & History* 15 (2003): 1–31; Martina Kessel, ed., *Kunst, Geschlecht, Politik: Männlichkeitskonstruktionen und Kunst im Kaiserreich und in der Weimarer Republik* (Frankfurt/M., 2005).

49. Birthe Kundrus, *Kriegerfrauen: Familienpolitik und Geschlechterverhältnisse im Ersten und Zweiten Weltkrieg* (Hamburg, 1995); Ute Frevert, ed., *Militär und Gesellschaft im 19. und 20. Jahrhundert* (Stuttgart, 1997); Karen Hagemann and Ralf Pröve, eds., *Landsknechte, Soldatenfrauen und Nationalkrieger: Militär, Krieg und Geschlechterordnung im historischen Wandel* (Frankfurt/M., 1998); Karen Hagemann and Stefanie Schüler-Springorum, eds., *Heimat-Front: Militär und Geschlechterverhältnisse im Zeitalter der Weltkriege* (Frankfurt/M., 2002); Ute Daniel, "Frauen," in *Enzyklopädie Erster Weltkrieg*, ed. Gerhard Hirschfeld (Paderborn, 2004), 116–134.

50. Gabriele Boukrif et al., eds., *Geschlechtergeschichte des Politischen: Entwürfe von Geschlecht und Gemeinschaft im 19. und 20. Jahrhundert* (Münster, 2002), vii.

51. Christiane Eifert, *Paternalismus und Politik: Preußische Landräte im 19. Jahrhundert* (Münster, 2003).

52. Susanne zur Nieden, ed., *Homosexualität und Staatsräson: Männlichkeit, Homophobie und Politik in Deutschland 1900–1945* (Frankfurt/M., 2005); Susanne Zantop, *Kolonialphantasien im vorkolonialen Deutschland (1770–1870)* (Berlin, 1999).

53. George L. Mosse, *The Nationalization of the Masses: Political Symbolism and Mass Movements in Germany from the Napoleonic War through the Third Reich* (New York, 1975).

54. See, for example, Hans-Ulrich Wehler's fundamental critique of the new cultural history in his "Review of Ute Daniel's *Kompendium Kulturgeschichte. Theorien, Praxis, Schlüsselwörter*," *Die Zeit*, 26 July 2001.

55. Etienne François and Hagen Schulze, eds., *Deutsche Erinnerungsorte*, vol. 1 (Munich, 2001), 15–16.

56. Ibid., 18–19.

57. Ibid., 14 (using a quotation from Roger Chartier, "Le XXe siècle des historiens," in *Le Monde*, 18 August 2000, 11).

58. Thomas Nipperdey drew attention to this field of research early on. See Thomas Nipperdey, "Nationalidee und Nationaldenkmal in Deutschland im 19. Jahrhundert," *Historische Zeitschrift* 206 (1968): 529–585. For two more recent examples of this scholarship, see Reinhard Alings, *Monument und Nation: Das Bild vom Nationalstaat im Medium Denkmal—zum Verhältnis von Nation und Staat im deutschen Kaiserreich 1871–1918* (Berlin, 1996); and Charlotte Tacke, *Denkmal im sozialen Raum: Nationale Symbole in Deutschland und Frankreich im 19. Jahrhundert* (Göttingen, 1995).

59. Bernhard Giesen, *Nationale und kulturelle Identität* (Frankfurt/M., 1991); Helmut Berding, ed., *Nationales Bewusstsein und kollektive Identität* (Frankfurt/M., 1994); idem, *Mythos*

und Nation (Frankfurt/M., 1996); Wolfgang Frindte and Harald Pätzold, eds., *Mythen der Deutschen: Deutsche Befindlichkeiten zwischen Geschichten und Geschichte* (Opladen, 1994); Kristin Platt and Mihran Dabag, eds., *Generation und Gedächtnis: Erinnerungen und kollektive Identitäten* (Opladen, 1995); Hans Hattenhauer, *Deutsche Nationalsymbole: Geschichte und Bedeutung*, 3rd ed. (Cologne, 1998); Horst-Alfred Heinrich, *Kollektive Erinnerungen der Deutschen. Theoretische Konzepte und empirische Befunde zum sozialen Gedächtnis* (Weinheim, Munich, 2002); Werner Freitag, ed., *Das Dritte Reich im Fest: Führermythos, Feierlaune und Verweigerung in Westfalen 1933–1945* (Bielefeld, 1997).

60. See Nancy R. Reagin's review essay, "Recent Work on German National Identity: Regional? Imperial? Gendered? Imaginary?" *Central European History* 37 (2004): 273–289.

61. Etienne François et al., eds., *Nation und Emotion: Deutschland und Frankreich im Vergleich 19. und 20. Jahrhundert* (Göttingen, 1995); Celia Applegate and Pamela Potter, eds., *Music and German National Identity* (Chicago, 2002); Lorie A. Vanchena, *Political Poetry in Periodicals and the Shaping of German National Consciousness* (New York, 2000); Svenja Goltermann, *Körper der Nation: Habitusformierung und die Politik des Turnens, 1860–1890* (Göttingen, 1998); Martina Kessel, *Langeweile: Zum Umgang mit Zeit und Gefühlen in Deutschland vom späten 18. bis zum frühen 20. Jahrhundert* (Göttingen, 2001).

62. Celia Applegate, *A Nation of Provincials: The German Idea of Heimat* (Berkeley, 1990).

63. Alon Confino, "The Nation as a Local Metaphor: Heimat, National Memory and the German Empire, 1871–1918," *History and Memory* 5 (1993): 72.

64. Ibid., 72.

65. Tacke, *Denkmal*, 15.

66. Ibid., 291.

67. Jean Quataert, *Staging Philanthropy: Patriotic Women and the National Imagination in Dynastic Germany, 1813–1916* (Ann Arbor, 2001), 294.

68. Ibid.

69. On the cooperation of patriotic and charitable women's associations with the BDF, see Angelika Schaser, "Women," 250–255.

70. Abigail Green, *Fatherlands: State Building and Nationhood in Nineteenth-Century Germany* (Cambridge, 2001).

71. Ulrike Jureit, ed., *Politische Kollektive: Die Konstruktion nationaler, rassischer und ethnischer Gemeinschaften* (Münster, 2001).

72. Aleida Assmann, "Vier Formen des Gedächtnisses," *Erwägen Wissen Ethik* 13 (2002): 183–190. See also the critiques of Assmann's categories and her responses in the same journal volume.

73. See the contributions by Kirsten Heinsohn, Heide-Marie Lauterer, and Angelika Schaser in *Erinnerungskartelle: Zur Konstruktion von Autobiographien nach 1945*, ed. Angelika Schaser (Bochum, 2003); and, as a case study, Karen Hagemann, "Die Perthes im Krieg: Kriegserfahrungen und–erinnerungen einer Hamburger Bürgerfamilie in der 'Franzosenzeit,'" in *Eliten im Wandel. Gesellschaftliche Führungsschichten im 19. und 20. Jahrhundert*, ed. Karl Christian Führer et al. (Münster, 2004), 72–101.

74. Helmut Walser Smith, *German Nationalism and Religious Conflict: Culture, Ideology, Politics* (Princeton, 1995); Gerd Krumeich and Hartmut Lehmann, eds., *"Gott mit uns": Nation, Religion und Gewalt im 19. und frühen 20. Jahrhundert* (Göttingen, 2000); Heinz-Gerhard Haupt and Dieter Langewiesche, eds., *Nation und Religion in der deutschen Geschichte* (Frankfurt/M., 2001).

75. See the contribution by Ann Taylor Allen in this volume.

76. Karin Hausen, "Die Nicht-Einheit der Geschichte als historiographische Herausforderung. Zur historischen Relevanz und Anstößigkeit der Geschlechtergeschichte," in *Geschlechtergeschichte und Allgemeine Geschichte: Herausforderungen und Perspektiven*, ed. Hans Medick and Anne-Charlott Trepp (Göttingen, 1998), 17–55.

77. Ibid., 25–26.
78. Ibid., 36.
79. Ibid., 37.
80. Ida Blom, "Gender and Nation in International Comparison," in Blom et al., *Gendered Nations*, 21.
81. Geoff Eley, "Culture, Nation and Gender," in Blom et al., *Gendered Nations*, 37. "Dramatic moments of political rupture . . . deliver some of the best answers to this question."
82. Sebastian Conrad and Jürgen Osterhammel, "Einleitung," in *Das Kaiserreich transnational: Deutschland in der Welt 1871–1914*, ed. Sebastian Conrad and Jürgen Osterhammel (Göttingen, 2004), 14.
83. Karin Hausen, "Die Nicht-Einheit," 46.
84. See also the contribution by Birthe Kundrus in this volume.

3

MILITARY, WAR, AND THE MAINSTREAMS
Gendering Modern German Military History

Karen Hagemann

In 1832 Carl von Clausewitz's famous book *On War* was published posthumously with an introduction by his widow, Marie von Clausewitz. She began modestly, stating that bewilderment at the fact that a female hand had dared to preface a work of such nature was entirely justified. She nonetheless asked readers to excuse her writing and involvement in the publication of her husband's book. He had not wished to publish the work during his lifetime, she claimed, but had wanted her to do so after his death. Even so, it had taken the persuasion of friends to convince her that Clausewitz's words obliged her to overcome timidity and introduce his book to the world.[1]

Fortunately I am no longer required today to provide long-winded justifications for dealing with the topics of the military and war. Nevertheless, even today the subject appears to be conceived of as genuinely masculine. The maleness of the military and war continues to be so self-evident to most military historians as to require no critical scrutiny. This is hardly surprising in regard to traditional military historiography, which generally is written from a politically conservative perspective. In this field of the discipline, the objects of study—wars, battles, weapons systems, generals, military organization, and military tactics—remain a male affair in a dual sense: in actual historical practice (most researchers are men) and in the scholarly focus (the research is on men). This bias is all the more surprising in the context of recent military historiography. The dual maleness of military history has been little affected by its receptivity to questions from social and economic history, which began in the 1970s among Anglo-American scholars and became known as the "New Military History." The same shift occurred somewhat later among German-speaking historians as well.[2] To be sure, researchers working in the framework of the "New Military History" are now also beginning to examine economic structures, military mentalities, and networks of relationships within the military, as well as relations between the military and civilian society, but the maleness of the subject remains unquestioned. Even the increasing integration of the perspectives of cultural history and the history of everyday life into military history since the early 1990s has changed little in this regard.[3] To be sure, historians now begin to pay attention to the life-worlds, mentalities, and experiences of ordinary men in the military and war, which had been neglected previously, but these studies also persist in accepting the maleness of the subject as a quasi-natural given, which thus does not need to be addressed. The same may be said for many cultural historical studies of the military and war undertaken on both sides of the Atlantic. Even in the analysis of military symbols, rituals, and festivities, of bellicose discourses, and of the culture of war before, during, and after a war, the majority of studies do not integrate gender. Most works of military history have focused on male actors, to be sure, but without addressing their gender, their culturally and socially constructed masculinity, or their relationships, as men to other men as well as to women.

Research in military history also has long neglected women—whether as soldiers' wives, members of the *Wehrmacht*, battlefield nurses of the Red Cross, or workers in the armaments industry or wartime welfare institutions. Thus, for example, Geoffrey Best was able to limit the subject of his study on war and society in Revolutionary Europe (1770–1870), to men without fear of being challenged. He noted succinctly: "We need not concern ourselves with women, who had very little part in our story."[4] On both sides of the Atlantic, German military history belongs to the fields of historiography that have confronted the challenge of women's and gender history only on the margins and only recently begun to integrate this promising perspective.

This omission is all the more remarkable given the fact that women's and gender studies began addressing the theme of the military and war already in the 1980s. Initially, a rapidly growing body of literature appeared mainly in the English-speaking countries. At first, the majority of authors and editors in this field came from the social and political sciences. Most influential were the works of scholars such as Cynthia Enloe and Jean Bethke Elshtain in North America and Ruth Seifert in Germany.[5] Later on, women's and gender historians began to address the subject. Since the early 1990s, the military and war have become increasingly important topics for women's and gender history in the United States and Germany. At first, research focused more on the question of women's place in the history of the military and war. One of the path-breaking studies in the field of German history was Ute Daniel's *The War from Within: German Working-Class Women in the First World War*, first published in 1989.[6] But the dimension of men and masculinity played an important role from early on as well. The earliest and most influential studies here were Klaus Theweleit's *Male Fantasies*, which came out in 1980, and George Mosse's *Fallen Soldier: Reshaping the Memory of the World Wars*, which appeared in 1990.[7] The history of the military and war belonged to the first fields in which gender history began expanding into a history of men and masculinities.[8]

Nowadays it is impossible to overlook the substantial changes in the past fifteen years in the historiography of the military and war, which has become a burgeoning research field and thus gained growing recognition even outside the circle of military history experts. Two main factors have contributed to this trend: primarily the development of world politics since the collapse of the Socialist system of states, which has because of the increasing number of military conflicts not only in Eastern Europe but elsewhere strongly underscored the continued relevance of the theme of the military and war and its influence on all areas of the economy, politics, society, and culture. Alongside also are innovations first introduced in the history of the military and war by social and later by cultural and gender historians. They challenged this field with new questions and methods. As a consequence, with these new approaches the military and war have become attractive subjects even for historians who are put off by the kind of traditional military history that Dennis E. Showalter has so aptly dubbed "drum and trumpet history."[9] The wide variety of methods and questions with which scholars in the United States and Germany are currently studying the military and war in German history is remarkable. These studies reach from military and operational history in the conventional sense to political, economic, and social history, the history of technology, art and cultural history, and film studies. For that reason, Thomas Kühne and Benjamin Ziemann speak of a "military history in extension" in the introduction to their historiographical anthology entitled *What Is Military History?*, published in 2000. The book presents state-of-the-art essays on all modern historiographical approaches in the field of the history of military and war, and includes a report on gender, military, and war.[10]

Against the background of this general development of the field, this chapter provides an overview of the state of research on the military, war, and gender in German history in the period from the introduction of general conscription at the beginning of the nineteenth century until the end of the Second World War and discusses some of the main deficits of this research. At the end, I will pursue the question of whether this research has succeeded in rewriting the mainstreams of military history.

An Unbalanced Field:
The Gender History of Modern German Military History

The gender historical research published so far indicates that reflecting on the "gender" of the military and war can only be fruitful and yield new insights if we abandon the notion, still so common among military historians, that gender is something natural, which can be taken for granted and does not need to be questioned. Furthermore, "gender" should not simply be equalized with women as is still so often the case. The most productive approach for research on the history of the military and war is an understanding of gender as a knowledge of sexual differences produced by culture and society—a knowledge that is neither absolute nor true, but always relative and produced in complex ways in specific historical discursive contexts. This knowledge refers not only to ideas but also to institutions and structures, to everyday behavior as well as symbolic interactions, to everything that helps to shape political and social relationships. "Gender" operates, thus, in relation to "categories of difference" such as class, race, ethnicity, age, and sexuality in a manner of ordering the world asymmetrically and hierarchically, which is inseparable from its political and social organization.[11]

The shift from "women" to "gender" and with it the development of a more sophisticated theoretical and methodological framework for historical analysis was extremely fruitful for the research on the history of military, war, and gender, because it has enabled us to make men and masculinity objects of historical research too. This opening helped us to understand better the male-dominated historical phenomena of military and war. The history of nineteenth- and twentieth-century Germany belongs to the research fields of the military history first impacted by the gendered perspective. This is hardly surprising, because of the special importance of military and war topics in modern German history. The focus of the research tended to be from the very beginning quite lopsided, however.[12] The twentieth century has been much better studied than the nineteenth: particularly in North America, research interest has concentrated on the period of the world wars and, more recently, also on the postwar history of the two Germanys.[13]

Military, War, and Gender in Nineteenth-Century Germany

The two central themes for the gender history of the military and war in the nineteenth century are the relationship between the nation, war, and the gender order on the one hand,[14] and between universal conscription, political citizenship rights, and images of masculinity on the other.[15] So far, mainly German scholars have been interested in these questions. The gender history of military and war in nineteenth-century Germany—with few exceptions—did not attract much attention by American scholars. The German scholarship—most recently the new book by Ute Frevert, *A Nation in Barracks: Modern Germany, Military Conscription and Civil Society*[16] and "my own study, "Manly Valor and German Honor": The Nation, Military and Gender during Prussia's Anti-Napoleonic Wars*[17]—has stressed that the introduction and implementation of universal male conscription, which was common in the nineteenth century at least during wartime, was everywhere closely associated with the process of modern nation building, regardless of the concrete forms it took. It had far-reaching consequences not just for the military and warfare, but also for the relationship between the military and civilian society.[18] In its wake, large groups of men were drafted for military and wartime service for the first time and had to be motivated and trained. Because of the altered form of warfare that accompanied the introduction of universal conscription, more was expected of these men than simple "subordination," "discipline," and "soldierly courage." They were expected to fight and die for their "fatherland" in a spirit of self-reliance and self-sacrifice. This national rhetoric of sacrifice culminated in the myth of the freely chosen patriotic hero's death, which was processed and disseminated in the cult surrounding the veneration and commemoration of heroes. This cult had to be universalized in the course of the introduction of universal conscription, since now any man liable for military service could die for his country. Thus from the beginning, wars conducted on the basis of universal conscription needed to be prepared for and accompanied by intensive patriotic-national propaganda, which motivated men to perform military service. A central element of this propaganda was the image of the man as "protector" and "defender" of family, home, and fatherland. Increasingly in the course of the nineteenth century in Germany, the military appears to have become not a "school of the nation" but rather a "school of masculinity."[19] One of the interesting paradoxes is that with the introduction of universal conscription, it was always young men who were drafted for military service and shaped by it. They were not just the first to be prepared mentally for the next war and the primary addressees of the propaganda of "valorous masculinity." They also did most of the fighting. Nevertheless, in the propaganda the conscript was mostly depicted as a "husband and father" who protects the loved ones.[20]

For an understanding of the military as an institution with inherent paradoxes, the notion of "military culture," the inner life of the military, is extremely important. The most recent study of this subject is Isabel Hull's book *Absolute Destruction: Military, Culture and the Practice of War in Imperial Germany*. Her main thesis is that at least since 1870–1871 in Germany there emerged a "military culture," which enhanced the unlimited acceptance of the exercise of military power in war and peacetime and the separation of the military from politics.[21] Interestingly, new parallel studies, like the work by

Marcus Funck on the officer corps of the Wilhelmine Army, underline that mainly civilians from the middle class were pushing for a harder masculinity more suited to fighting a modern war.[22]

The increasing number of publications is a beginning, to be sure, but many questions remain unanswered. One of the most glaring desiderata is the absence of an analysis of the relationship between the military and civilian society in the long nineteenth century that systematically links social history, the history of everyday life, and gender history.[23] We also lack a study of the institution of the military and the changing forms of military service in the nineteenth century that not only brings together approaches from social history, gender history, and the history of experience, but also includes and compares the differences among German territorial states.[24] We urgently need an analysis of military training and its effects on recruits as well as of the mental and physical requirements and consequences of battle, combining the history of mentalities with the history of the body. Such studies would be important not only for the nineteenth but also for the twentieth century. They would need to examine, among other things, which images of masculinity the military aspired to and sought to enforce at a given time and how recruits reacted to these attempts to (re)shape them. More generally, it seems important to historicize models of masculinity, and also to differentiate among them more than historians have done until now.[25] In this vein, Rene Schilling has recently published a monograph examining the transformation of the *Construction of the War Hero between 1813 and 1945*.[26]

Parallel to the introduction of universal conscription and the necessary reorganization of armies that accompanied it, military-strategic and fiscal motives ultimately led to the exclusion of all women from military society. This included even the soldiers' and officers' wives who in the early modern period had been subject to military law, and who in the eighteenth century had still sometimes accompanied fighting armies in order to cater to the everyday needs of the troops. Only with universal conscription, and limited to the nineteenth century, did the armies develop into a largely masculine institution. The right to bear arms as well as the business of warfare became an exclusively male affair. Aside from military strategy and fiscal concerns it was above all political motives that played a role here, since universal conscription and citizenship rights were closely linked in political discourse. In this way women could be excluded from the newly emergent "society of citizens of the state" and kept out of central areas of political power.[27]

This development had paradoxical consequences for the gender order and gender relations. While women were systematically excluded from central institutionalized political arenas during the nineteenth century, they nevertheless remained indispensable for the functioning of wartime society. Indeed, the introduction of universal conscription made broad support for war among

what's missing?

civilian society more important than ever. This already became evident in Prussia during the anti-Napoleonic wars of 1813–1815. The Prussian government could never have conducted these wars successfully without the broad support of middle- and upper-class circles. The incorporation of civilian society into the "nation at arms" was facilitated by the widely propagated model of the "*Volk* family." This model constructed the nation as a family organized along patriarchal and hierarchical lines, with a complementary gender-specific division of labor, which in times of looming war also had to be a military fighting community whereby each member had to fulfill the duties specific to his or her rank, gender, age, and marital status.[28] This model continued to be promoted during the First and Second World Wars, in forms modified to suit the changing times.

As the 1998 study by Dirk Reder, *Women's Movement and Nation,* on the patriotic women's associations between 1813 and 1830, and Jean Quataert's 2001 book, *Staging Philanthropy: Patriotic Women and the National Imagination in Dynastic Germany, 1813–1916,* show, women were active in preparations for war and wartime welfare throughout the nineteenth century—mainly, but not exclusively, in the areas of nursing and war relief.[29] The patriotic women's associations of the wars of 1813–1815 and their successor organizations continued in a new institutional form to perform a large portion of the work soldiers' wives had done in the baggage trains of early modern armies and that earlier had been the duty of aristocratic officers' and landowners' wives, as well as church women. The work of the patriotic women's associations was largely performed by aristocratic and bourgeois women. Women's organized activities in war relief in the "National Women's Front" and in military nursing through the German Red Cross during the First World War thus had a long tradition.[30]

In examining the research on the military, war, and gender in the long nineteenth century, a basic pattern of the gender order becomes evident: as soon as wars were conducted as "national wars" on the basis of broad mobilization, the discursively constructed gender differences intensified over the course of these wars, while at the same time women's scope of action expanded. These two at first sight paradoxical developments appear to be directly related. Since women's scope of action had to be extended because of the specific exigencies of war on the basis of universal mobilization and this at least potentially jeopardized the gender order, gender images had to be drawn all the more strictly; and after the war, in particular, efforts had to be made to restore the previous gender order. This paradox should be analyzed more intensively and in temporal, regional, and national comparison. As part of the research that focuses on women, the military and war in the long nineteenth century, we need an analysis of the changing position of women of different social strata in the military and towards the military. For instance, we know next to nothing about the situation of soldiers' and officers' wives and widows. Moreover, we need social and everyday life histories of the anti-Napoleonic wars and the wars of unification that systematically integrate the relationship between home and front and thereby explore its gender dimension.

The Gender Order of the Era of the Two World Wars

The history of military and war of the twentieth century has received in general much more scholarly and public attention than the history of the long nineteenth century. The period of the two world wars is obviously also more interesting for American scholars. Next to the importance of both wars for the global history of the twentieth century, one reason might be that the United States participated in both wars. At the beginning researchers on both sides of the Atlantic were mainly interested in the role of women. Later in particular German scholars started to work on the theme of military and masculinity. Today it is commonly understood that the analysis of both—the propagated concepts of femininity and masculinity and the practical role of women and men in war societies—is necessary if we want to understand the gender order of "total war" societies. Scholars agree furthermore that the two world wars presented additional challenges to the wartime gender order. But the major question of whether the paradoxical basic pattern of the gender order described for the nineteenth century applies, in modified form, to the period of the world wars needs to be investigated further. The previous research on the First and Second World War and the two postwar periods indicate that this is indeed the case.

The most important books on the gender order of World War I are, apart from Ute Daniel's *War from Within*, Birthe Kundrus's book *Soldiers' Wives: Family Policy and the Gender Relations in the First and Second World War*, published in 1995, which compares in an innovative way the two world wars, and Benjamin Ziemann's *Front und Heimat*, which came out in 1997 and analyzes the war experiences, perceptions, and memories of men and women in rural southern Bavaria between 1914 and 1923.[31] These three studies question in different ways the old view of the First World War as a catalyst for women's emancipation and point to the diversity of war experiences and perceptions. Furthermore, they show the close ties between "home" and "the front." Roger Chickering's 1998 *Imperial Germany and the Great War, 1914–1918*[32] also systematically analyzes the relationship between both. His study reveals the significance of the gender dimension for the analysis of "total wars," which are marked ideal—typically by the interplay of four elements—the "totality" of war aims, methods, mobilization, and control.[33] The consequence is the blurring of the line between military and civilian spheres.[34] Gender relations are a key indicator of this process of blurring.[35]

The extensive scholarship on the First World War has underlined that industrialized mass war demanded a previously unknown degree of patriotic national mobilization among soldiers and civilians alike.[36] As it became increasingly industrialized, war became more strongly determined than ever by the readiness of the civilian population at home, both male and female, to support the war, not just with material sacrifices and involvement in war relief and nursing but also, and above all, by working in wartime industry.[37] The "second front" at home was expected to provide endless streams of material and people for the war on the "first front" and at the same time process its losses materially and psychologically. Thus, the war was increasingly waged in the economic arena as well—among other things by the blockade policies of the Allies, which dramatically worsened the supply situation of the German civilian population.[38]

In the face of the increasingly catastrophic shortage of everyday necessities at home and the dramatically rising casualties at the front, the "social and political truce" (*Burgfrieden*) that had been declared at the beginning of the war soon crumbled, and social protest and opposition to the war grew among both women and men. The important political role that women played in the increasing street protests against wartime food shortages is revealed by Belinda Davis in her 2000 study *Home Fires Burning: Food, Politics, and Everyday Life in World War I Berlin*.[39] At least in Berlin, these protests met with a good deal of public sympathy. Could the same be said of other regions in the Reich, or was this a phenomenon specific to Berlin? The new book by Maureen Healy, *Vienna and the Fall of the Habsburg Empire: Total War and Everyday Life in World War I*, describes nearly the same social problems due to food shortages, but the working-class population acted differently than in Berlin, even if many in the population increasingly disliked the war. Vienna did not experience such a large outbreak of food riots.[40] Like other studies, both authors demonstrate the social and political consequences of the Allied food blockade of Austria and Germany. Its main target was the civilian population. With the blockade the Allies successfully destabilized the home front.[41]

If we follow Belinda Davis, working-class women's food riots only came under fire in Germany with the defeat and the Revolution, at the time when the legend of the "stab in the back" was constructed and propagated, largely by leading military officers, in order to mask their own failure and project responsibility onto their civilian political opponents.[42] It would be interesting to compare the discourses after the First and the Second World Wars and test Susanne zur Nieden's thesis that the myth of German women's "quick surrender" after the Second World War was a variation on the stab-in-the-back legend of the First World War—an idea outlined in her article in the recent anthology *Home/Front: The Military, War and Gender in 20th Century Germany*—edited by Stefanie Schüler-Springorum and Karen Hagemann.[43]

One growing field in the gendered history of the military and war is the interwar period. The war lived on long after it was officially ended, initially as part of the necessary process of coping with the effects of war and defeat. Apart from political debates on the question of responsibility for the defeat,[44] which was associated with the collapse of the political and social order of Imperial Germany, the focus in the early postwar years was on the problem of economic and social demobilization. And this demobilization was—as several older studies by scholars such as Richard Bessel, Karin Hausen, and Susanne Rouette show—as gendered as the cultural demobilization.[45]

As part of this demobilization processes the national-conservative political spectrum propagated increasingly heroicized memories of the First World War. The violent experiences of the war were more and more idealized in the postwar period in these memories and with them the men who fought during the war on the front line. Parallel violence increasingly became an accepted instrument of politics.[46] This development already began in the November Revolution of 1918, continued with the founding of paramilitary "Protection and Defense Leagues" across almost the entire political spectrum[47] and the militarization of demonstration culture,[48] and ended with terror in the streets and meeting halls and also political assassinations.[49] It is striking that in all political camps, it was mainly young men who used violence: not the generation of war veterans, but mainly their younger brothers and sons drove the process which culminated in the militarization of political culture and the acceptance of violence as a political tool.[50]

The development was accompanied by the growing popularity of an image of "martial masculinity."[51] This model of masculinity, most prominently proposed by Ernst Jünger, set the terms for the discussion of male war experience by historians for many years. Its dominance has increasingly been challenged, by Sabine Kienitz and Paul Lerner, among others, who have been studying the physical and mental effects of the war on various groups of men.[52] Kienitz analyses in her book *Damaged Heroes* the cultural perception of war invalids between 1914 and 1923. Lerner explores in his study *Hysterical Men* the changing perceptions and representations of men, who were mentally affected by military service between 1890 and 1930. Their research is an important contribution to the repeatedly invoked but as yet—at least in German history—unwritten gender history of violence and deformation, dying, and death in war.[53]

Part of a critical confrontation with the image of "martial masculinity" should also be an analysis of an alternative model of masculinity such as was developed in the context of the peace movement in the Weimar Republic.[54] Until now, scholarship has tended to overlook the (admittedly far less influential) pacifist culture that existed alongside militarist culture.[55] It would be important in general to take a more systematic look at peace movements and international peace and security policy from the gender perspective, with a comparative analysis of policies and practices in their international context.[56]

Apart from the First World War, the Second by now doubtless is one of the best-researched military conflicts. Scholars on both sides of the Atlantic agree that the groundwork for the Second World War was laid long before actual hostilities began, and that during this war, far more than during the First World War, the conduct of war was determined by the mobilization of huge masses of people, the massive deployment of highly technological weapons, powerful equipment, and newly developed communications technologies.[57] At the same time, the Second World War was the first war of conquest and annihilation primarily legitimated by racist motives. A murderous will to exterminate characterized the military practice of the Third Reich. A particularly horrific aspect of the "barbarization of war" in the years 1939 to 1945 is the fact that the Wehrmacht was a conscript army. Not all soldiers of the Wehrmacht were involved in the murderous logic of the war of annihilation and the Holocaust, but many participated when the situation arose, if for varying reasons.[58] In the *Endkampf* of 1945 some of them were even willing to fight against their own civilian populations, that is, suppress their willingness to make peace with the victorious enemy and force themselves to fight till the bitter end, as the new study by Stephen G. Fritz shows.[59] What role the "model of martial masculinity" and the male bonding concept of "comradeship" played here is subject of research. Klaus Latzel and Thomas Kühne have written important studies in this area.[60] In particular Kühne points to the significance of "comradeship" for the integration of normal men not only into the Wehrmacht, but also for their exercise of military violence. He argues in his recent book, *Kameradschaft: Die Soldaten des nationalsozialistischen Krieges und das 20. Jahrhundert,* on soldiers and the national socialist war in twentieth century Germany—as in earlier articles—that the model of comradeship could fulfill this function above all because it tended to be open and included "soft," "womanly" elements of masculinity. On the one hand, this allowed men at the front to communicate verbally about the tensions between the heterosexual norm and the sublimated homosexuality characteristic of any male community, thus safeguarding the men's individual and biographical identities. On the other, it also facilitated communication with those back home, since it incorporated the idea of "comradeship" between the homeland and the front. The malleability of the concept made it easier for Kühne to symbolically bridge disparate experiences. At the same time, according to him, comradeship functioned as a symbolic hinge between violence and harmony, war and peace, because it bridged the contradiction between military violence and the civilian norm of nonviolence and offered soldiers emotional relief from their violent tasks at the front.[61]

Only relatively few men sought to escape conscription, for example by "self-mutilation," or went so far as to desert. During the Second World War, ten thousand Wehrmacht soldiers alone were convicted of "self-mutilation" by a military tribunal. More than half of them were sentenced to death. The law on special military tribunals treated self-mutilation as fulfilling the offense of "undermining military strength." We know very little about this group of men and their male self-images. Moreover, the research done so far did not include systematically the important dimension of gender images.[62] This is a promising field for future research. One of the questions that should be analyzed is how these men defined their identities as men in wartime and postwar societies, which regarded desertion, "malingering," and self-mutilation as "cowardly, unmanly behavior" and "treasonous."

More research is done for World War II on the role of German women on the "homefront." This research shows that far more than in the World War I, the line between the front and home was abolished. This further increased the importance of the economic and political-moral support for the progress of the war. Leila A. J. Rupp, in her early studies on the mobilization of German women for war, and Birthe Kundrus in her more recent book, *Soldiers' Wives*, have shown that the National Socialists, in order to prevent the sort of "stab in the back at home" they believed had occurred in the last war, never fully exploited the opportunities for conscripting women for national service that the Defense Law of 1935 opened up.[63] Instead, they propped up the livelihood of soldiers' wives and families as far as possible. Far more thoroughly than the Wilhelmine state, the Nazi state closed the gap left by husbands serving in the army in their role as breadwinners, and thus sought at the same time to stabilize the "home front." This support was highly selective, however, in accordance with racial and class politics. Moreover, the Nazis differentiated carefully between German women of different age and familial status.[64] Newer studies by Elizabeth Heinemann and Lisa Pine have confirmed the results of Rupp and Kundrus.[65] What is more, they all agree that this labor market and family policy, which was shaped on the one hand by population and racial policy motives and on the other by the demands of the wartime economy, was only possible during the war years because of the massive deployment of forced labor, which kept the economy going.[66]

Through their persistent willingness to maintain everyday life on the "home front" even under the conditions of constant bombing raids, women bore substantial responsibility for the continuation of the war and with it the racist policy of murder. Not only did they "wear the trousers" in many areas of the wartime economy,[67] but a rapidly growing number of "German women" became active as nurses and Wehrmacht auxiliaries in the occupied territories and on the front itself. It is true that at the end of the First World War, women also had been deployed as auxiliaries in the offices of the communications zone (*Etappendienst*). The Wehrmacht auxiliaries of the Second World War, however, were far more important, and in the final phase of the war their duties included regular military service in the air defense: Between 450,000 and 500,000 were deployed in various areas of the military—one woman to every twenty soldiers. Only one-third of these women was performing compulsory service; the majority volunteered.[68] Women's participation in the Nazi system and the Wehrmacht was one of the longest repressed and ignored subjects after 1945. One reason is surely that it demonstrated most clearly the everyday involvement of many people in the Nazi state, its war of annihilation and the Holocaust, and thus profoundly challenged the postwar rhetoric of victimization.[69] Until today, women's role in the Wehrmacht, and even in the medical service,[70] and the perception of this service during and its suppression after the war has not yet been studied systematically—neither by American nor by German scholars.

At present, we also do not know much about women's participation in the Nazi regime of occupation and extermination. Elizabeth Harvey makes a start with her recent book *Women and the Nazi East: Agents and Witnesses of Germanization,* which deals with the deployment of German women in occupied Poland.[71] The women she studies were not obvious perpetrators such as the female employees of the SS troop task forces, SS telecommunications and staff auxiliaries, SS doctors and nurses, and SS concentration camp guards, or the wives of SS men.[72] Rather, she analyzes the motives that led young, single "German women" to go to occupied Poland to work as teachers and counselors for the ethnic German community as part of the "ethnic struggle" (*Volkstumskampf*) against Poland's "non-German" population. Harvey makes it clear that these women went to Poland because working within the occupation regime promised them a wider scope of action, more responsibility, and greater privileges than employment in Germany proper. Like many women on the "home front," she shows also that they focused their attention and awareness on their narrow personal interests, daily tasks, and duties, and ignored the wider genocidal context.

The occupation regime is an area that, by and large, has only quite recently begun to be studied from the perspective of social history and the history of everyday life. Particularly promising is a focus on the interactions between occupied and occupiers.[73] One of the pioneering studies here is Bernhard Chiari's *Everyday Life behind the Front: Collaboration and Resistance in Belarus, 1941–44,* which came out 1998. His book has not only drawn attention to the everyday functioning of dictatorship, but also addresses collaboration, defiance, and armed resistance on the part of the occupied. Unfortunately, he did not incorporate the gender dimension sufficiently. The first studies devoted to relations between male occupiers and the female occupied is Ebba D. Drolshagen's book on women in the occupied Western and Northern European territories who were true loves of German soldiers.[74] Her picture is surprisingly positive. These women had mainly problems with their non-German neighbors, who perceived them as "collaborators," but not with German soldiers. The German army command accepted relations between soldiers and "Aryan" women in the occupied Scandinavian and Western European regions. If Drolshagen would have included the occupied regions of Eastern Europe her study would certainly have yielded a different, much darker picture since the concrete occupation policies were very much informed by the racist images of the enemy and the different objectives that arose from them. The substantial differences in occupation policy are amply evident in Birgit Beck's new book, *Wehrmacht and Sexual Violence*, which analyzes the military trials of sexual crimes committed by German soldiers and thereby treats a largely unwritten chapter in the history of war crimes.[75] By studying Wehrmacht court-martial records she succeeds not just in refuting the common thesis that rapes by soldiers went unpunished, but also in showing how differently such offenses were dealt with by military tribunals on the Eastern and Western fronts, reflecting the respective intentions of an occupation policy formed by a racial ideology, which was shared by the judges. On both the Eastern and Western fronts sentencing was strongly influenced by the racist thinking of judges, who primarily represented the interests of the Wehrmacht and its male members. This circumstance is reflected in the more severe punishment of the far less serious crimes against property because they were considered to "undermine military strength." Hopefully, further empirical studies will deal more intensively with the problem of sexual violence in the First and Second World Wars, which includes forced prostitution.[76] A start are the publications by Christa Paul on *Forced Prostitution* by the NS state and Insa Meinen on the *Wehrmacht and Prostitution in the Occupied France*. These studies demonstrate how intensively the NS state supported by the military sexually exploited women in the occupied territories and tried to control the relations between soldiers and women to prevent sexual diseases but also "fraternization with the enemy." Until the publication of the books by Beck, Meinen and Paul the research on sexual violence during World War II has succeeded only in fixing in the public mind the mass rapes of German women by soldiers of the Red Army at the end of the war in 1945, which subsequently became a portent of defeat and capitulation in the collective memory of the German nation.[77]

Conclusion: The Integration and Separation of Gender

The research of the last decade on the themes of military, war, and gender in modern German history is impressive, but more has to be done. A gendered rewriting of this history in the future should include the following four key dimensions: Firstly, because of the close interrelationship between civilian and military society, home and the front, we need to analyze both more concretely in their interdependence and their historical contexts and—depending upon the questions we are asking—examine the links to politics, the economy, society, and culture. Secondly, since the boundaries between military and civilian society, and between war and peace, are relative and fluid, it is important to abandon obsolete periodizations and to compare different periods far more than we have until now, paying attention to continuities and discontinuities, commonalities as well as differences. Thirdly, we need to focus more on the ambivalences and ruptures, the contradictions in the phenomena of the military and war, which can best be done by adopting a multiperspective approach that combines political, social, and cultural history; one example here is the discussed paradoxical relation between propaganda and practices. Fourthly and finally, we need many more regional and national comparative studies and transnational research, in order, for example, to work out what is specific or common to the gender order of a specific wartime society. The most important desiderata for comparative studies in the field of a gendered history of modern military and war are: the differences and similarities in the gendered military culture; the cultural strategies that were used to mobilize men for war; the forms of integration and the rhetorical legitimation of different groups of women not only in the home front but also, for the First and in particularly Second World Wars, in the military front, especially in the auxiliary corps; the discourses and practices, experiences and perceptions of sexual violence—of rape and prostitution—during and after the wars as part of the occupation; the economic, social, political, and cultural demobilization, and also as part of this agenda the different ways how postwar societies dealt with war destruction and postwar violence in the home and in the public; and last but not least, the peace movements and international peace and security policies.

Even though gender research is relatively recent, we have gained in many fields new insights that differentiate and modify the conventional knowledge about military and war. Despite the importance of these new insights, the degree of integration of the findings of women's and gender history into mainstream scholarship on the military and war is still surprisingly limited. At first sight, however, the situation, at least in Germany, appears to be better here than in other fields of history, and even better than in the United States. The growing inclusion of gender history themes is evident above all at conferences and in collections of essays on the history of the military and war. Today, at least one or two contributions on women's and gender history are obligatory, it seems. In Germany, the activities of three working groups, which were founded in the 1990s, have had substantial influence: the *Arbeitskreis Historische Friedensforschung* (Working Group on Peace Studies),[78] the Working Group on Military and Society in the Early Modern Period,[79] and the Working Group of Military History.[80] All three have organized a conference on different aspects of gender, military, and war/peace. The results are published in essay collections.[81]

Even the Institute for Military History Research (MGFA), which is attached to the German Ministry of Defense, is turning, if slowly and hesitantly, to questions of gender history, which can be seen from its most recent conference publications.[82] Moreover, in 2002 the military history journal *Militärhistorische Zeitschrift* for the first time put out a special issue on gender history entitled *Post-War-Heroes: Political and Cultural Demobilization in German Postwar Histories*.[83] The work of the MGFA however also shows quite clearly the limits to the integration of gender history. The largest historical research institute in Germany continues to be a nearly exclusively male bastion.[84] Nobody on the staff specializes in the gender history of the military. As a consequence gender has remained largely neglected in all large-scale research projects of the MGFA.[85]

A glance at the many new German and English monographs and general histories of the military and war in nineteenth- and especially twentieth-century German history that have appeared in the past few years yields a similar picture. There is a marked tendency towards separated spheres: despite the increasing research by gender historians on military and war, the gender dimension remains a marginal theme at best in so-called general accounts written by male historians on both sides of the Atlantic. The answer to one of the central questions of this volume, of whether gender history today is increasingly recognized by military historians and how far gender historians have succeeded in rewriting the mainstreams on both sides of the Atlantic, is highly ambivalent. The results of more than a decade of women's and gender history research are quite respectable on the whole, but neither in Germany nor in the United States have gender historians managed to do more than dip their toes in the mainstreams. Within military history, gender history is increasingly recognized as interesting and innovative. But there has been inadequate integration of both—the insights and the developed theoretical and methodological reflections of gender history—into mainstream research on the military and war.

Notes

I would like to thank Jean Quataert warmly for her criticism and careful work on the text and Pamela Selwyn for her translation.

1. Carl von Clausewitz, *Vom Kriege: Hinterlassenes Werk* (Berlin, 1999), 13.
2. See Torbjörn L. Knutsen, "Old, Unhappy, Far-Off Things: The New Military History of Europe," *Journal of Peace Research* 24 (1987): 87–98.
3. Wolfram Wette, "Militärgeschichte von unten: Die Perspektive des 'kleinen Mannes,'" in *Der Krieg des kleinen Mannes: Eine Militärgeschichte von unten*, ed. Wette (Munich, 1992), 9–47.
4. Geoffrey Best, *War and Society in Revolutionary Europe, 1770–1870* (London, 1982), 18.

5. Cynthia Enloe, *Does Khaki Become You? Militarization of Women's Lives* (London, 1988); Cynthia Enloe, *Maneuvers: The International Politics of Militarizing Women's Lives* (Berkeley, 2000); Jean Bethke Elshtain, *Women and War* (New York, 1987); Jean Bethke Eshtain and Sheila Tobias, eds., *Women, Militarism, and War: Essays in History, Politics, and Social Theory* (Savage, Md., 1990); Ruth Seifert, *Militär—Kultur—Identität: Individualisierung, Geschlechterverhältnisse und die soziale Konstruktion der Soldaten* (Bremen, 1996); Joshua Goldstein, *War and Gender: How Gender Shapes the War System and Vice Versa* (Cambridge, 2001).

6. Ute Daniel, *The War from Within: German Working-Class Women in the First World War* (Oxford, 1997) (in German: 1989).

7. See Klaus Theweleit, *Male Phantasies*, 2 vols. (Minneapolis, 1987) (in German: 1980); George Mosse, *Fallen Soldiers: Reshaping the Memory of the World Wars* (New York, 1990); Ute Frevert, *Men of Honor: A Social and Cultural History of the Duel* (Cambridge, 1995) (in German: 1991).

8. Early studies are: Michael C. Adams, *The Great Adventure: Male Desire and the Coming of World War I* (Bloomington, 1990); Graham Dawson, *Soldier Heroes: British Adventures, Empire and the Imagining of Masculinities* (London, 1994); Joanna Bourke, *Dismembering the Male: Men's Bodies, Britain and the Great War* (London, 1996). Introductory anthologies include: Thomas Kühne, ed., *Männergeschichte—Geschlechtergeschichte: Männlichkeit im Wandel der Moderne* (Frankfurt/M., 1996); Stefan Dudink et al., eds., *Masculinities in Politics and War: Rewritings of Modern History* (Manchester, 2004).

9. Dennis E. Showalter, "History, Military," in *The Reader's Companion to Military History* (Boston, 1996), 205.

10. Thomas Kühne and Benjamin Ziemann, "Militärgeschichte in der Erweiterung: Konjunkturen, Interpretationen, Konzepte," in *Was ist Militärgeschichte?* ed. Kühne and Ziemann (Paderborn, 2000), 9–48; Christa Hämmerle, "Von den Geschlechtern der Kriege und des Militärs: Forschungseinblicke und Bemerkungen zu einer neuen Debatte," in Kühne and Ziemann, *Was ist Militärgeschichte*, 229–262.

11. See Joan W. Scott, *Gender and the Politics of History* (New York, 1988), 2; idem, "Gender: A Useful Category of Historical Analysis," in Scott, 28–50; Gisela Bock, "Women's History and Gender History: Aspects of an International Debate," *Gender & History* 1 (1989): 7–30; Hans Medick and Anne-Charlotte Trepp, eds., *Geschlechtergeschichte und Allgemeine Geschichte. Herausforderungen und Perspektiven* (Göttingen, 1998).

12. For research overviews see: Karen Hagemann, "Militär, Krieg und Geschlechterverhältnisse: Untersuchungen, Überlegungen und Fragen zur Militärgeschichte der Frühen Neuzeit," in *Klio in Uniform? Probleme und Perspektiven einer modernen Militärgeschichte der Frühen Neuzeit*, ed. Ralf Pröve (Cologne, 1997), 35–88; Karen Hagemann, "Venus und Mars: Reflexionen zu einer Geschlechtergeschichte von Militär und Krieg," in *Landsknechte, Soldatenfrauen und Nationalkrieger: Militär, Krieg und Geschlechterordnung im historischen Wandel*, ed. Karen Hagemann and Ralf Pröve (Frankfurt/M., 1998), 13–48; Karen Hagemann, "The Military, Violence and Gender Relations in the Age of the World Wars," in *Home/Front: The Military, War and Gender in Twentieth Century Germany*, ed. Karen Hagemann and Stephanie Schüler-Springorum (Oxford, 2002), 1–42; Hämmerle, "Von den Geschlechtern."

13. For more on the postwar period, see the selected bibliography in Hagemann and Schüler-Springorum, *Home/Front*, 379–382.

14. On the state of research on "Gender and Nation," see the article by Angelika Schaser in this volume. Important for the relation of military, war, and nation in German history are: Ute Frevert, *A Nation in Barracks: Modern Germany, Military Conscription and Civil Society* (Oxford, 2004) (in German: 2001); Karen Hagemann, "Nation, Krieg und Geschlechterordnung: Zum kulturellen und politischen Diskurs in der Zeit der antinapoleonischen

Erhebung Preußens, 1806–1815," *Geschichte und Gesellschaft* 22 (1996): 562–591; Karen Hagemann, *"Mannlicher Muth und Teutsche Ehre": Nation, Militär und Geschlecht zur Zeit der antinapoleonischen Kriege Preußens* (Paderborn, 2002).

15. See Frevert, *A Nation in Barracks;* Frevert, ed., *Militär und Gesellschaft im 19. und 20. Jahrhundert* (Stuttgart, 1997); Karen Hagemann, "Of 'Manly Valor' and 'German Honor': Nation, War and Masculinity in the Age of the Prussian Uprising against Napoleon," *Central European History* 30 (1997): 187–220; Hagemann, *Mannlicher Muth;* Martin Lengwiler, *Zwischen Klinik und Kaserne: Die Geschichte der Militärpsychiatrie in Deutschland und der Schweiz 1870–1914* (Zurich, 2000); Thomas Rohrkrämer, "Mannesstolz und Kriegsverdrossenheit: Autobiographische Erinnerungen an die Einigungskriege," *Krieg und Literatur* 2 (1990): 19–36; Thomas Rohrkrämer, "Das Militär als Männerbund? Kult der soldatischen Männlichkeit im Deutschen Kaiserreich," *Westfälische Forschungen* 45 (1995): 169–187; René Schilling, *Heroische Männlichkeit: Die Konstruktion des Kriegshelden in Deutschland zwischen 1813 und 1945 am Beispiel der Rezeptionsgeschichte Körners, Friesens, Richthofens und Weddigens,* Paderborn, 2002; René Schilling, "Die 'Helden der Wehrmacht'—Konstruktion und Rezeption," in *Die Wehrmacht: Mythos und Realität* (Munich, 1999), ed. Rolf-Dieter Müller and Hans-Erich Volkmann (Munich, 1999), 550–572.

16. Frevert, *Nation in Barracks.*

17. Hagemann, *Mannlicher Muth.*

18. See for a comparative perspective: Dudink et al., *Masculinities;* Christian Jansen, ed., *Der Bürger als Soldat: Die Miliarisierung europäischer Gesellschaften im langen 19. Jahrhundert: Ein internationaler Vergleich* (Hamburg, 2004); Daniel Moran and Arthur Waldron, eds., *The People in Arms: Military Myth and National Mobilization since the French Revolution* (Cambridge, 2003).

19. Ute Frevert, "Das Militär als 'Schule der Männlichkeit': Erwartungen, Angebote, Erfahrungen im 19. Jahrhundert," in Frevert, *Militär,* 145–173.

20. Karen Hagemann, "German Heroes: The Cult of the Death for the Fatherland in 19th Century Germany," in Dudink et al., *Masculinities,* 116–134.

21. Isabel V. Hull, *Absolute Destruction: Military Culture and the Practice of War in Imperial Germany* (Ithaca, 2005).

22. Marcus Funck, "Ready for War? Conceptions of Military Manliness in the Prussio-German Officer Corps before the First World War," in Hagemann and Schüler-Springorum, *Home/Front,* 43–68.

23. Ute Planert's *Habilschrift Der Mythos vom Befreiungskrieg: Der deutsche Süden und die französischen Kriege, 1790–1840* (Paderborn, 2007, forthcoming). It will be one of the first publications on German war experiences of this period.

24. Christa Hämmerle's *Habilschrift,* "Die Allgemeine Wehrpflicht zwischen Akzeptanz und Verweigerung: Militär und Männlichkeiten in der Habsburgermonarchie (1868–1914/18)," will be an important step to a regionally differentiated knowledge that integrates gender. See also Christa Hämmerle, "Die k. (u.) k. Armee als 'Schule des Volkes'? Zur Geschichte der Allgemeinen Wehrpflicht in der multinationalen Habsburgermonarchie (1866 bis 1914/18)," in Jansen, *Der Bürger,* 175–213.

25. See Hagemann, "German Heroes."

26. See Schilling, *Heroische Männlichkeit.*

27. Important, but without the gender dimension, is Ralf Pröve, *Stadtgemeindlicher Republikanismus und "bewaffnete Macht des Volkes": Civile Ordnungsformationen und kommunale Leitbilder politischer Partizipation in Spätaufklärung, Vormärz und Revolution* (Göttingen, 2000).

28. See Hagemann, *Muth.* 583–591; Karen Hagemann, "A Valorous *Volk* Family: The Nation, the Military, and the Gender Order in Prussia in the Time of the Anti-Napoleonic Wars,

1806–15," in *Gendered Nations: Nationalisms and Gender Order in the Long Nineteenth Century*, ed. Ida Blom et al. (Oxford, 2000), 179–205.

29. Dirk A. Reder, *Frauenbewegung und Nation: Patriotische Frauenvereine in Deutschland im frühen 19. Jahrhundert (1813–1830)* (Cologne, 1998); Jean H. Quataert, *Staging Philanthropy: Patriotic Women and the National Imagination in Dynastic Germany, 1813–1916* (Ann Arbor, 2001); Rita Huber-Sperl, "Organized Women and the Strong State: The Beginnings of Female Associational Activity in Germany, 1810–1840," *Journal of Women's History* 13, no. 4 (2002): 81–105; Karen Hagemann, "Female Patriots: Women, War and the Nation in the Period of the Prussian-German Anti-Napoleonic Wars," *Gender & History* 16, no. 3 (2004): 396–424.

30. On the National Women's Service see Barbara Greven-Aschoff, *Die bürgerliche Frauenbewegung in Deutschland, 1894–1933* (Göttingen, 1981), 150–158; Birthe Kundrus, *Kriegerfrauen: Familienpolitik und Geschlechterverhältnisse im Ersten und Zweiten Weltkrieg* (Hamburg, 1995), 98–123.

31. See Daniel, *War from Within*; Ute Daniel, "Zweierlei Heimatfronten: Weibliche Kriegserfahrungen 1914 bis 1918 und 1939 bis 1945 im Kontrast," in *Erster Weltkrieg—Zweiter Weltkrieg: Vergleich: Krieg, Kriegserlebnis, Kriegserfahrung in Deutschland*, ed. Bruno Thoss and Hans-Erich Volkmann (Paderborn, 2002), 391–410; Kundrus, *Kriegerfrauen*; Benjamin Ziemann, *Front und Heimat: Ländliche Kriegserfahrungen im südlichen Bayern 1914–1923* (Essen, 1997).

32. Roger Chickering, *Imperial Germany and the Great War, 1914–1918* (Cambridge, 1998).

33. On the concept of "total war," see Stig Förster, "Das Zeitalter des totalen Krieges, 1861–1945," *Mittelweg 36* 8, no. 6 (1999): 12–29.

34. See Roger Chickering, "Militärgeschichte als Totalgeschichte im Zeitalter des totalen Krieges," in Kühne and Ziemann, *Militärgeschichte*, 306; Roger Chickering, "Total War: The Use and Abuse of a Concept," in *Anticipating Total War: The German and American Experiences, 1871–1914*, ed. Manfred F. Boemeke et al. (Cambridge, 1999), 3–28.

35. See also Ute Daniel, "Women," in *Enzyklopädie Erster Weltkrieg*, ed. Gerhard Hirschfeld et al. (Paderborn, 2003), 116–134.

36. See Wilhelm Deist, "Das Militär an der Heimatfront 1914–1918 und 1939 bis 1945," in Thoss and Volkmann, *Erster Weltkrieg*, 375–390.

37. See Kundrus, *Kriegerfrauen*; Daniel, *War from Within*; Ursula v. Gersdorff, *Frauen im Kriegsdienst 1914–1945* (Stuttgart, 1969), 15–37; Christa Hämmerle, "'Habt Dank, Ihr Wiener Mägdelein . . . ': Soldaten und weibliche Liebesgaben im Ersten Weltkrieg," *L'Homme* 8 (1997): 132–154; Hämmerle also edited together with Susanna Burghartz a special issue of the journal *L'Homme* on the topic "Soldiers," 12, no. 1 (2001).

38. Gerald D. Feldman, *Army, Industry and Labor in Germany, 1914–1918* (Oxford, 1992) (in German: 1985).

39. Belinda Davis, *Home Fires Burning: Food, Politics, and Everyday Life in World War I Berlin* (Chapel Hill, 2000); idem, "Geschlecht und Konsum: Rolle und Bild der Konsumentin in den Verbraucherprotesten des Ersten Weltkrieges," *Archiv für Sozialgeschichte* 38 (1998): 119–139.

40. Maureen Healy, *Vienna and the Fall of the Habsburg Empire: Total War and Everyday Life in World War I* (Cambridge, 2004).

41. See also N. P. Howard, "The Social and Political Consequences of the Allied Food Blockade of Germany, 1918–19," *German History* 11, no. 2 (1993): 161–188.

42. See Elisabeth Domansky, "Militarization and Reproduction in World War I Germany," in *Society, Culture, and the State in Germany, 1870–1930*, ed. Geoff Eley (Ann Arbor, 1996), 426–454.

43. Susanne zur Nieden, "Erotic Fraternization: The Legend of the German Women's Quick Surrender," in ed. Hagemann and Schüler-Springorum, *Home/Front*, 297–310.

44. See Jörg Duppler and Gerhard P. Groß, eds., *Kriegsende 1918: Ereignis, Wirkung, Nach-wirkung* (Munich, 1999); Bernd Ulrich and Benjamin Ziemann, eds., *Krieg im Frieden: Die umkämpfte Erinnerung an den Ersten Weltkrieg*) Frankfurt/M., 1997).

45. See Robert Weldon Whalen, *Bitter Wounds: German Victims of the Great War, 1914–1939* (Ithaca, 1984); Karin Hausen, "The German Nation's Obligations to the Heroes' Widows of World War I," in *Behind the Lines: Gender and the Two World Wars*, ed. Margaret Randolph Higonnet et. al. (New Haven, 1987), 126–140; Hausen, "Die Sorge der Nation für ihre 'Kriegsopfer': Ein Bereich der Geschlechterpolitik während der Weimarer Republik," in *Von der Arbeiterbewegung zum modernen Sozialstaat*, ed. Jürgen Kocka et. al. (Munich, 1994), 719–739; Richard Bessel, "'Eine nicht allzu große Beunruhigung des Arbeitsmarktes': Frauenarbeit und Demobilmachung in Deutschland nach dem Ersten Weltkrieg," *Geschichte und Gesellschaft* 9 (1983): 211–229; Susanne Rouette, *Sozialpolitik als Geschlechterpolitik: Die Regulierung der Frauenarbeit nach dem Ersten Weltkrieg* (Frankfurt/M.,1993); Susanne Rouette, "Mothers and Citizens: Gender and Social Policy in Germany after the First World War," *Central European History* 30 (1997): 48–66.

46. Bernd Weisbrod, "Gewalt in der Politik. Zur politischen Kultur in Deutschland zwischen den beiden Weltkriegen," *Geschichte in Wissenschaft und Unterricht* 43 (1992): 391–404; Dirk Schuhmann, *Politische Gewalt in der Weimarer Republik 1918–1933: Kampf um die Straße und Furcht vor dem Bürgerkrieg* (Essen, 2001).

47. James M. Diehl, *Paramilitary Politics in Weimar Germany* (Bloomington, 1977); Benjamin Ziemann, "Republikanische Kriegserinnerungen in einer polarisierten Öffentlichkeit: Das Reichsbanner Schwarz-Rot-Gold als Veteranenverband der sozialistischen Arbeiterschaft," *Historische Zeitschrift* 267 (1998): 357–398.

48. Karen Hagemann, "Men's Demonstrations and Women's Protest: Gender in Collective Action in the Urban Working-Class Milieu during the Weimar Republic," *Gender & History* 5 (1993): 101–119.

49. Eve Rosenhaft, *Beating the Fascists? The German Communists and Political Violence, 1929–1933* (Cambridge, 1983).

50. Richard Bessel, "The 'Front Generation' and the Politics of Weimar Germany," in *Generations in Conflict: Youth Revolt and Generation Formation in Germany 1770–1968*, ed. Mark Roseman (Cambridge, 1995), 121–136.

51. Bernd Weisbrod, "Military Violence and Male Fundamentalism: Ernst Jünger's Contribution to the Conservative Revolution," *History Workshop Journal* 49 (2000): 69–94; Gabriele Kämper, "Der 'Kult der Kälte': Figurationen von Faszination und Männlichkeit im Rückblick auf Ernst Jünger: Ein Nachruf auf die Nachrufe," *Feministische Studien* 18, no. 2 (2000): 20–34.

52. Sabine Kienitz, "War Disability and Construction of Masculinity in Weimar Germany," in Hagemann and Schüler-Springorum, *Home/Front*, 181–204; Paul Lerner, "Hysterical Cures: Hypnosis, Gender and Performance in World War I and Weimar Germany," *History Workshop Journal* 45 (1998): 79–101; Sabine Kienitz, *Beschäftigte Helden: Kriegsinvalide Körper in der Kultur. Deutschland 1914–1923.* (Paderborn 2007, forthcoming); Paul Lerner, *Hysterical Men: War, Psychiatry and the Politics of Trauma in Germany, 1890–1930* (Ithaca, 2003).

53. A pioneering British study is that of Joanna Bourke, *An Intimate History of Killing: Face-to-Face Killing in Twentieth-Century Warfare* (London, 1999); see also Martin Lengwiler, "Jenseits der 'Schule der Männlichkeit': Hysterie in der deutschen Armee vor dem Ersten Weltkrieg," in Hagemann and Pröve, *Landsknechte*, 145–170.

54. For a first overview on recent gender research on the history of the German peace movements, see the articles by Belinda Davis, Jennifer Davy, Ute Kaetzel, Irene Stoehr, and Annika Wilmers in Jennifer A. Davy et al., eds., *Frieden—Gewalt—Geschlecht: Friedens- und Konfliktforschung als Geschlechterforschung* (Essen, 2005).

55. See Karl Holl and Wolfram Wette, eds., *Pazifismus in der Weimarer Republik: Beiträge zur Historischen Friedensforschung* (Paderborn, 1981).

56. For more see Davy et al., *Frieden.*

57. New overviews on the state of gender research on World War II include Birthe Kundrus, "Nur die halbe Geschichte: Frauen im Umfeld der Wehrmacht zwischen 1939 und 1945–Ein Forschungsbericht," in Müller and Volkmann, *Die Wehrmacht,* 719–735; idem, "Loyal, weil satt: Die innere Front im Zweiten Weltkrieg," *Mittelweg 35,* no. 5 (1997): 80–93; Gaby Zipfel, "Wie führten Frauen Krieg?" in *Vernichtungskrieg: Verbrechen der Wehrmacht 1941 bis 1944,* ed. Hannes Heer and Klaus Naumann (Hamburg, 1995), 460–474; Thomas Kühne, "Der nationalsozialistische Vernichtungskrieg und die 'ganz normalen' Deutschen: Forschungsprobleme und Forschungstendenzen der Gesellschaftsgeschichte des Zweiten Weltkriegs," *Archiv für Sozialgeschichte* part I, 39 (1999): 580–662; part II, 40 (2000): 440–486.

58. See Omer Bartov, *Hitler's Army: Soldiers, Nazis, and War in the Third Reich* (Oxford, 1991); Christopher R. Browning, *Ordinary Men: Reserve Police Battalion 101 and the Final Solution in Poland* (New York, 1992).

59. Stepen G. Fritz, *Endkampf: Soldiers, Civilians, and the Death of the Third Reich* (Lexington, 2004).

60. See Klaus Latzel, *Deutsche Soldaten—nationalsozialistischer Krieg: Kriegserlebnis—Kriegserfahrung, 1939–1945* (Paderborn, 1998); Thomas Kühne, "Comradeship: Gender Confusion and Gender Order in the German Military, 1918–1945," in Hagemann and Schüler-Springorum, *Home/Front,* 233–254; Thomas Kühne, "'Kameradschaft—Das Beste im Leben des Mannes': Die deutschen Soldaten des Zweiten Weltkrieges in erfahrungs- und geschlechtergeschichtlicher Perspektive," *Geschichte und Gesellschaft* 22 (1996): 504–529; Thomas Kühne, "Zwischen Männerbund und Volksgemeinschaft: Hitlers Soldaten und der Mythos der Kameradschaft," *Archiv für Sozialgeschichte* 38 (1998): 165–189.

61. See Thomas Kühne, *Kameradschaft: Die Soldaten des nationalsozialistischen Krieges und das 20. Jahrhundert* (Göttingen, 2006).

62. Wolfram Wette, ed., *Deserteure der Wehrmacht: Feiglinge—Opfer—Hoffnungsträger: Dokumentation eines Meinungswandels* (Essen, 1995); Benjamin Ziemann, "Flüchten aus dem Konsens zum Durchhalten: Ergebnisse, Probleme und Perspektiven der Erforschung soldatischer Verweigerungsformen in der Wehrmacht 1939–1945," in Müller and Volkmann, *Wehrmacht,* 589–613; Maria Fritsche, *Entziehungen: Österreichische Deserteure und Selbstverstümmler in der Deutschen Wehrmacht* (Vienna, 2004); on World War I: Christoph Jahr, *Gewöhnliche Soldaten: Desertion und Deserteure im deutschen und britischen Heer 1914–1918* (Göttingen, 1998); Benjamin Ziemann, "Fahnenflucht im deutschen Heer 1914–1918," *Militärgeschichtliche Mitteilungen* 55 (1996): 93–130.

63. Leila A. J. Rupp, *Mobilizing Women for War: Germany and American Propaganda, 1939–1945* (Princeton, 1980); Rupp, "'I Don't Call that Volksgemeinschaft': Women, Class and War in Nazi Germany," in *Women, War, and Revolution,* ed. Carol R. Berkin and Clara M. Lovett (London, 1980), 37–53; Kundrus, *Kriegerfrauen,* 322–351.

64. See Elizabeth D. Heineman, "Whose Mothers? Generational Differences, War and the Nazi Cult of Motherhood," *Journal of Women's History* 12, no. 4 (2001): 139–163.

65. Lisa Pine, *Nazi Family Policy, 1933–1945* (Oxford, 1997); Elizabeth D. Heineman, *What Difference Does a Husband Make? Marital Status in Germany, 1933–1961* (Berkeley, 1999).

66. See also: Rüdiger Hachtmann, "Industriearbeiterinnen in der deutschen Kriegswirtschaft 1936–1944/45," *Geschichte und Gesellschaft* 19 (1993): 332–366; Dörte Winkler, *Frauenarbeit im "Dritten Reich"* (Hamburg, 1977).

67. Hachtmann, "Industriearbeiterinnen."

68. Gersdorff, *Frauen,* 49–77; for an overview of the state of research, see Kundrus, "Nur die halbe Geschichte"; Hagemann, "'Jede Kraft wird gebraucht': Militäreinsatz von Frauen im Ersten und Zweiten Weltkrieg," in Thoss and Volkmann, *Erster Weltkrieg,* 79–107. In a comparative

perspective: D'Ann Campbell, "Women in Combat: The World War II Experience in the United States, Great Britain, Germany, and the Soviet Union," *Journal of Military History* 57 (1993): 301–323.

69. See on war memories for example: Robert Moeller, *War Stories: The Search for a Usable Past in the Federal Republic of Germany* (Berkeley, 2001); Moeller, "What Did You Do in the War, *Mutti?* Courageous Women, Compassionate Commanders, and Stories of the Second Word War," *German History* 22, no. 4 (2004): 563–659; Klaus Naumann, *Der Krieg als Text: Das Jahr 1945 im kulturellen Gedächtnis* (Hamburg, 1998).

70. So far, studies on war nurses only exist on World War I: Bianca Schönberger, "Motherly Heroines and Adventurous Girls: Red Cross Nurses and Women Army Auxiliaries in the First World War," in Hagemann and Schüler-Springorum, *Home/Front*, 87–115; Regina Schulte, "Die Schwester des kranken Kriegers: Verwundetenpflege im Ersten Weltkrieg," in *Die verkehrte Welt des Krieges: Studien zu Geschlecht, Religion und Tod*, ed. Regina Schulte (Frankfurt/M., 1998), 95–116.

71. Elizabeth Harvey, *Women and the Nazi East: Agents and Witnesses of Germanization* (New Haven, 2003); idem, "'We Forgot All the Jews and Poles': German Women and the 'Ethnic Struggle' in Nazi-Occupied Poland," *Contemporary European History* 10, no. 3 (2001): 447–461; idem, "'Die deutsche Frau im Osten': 'Rasse,' Geschlecht und öffentlicher Raum im besetzten Polen 1940–1944," *Archiv für Sozialgeschichte* 38 (1998): 191–214.

72. See for example Angelika Ebbinghaus, ed., *Opfer und Täterinnen: Frauenbiographien des Nationalsozialismus* (Nördlingen, 1987); Gudrun Schwarz, *Eine Frau an seiner Seite: Ehefrauen in der "SS-Sippengemeinschaft"* (Hamburg, 1997). For more see the article by Claudia Koonz in this volume.

73. Bernhard Chiari, *Alltag hinter der Front: Besatzung, Kollaboration und Widerstand in Weißrußland 1941–44* (Düsseldorf, 1998); with the inclusion of gender: Madeleine Bunting, *The Model Occupation: The Channel Islands under German Rule, 1940–1945* (London, 1996).

74. Ebba D. Drolshagen, *Nicht ungeschoren davongekommen: Das Schicksal der Frauen in den besetzten Ländern, die Wehrmachtssoldaten liebten* (Hamburg, 1998).

75. Birgit Beck, *Wehrmacht und sexuelle Gewalt, Sexualverbrechen vor deutschen Militärgerichten, 1939–1945* (Paderborn, 2004); idem, "Rape: The Military Trials of Sexual Crimes Committed by Soldiers of the Wehrmacht, 1939–1944," in Hagemann and Schüler-Springorum, *Home/Front*, 255–274.

76. Christa Paul, *Zwangsprostitution: Staatlich errichtete Bordelle im Nationalsozialismus* (Berlin, 1994); Insa Meinen, "Wehrmacht und Prostitution—Zur Reglementierung der Geschlechterbeziehungen durch die deutsche Militärverwaltung im besetzten Frankreich 1940–1944," *Zeitschrift für Sozialgeschichte des 20. und 21. Jahrhunderts* 14, no. 2 (1999): 35–55; Insa Meinen, *Wehrmacht und Prostitution im besetzen Frankreich* (Bremen, 2002); Annette Timm, "Sex with a Purpose: Prostitution, Venereal Disease, and Militarized Masculinity in the Third Reich," *Journal of the History of Sexuality* 11, no. 2 (2002): 223–255.

77. Atina Grossmann, "A Question of Silence: The Rape of German Women by Occupation Soldiers," *October* 72 (1995): 43–63; Regina Mühlhäuser, "Massenvergewaltigungen in Berlin 1945 im Gedächtnis betroffener Frauen: Zur Verwobenheit von nationalistischen, rassistischen und geschlechtsspezifischen Diskursen," in *Geschlecht hat Methode: Ansätze und Perspektiven in der Frauen- und Geschlechtergeschichte*, ed. Veronika Aegerter et al. (Zurich, 1999), 235–246; Hsu-ming Teo, "The Continuum of Sexual Violence in Occupied Germany, 1945–49," *Women's History Review* 5, no. 2 (1996): 191–218.

78. See http://www.afk-web.de/html/historie_frieden.html.

79. See http://akmilitaergeschichte.de/.

80. See http://www.amg-fnz.de/.

81. Hagemann and Pröve, *Landsknechte;* Hagemann and Schüler-Springorum, *Home/Front;* Davy et al., *Frieden.* See from a similar conference in Zurich: Christoph Dejung and Regula Stämpfli, eds., *Armee, Staat und Geschlecht: Die Schweiz im internationale Vergleich* (Zurich, 2003).

82. See Müller and Volkmann, *Die Wehrmacht;* Thoss and Volkmann, *Erster Weltkrieg.*

83. Karen Hagemann, ed., *Nach—Kriegs—Helden: Kulturelle und politische DeMobilmachung in deutschen Nachkriegsgeschichten,* special issue, *Militärgeschichtliche Zeitschrift* 60, no. 2 (2001).

84. Only the academic director was for a brief period a woman (Beatrice Heuser).

85. See ibid. One example is the ten-volume magisterial work, Militärgeschichtliches Forschungsamt, ed., *Das Deutsche Reich und der Zweite Weltkrieg.* No article so far has discussed the role of women during the war. This is even true for the most recent volume: Jörg Echternkamp, ed., *Die deutsche Kriegsgesellschaft, 1939 bis 1945, Zweiter Halbband: Ausbeutung, Deutungen, Ausgrenzung* (Munich, 2005); See as a critique of the MGFA research by Wolfram Wette, "Militärgeschichte zwischen Wissenschaft und Politik," in Kühne and Ziemann, *Militärgeschichte,* 50–71.

4

BLIND SPOTS

Empire, Colonies, and Ethnic Identities in Modern German History

Birthe Kundrus

The nineteenth century saw the emergence of close links between nationalism and colonialism in all European nations. Most proponents of colonialism
aspired to two goals: to heighten and secure the nation's honor and to become a world power. To be a nation meant owning colonies, colonies meant
world power, and being a world power was proof of the superiority of national culture.[1] Although the *Schutzgebiete* (protectorates) were hardly profit-
able economically, except for a few individual entrepreneurs, and although
hopes they would lure millions of German settlers were not fulfilled,[2] they
did serve as a screen on which to project personal as well as collective desires
and concepts that ranged from the notion of "New Germanies" overseas to
the mission of disseminating the achievements of civilization in the name of
medicine and Christianity to a space for adventure or for concrete designs of
scholars, planners, civil servants, and women's organizations. This conglom-
erate of phantasmagoric desires, absolute pretensions to power, and their un-
restrained pursuit regularly lead to conflicts with the indigenous societies that
ended all too often in extreme forms of violence. Imperial "self-fulfilment" at
the expense of those who were colonized affected not only the annexed states
but also Germany. Colonialism left its mark on such diverse spheres as literature, film, the academic world, advertising, urban topography, legislation,
and clubs and associations as well as influencing political and administrative
planning and the demands of the women's movement. Moreover, subjects

from the (former) colonies, especially those in Africa, immigrated to Germany, although only in small numbers. In short, colonialism found its way into the emotions and thoughts of German society.

Until quite recently, the question of what traces colonialism left on the mental maps of the colonized[3] as well as on colonists was an issue that was seldom addressed by German research on the colonial period.[4] This lack of interest reflected the fact that, for many years, the country's colonial era was perceived as a marginal phenomenon and its career as a colonial power was judged too late, superficial, and short-lived to have made a profound impression. This view did not change until German scholars began addressing the themes and approaches that previously had surfaced in international colonial and postcolonial studies. Since the late 1970s, scholars in this field have contributed to creating a heightened awareness—especially in the Anglo-American academic world—of the interactive nature of relations between colonial powers and those who are colonized. What is more, they have emphasized the significance of cultures outside of Europe for the self-perception of Western European "civilization."[5] As conceptual foundations in the field of cultural studies, these approaches focus on the heterogeneity of pluricultural societies; as sociopolitical concepts, they also endeavor to analyze power structures. Thus, issues of nation building and the formation of identity with reference to both colonialists and colonized, rather than political or economic aspects, are at the center of attention. Concepts of "identity," as a collective construction of meaning that aims to guide actions, and "culture" are key theoretical elements of colonial and postcolonial studies. Culture, conceptualized as a system of self-interpretation and interpretation by others, seems best suited to mark the way that difference, race, and gender are constantly constructed and performed. Simultaneously, culture, as a set of practices, takes into account the structural and social realities created by these ideas.[6] Thus, scholars from the United States were generally the first who, equipped with these new methods and theoretical tools, began scrutinizing German colonial and postcolonial history.[7] Susan Zantop's work in the field of literary studies offered decisive inputs, uncovering the German precolonial fantasies that "provided Germans an arena for creating an imaginary community and constructing a national identity."[8] Moreover, her results revealed that the historical caesura of 1884 or 1918 did not, in fact, mark decisive turning points. Although Germany's history as a colonial power ended in 1918, the influence of colonial desires and projections was still felt and proved to be astonishingly persistent under varying historical conditions.

In recent years, research conducted in the German-speaking countries has increased significantly; much of this work reflects an interest in interdisciplinary exchange between historical, cultural, and literary studies.[9] Scholars in the Federal Republic of Germany had begun to realize that one must explore the construction of the Other in order to better understand one's own self-image.

This search for new points of reference was reinforced by the political developments of 1989 and continues to enhance the relevance of German colonial history and the issue of what is seen as "foreign" in German historiography. Appreciably, the days of "official" colonial amnesia are now gone for good.[10] This development has been fostered by recent commemorative dates such as the one hundredth anniversary—observed in 2004—of the war Germany waged against the Herero in Namibia and recently emerging debates about global and world history.[11] But if we consider the amount of catching up that the "new German colonial history" still has to do, it seems premature to announce the end of national history (or histories), as some scholars from the English-speaking world have.[12] Since colonialism is a global, typically European, and national phenomenon, it should remain situated within these three coordinates.

This contribution will retrace various stages in this process of establishing a "new German colonial history" and sketch focal points and results of research, as well as indicate areas for future work. To date, the majority of investigations that employ a gender history approach proceed from an actor-centred perspective and choose the organized women's colonial movement in the Kaiserreich as their starting point. Some of the findings from this work are presented in the first section. This focus calls to mind the first phase of British historical work on gender and colonialism that, "once associated with the narrow definition of white women in the colonies . . . now encompasses a much wider framework, concerned with the ways in which colonialism restructured gender dynamics of colonizing and colonized societies."[13] Similarly, research perspectives on the German colonies have broadened noticeably since the mid 1990s, but it is still too early to refer to German colonial history as a complete edifice. Rather, the field can be seen as a collection of construction sites where work is proceeding in various stages simultaneously. For example, the issue of *Mischehen* (mixed marriages) and the regulations banning such unions were one focus of increased attention. The reason for this preoccupation may lie in this particular topic, linking as it does the issues of race and sexuality, or in the impression that the prohibitions in some German colonies seemed to go beyond the usual imperial practices and suggested disturbing signs of continuity with Nazi policies of persecution and extermination. The second section is devoted to these questions. A subject that has recently yielded an impressive body of literature—thanks to a considerable extent to the work of Afro-German scholars—will be taken up in the final section: the experiences and activities of "black Germans." Looking at the experiences of African Germans provides an opportunity for exploring another long-ignored dimension of the nineteenth- and twentieth-century ideas of race as well as the life-worlds of "other" Germans. In addition, the experience of black Germans and blacks in Germany offers insights into the transformation of society in contemporary Germany. Although the following survey of the "youngest" field included in this volume may be somewhat premature, it seems that despite ambitious theoretical announcements the status of gender history approaches within this field appears still uncertain.

Female Imperialism: German Women in the Colonies

In the earliest phase of development, gender history of German colonialism was in fact exclusively the history of "German women in the colonies." Economist and sociologist Martha Mamozai was one of the first to retrace German women's participation, as members of the master race, in the brutal oppression and exploitation of colonized peoples.[14] According to Mamozai, they were frequently motivated by hopes of acquiring more power, privileges, and options. They identified themselves with the goals and values of the male colonial movement, suppressed the recognition of their own oppression and thus became perpetrators themselves. Perhaps this disillusionment with female "innocence," brought forward with considerable moral force in Mamozai's books, helps explain why the topic virtually disappeared from view in West Germany after publication of her work.

It was not until the late 1990s that Lora Wildenthal again took up the central question of what fascinated German women about the colonies.[15] In her reading, the colonies became a mirror of individual and collective power fantasies and the desire to belong. These findings have been complemented and enhanced by Rosa B. Schneider's work in literary studies and by my own investigations.[16] For example, women who chose to go to *Deutsch-Südwestafrika* (German Southwest African colony) imagined that Africa's natural environment—untainted as it seemed by civilization—would offer opportunities to lead a less constrained life, and to transcend or redefine the boundaries set, internally and externally, by bourgeois ideals of femininity.[17] Like their male counterparts, women who followed this path of colonialist reasoning associated the colony with the dream of newly acquired individualism as well as a new self-understanding and tied a critique of civilization to hopes for progress. Further research is needed to explore how these hopes shared by white men and women were fractured in the course of everyday life in the colonies and confrontations with colonized peoples and what this meant for the hegemonic practices in the Schutzgebiete. Recently, Gesine Krüger has supplied a detailed analysis of how rumours about purported abuse of German women and children by the Herero radicalized German warfare in Deutsch-Südwestafrika in the years 1904 to 1907 because of their exculpatory effect.[18] Atrocity fantasies about African women as "black beasts" who mutilated German soldiers also served to rationalize and legitimize violence and cruelty in the Germans' treatment of African men and women and the creation of a "racial order"—a separation of "white" and "black" in a rigid form that had not been practiced in the social life of the colony before 1904. Furthermore, the self-interpretations and worldviews of German female missionaries have received little attention in research thus far.[19]

With Roger Chickering's pioneering study in 1988,[20] and, increasingly in the late 1990s, with work done by Ute Planert, Karin Bruns, Elizabeth A. Drummond, Jean H. Quataert, and Andrea Süchting-Hänger, nationalist-imperialist women and their organizations in the metropoles, rather than the female settlers and planters in the colonies, become the focus of interest.[21] Summing up her findings in a literature report on "Women in the Political Right," Christiane Streubel asserted that these organizations must be considered part of the new right-wing movement that began intervening in politics as part of associations of bourgeois agitators around 1900, as German society and the country's traditional party system experienced a period of crisis and structural change.[22] German society underwent a process of politicization that affected all parts of the political spectrum and both sexes.[23] National women's organizations, which have only gradually been discovered by gender historiography and remain for the most part unnoticed by mainstream research on the Kaiserreich,[24] took up both of these developments. They recruited their members from Protestant, nationalist, and housewives' circles and from charities and attracted an impressive following. Besides these independent women's alliances, the *Flottenverein* (Naval Association), *Ostmarkenverein* (Association for the Eastern Provinces), and colonial associations created their own women's divisions; membership and social relevance of these organizations increased considerably, especially after the turn of the century. In 1914, for example, membership in the *Frauenbund der Deutschen Kolonialgesellschaft* (Women's League of the German Colonial Society) numbered about 18,700, nearly 50 percent of that of the men's division and equal to that of the *Alldeutscher Verband* (Pan-German League). These colonial organizations were by no means all male, in contrast to the *Alldeutscher Verband*, which did not accept women until World War I.[25] And the associated women's divisions were anything but insignificant; the Women's League, in particular, gradually occupied an increasingly prominent position in the public sphere.

Karen Smidt and especially Lora Wildenthal have authored comprehensive analyses of the Women's League of the German Colonial Society, which provide a foundation for further work.[26] The Women's League aimed to promote women's interests in the colonies, enlist women and girls to emigrate to the colonies, and stabilize economic and intellectual relations between the metropole and the colonies. This latter objective, fostering close ties between the colony and the homeland (*Kolonie und Heimat*), was reflected in the pages of the League's high-circulation journal of the same name. The periodical was run by the radical faction within the German Colonial Society (*Deutsche*

Kolonialgesellschaft [DKG]), which took a critical stance towards "old" conservatism and nationalism. Other interests pursued by the League included the provision of nannies, kindergartens, and schools for white children and promotion of appropriate training in home economics and agricultural affairs. This last aim led to activities such as the cooperation with the *Koloniale Frauenschulen* (Colonial Schools for Women) in Carthaus near Trier and Witzenhausen (later Bad Weilbach) or the establishment of the *Heimathaus* (Homeland House) in Keetmanshoop, envisioned as a base for newly immigrated women and—in the words of League official Leonore Niessen-Deiters—a stronghold against "*Verburung, Verengländerung und Verkafferung*"[27] in Southwest Africa. In the metropole, women organized costume balls, bazaars, lotteries, colonial coffee parties, slide presentations, and plays as fundraisers for the DKG. As Wildenthal points out, the League's activities changed little from its beginnings until it was disbanded in 1945. During the Weimar Republic, the men and women active in the colonial movement were anti-republican and part of the nationalist opposition. Although there were large areas of consensus with the Nazi movement, Wildenthal notes that some colonial functionaries criticized the fact that German women were excluded from positions of power in the Nazi hegemonic system. Colonial aspirations were not rendered an anachronism until Germany attacked the Soviet Union in 1941, but this event did not threaten the continued existence of the Colonial School for Women in Rendsburg and its cooperation with the SS.[28]

Whereas the women's movements employed nationalist arguments in their drive for improvements in individual rights for women, the imperialist women's societies pursued a program of nationalist agitation of and with women. As Germany's political landscape became increasingly nationalistic around the turn of the century, these different forms of female politicization linked up. Recurrent controversies with the DKG led to the suspicion on the part of the male members that, with the establishment of the Women's League, a suffragette cuckoo's egg had been laid in the organization's nest. In fact, there were diverse links to the *Bund Deutscher Frauenvereine* (German Women's Associations), which the Women's League of the DKG joined in 1911.[29] Unfortunately, none of the studies mentioned above elucidates this close relationship.

How did the Women's League of the DKG attain a unique position as part of the politicization of German society? Wildenthal has drawn our attention to the fact that the "women's question" was connected to the issues of settlement policy.[30] New Germany was to be established overseas in Deutsch-Südwestafrika, with German farmer families as the germ cell of this new entity. But German colonists who acquired "African" habits and entered into relationships with African women—behavior branded by their contemporaries as *Verkaffern*—posed a threat to the settlement project and, indeed, to the purity of German nature. In terms of the colonial narrative, "German culture" and "German women" were needed to counteract these foreign powers. Unstable German men, vacillating between whiteness and masculinity, between intellect and sex, would not be capable of constituting and experiencing themselves as truly German males without the presence of their stable white German female counterparts. Such narratives are evidence of contrasting images of masculinity circulating even in the seemingly militaristic Kaiserreich; these images, their precise scope and foundations in society call for further investigation.[31] Although women's participation in the colonial movement—and, as a result, in other sectors of society—was extended, as Wildenthal emphasizes, the range of activities that was open to them remained limited to those with feminine connotations.[32] Roger Chickering's contention that in Imperial Germany emancipatory positions were supported only by a minority of women in organizations on the political right remains plausible. Nonetheless, in the estimation of Elizabeth A. Drummond, Lora Wildenthal, Andrea Süchting-Hänger, and Claire Venghiattis, women in these nationalist associations were more eager to assert themselves than Chickering recognizes. Debates about suffrage for white German farm wives in Deutsch-Südwestafrika[33] seem to support the assessment that, in the course of time, autonomy became an increasingly significant topos within right-wing women's organizations.

Equality, Difference, and Otherness

The Women's League and the discussion about German women in the colonies produced, with the help of the traditional dualism of nature and culture, constructions of gender, race, and class differences; in the end these same processes successfully and inevitably confirmed the importance of the female imperialists. The formation of civilization as cultural progress could be achieved only if women were integrated into this process, for German women were the embodiment of culture, in contrast to the "cultureless" societies of the southern hemisphere. Female "emancipation" was therefore simultaneously an indicator of the developmental status of a specific society and marked the distance between it and "primitive" societies. In all these constructions, the "German woman" remained a flexible metaphor of delineation; as a self-description, its chief purpose was to mark an antipode to "the" woman from Poland, Africa, and Oceania. In fact, the supposedly fixed national character of the German female remained indeterminate, aside from such social formations as the "white Christian wife" and some cultural practices considered to be traditionally German, that is, clubs and societies, German homemaking and cooking, and holiday traditions such as those associated with Christmas.[34]

This "coexistence of nationalism, imperialism, and feminism,"[35] as Claire Venghiattis has called it, successfully allayed some of the fears that the recoding of femininity might be interpreted as support for the aims of the women's emancipation movement. "Female cultural imperialism,"[36] as Drummond has referred to it, became inextricably linked to the drive for national expansion.

Although scholarship on the imperialist women's societies has made considerable progress, numerous questions remain unanswered. Further research is needed to clarify how these societies were situated in the contemporary political context of Imperial Germany. What appears most remarkable about the imperial women's organizations is their attempt to position themselves with respect to both decisive political debates of their time—those on equality and on difference—an undertaking that was no doubt motivated by the perception of German women's status as the "inferior sex of a superior race," as Frances Gouda has quite fittingly noted.[37] The schemes of societal structure favored by the political right centered on the notion of inequality, whether with respect to class, nation, race, gender, or religion.[38] The relatively new sphere of formal colonial hegemony gave a fresh impetus to such hierarchical and racist models of social order around the turn of the century, at a time when liberal-democratic and socialist demands for individual freedom, equality, and political participation were being articulated with increasing vehemence by the women's movement, social democrats, and others. In this practical test in the political arena, the political right "took possession" of the colonies and was eager to gain control of colonialism as a field of public discourse. Race ideology became the dominant principle, as a means of discriminating between center and periphery, between the German population of the nation-state and the colonized peoples. On the domestic level, however, the intimation was that equality reigned—albeit, the equality of those who had established this order. And the imperialist women's societies appealed to precisely this promise of equality. By occupying imperialism as a field for political agitation, they transcended the borders between white German bourgeois men and women, between nation and state,[39] and between the private and the public sphere.

As Wildenthal has written: "Race was a powerful language with which to argue for inclusion."[40] Instrumentalizing colonial racism to underpin and legitimize German middle- and upper-class women's demands for political participation was paid for with the loss of bourgeois promises of equality and the renouncement of all universalisms. This was perhaps the most decisive factor that distinguished German from British "female imperialists"[41]: the fact that German women almost completely omitted the altruistic elements that, despite their problematic background in ideas of cultural supremacy and racial difference, nonetheless tempered British colonialism. The "white woman's burden" (Antoinette Burton), as a condescending but binding responsibility to "civilize" and support nonwhite women in the colonies, rarely surfaced in the German debate. A possible explanation for this omission might lie in the unique nature of German clubs and societies, which resulted in a diverse landscape of milieus and prevented the development of a general liberal culture similar to the one that evolved in Great Britain. Moreover, the right dominated the imperial discussion, leading to a narrow focus on an extremely nationalistic and racist worldview into which egalitarian models could hardly be integrated, except in the relationship between men and women of the superior group. This description is not meant to revive the old model of the German *Sonderweg*; rather, the aim is to record one specific characteristic of the German debate on colonialism, a development that might be explained by the political milieu of Germany under Kaiser Wilhelm II.

However, to date, in-depth studies on the German critique of the country's colonial politics as well as research on the few who pursued a more philanthropic mode of colonialism are lacking.[42] The impression of a uniform worldview of German female imperialists could conceivably require revision if an intercolonial comparison of current findings and hypotheses scrutinized, for example, German acquisitions in the South Pacific. It appears that these colonies were linked, at least in part, to much more positive visions than those associated with the "dark continent." Moreover, the question might be raised to what extent these colonial visions and practices of women (and men) were indeed uniquely German. An obsessive preoccupation with white national prestige, the complex attempts to form a national identity in and through overseas possessions, "the white woman" as a savior of culture, or the radicalization of racist attitudes around 1900—all these elements can also be found in the British discussion about colonial history.[43] Comparisons with other settler societies and settler colonialism might throw light on the question of whether all these societies generally tend to resolve the basic dilemma of all colonists—the "ambivalence of triumphal and traumatic experience"[44]—by eliminating ambiguity; in other words, by seeking to establish societal models that are radical, in the sense that they aim for social, cultural, and ethnic homogeneity.[45]

Race and Male Sexuality

In 1905, the vice-governor of *Deutsch-Südwestafrika*, Hans Tecklenburg, declared that marriages between Africans and Germans before justices of the peace in the colony were officially prohibited. A similar regulation was passed down in *Deutsch-Ostafrika* (German East Africa) in 1906, and on Samoa, Colonial State Secretary Wilhelm Solf banned mixed marriages on 17 January 1912.[46] These proscriptions evoked vehement and highly contradictory reactions. While one side justified the new regulations with the specter of racial and political threats to the protectorates, the other urged that "coloured girls and women" should not be unscrupulously degraded to "instruments of lust," since a ban on marriage would merely signal official approval for "concubinage." The centerpiece of this discourse was thus the figure of the white male in the colonial contact zone and the issue of disciplining his sexual desires. There was general agreement among all those involved that "mixed marriages" were undesirable; what was controversial was whether a strict ban or a strategy of appealing to the self-discipline of German colonists was the more effective course of action. Ultimately, the Reichstag passed a resolution addressed to the Bundesrat on 21 March 1912, calling on that body to draft a law that would guarantee that all marriages between "whites and natives" in all German colonies would be considered valid. The result was a wave of indignation in the right-wing press. Outside of the Reichstag, developments followed a different course. Solf refused to act in accordance with the resolution and the colonists showed little inclination to tolerate state interventions into their intimate affairs.

The issue of whether the state should meddle in the private lives of its male citizens elicited passionate responses. Lora Wildenthal and Pascal Grosse agree that the clash over mixed marriages pivoted on the question of how the eugenic principle of racial purity was to be aligned with men's sexual autonomy: "Limiting the patriarchal rights of German men proved to be the most controversial aspect of the debate over mixed marriages."[47] No solution of this problem was found before German rule ended. While the official bans curtailed the rights and the autonomy of German men, extramarital relationships were left untouched. Nevertheless, Grosse suggests that the category of race changed the understanding of public and private in German society and that the state used race to legitimize increasing involvements in the private sphere by claiming the need to protect public interests—a process that ended in the eugenic totalitarianism of the Nazi period.

On the background of this discussion about mixed marriage, Lora Wildenthal has developed two opposing models of colonial masculinity: the imperial patriarch and the liberal nationalist. The first model is applicable in particular to representatives of the early phase of colonial conquest who viewed officially sanctioned sexual relations with indigenous women as part of German conquest and consolidation strategies. The liberal nationalist, in contrast, perceived sexual matters as related solely to questions of race policy and was a resolute opponent of any form of racial mixing that might endanger German identity and rule. Colonialism reformulated the issue of the form of hegemonial masculinity in modernity: the colonial project of subjugation was clearly masculine in nature. Did this mean that giving free rein to male passions was to become a central objective when territorial borders were violated? Or should the renunciation of instinct form the core of the colonial project? The latter was thought to testify to the superiority of bourgeois white civilization in comparison to the colonized people and their notorious hedonism.

In the many studies on "mixed marriages," the perspective of those colonized, including both the women involved and their relatives, is generally lacking. Presumably, they held a variety of attitudes; some tried to minimize sexual contacts with the white oppressors whereas those who were interested in establishing closer ties were more willing to accept marriages. Such considerations do not aim to gloss over the power hierarchies and at times brutal personal relations in the colonies; rather, they are a reminder that the options available to male and female Africans and Asians should also be taken into account. One notable example of such an approach is Dag Henrichsen's sensitive micro study (which unfortunately has no references) about Karera Ida Getzen-Leinhos, a Herero-Canadian woman who was married to a German.[48]

The concentration on the limited number of marital unions—in 1907–1908, there was presumably a total of 166 "mixed marriages" in all German colonies, including marriages of indigenous women to white non-German men—testifies to the fact that, as Grosse and Wildenthal have surmised, the goal of securing a "racially pure" nation-state lay at the heart of the German debate, since African women became German citizens by marriage. But most advocates of colonialism were less concerned with questions of race eugenics, for in the logic of this model, the "body of the people" (*Volkskörper*) and the "body of the state" (*Staatskörper*) were (as yet) separate. After all, the majority of sexual contacts occurred outside of marriage. Concerns centered instead on the issues of reputation, hegemonic position, and, as a result, Germany's self-image as a (colonial) power that was destined to rule. Conjugal unions with indigenous women were obviously a sustained source of irritation for such feelings of superiority. Thus, the stability of the paradigm of racial purity should not be overestimated, for it did not see its greatest triumph until the rise of National Socialism. And preliminary studies have revealed that it would be incorrect to assume simple continuities between colonial bans on intermarriage and the Nuremberg laws; the latter were based on an anti-Semitic discourse that employed very specific argumentative figures to justify demands for a strict separation of "Aryans" and "Jews."[49] Furthermore, in enacting marriage bans, the "Third Reich" made use of a tool that had been used not only in the colonial era but also in earlier periods and in other countries and prepared to apply it as part of its politics of persecution. Comparing prohibitions against intermarriage enforced in such places as Mexico, Cuba, India, Indonesia, South Africa, and the U.S. South at various times would seem to be a fruitful undertaking—not only as a means of determining parallels and differences with respect to intentions, the groups sanctioned, and relevant implementation practices, but also to elucidate possible transfers of such policies between governments.[50] German debates about mixed marriages were not limited to intermarrying in the colonies: the "problem" of such unions and of cultural "decline" was also discovered in East Prussia with its large Polish population. Once again, a comparison of these discourses about the "cultural crisis on the periphery" remains a topic for future work.

The white colonial rulers' claim to superiority and hegemony was based on a racist construction of the separation and hierarchical order of "races" from which was deduced the idea that any contact between the two would "contaminate" whites and "natives." In practice, this contact meant *Verkaffer-ung*. This category brought together the fantasies of transgression and downfall that plagued the proponents of colonialism into a single, vivid image. It appeared that, in the colonial realm, race, masculinity and national origin no longer sufficed as reliable reference points for stable identities. This loss of orientation threatened to destroy the colonial order: white German men could become black Africans. Strikingly, the problem was ascribed to men only and it could only be overcome with the help of German women. An investigation of *Verkafferung* that would succeed in incorporating the various dimensions of the feminization of the German cultural nation and the ignoble colonization of the German male body is sorely needed.[51]

Work by Sandra Maß has demonstrated how productive an approach founded in the history of masculinity can be.[52] Her innovative reconstruction of German descriptions of African soldiers and the function of these descriptions for the colonial construction of heroic German masculinity in the Weimar Republic fulfills one of the goals set by recent comparative history. In the wake of World War I, the two dominant fantasies about African soldiers, the "barbaric French colonial soldier" and the "loyal German Askari," collided with one another as part of rival propaganda campaigns. One narrative assailed the occupation of the Rhineland by marauding, rapist hordes of African soldiers; the other popularized the legend of the undefeated German army in Deutsch-Ostafrika that, together with loyal African soldiers, had prevailed despite being outnumbered by the Allied forces. In both discourses, the African soldier served as a mirror to reflect white, soldierly colonial masculinity. Maß reads propaganda texts about World War I as a German attempt to "heal," that is as attempts to "broach the topic of the psychological and physical fragmentation of the male body, without having to speak directly about the traumata."[53] The "black barbarians," rather than the cruel weapons of war, dismembered these white bodies and robbed them of their sacrificial deaths and honor. With this new focus, Maß redirects our gaze away from the much-cited connection between women's bodies and *Volkskörper* to the bodies of men.

Black Germans and the Politics of Race and Gender

Until the early 1980s, African men and women living in Germany were perceived as a very small minority whose presence was without relevance for

German society. Sander L. Gilman even argued that the uniqueness of the German conception of blackness lay in its paradoxical development in the absence of a black presence.[54] This reductionist view changed in 1984 with a creative writing course for women of color taught at Berlin's Free University by African-American poet Audre Lorde. An anthology of texts resulting from the seminar, appeared in 1986 and was the source of decisive new impulses, as black Germans began uncovering and writing their own history.[55] In the interim, a growing number of scholarly studies that investigate the past and present experiences of the black populations of Germany has appeared. Other authors have attracted substantial public attention with autobiographical works, such as Hans J. Massaquoi's memoir about his childhood in Nazi Germany.[56] This body of work documents how diverse and complex the history of black Germans and of blacks in Germany was and is.[57] Continuing public interest in this literature or in the exhibition *Besondere Kennzeichen: Neger—Schwarze im NS-Staat* presented in 2002–2003 in Cologne presumably has to do with the recognition that Germany is a multinational and multiethnic country.[58] Nonetheless, scholars from Africa and Asia remain underrepresented in research on German colonialism; while the reasons for this are complex, existing power structures within academia no doubt constitute one aspect.

The majority of studies aim "to analyze the way African Germans have presented themselves and the way others have viewed them."[59] Most of the authors address issues of identity, ethnicity, and self-perception within the context of German history and thus position themselves within a scholarly, political, and mental tradition of theorizing African life in the diaspora. One recurrent theme is the ambivalence of African German lives in the face of the ethnic conceptualization of "nation" in Germany. They are German nationals, but they persistently function as a representation of the "Other," or, as Tina Campt has phrased it, they serve in the process of "identifying the other within."[60] Yara-Colette Lemke Munz de Faria has scrutinized how Germany has dealt with this "unloved" minority by focusing on a particularly moving chapter of recent history—the children of African American soldiers and German women in the post-World War II period.[61] Although the volume is for the most part descriptive, it demonstrates the extent to which racist attitudes and patterns survived in the general population as well as in the minds of supposedly well-meaning physicians and politicians in the postwar era. Two contradictory concepts determined the treatment of African German children: separation from their white, German environment and integration into the society of the Federal Republic of Germany.

Lately, there have been signs of two newly emerging focal points for research, both of which effectively call into question established perspectives on the role of black Germans as victims. The first explores the situation of and the options available to Africans living in the German-speaking parts of Europe before colonial rule formally began.[62] The second focuses on the "extraordinary" circumstances surrounding African Germans and Africans during the Third Reich.[63] In contrast to widespread assumptions, they did not face the same fate as the Jews or the Roma and Sinti during Nazi rule. There was neither a comparable mass murder of blacks, nor was there systematic persecution of them in Germany or the rest of Europe. The situation was more complex and reflected the structure of the black population in Germany as a highly diverse group. Status, origin, nationality, the specific circumstances, and numerous other factors had a decisive influence on the fate of individuals. Some were indeed victims of race hygiene policies, forced to work as slave laborers or interned in concentration camps. Many but not all of the black victims of forced sterilization were African Germans.[64] African prisoners of war serving in the French Army were subject to especially cruel treatment. In the spring of 1940 alone, the Wehrmacht killed between one and four thousand of these prisoners.[65] Many blacks participated—by force or for lack of employment alternatives—in creating colonial film propaganda.[66] Some blacks joined the resistance movement, some were drafted into the Wehrmacht, a few became Nazi spies or admirers of Hitler. The interests of the Nazi state and its authorities with respect to people of African descent in Germany remained contradictory. On the one hand, their presence in the Reich undermined the "purity of the blood"; on the other, they were considered a potentially useful pawn in negotiations about establishing a "Middle African Colonial Empire" under German domination. In any case— and Tina Campt, in particular, has highlighted this question in her work—the perspective of the Nazi regime and of the social environment in which African Germans lived was determined by two interwoven processes: the racializing of gender and the gendering of race. African German women were treated differently than African German men, and they had other options for behavior. However, since Campt conducted only two interviews, the empirical base for her findings is limited. She also fails to acknowledge that most African Germans were considered *Mischlinge*, a category the Nazis also had great difficulties with in the case of Jewish and "gypsy" counterparts. Despite the shortcomings of Campt's study, her work points to paths to be followed in future investigations. A central focus should be the question of images of the "Other" that German society has constructed in the course of modernity and thus also of itself.

Conclusion

German society, like the societies of Britain, France, or Spain, is a postcolonial society. Although the epoch of colonial rule was quite short, the "colonial" mentalities and practices that developed in Germany even without formal colonial possessions continue to have a lasting effect up to the present day. This impact clearly is marked by the persistent self-image of German society as a "white" collective. Recognition of this phenomenon and the desire to further explore its implications has lead to a renaissance of "colonial" themes in Germany that is especially apparent among younger historians. Modern approaches from cultural studies originally developed in the United States have been adopted and adapted to new issues. Contextualizing phenomena in broader societal, socioeconomic, and political landscapes on a European and a global level is another important direction of research. To this day, one process by which "Europe" is constituted is by delimiting its borders and its difference with respect to the Near East, Africa, or the wider Muslim world. Those who seek to uncover the traces of national colonialism will no doubt analyze what unique features have resulted—especially in comparison to the other European colonial powers—from Germany's special constellation as a country with a long history of colonialism without colonies and a short imperial phase. Presumably, the prospects for further progress in the field of colonial studies will depend to a considerable extent on whether researchers succeed in effectively broadening their application of the category of gender so that it applies not only to women and femininity but to investigating and illuminating historical actors, practices, and representations of self and other in the history of masculinities.

Notes

Translation by Paula Bradish

1. See as recent critical surveys of the field Lora Wildenthal, "The Places of Colonialism in the Writing and Teaching of Modern German History," *The European Studies Journal* 16, no. 2 (1999): 9–23; Sebastian Conrad, "Schlägt das Empire zurück? Postkoloniale Ansätze in der deutschen Geschichtsschreibung," *Werkstatt Geschichte* 30 (2001): 73–83; and "Doppelte Marginalisierung: Plädoyer für eine transnationale Perspektive auf die deutsche Geschichte," *Geschichte und Gesellschaft* 28 (2002): 145–169.
2. Horst Gründer, *Geschichte der deutschen Kolonien* (Stuttgart, 2004); Dirk van Laak, *Über alles in der Welt: Deutscher Imperialismus im 19. und 20. Jahrhundert* (Munich, 2005).
3. Ulrich van der Heyden, "Kolonialgeschichtsschreibung in Deutschland: Eine Bilanz ost- und westdeutscher Kolonialhistoriographie," *Neue Politische Literatur* 48 (2003): 401–429.
4. That the colonies are hardly an element of national history in Germany is documented by the fact, for example, that in Etienne François and Hagen Schulze, eds., *Deutsche Erinnerungsorte*, vols. 1–3 (Munich, 2001), there is no listing of the colonies as a site of memory in their own right. Colonial history is only dealt with as a part of the texts on the topics "*Volk*" and ethnological museums.

5. Pioneering works range from Edward Said, *Orientalism* (New York, 1978); to Tzvetan Todorov, *The Conquest of America: The Question of the Other* (New York, 1984); and Paul Gilroy, *The Black Atlantic: Modernity and Double Consciousness* (Cambridge, Mass., 1993).

6. See the reviews of research in Ann Laura Stoler and Frederick Cooper, "Between Metropole and Colony: Rethinking a Research Agenda," in *Tensions of Empire: Colonial Cultures in a Bourgeois World*, ed. Stoler and Cooper (Berkeley, 1997), 1–56; Ann Laura Stoler, "Rethinking Colonial Categories: European Communities and the Boundaries of Rule," in *Colonialism and Culture*, ed. Nicholas B. Dirks (Ann Arbor, 1992), 319–352; for a differentiated perspective: Patrick Wolfe, "History and Imperialism: A Century of Theory from Marx to Postcolonialism," *American Historical Review* 102 (1997): 388–420; see also Boris Barth, "Internationale Geschichte und europäische Expansion: Die Imperialismen des 19. Jahrhunderts," in *Internationale Geschichte: Themen—Ergebnisse—Aussichten*, ed. Wilfried Loth and Jürgen Osterhammel (Munich, 2000), 309–327.

7. See for example Russell A. Berman, *Enlightenment or Empire: Colonial Discourse in German Culture* (Lincoln, Neb., 1998); Johannes Fabian, *Im Tropenfieber: Wissenschaft und Wahn in der Erforschung Zentralafrikas* (Munich, 2001); Marcia Klotz, "White Women and the Dark Continent: Gender and Sexuality in German Colonial Discourse from the Sentimental Novel to the Fascist Film," Ph.D. diss., Stanford University, 1995; Suzanne Marchand, "Orientalism as Kulturpolitik: German Archeology and Cultural Imperialism in Asia Minor," in *Volksgeist as Method and Ethic: Essays on Boasian Ethnography and the German Anthropological Tradition*, ed. George W. Stocking, Jr. (Madison, 1996), 298–336; John Noyes, *Colonial Space: Spatiality in the Discourse of German South West Africa 1884–1915* (Chur, 1992); Lora Wildenthal, *German Women for Empire, 1884–1945* (Durham, 2001); Sara Friedrichsmeyer et al., eds., *The Imperialist Imagination: German Colonialism and Its Legacy* (Ann Arbor, 1998).

8. Susanne Zantop, *Colonial Fantasies: Conquest, Family, and Nation in Precolonial Germany, 1770–1870* (Durham, 1997), 7.

9. See for example Nina Berman, *Orientalismus, Kolonialismus und Moderne: Zum Bild des Orients in der deutschsprachigen Kultur um 1900* (Stuttgart, 1997); Kerstin Gernig, ed. *Fremde Körper: Zur Konstruktion des Anderen in europäischen Diskursen* (Berlin, 2001); Alexander Honold and Oliver Simons, eds., *Kolonialismus als Kultur: Literatur, Medien, Wissenschaft in der deutschen Gründerzeit des Fremden* (Tübingen, 2002); Alexander Honold and Klaus R. Scherpe, eds., *Mit Deutschland um die Welt: Eine Kulturgeschichte des Fremden in der Kolonialzeit* (Stuttgart, 2004); Birthe Kundrus, *Moderne Imperialisten: Das Kaiserreich im Spiegel seiner Kolonien* (Cologne, 2003); Birthe Kundrus, ed., *Phantasiereiche: Zur Kulturgeschichte des deutschen Kolonialismus* (Frankfurt/M., 2003); Jürgen Osterhammel, *Die Entzauberung Asiens: Europa und die asiatischen Reiche im 18. Jahrhundert* (Munich, 1998); Ulrich van der Heyden and Joachim Zeller, eds., *Kolonialmetropole Berlin: Eine Spurensuche* (Berlin, 2002); van der Heyden and Zeller, eds., *Macht und Anteil an der Weltherrschaft: Berlin und der deutsche Kolonialismus* (Berlin, 2005).

10. See Lora Wildenthal, "Notes on a History of 'Imperial Turns' in Modern Germany," in *After the Imperial Turn: Thinking With and Through the Nation*, ed. Antoinette M. Burton (Durham, 2003), 144–156.

11. Christoph Conrad and Sebastian Conrad, eds., *Die Nation schreiben: Geschichtswissenschaft im internationalen Vergleich* (Göttingen, 2002); Sebastian Conrad and Shalini Randeria, eds., *Jenseits des Eurozentrismus: Postkoloniale Perspektiven in den Geschichts- und Kulturwissenschaften* (Frankfurt/M., 2002); Sebastian Conrad and Jürgen Osterhammel, eds., *Das Kaiserreich transnational: Deutschland in der Welt 1871–1914* (Göttingen, 2004).

12. Durba Ghosh, "Gender and Colonialism: Expansion or Marginalization?" *The Historical Journal* 47, no. 3 (2004): 738; also Wildenthal, "Notes."

13. Ghosh, "Gender," 737.

14. Martha Mamozai, *Herrenmenschen: Frauen im deutschen Kolonialismus* (Reinbek, 1982); idem, *Schwarze Frau, weiße Herrin: Frauenleben in den deutschen Kolonien* (Reinbek, 1988); and idem, *Komplizinnen* (Reinbek, 1990).

15. Wildenthal, *German Women.*

16. Rosa B. Schneider, *"Um Scholle und Leben": Zur Konstruktion von "Rasse" und Geschlecht in der deutschen kolonialen Afrikaliteratur um 1900* (Frankfurt/M., 2003); Kundrus, *Imperialisten,* 77–96.

17. See Wildenthal, *German Women,* 151–156; Berman, *Enlightenment,* 171–194.

18. Gesine Krüger, "Bestien und Opfer: Frauen im Kolonialkrieg," in *Völkermord in Deutsch-Südwestafrika: Der Kolonialkrieg in Namibia (1904–1908) und seine Folgen,* ed. Jürgen Zimmerer and Joachim Zeller (Berlin, 2003), 142–159.

19. See Kathrin Roller, "Mission und 'Mischehen,' Erinnerung und Körper—geteiltes Gedächtnis an eine afrikanische Vorfahrin: Über die Familie Schmelen-Kleinschmidt-Hegner," in *Namibia—Deutschland. Eine geteilte Geschichte Widerstand—Gewalt—Erinnerung,* ed. Larissa Förster et al. (Cologne, 2004), 194–211; Kathrin Roller, "'Statt dessen schwang sie eine andere Waffe': Gewalt und Geschlecht in Texten der Berliner Mission über Südafrika aus der Zeit um 1900," in *Mission und Gewalt: Der Umgang christlicher Missionen mit Gewalt und die Ausbreitung des Christentums in Afrika und Asien in der Zeit von 1792 bis 1918/19,* ed. Ulrich van der Heyden and Jürgen Becher (Stuttgart, 2000), 301–326; Vera Boetzinger, *"Den Chinesen ein Chinese werden": Die deutsche protestantische Frauenmission in China 1842–1952* (Stuttgart, 2004).

20. Roger Chickering, "'Casting Their Gaze More Broadly': Women's Patriotic Activism in Imperial Germany," *Past & Present* 118 (1988): 156–185.

21. Elizabeth A. Drummond, "'Durch Liebe stark, deutsch bis ins Mark': Weiblicher Kulturimperialismus und der Deutsche Frauenverein für die Ostmarken," in *Nation, Politik und Geschlecht: Frauenbewegungen und Nationalismus in der Moderne,* ed. Ute Planert (Frankfurt/M., 2000, 147–164); Ute Planert, *Antifeminismus im Kaiserreich: Diskurs, soziale Formation und politische Mentalität* (Göttingen, 1998), 232–234; Andrea Süchting-Hänger, *Das "Gewissen der Nation": Nationales Engagement und politisches Handeln konservativer Frauenorganisationen, 1900 bis 1937* (Düsseldorf, 2002), 23; Karin Bruns, "Völkische und deutschnationale Frauenvereine im 'zweiten Reich,'" in *Handbuch zur Völkischen Bewegung 1871–1918,* ed. Uwe Puschner et al. (Munich, 1996), 376–394; Jean H. Quataert, *Staging Philantropy: Patriotic Women and the National Imagination in Dynastic Germany, 1813–1916* (Ann Arbor, 2001).

22. Christiane Streubel, "Sammelrezension: Literaturbericht: Frauen der politischen Rechten," retrieved 10 June 2003 from http://hsozkult.geschichte.hu-berlin.de/rezensionen/2003-2-141h; idem, "Ihrem Volk verantwortlich," in *Frauen der politischen Rechten 1890–1937. Organisation—Agitation Ideologien,* ed. Eva Schöck-Quinteros and Christiane Streubel (Berlin, 2007). See also Kevin Passmore, ed., *Women, Gender and Facism in Europe, 1919–45* (Manchester, 2003); Raffael Scheck, *Mothers of the Nation: Right-Wing Women in Weimar Germany* (Oxford, 2004); Heidrun Zettelbauer, *Die "Liebe sei Euer Heldentum": Geschlecht und Nation in völkischen Vereinen der Habsburgermonarchie* (Frankfurt/M., 2005).

23. See Angelika Schaser's contribution to this volume.

24. In the recently published Gebhardt handbook, again, these associations were not mentioned: Volker Berghahn, *Das Kaiserreich (1871–1914): Industriegesellschaft, bürgerliche Kultur und autoritärer Staat,* Handbuch der deutschen Geschichte, Gebhardt Band 16 (Stuttgart, 2003).

25. See Rainer Hering, *Die konstruierte Nation: Der Alldeutsche Verband 1890–1939* (Hamburg, 2003), 380–394.

26. Karen Smidt, *Germania führt die deutsche Frau nach Südwest: Auswanderung, Leben und soziale Konflikte deutscher Frauen in der ehemaligen Kolonie Deutsch-Südwestafrika 1884–1920*

(Magdeburg, 1997), 55–74; Wildenthal, *German Women*, 131–171; Lora Wildenthal, "Rasse und Kultur: Koloniale Frauenorganisationen in der deutschen Kolonialbewegung des Kaiserreichs," in Kundrus, *Phantasiereiche*, 202–219; Katharina Walgenbach, *Die weisse Frau als Trägerin deutscher Kultur: Koloniale Diskurse über Geschlecht, Rasse und Klasse im Kaiserreich* (Frankfurt/M., 2006); Cornelia Carstens, Gerhild Vollherbst, "'Deutsche Frauen nach Südwest!'—Der Frauenbund der Deutschen Kolonialgesellschaft," in van der Heyden, *Kolonialmetropole*, 50–56; K. Molly O'Donnell, "German Women's Letters from Southern Africa," in *Lives and Voices: Sources in European Women's History*, ed. Merry Wiesner and Lisa DiCaprio (Boston, 2000); Wiesner and DiCaprio, "Poisonous Women: Danger, Illicit Violence, and Domestic Work in German Southwest Africa, 1904–1915," *The Journal of Women's History* 11, no. 3 (1999): 31–54; Daniel Joseph Walther, *Creating Germans Abroad: Cultural Policies and National Identity in Namibia* (Athens, 2002), 46–64; Claire Venghiattis, "Mobilising for Nation and Empire: A History of the Women's Association of the German Colonial Society, 1907–45," Ph.D. diss., Columbia University, 2005; Else Frobenius, *Erinnerungen einer Journalistin: Zwischen Kaiserreich und Zweitem Weltkrieg*, ed. Lora Wildenthal (Cologne, 2005).

27. Negative German terms for "going native," literally becoming Englishmen, Boers, or kaffirs. Leonore Niessen-Deiters, *Die deutsche Frau im Auslande und in den Schutzgebieten: Nach Originalberichten aus fünf Erdteilen* (Berlin, 1913), 63.

28. Mechthild Rommel, Hulda Rautenberg, "Die Kolonialen Frauenschulen von 1908–1945," *Der Tropenlandwirt*, Beiheft 16 (1983); Smidt, *Germania*, 74–82; Dorothea Siegle, *"Trägerinnen echten Deutschtums": Die Koloniale Frauenschule Rendsburg* (Rendsburg, 2004); see also the film *Wir hatten eine Dora in Südwest*, by Christina Tink Diaz, documentary combining historical archival materials and interviews, BRD, 1991, 70 mins.

29. See Süchting-Hänger, *Gewissen*, 75. There are no studies that analyze the German women's movement's relationship to imperialism, but see Anette Herlitzius, *Frauenbefreiung und Rassenideologie: Rassenhygiene und Eugenik im politischen Programm der "Radikalen Frauenbewegung" (1900–1933)* (Wiesbaden, 1995); Christian Geulen, *Wahlverwandte: Rassendiskurs und Nationalismus im späten 19. Jahrhundert* (Hamburg, 2004), 232–245.

30. Wildenthal, *German Women*, 151–156; Wildenthal, "Rasse," 203–206.

31. See Christian Jansen, ed., *Der Bürger als Soldat: Die Militarisierung europäischer Gesellschaften im langen 19. Jahrhundert: Ein internationaler Vergleich* (Essen, 2004).

32. Wildenthal, *German Women*, 170–171.

33. Birthe Kundrus, "Weiblicher Kulturimperialismus: Die imperialistischen Frauenverbände des Kaiserreichs," in Conrad and Osterhammel, *Das Kaiserreich transnational*, 230–232.

34. See Nancy Ruth Reagin, "The Imagined Hausfrau: National Identity, Domesticity, and Colonialism in Imperial Germany," *The Journal of Modern History* 73 (2001): 54–86.

35. Venghiattis, "Mobilising."

36. Drummond, "Liebe," 147.

37. Frances Gouda, "Das 'unterlegene' Geschlecht der 'überlegenen' Rasse: Kolonialgeschichte und Geschlechterverhältnisse," in *Geschlechterverhältnisse im historischen Wandel*, ed. Hanna Schissler (Frankfurt/M., 1993), 185–203.

38. See Kathleen Canning, "Class vs. Citizenship: Keywords in German Gender History," *Central European History* 37, no. 2 (2004): 225–244.

39. See Ida Blom et al., eds., *Gendered Nations: Nationalisms and Gender Order in the Long Nineteenth Century* (Oxford, 2000).

40. Wildenthal, *German Women*, 10.

41. See Antoinette Burton, *The Burdens of History: British Feminists, Indian Women, and Imperial Culture, 1865–1915* (Chapel Hill, 1994), 2–3; Vron Ware, *Beyond the Pale: White Women, Racism and History* (London, 1992), 117–166.

42. Van der Heyden, *Kolonialgeschichtsschreibung.*
43. From the copious body of literature in English see, among others: Mary Procida, *Married to the Empire: Gender, Politics, and Imperialism in India, 1883–1947* (Manchester, 2002); Helen Callaway, *Gender, Culture and Empire: European Women in Colonial Nigeria* (Houndmills, city1987); Catherine Hall, ed., *Cultures of Empire: Colonizers in Britain and the Empire in the Nineteenth and Twentieth Centuries* (Manchester, 2000); Philippa Levine, ed., *Gender and Empire* (Oxford, 2004).
44. Benedikt Stuchtey, "Nation und Expansion. Das britische Empire in der neuesten Forschung," *Historische Zeitschrift* 274 (2002): 112.
45. See for example Daiva Stasiulis and Nira Yuval-Davis, eds., *Unsettling Settler Societies: Articulation on Gender, Race, Ethnicity and Class* (London, 1995); Marilyn Lake, "The Ambiguities for Feminists of National Belonging: Race and Gender in the Imagined Australian Community," in Blom et al., *Gendered Nations*, 159–176; on the ideal of women as the representative of culture in German-American women's clubs see Anke Ortlepp, *"Auf denn, Ihr Schwestern!": Deutschamerikanische Frauenvereine in Milwaukee, Wisconsin, 1844–1914* (Stuttgart, 2003).
46. See Helmut Bley, *Kolonialherrschaft und Sozialstruktur in Deutsch-Südwestafrika 1894–1914* (Hamburg, 1968); 249–256; Fatima El-Tayeb, *Schwarze Deutsche: Der Diskurs um "Rasse" und nationale Identität 1890–1933* (Frankfurt/M., 2001), 83–141; Cornelia Essner, "'Wo Rauch ist, da ist auch Feuer': Zu den Ansätzen eines Rassenrechts für die deutschen Kolonien," in *Rassendiskriminierung, Kolonialpolitik und ethnisch-nationale Identität*, ed. Wilfried Wagner (Münster, 1992), 145–160; Cornelia Essner, "Zwischen Vernunft und Gefühl: Die Reichstagsdebatten von 1912 um koloniale 'Rassenmischehe' und 'Sexualität,'" *Zeitschrift für Geschichtswissenschaft* 45, no. 6 (1997): 503–519; Franz-Josef Schulte-Althoff, "Rassenmischung im kolonialen System: Zur deutschen Kolonialpolitik im letzten Jahrzehnt vor dem Ersten Weltkrieg," *Historisches Jahrbuch* 105, no. 1 (1995): 52–94; Helmut Walser Smith, "The Talk of Genocide, the Rhetoric of Miscegenation: Notes on Debates in the German Reichstag Concerning Southwest Africa, 1904–1914," in Friedrichsmeyer et al., *Imperialist Imagination*, 107–123; Zimmerer, *Herrschaft*, 94–109; Kundrus, *Imperialisten*, 219–280; Frank Becker, ed., *Rassenmischehen—Mischlinge—Rassentrennung: Zur Politik der Rasse im deutschen Kolonialreich* (Stuttgart, 2004); Thomas Schwarz, "Bastards. Juli 1908: Eugen Fischer bringt die 'Rassenkunde' nach Afrika." in Honold and Scherpe, *Deutschland*, 373–380; Wolfram Hartmann, "Sexual Encounters and Their Implications on an Open and Closing Frontier: Central Namibia from the 1840s to 1905," Ph.D. diss., Columbia University, 2002; K. Molly O'Donnell, "The First Besatzungskinder: Afro-German-Children, Colonial Childrearing Practices, and Racial Policy in German Namibia, 1890–1914," in *Not So Plain as Black and White: Afro-German History and Culture, 1890–2000*, ed. Reinhild Steingroever and Patricia Mazon (Rochester, 2005).
47. Wildenthal, "Race," 268; Pascal Grosse, *Kolonialismus, Eugenik und bürgerliche Gesellschaft in Deutschland, 1850–1918* (Frankfurt/M., 2000), 145–192; Grosse, "Zwischen Privatheit und Öffentlichkeit: Kolonialmigration in Deutschland, 1900–1940," in Kundrus, *Phantasiereiche*, 91–109.
48. Dag Henrichsen, "Heirat im Krieg: Erfahrungen von Kaera Getzen-Leinhos," in Zimmerer, *Völkermord*, 160–170.
49. Birthe Kundrus, "Von Windhoek nach Nürnberg?: Koloniale 'Mischehenverbote' und die nationalsozialistische Rassengesetzgebung," in Kundrus, *Phantasiereiche*, 110–131.
50. See also Ann Laura Stoler, "Rethinking," 339; Stoler, "Sexual Affronts and Racial Frontiers: European Identities and the Cultural Politics of Exclusion in Colonial Southeast Asia," in Cooper and Stoler, *Tensions*, 198–237.

51. Felix Axster, "Die Angst vor dem Verkaffern—Politiken der Reinigung im deutschen Kolonialismus," *WerkstattGeschichte* 39 (2005): 39–53.

52. Sandra Maß, *Weiße Helden, schwarze Krieger: Zur Geschichte kolonialer Männlichkeit in Deutschland 1918–1964* (Cologne, 2006); idem, "Das Trauma des weißen Mannes: Afrikanische Kolonialsoldaten in propagandistischen Texten, 1914–1923," *L'Homme* 12, no. 1 (2001): 11–33.

53. Maß, "Trauma," 15.

54. Sander L. Gilman, *On Blackness without Blacks* (Boston, 1982).

55. Katharina Oguntoye et al., eds., *Farbe bekennen: Afro-deutsche Frauen auf den Spuren ihrer Geschichte* (Berlin, 1986). English translation: *Showing Our Colors: Afro-German Women Speak Out* (Amherst, 1992).

56. Hans J. Massaquoi, *Neger, Neger, Schornsteinfeger: Meine Kindheit in Deutschland* (Bern, 1999). First published as *Destined to Witness* (New York, 1999).

57. Marianne Bechhaus-Gerst and Reinhard Klein-Arendt, eds., *Die Koloniale Begegnung: Afrikaner in Deutschland—Deutsche in Afrika* (Bern, 2002); idem, *AfrikanerInnen in Deutschland und schwarze Deutsche—Geschichte und Gegenwart* (Münster, 2004); Tina Campt, "Converging Spectres of an Other Within: Race and Gender in Prewar Afro-German History," *Callaloo* 26, no. 2, (2003): 322–341; El-Tayeb, *Schwarze Deutsche*; Katharina Oguntoye, *Eine afro-deutsche Geschichte: Zur Lebenssituation von Afrikanern und Afro-Deutschen in Deutschland von 1884 bis 1950* (Berlin, 1997); Paulette Reed-Anderson, *Eine Geschichte von mehr als 100 Jahren: Die Anfänge der afrikanischen Diaspora in Berlin* (Berlin, 1995); May Ayim, "Die afrodeutsche Minderheit," in *Ethnische Minderheiten in der Bundesrepublik Deutschland: Ein Lexikon*, ed. Cornelia Schmalz-Jacobsen and Georg Hansen (Munich, 1995); Tina Campt et al., "Blacks, Germans, and the Politics of Imperial Imagination, 1920–60," in Friedrichsmeyer et al., *Imperialist Imagination*, 205–229; Pascal Grosse, "Koloniale Lebenswelten in Berlin 1885–1945," in van der Heyden, *Kolonialmetropole*, 195–200; van der Heyden, "Zwischen Privatheit und Öffentlichkeit: Kolonialmigration in Deutschland, 1900–1940," in Kundrus, *Phantasiereiche*, 91–109; Eve Rosenhaft, "Afrikaner und 'Afrikaner' im Deutschland der Weimarer Republik: Antikolonialismus und Antirassismus zwischen Doppelbewusstsein und Selbsterfindung," in Kundrus, *Phantasiereiche*, 282–301; Susan Arndt, ed. *AfrikaBilder: Studien zu Rassismus in Deutschland* (Münster, 2001).

58. Peter Martin and Christine Alonzo, eds., *Zwischen Charleston und Stechschritt: Schwarze im Nationalsozialismus* (Hamburg, 2004).

59. Carol Aisha Blackshire-Belay, *The African German Experience: Critical Essays* (Westport, 1996), ix.

60. Campt, "Other German," 136.

61. Yara-Colette Lemke-Muniz de Faria, *Zwischen Fürsorge und Ausgrenzung: Afrodeutsche Besatzungskinder im Nachkriegsdeutschland* (Berlin, 2002); idem, "'Germany's "Brown Babies" Must Be Helped! Will You?': U.S. Adoption Plans for Afro-German Children, 1950–1955," *Callaloo* 26, no. 2, (2003): 342–362; see now Heide Fehrenbach, *Race after Hitler: Black Occupation Children in Postwar Germany and America* (Princeton, 2005).

62. See especially Peter Martin, *Schwarze Teufel, edle Mohren: Afrikaner in Geschichte und Bewusstsein der Deutschen* (Hamburg, 1993); for an opposing position, see Monika Firla, "Exotisch—höfisch—bürgerlich: Afrikaner in Württemberg vom 15. bis zum 19. Jahrhundert," *Katalog zur Ausstellung des Hauptstaatsarchivs Stuttgart* (Stuttgart, 2001); Firla, "AfrikanerInnen und ihre Nachkommen im deutschsprachigen Raum vor der Zeit der Kongokonferenz und ihrer Folgen: Bemerkungen zur Forschungsproblematik," in Bechhaus-Gerst, *AfrikanerInnen*, 9–24.

63. Marianne Bechhaus-Gerst, "Afrikaner in Deutschland 1933–45," *1999, Zeitschrift für das 21. Jahrhundert* 12, no. 4 (1997): 10–31; Tina Campt, *Other Germans: Black Germans and the*

Politics of Race, Gender and Memory in the Third Reich (Ann Arbor, 2003); Clarence Lusane, *Hitler's Black Victims: The Historical Experiences of Afro-Germans, European Blacks, Africans, and African Americans in the Nazi Era* (New York, 2002); Elisa von Joeden-Forgey, "Nobody's People: Colonial Subjects, Race Power, and the German State, 1884–1945," Ph.D. diss., University of Pennsylvania, 2004; Susann Lewerenz, *Die Deutsche Afrika-Schau (1935–1940): Rassismus, Kolonialrevisionismus und postkoloniale Auseinandersetzungen im nationalsozialistischen Deutschland* (Frankfurt/M., 2005).

64. Reiner Pommerin, *Die Sterilisierung der Rheinlandbastarde: Das Schicksal einer farbigen deutschen Minderheit 1918–37*, (Düsseldorf, 1979); Campt, *Other Germans*, 63–80; Bastian Breiter, "Der Weg des 'treuen Askari' ins Konzentrationslager—Die Lebensgeschichte des Mohamed Husen," in van der Heyden, *Kolonialmetropole*, 215–220.

65. Raffael Scheck, *Hitler's African Victims: The German Army Massacres of 1940* (Cambridge, 2006).

66. Tobias Nagl, "Von Kamerun nach Babelsberg—Louis Brody und die schwarze Präsenz im deutschsprachigen Kino vor 1945," in van der Heyden, *Kolonialmetropole*, 220–225; idem, "'Sieh mal den schwarzen Mann da!'—Komparsen afrikanischer Herkunft im deutschsprachigen Kino vor 1945," in Martin and Alonzo, *Charleston*, 81–99.

5

The Personal Is Political

Gender, Politics, and Political Activism in Modern German History

Belinda Davis

"Women's history" grew out of the feminist movement. Therefore it comes as no surprise that the history of women's activism and politics was from the beginning a major topic of interest for women's historians. Many of these researchers, reflecting a range of professional training, sought to connect the activism of the past with their own, looking to learn from that history, reinterpret it, integrate it, and trace the longer continuum of its existence. In doing so, these scholars accomplished several goals. First, they helped initiate a challenge to what history was and who "did" it. From the beginning, feminists writing the history of women's politics extended their coverage from the early nineteenth century through the Second Wave. This contributed to widespread recognition of "contemporary" history, suggesting that methodology was more relevant to the writing of history than any artificial chronological cut-off. Second, feminists in West Germany in particular, as throughout Western Europe, were seminal in advancing the "history workshop" notion, whereby nonprofessional historians sought, alongside their counterparts with advanced degrees, to "dig where they stood," discovering their "own" histories, however defined.[1] They thereby also challenged the purposes of history, insisting that its pursuit was politicized and rightfully political, and questioning the notion of its "objectivity" and simple facticity. These researchers interrogated definitions of political history, as they raised for consideration the definition of "politics" *tout court*. Transcending political histories that turned on specific governments in power, these writers confronted standing periodizations. By explicitly introducing the notion of gender into politics, finally, this work instigated study of masculinity and maleness in politics as well as femaleness, and included consideration of the role played by gendered imagery and representation in politics. This body of work has, then, from the beginning contributed to the transformation of historical methodology and the very understanding of history, as well as playing a critical role in inspiring activists and activism. And, naturally, this work itself was one form of activism.

The first formally scholarly works on the topic were written in English, and these few studies have remained seminal.[2] While the history of German women and gender has thrived in the English-speaking world since that time, the topic of women's politics and activism has remained a relatively small subfield of this work, in contrast for example with the social or even cultural history of women, or with their treatment as the objects of political policy. By contrast, the topic exploded in West Germany alongside the rise of the women's movement in the 1970s, though almost entirely among scholars with less formal training in history. By the 1980s, this work flourished as well among professional historians in West Germany, contributing new nuance and understanding of women's activism, particularly of the broader bourgeois women's movement, in addition to women's roles in formal political parties. In this era too scholars began to undertake the question of gender in politics more broadly, a literature that has also continued to grow. There are concerns however for this literature's continued returns, both in scholarly and political terms. These historians converge on a number of conclusions, many of which apply outside Germany as well. We may now be at a kind of standstill, having rediscovered women's roles, strategies, and thinking in so many stories, but unable to use these histories' conclusions in present-day politics to move past the obstacles the literature has identified.

These conclusions include the following: (1) Women in modern politics have always confronted seeking equal standing with men in "male" structures (political parties, parliaments), working entirely outside such structures, or working to modify "men's" structures, which may be fundamentally unmodifiable. (2) Gender structures how women and men have operated across the range of political and social movements and usually puts women in a disadvantageous position vis-à-vis men, though recent redefinitions of politics have challenged this view. (3) Women are regularly part of protest and political movements, but have rarely been part of politics in power. (4) When women do gain political power, it is most frequently in the form of control over "women's issues," however defined. (5) Women who have gained the most political power often represent very conservative points of view, which have sometimes served to reinforce particular and limited views of women and their roles. (6) Women's movements have originated in women's disaffection in mixed-gender groupings. (7) When women have organized qua women, however, they have discovered the "paradox" by which their organization as women threatens to refute their political equality and/or equivalent value. (8) Organizing as women has also exposed divisions among women, often causing conflicts of "identity politics," including but not limited to class, sexual orientation, confession/religion, and ethnicity, as well as ideological predilection and views of gender essentialism. Among historians' next task might be to speculate more willingly on how we might draw on the past to overcome some of these stumbling blocks in the present and future.

The following essay offers an overview of the historiography of women, gender, and politics in West Germany at all levels since the 1970s, from both sides of the Atlantic. The essay proceeds chronologically, mapping out the major trends and achievements in each of the last three decades. It highlights the nuanced "expert" historical influences from the beginning, as well as the lively and exciting nonprofessional scholarship that has remained so inspirational in the literature. The piece focuses particularly on debates concerning appropriate emphasis on political difference or sameness, as well as women's role as agent and/or object of official policy, and the nature of femininity, masculinity, and politics. These foci are closely related to contemporary concerns of the authors themselves. Acknowledging thus the contribution historical work has made both to broader scholarship and to strategic assessments of present-day politics, this piece ends with suggestions for where historians might turn next.

First Engagements: The 1970s and Equality versus Difference

Aside from such exceptions as a precocious 1964 dissertation, women's history began with the women's movement, commencing full force in the 1970s.[3] The differences between what was produced in the United States and England on the one hand and West Germany on the other are most striking in this period.[4] From the beginning, the literature on both sides of the Atlantic took up study of women in both women-only groups and in mixed groups, including political parties. Particularly in the West German work, authors also adopted in their writings the far broader view of what constituted politics and political work that characterized the feminist movement and the broader extraparliamentary opposition. This work challenged contemporary views of women's activism as apolitical or politically "neutral," as many activist women in the nineteenth century themselves characterized it, thereby demonstrating how these women's efforts must be viewed as a relevant piece of German political history. Many of the contributions of the era traced out political differences among women. At the same time, visible from the earliest work are differing estimations of the "equality versus difference" question, relevant to

both contemporary feminist strategies and to assessments of the intervening Nazi era. From the beginning this work consistently challenged standard periodizations in modern German history, writing even from the newly
rediscovered early nineteenth-century origins of "the women's movement"
through the present.

Four American historians, Amy K. Hackett, Karen Honeycutt, Marion A.
Kaplan, and Jean Quataert, completed dissertations on feminism and German women's activism in the mid-1970s. Two of these studies appeared with
scholarly presses and remain seminal texts.[5] A fifth Anglophone study by Brit-
isher Richard J. Evans also appeared in this period, the first contribution by
a man to this work.[6] All five studies came out of major history department
programs, providing a degree of legitimacy and visibility from the beginning,
though sometimes belied by the subsequent professional experience of their
authors. Jean Quataert's *Reluctant Feminists in German Social Democracy* took
up the thorny question: what is feminism? Looking at "competing identities
and loyalties," Quataert finds in her study of female activists in the Social
Democratic Party (SPD) straddling World War I that these women did not
see themselves as "feminist." They regarded themselves rather as unified with
their male party counterparts in pursuing socialism. She asserts however that
their actions and even many of their ends can be characterized as radically
"feminist." This was the cause of some of their frictions with their male colleagues, though they did not see it as such. Testing, arguing over, and refining
definitions of feminism was a hallmark of the contemporary historiography,
usefully contributing to contemporary discussion in the women's movement.[7]
Quataert's study traces the lives of eight major female figures in the SPD,
whose existence had been largely lost to memory in the intervening years.
This effective group biography permitted Quataert to depict a milieu in detailed fashion. She highlights the ways in which these women interacted with
one another and with the men in the party to pursue their goals—and how
they succeeded or failed. This methodological strategy, like the fording of political periods, would be emulated in future works. The approach transcended
"great man" strategies in both the multiplicity and the lack of status of her
subjects, without losing individuality and agency as was the case in some contemporary institutional and social histories.

That Quataert characterized her subjects as feminists in the SPD also spoke
to contemporaneous concerns: finding a model of women's activism outside
the somewhat better-known "bourgeois" German women's movement. The
political as well as scholarly utility of this perspective was clear. If the subjects of Quataert's work grew up in bourgeois households, their adult lives
were committed to the pursuit of a socialist future; such work helped challenge contemporary assumptions by historians concerning linkages between
class position and ideological and party proclivities. For many feminists in

the 1970s in both the United States and West Germany, this past offered legitimacy for the present, as splits in the women's movement, including political philosophy and the primacy of gender and of patriarchy, threatened to sap the movement of its strength, and as feminism was still often associated outside the movement with a kind of exclusive separatist "man-hating." The other contemporary Anglophone studies pursued similar topics and questions, looking at "feminists" in and out of explicitly women's movements, and examining divisions within the women's movement, boundaries of ethnicity as well as of political philosophy. Thus Marion Kaplan's study of the Jewish Women's Federation introduced early discussion of "identity politics," as she describes the efforts of her subjects to identify their interests as "women" and as "Jews."[8]

The political utility of such work was for some in contrast with Richard Evans's study, which drew challenge particularly among West German feminists because of his broad criticism of the larger German bourgeois women's movement. Evans viewed movement leaders' approach to "difference" versus "equality" as permitting the movement's rightward move in the first decades of the twentieth century. But this speaks to one of the most significant ongoing variations between Anglophone and (a significant portion of the) West German scholarship, addressing the different relation to contemporary West German feminist politics and respective political traditions at least as much as differences in gendered perspective. Evans's work, as well as Amy Hackett's, questioned feminists in West Germany who emphasized difference (though not to the exclusion of "equal rights"), and who drew in their own politics on Germany's long tradition of "spiritual motherhood" and other aspects of women's collectives that were quite apart from "men's politics." West German feminists saw this stance as the basis for a radical critique of "men's politics." Evans's assertion was all the more painful for some of these West German researchers as they experienced often rancorous relations (or no relations at all) with "equal rights" feminists in their own country. This scholarly divide arose again in the "women historians quarrel" (*Historikerinnenstreit*) of the 1980s. Following soon after publication of his first book, Richard Evans's second monograph, *The Feminists: Women's Emancipation Movements in Europe, America, and Australasia, 1840–1920*, was the first to offer a comparative and transnational approach to this movement, another important new trend that other scholars would follow. He quite purposely identified common liberal roots in the German and other national women's movements he explored, inter alia challenging contemporary assertions regarding Germany's "peculiarity" and, specifically, lack of liberal tradition, if simultaneously warning against celebration of the turn away from this tradition by others in the German movement.[9]

There were considerably more titles on women's activism, gender and politics, and feminism issuing from West Germany in this period, though fewer from professionally trained historians. Those who were soon to become West Germany's first leading historians of women and gender, such as Karin Hausen and Gisela Bock, were in this period writing dissertations on more traditional or more typical topics of the period.[10] But the results were nonetheless impressive and important. Perhaps precisely because unconstrained by standard historical periodizations, these authors shared a freedom in creating a long trajectory of activism leading to their own. Petra Schneider's study of the Weimar-era campaign against §218, which criminalized abortions, offered in 1975 a past for a burning issue of the new women's movement as well.[11] Gerontologist Herrad Schenk published in 1979 a book on "150 years of the women's movement." Schenk's concise overview traced long trajectories on issues from sexuality and reproduction through the building of "alternative cultures," concluding with specific recommendations for feminism's present and future. For her as for many, the first-wave movement validated contemporary "difference" feminism. Literary critic Renate Wiggershaus published in the same year an historical overview on the women's movement "since 1945"—in the Federal Republic and also in the German Democratic Republic.[12] In 1978, sociologist Ute Gerhard published an historically informed treatment of women's rights in Germany; she and other historical sociologists have constituted a significant thread of discussion on the "difference" question.[13] Beyond book- and pamphlet-length studies, in and out of the vast new feminist press and other alternative publications, feminists practiced this work in a great range of forms, including exhibitions and films concerning women's activism, past and present.[14]

As in the Anglophone literature, many German-language studies emphasized histories of women's politics in alliance with or as part of left-wing movements, including for example the council movement that developed in World War I, itself a history newly recuperated by men and women in the broader West German extraparliamentary movement.[15] But women's historic difficulties in practicing politics within structures dominated by men, likewise reflecting present-day concerns, were also a dominant theme, as in studies on women's struggles working in the Free Trade Unions and the Communist Party, as well as more broadly in the "*Männerstaat*," including under Social Democratic control. Collectively, this work recaptured women's presence especially in the history of Germany's political left as well as identifying the long trajectory of women's organization as such. It pinpointed their accomplishments and also the many obstacles they faced; the balance sheet seemed to indicate the limits of these women's achievements, of the sort adumbrated above. This included examination of the most repressive "male state," the National Socialist regime—and of the total collapse the regime represented for the formal women's movement, at least temporarily.[16] But these works offered a kind of hopefulness that awareness of these limitations would provide a means to supercede them.

New Subtleties:
The 1980s, Agency, Politics, and the Gender Question

The 1980s were a surprisingly quiet time for publication among American historians of German women's history overall, particularly concerning activism and politics, though a new generation of graduate students in history was beginning to undertake research. Renate Pore's 1981 study of women in Weimar-era Social Democracy usefully extended earlier discussions by focusing on this critical era that saw new power for, then the demise of, both Social Democratic and feminist interests. Pore, like her predecessors writing as a scholar and feminist activist, further analyzed the quandary of women's activism within male-dominated organizations, explicitly linking both the "opportunities and dangers" to contemporary women's liberation.[17] The new work went still further too in emphasizing the close and mutually informing ties of the "personal" and the "political," the mantra of the women's movement. Renate Bridenthal's 1977 article, reworked with Claudia Koonz in the seminal 1984 collection *When Biology Became Destiny*, addressed head-on the overwhelmingly conservative voting habits of rural women in the Weimar Republic, who were first exercising their franchise.[18] Bridenthal and Koonz argued that one could not simply look at the level of political ideals and high theory, but must rather examine the everyday lives, experiences, and worldviews of the women they studied; doing so made more unpalatable and uncomprehended practices comprehensible. Such scholarship was at the forefront of new methodological practices visible all the more in West Germany and England. It reflected a move away from both historicism and from the newly dominant social science history toward a return to agency, but not just among "great men," and toward a consideration of experience, as other major feminist historians later emphasized.[19] These methods must be seen in turn as inspired by feminism and the women's movement. Roger Chickering likewise addressed the paradoxes of "right wing" women, whose own activism included exhortations to other women to adhere to "traditional" women's roles.[20] Such work challenged the ability of contemporaries—and also present-day women activists—to claim that radical nationalism was "men's politics" only, related to women only insofar as it was a source of their oppression. This work also began to make important distinctions. If some scholars had argued earlier that "difference" feminists had permitted a rightward drift, precisely into the worst of "men's" politics, still even these feminists had not argued against women's rights conceptually. But this newly discussed category of women activists did just that; they were not "feminists" by any contemporary definition.

In turn, this new work also contributed to still-rising general historical interest in the Nazi era, and in the role of "average" Germans. Scottish historian Jill Stephenson demonstrated inter alia that Nazi women's organizations were means by which the Nazi state turned women into subjects only, subjecting them collectively to the most repressive measures.[21] But if Renate Wiggershaus's 1984 work included attention as well to women's role in supporting the Third Reich, both individually and in groups, this was the major theme of Claudia Koonz's study of the same year. This volume emphasized moreover the significance of women's support for the Nazis already in the Weimar period.[22] The emphatic nature of Koonz's assertion unleashed a firestorm of criticism particularly from many German feminist historians, on both scholarly and political grounds.[23] The "women historians' quarrel" stemmed from the ongoing differences in the West German and Anglophone literature. First, some responded, how could one emphasize women's agency and even role as "perpetrator" when their victimization was so overwhelming, and presumably so overwhelmingly a part of any active role they played? Secondly, what was the political utility of this emphasis, when feminists were at such pains to provide historical models for women's positive and successful activism and political life? The scholarly and political utility was noteworthy, however, as the cumulative awareness of the recent work. The work made explicit in this extreme case the limits of "identity politics," and of assumptions that women as a group followed political ideas entirely different from and independent of men's, as well as that they held inherent, primary concern for the interests of other women. It also challenged presumptions that if women were victims they could hardly be "perpetrators," except, perhaps, as a consequence of their victimization. One can aver that, whatever other criticisms historians leveled, these arguments played a positive role ultimately in complicating women's politics. Certainly scholarly work on right-wing German women's politics from the Second Empire into the Federal Republic soon burgeoned on both sides of the Atlantic.

If the American scholarly contribution to the field in this decade was small as measured in numbers, the offerings of West Germans took off, now including among trained historians as well as other scholars and authors. Topically, many of these works continued the explorations begun in the previous decade, concerning the "proletarian" and socialist women's movement and especially the three wings (conservative, liberal, radical) of the bourgeois women's movement, as well as, to a lesser degree, women's activism in other organizations and institutions.[24] Scholars continued to explore the question: how "feminist" were these women of the past? West German scholars particularly also continued to explore contemporary views of the relation between difference and equality, seen as so closely related to West German feminists' own political strategies, including now as inspired by the new peace movement, such as Barbara Greven-Aschoff's detailed study on the bourgeois women's movement between 1894 and 1933.[25] This work addressed the paradox of women's organizations, emphasizing the difficulties women inevitably ran up against in the "male" political world, even as they tried to organize apart from this, including through perceived "women's issues."

Among the first male West German historians to engage in the discussion, Christophe Sachße explored "maternalist" politics: the notion that women who took on roles in Wilhelmine public policy did so largely in public versions of women's "traditional" roles, not only as "spiritual mothers" but also as "social mothers," developing and reforming social welfare.[26] This was a significant contribution to a major new German historical literature that otherwise almost entirely ignored the gender element, certainly among the practitioners if not the recipients of welfare reform. This historical practice had reflected in part a lack of alternative for contemporaries, as women were shunted off into these areas. But Sachße also emphasizes women's particular interest in welfare, precisely as part of demonstrating their distinct and worthy abilities, once more highlighting the debate on difference. Sachße's rich study reflects too the new attention to women across the political spectrum, emphasizing how welfare provided a site for a great variety of political practices and ideals. Just as women gained formal political power in the Weimar Republic, however, women actually lost their position as leaders in this area, as the state took on distribution of entitlements. This reflected yet another broader conclusion of this literature.

These new studies also challenged the very definition of politics still more fundamentally than the earlier works. This was inspired by and contributed to contemporary feminist practices, as well as to new views of politics more broadly coming out of the 1970s counterculture. Herrad-Ulrike Bussemer argued in her social historical study of the bourgeois women's movement that the movement had been deeply political and politically oriented, even if the women involved steadfastly characterized themselves as nonpolitical and as "neutral."[27] But new definitions of the political went further than this, for example, taking up women's popular protest as explicitly political. Ethnologist Carola Lipp's work on women in bread riots in *Vormärz* (the period before 1848) asserted, alongside new studies on the French revolution, that such riots must be constituted as political by a variety of measures, although others characterized them as "apolitical" and "prepolitical," and that gender played a central role in these politics.[28] In the same vein, Anna Bergmann's research on the working-class women's "birth strike" in 1913, likewise observing unorganized underclass women (though through the eyes of SPD leaders), offered another example of politics not heretofore constituted as such. These politics of sexuality and reproduction, identified at still more a "grassroots" level than even study of the mass anti-§218 movement in the 1920s, were of particular relevance to contemporary feminism in addition to reflecting its influence.[29] In different fashion, we also understand this broader sense of politics from leading German historian Ute Frevert's *Women in German History: From*

Bourgeois Emancipation to Sexual Liberation. While not exclusively a study of women's politics and activism, this remarkably compact study of "women's history" includes the narrative of women's politics as part of their larger story, from the early nineteenth century through the institution of women's centers and "women's houses" in the 1970s.[30]

Published at the very end of this period, Karen Hagemann's ironically titled *Frauenalltag und Männerpolitik* ("women's everyday lives and men's politics") made clear the presence and significance of Social Democratic working-class women's formal politics and informal political activism during the Weimar Republic and how they were engendered by these women's everyday life experiences, working conditions, and social and familial positions.[31] Drawing on a great range of sources including sixty interviews with working-class women, Hagemann provides the broadest definition of politics, encompassing activities from efforts at reproductive rights and education within the family, to consumer and welfare actions, to membership in the trade unions and political parties. At the same time, she makes visible women's rapidly narrowing room for maneuver, including precisely within Social Democratic structures. This work made clearer still the paradox Sachße observed that, despite the formal granting of equal rights to women, men worked continuously to narrow women's space in the political arena, increasingly masculinizing that space in all senses.[32] Ultimately this male antifeminism, including among Social Democrats, along with the limiting structures of their lives, radicalized women in late Weimar, pushing younger ones to the left and older ones to the far right. Hagemann makes explicit the comparison between the past and present, arguing along with Ute Gerhard for the limitations that obtained in equality, which operated only in a broad legal sense.

This was then perhaps the most exciting decade in the history of German women's politics and activism. Deepening and complicating the histories of the previous decade, this work continued to emphasize its close connection to contemporary feminist concerns. The politics of women writing women's politics is implicit and explicit in many of these books. This is all the more the case in the new West German practice of anthologies written and even often edited entirely by graduate students, not only offering those early in their career a critical chance to publish, but also providing some of the leading work on the topic.[33] But if women were no longer the only practitioners of this scholarship, they were also no longer the only subjects. New study of "femininity" and "masculinity" transcended individual gendered bodies altogether. Hagemann's work, among others, also raised the issue of "masculinity" in politics and gender more broadly, signaling a new key topic. Social historian Jürgen Reulecke began publishing on "*Männerbünde*," groups exclusively of men in which inter alia notions of a masculine political dominance (as well as of a muscular nationalism) were reproduced and nourished among successive generations.[34] This also inspired new work on gender in politics in a broader sense, and represented in the event a move by men in the academy into gender studies. Already in the 1970s, such themes were telegraphed in the title of Silvia Kontos's *Die Partei kämpft wie ein Mann* (the party fights like a man)."[35] Now in the late 1980s and early 1990s historians began looking at gendered imagery and symbolism in both more and less formal politics, from the official propaganda of the Nazi party to the "balled fist" of Weimar street demonstrators, also transcending thereby more fixed notions of men and women in useful fashion. By the next decade this too would burgeon as a major topic of the literature.

"Catching One's Breath"?: The 1990s and Beyond

Historical work on women, gender, politics, and activism appearing in the 1990s reflected the 1989 *Wende*, but perhaps not as centrally as did other historical topics—or as did the subject of women and politics in other disciplines. For Americans, the relative quiet in the 1980s was replaced by the publication of numerous dissertations on women's and gender history in general in Germany. But relatively few focused centrally on politics and activism. Dagmar Herzog's 1996 *Intimacy and Exclusion* offered new insight into the complex range of influences and identities including gender guiding women as well as men in the heady liberal politics of pre-1848, resulting in the establishment of the first women's movement in the German lands as elsewhere in Europe and the United States.[36] Along with her predecessors documenting the origins of the women's movement in this early period, Herzog also contributed to work challenging estimations of the 1848 revolution and of German liberalism as complete failures. This study was significant too for "mainstreaming" gender: this was no "women's history," nor even "just" a gender history. Rather, gender was one category among a range, permitting, in the fashion established in the preceding decades, an increasingly nuanced and complex vision of the workings of gender and of identity in politics more broadly. Herzog's study was a promising manifestation of a new move to talk about "difference."

Other topics raised in earlier years saw revisitation and development. Ann Taylor Allen's work on feminism and "maternalism" in the long nineteenth century challengingly offered a more salutary view of the "mother" identity than most Anglophone writers had at least. This work reflected continued disputes over the practical effects of the politics of difference.[37] New work on the activism of sexuality and reproduction deepened our understanding of both the great relevance of these issues in the past as in the present and the complex fashion in which these issues were intertwined with the range of social, "moral," and political questions.[38] This literature further challenged fixed notions of political "right" and "left," for example through new looks at Weimar-era conversations concerning eugenics and Wilhelmine discussions of prostitution. There were also efforts, inspired both by feminists and by historians of everyday life, to understand politics still more expansively, to better account for a still broader range of women's as well as men's activities, and for the gendered representations of politics.[39] This practical openness is rendered transparent in Nancy Reagin's focus on the German Protestant Women's League, which anticipated some women's increasingly rightward turn into the radical nationalist politics of Weimar. The group's activities also offered further evidence both of women's willing place at "men's" political table, and their readiness to choose class and other identities over "sisterhood." Continuing discussion of the paradox observed by Roger Chickering, Reagin notes that her subjects, though women activists, were not feminists: while they themselves moved perhaps closest to men's politics in power, they spoke out actively against political rights for women.[40]

German work on German women, gender, activism, and politics continued its growth into the 1990s and beyond. Scholars offer increasingly subtle and detailed studies of women's activism and the themes of equality versus difference; the role of religion, class, generation, and other crosscutting cleavages in dividing and uniting women within the first-wave feminist movement; women's less attractive political histories; and other key issues discussed above.[41] "Masculinity" and "femininity," as symbol and as affect, received renewed consideration: new attention to "political symbolism" as well as to the experience of gender in a very broad sense offered important new examples of where gender and politics might go methodologically.[42] This work became increasingly professionalized, as greater numbers of both graduate students and more senior scholars took on such topics, in turn as women's and gender history became both more legitimate and more mainstream. But for all its continued achievements this work also reflected relatively few innovative topics, methodologies, or theoretical contributions, at least relative to its earlier achievements. Quite traditional biographical histories became more commonplace than ever, in and out of the academy.[43] The first-wave women's movement continued to capture the lion's share of attention, but not in proportion to how much more we learned about it—or about the present day. And this raises perhaps the most discouraging aspect of this wave of writings: there is a certain depoliticization of this work, and, in the name of professionalism, some lesser willingness to speak to what the earlier experiences teach us about advancing feminist interests in the present.

For many, the original motivations remain: Christl Wickert notes at the outset of her definitive 1991 study of Helene Stöcker her own longstanding fascination and even identification with Stöcker, based precisely on the latter's relevance to more recent feminist concerns.[44] But what do we understand at the end of Wickert's study that gets us someplace new and different? To be sure, this standard puts an enormous onus on this scholarship. But the model itself seems limiting somehow. Angelika Schaser's excellent dual biography of Helene Lange and Gertrud Bäumer offers a real sense of the complexities of these women, their multiple allegiances, and constant and changing challenges, dealing frankly with the less palatable aspects of Bäumer's life.[45] Yet, in the end, it remains open how much more this format offers us as a window to the "complete inner transformation of power relations" that her subjects sought. Anne Dünnebier's and Ursula Scheu's dual biography of Anita Augsburg and Lida Heymann is written with an inspiring buoyancy and liveliness.[46] Showcasing these figures in the same way we have done so often with prominent male political leaders certainly sends an important message by itself. But there may be other useful approaches as well—including in the interest of moving beyond "individualist" views of how politics happen. This was after all one of the original innovations of West German feminist scholars. Can't we learn still more about the majority of those involved in the movement at any given stage, and how their views and motivations differed from those of the few leaders we now know so much more about? Other new work in this decade, on difference versus equality, and on working within or outside of "men's" institutions, likewise seems to bring little fresh perspective in this sense. Politically, feminists seem in many respects to have moved beyond this historiographical dichotomy by this time.[47]

Some inspiration may come once more from models outside the academy—and outside the historical "guild." The years since 1989–90, as a consequence of new directions in the social sciences as well as of the *Wende*, saw a plethora of publications that may offer some inspiration for historians. (To be sure, historians, feminist and otherwise, have in turn clearly influenced these other fields.) We might look at recent work concerning the women's movement in the late years of the German Democratic Republic. Political scientist Ingrid Miethe's research reflects a "group biographical" approach in considering East German women peace activists and successor groupings.[48] The liveliness and sense of a range of real people, their visions, emotional life, and everyday restraints seems drawn from the spirit of some of the earlier historical studies. Miethe analyzes the precipitous drop in these women's political involvement after the *Wende*, as a function of how her subjects understood politics: what it meant to go from East German activist "Bärbel [Bohley]'s kitchen table" to working within channels of formal politics in the Federal Republic—and to encounter perceived obstacles among West German feminists. Further such work might compare East German men and women activists' experience. But this research has brought with it a sense of proximity to the everyday workings of politics that, among other virtues, makes it easier to draw conclusions about the present—though Miethe stops short of doing this herself.

To be sure, the conclusion of much of this recent work matches up with earlier summations: that effective activism requires some work outside existing formal political channels but also necessitates efforts to increase a presence within these structures as well. But most recently it is overwhelmingly political scientists and other social scientists who have discussed these modalities specifically with reference to the present and future. If amateur and professional researchers were willing to do this with the earliest and some of the least sophisticated historical work, appearing in *Courage, Emma, Frankfurter Frauenblatt* and elsewhere in the 1970s, historians should be willing to do this now, based on work that is that much richer and more complex. As earlier, nonprofessional historians and/or historians at very early stages of training offer useful lessons in this regard. Recent scholarship on radical right women in contemporary Germany offers one example.[49] One consistent conclusion among these works is that if there is no essential "women's politics," there is no more a single "neofascist woman": these studies are fresh and insightful in their findings on how very different women are drawn to radical right-wing groups. There are many biographies, but not just of leaders, and there is a great deal of attention to experience, motivations, and strategies, as in the best earlier historical work. A second virtue that unifies these recent authors is their willingness, as in earlier days, to connect their work to current political concerns. While one should not overstate the success of such scholars in transforming the outcome of women's political activities in Germany, such willingness to speculate and apply lessons of the (more or less distant) past offers at least the possibility to have a real impact.[50] While to be sure our work as historians need not always be tightly tied to specific present-day conclusions, a willingness to draw conclusions for political ends can be one way in which our work is and can be still more meaningful, connecting closely with the original mission of women's history, women's studies, and the second-wave women's movement more broadly.

Conclusion: Something Old, Something New

This essay has traced the recuperation of a women's and gendered history of politics as a corollary of second-wave feminism itself and broader subsequent gender politics. The mutual influences of these pursuits have been transformative and salutary. A certain stagnation in recent years relates in part to a sundering of these links. Though women's and gender topics have continued to flourish among American and British historians of Germany now into the new millennium, there continue to be relatively few studies on women's and gendered politics and activism, except in the broadest sense. Excellent work on nationalist women and on women and social reform continues to emerge.

Women and the peace movement throughout the nineteenth and twentieth centuries (also very much focused on key biographies) has developed as an important new topic, without doubt inspired at least in part by more recent history.[51] More developed studies of the second-wave women's movement have begun to emerge, as well as discussions of activism, gender, and ethnicity.[52] German doctoral students particularly have continued to contribute to discussions of women's power and politics, often explicitly in relation to their own situations.[53] But while major German-language journals, including older, more conservative ones (e.g., *Historische Zeitschrift*), now at least periodically include pieces on women, if not on gender, special "women's history" theme issues in mainstream journals when they come out tend to contain very little on women's activism (compare *Geschichte und Gesellschaft*; *Archiv für Sozialgeschichte* [1997] obversely does include several). This has been little better among Anglophone journals of German history.[54] The results of this absence can be to reinscribe women's role as those to whom things are done, good or bad (mostly bad), rather than as actors and agents themselves. Among periodicals devoted to women's and gender studies, including *l'Homme* and *Aspekt*, leading journal *Feministische Studien* is also important as an exception to this pattern.(This problem is somewhat less true for counterpart Anglophone journals, such as *Gender & History, Journal of Women's History, Signs, Women's History Review*, etc.) Obviously there are many important topics relating to women and gender that cannot be neglected; I am concerned only that politics and activism remains among them—and remains growing and vital.

As historians, we take great care to avoid drawing simple-minded lessons, particularly those that generalize about very specific circumstances. But women's and gender history should not lose one of its original motivations: not just to put women back into the past, but to put them into the present, to understand the past in order to somehow move beyond some of these recurring problems, rather than simply observing their rather remarkable consistency across time and vastly different regimes. Topically, historians might move in to look at more extensive arenas in which women have made their own worlds, within and yet opposing the "men's world." This includes continued work on the second-wave West German women's movement itself and its enormous implications—despite of course what remains the still relatively dismal representation of women within formal politics, all too grossly demonstrated in the process of unification and beyond. Secondly, women's and gender historians could draw more explicitly on—and in turn contribute to—work by, for example, new social movement theorists and other scholars of popular political movements, who, in the best of their scholarship, open up to us an understanding of the democratizing effects of such movements. And, once more, historians might risk drawing more explicit conclusions for the present. If what we have learned from this work covering 150 years of German history is that the problems and paradoxes remain astonishingly constant, then what is the next step? How can we avoid writing these same tales of complete or near failure for the next 150 years? What has worked and why, among big and little changes? How is "politics" connected on an everyday level in Germany and beyond? Do "women" in particular contexts and moments want equal standing with men in "their" world, do women want to build their own world, or do women seek to modify the existing; if the latter, do they do so as women, and, if so, what does this mean? How has gender functioned within the range of political movements—and how should it function? When have women been successful in moving into politics in power, and what has this success meant? What are the implications we want to assert with attention to women and gender? Who and what gets left in and left out? I hope these may be some suggestions to help us move us beyond, in a broad sense, the current *"Atempause."*

Notes

1. Compare Britain's *History Workshop*, begun in London in the mid 1970s, and the Berlin *Geschichtswerkstatt*, among the first in West Germany, founded soon afterward. On the professionalization of historiography, and the simultaneous pushing out of women, see Bonnie Smith, *The Gender of History: Men, Women, and Historical Practice* (Cambridge, Mass., 1998).

2. I review here primarily American and West German, with more limited consideration of British and other Anglophone work, and without attention to East German and other Germanophone work. Compare among the relatively few relevant works from Canada Rosemarie Schade's useful studies. Space constraints dictate that works cited are exemplary rather than exhaustive.

3. Jacqueline Strain, "Feminism and Political Radicalism in the German Social Democratic Movement, 1890–1914," Ph.D. diss., University of California, Berkeley, 1964.

4. Less professionally trained American historians would likely have lacked the skills to pursue such topics. West German feminists regularly studied their American counterparts, partly because they had the language abilities to do so. Compare Carla MacDougall, "Councils of Women: Transnationality and the Shaping of Feminist Identity in West Germany 1967–1975," unpublished manuscript.

5. Jean H. Quataert, *Reluctant Feminists: Socialist Women in Imperial Germany, 1885–1917* (Princeton, 1979) (based on a 1974 UCLA dissertation); Marion A. Kaplan, *The Jewish Feminist Movement in Germany: The Campaigns of the Jüdischer Frauenbund, 1904–1938* (Westport, Conn., 1979) (from a 1977 Columbia University dissertation; published in German in 1981); Compare Karen Honeycutt, "Clara Zetkin: A Left-Wing Socialist and Feminist in Wilhelmian Germany," Ph.D. diss., Columbia University, 1975; and Amy K. Hackett,

"The Politics of Feminism in Wilhelmine Germany, 1890–1918," Ph.D. diss., Columbia University, 1976. These were never published, though circulated widely. Claudia Koonz's 1969 dissertation on women's political accommodation with the Third Reich was published in 1984; see below.

6. Richard Evans, *The Feminist Movement in Germany, 1894–1933* (London, 1976); idem, "German Women and the Triumph of Hitler," *Journal of Modern History* 48, 1 (March 1976), 123–175.

7. Among scholarly contributions, compare Richard Evans, "Feminismus als Forschungskonzept: Anmerkungen für die Praxis," in *Frauen in der Geschichte VI*, ed. Ruth-Ellen B. Joeres and Annette Kuhn (Düsseldorf, 1985); and Ruth-Ellen B. Joeres, "'Das Mädchen macht eine ganz neue Gattung von Charakter aus!' Ja, aber ist sie deshalb eine Feministin? Beobachtungen zu Sophie von la Roches 'Geschichte des Fräuleins von Sternheim,'" in Joeres and Kuhn, *Frauen in der Geschichte VI*; also, Herrad-Ulrike Schenk, *Die feministische Herausforderung: 150 Jahre Frauenbewegung in Deutschland* (Munich, 1980).

8. Kaplan, *The Jewish Feminist Movement.*

9. Evans, *The Feminists: Women's Emancipation Movements in Europe, America, and Autralasia, 1840–1920* (London, 1977); idem, *Comrades and Sisters: Feminism, Socialism and Pacifism in Europe, 1870–1945* (London, 1987); and Sabine Hering and Cornelia Wenzel, eds., *Frauen riefen, aber Man hörte Sie nicht: die Rolle der deutschen Frauen in der internationalen Frauenfriedensbewegung zwischen 1892 und 1933* (Kassel, 1986); also, Leila Rupp, *Worlds of Women: The Making of an International Women's Movement* (Princeton, 1997); Bonnie Anderson, *Joyous Greetings: The First International Women's Movement, 1830–1860* (Oxford, 2000); and Karen M. Offen, *European Feminisms 1700–1950: A Political History* (Stanford, 2000).

10. Karin Hausen, *Deutsche Kolonialherrschaft in Afrika: Wirtschaftsinteressen und Kolonialverwaltung in Kamerun vor 1914* (Freiburg, 1970); Gisela Bock, *Thomas Campanella: Politische Intention und philosophische Spekulation* (Tübingen, 1974). Both women were active in the women's movement. Compare Bock's "Frauenbewegung und Frauenuniversität: Die politische Bedeutung der Sommeruniversität," in *Frauen und Wissenschaft: Beiträge zur Berliner Sommeruniversität für Frauen*, ed. Gruppe Berliner Dozentinnen (Berlin, 1976), 15–22; also Eleanor Flexner, *Hundert Jahre Kampf: Die Geschichte der Frauenrechtsbewegung in den Vereinigten Staaten*, trans. Gisela Bock (Frankfurt/M., 1978).

11. Petra Schneider, *Weg mit dem §218! Die Massenbewegung gegen das Abtreibungsverbot in der Weimarer Republik* (Berlin, 1975). Like many of these works, this study was published by an "alternative" publisher.

12. Herrad Schenk, *Die feministische Herausforderung: 150 Jahre Frauenbewegung in Deutschland* (Munich, 1980); Renate Wiggershaus, *Geschichte der Frauen und der Frauenbewegung in der Bundesrepublik und in der Deutschen Demokratischen Republik nach 1945* (Wuppertal, 1979). See also Cordula Koepcke, *Frauenbewegung zwischen den Jahre 1800–2000* (Heroldsberg bei Nürnberg, 1979); Lottemi Doormann, ed., *Keiner schiebt uns weg: Zwischenbalanz der Frauenbewegung in der Bundesrepublik* (Weinheim, 1979).

13. Ute Gerhard, *Verhätnisse und Verhinderungen: Frauenarbeit, Familie und Recht der Frauen im 19. Jahrhundert* (Frankfurt/M., 1978) (her 1977 dissertation). Among Gerhard's many other works: *Unerhört: Die Geschichte der deutschen Frauenbewegung* (Reinbek, 1992); and *Atempause: Feminismus als demokratisches Projekt* (Frankfurt/M., 1999). Also, Irene Stoehr, *Emanzipation zum Staat? Der Allgemeine Deutsche Frauenverein-Deutscher Staatsbürgerinnenverband, 1893–1933* (Pfaffenweiler, 1990); Theresa Wobbe, *Gleichheit und Differenz: politische Strategien von Frauenrechtlerinnen um die Jahrhundertwende* (Frankfurt/M., 1989); Ulla Wischermann, *Frauenfrage und Presse: Frauenarbeit und Frauenbewegung in der illustrierten Presse* (Munich, 1983); and Elisabeth Meyer-Renschhausen, *Weibliche Kultur und soziale Arbeit: Eine Geschichte der Frauenbewegung am Beispiel Bremens 1810–1927* (Cologne, 1989).

14. Compare as a small sample exhibitions such as "'Andre Gehäuse': Frauen formen ihre Stadt," sponored by local women doing women's history, which toured West Germany and West Berlin in the late 1970s; films such as Helke Sander's *Der Subjektive Faktor* and *Redupers*; and such newspaper contributions as "Vaterlandsverteigigung—Pazifismus—Klassenkampf: Positionen in der Frauenbewegung zum 1. Weltkrieg," *Frauen auf die Barrikaden* 4 (1983), 1–9; and Kaethe Schumacher, "So kämpfen die Suffragetten!" *Emma* (September 1977), 18–25; as well as publication of historical documents.

15. Compare Gundula Bölke, *Die Wandlung der Frauenemanzipationsbewegung von Marx bis zur Rätebewegung* (Hamburg, 1975).

16. Gisela Losseff-Tillmanns, *Frauenemanzipation und Gewerkschaften* (Wuppertal, 1978); Mary Nolan, "Proletarischer Anti-Feminismus," in Gruppe Berliner Dozentinnen, *Frauen und Wissenschaft*, 356–377; Annemarie Tröger, "Dolchstoßlegende der Linken," in Dozentinnen, *Frauen und Wissenschaft*, 324–355; Silvia Kontos, *Die Partei kämpft wie ein Mann: Frauenpolitik der KPD in der Weimarer Republik* (Frankfurt/M., 1979).

17. Renate Pore, *A Conflict of Interest: Women in German Social Democracy, 1919–1933* (Westport, Conn., 1981).

18. Renate Bridenthal and Claudia Koonz, "Kinder, Küche, Kirche: Weimar Women in Politics and Work," in *When Biology Became Destiny: Women in Weimar and Nazi Germany*, ed. Renate Bridenthal et al. (New York, 1984), 33–65.

19. Compare Joan Scott, "Experience," in *Feminists Theorize the Political*, ed. Judith Butler and Joan Scott (New York, 1992), 22–38.

20. Roger Chickering, "'Casting Their Gaze More Broadly': Women's Patriotic Activism in Imperial Germany," *Past and Present* 118 (1988), 156–185.

21. Jill Stephenson, *Women in Nazi Society* (New York, 1975); idem, *The Nazi Organisation of Women* (London, 1981).

22. Renate Wiggershaus, *Frauen unterm Nationalsozialismus* (Wuppertal, 1984); Claudia Koonz, *Mothers in the Fatherland: Women, Family Life, and Nazi Ideology, 1919–1945* (New York, 1986). Also, Frigga Haug, ed., "Frauen—Opfer oder Täter? Diskussion," *Das Argument-Studienheft* 46 (1981); and Dorothee Klinksiek, *Die Frau im NS-Staat* (Stuttgart, 1982).

23. Compare on this "women historians' quarrel" (*Historikerinnenstreit*) Dagmar Reese, "Homo homini lupus-Frauen als Täterinnen," *International Wissenschaftliche Korrespondenz zur Geschichte der deutschen Arbeiterbewegung* 27 (1991): 25–34; Adelheid von Saldern, "Opfer oder (Mit-)täterinnen?: Kontroversen über die Rolle der Frau im NA-Staat," *Sozialwissenschaftliche Informationen* 20 (1991), 97–103; Atina Grossmann, "Feminist Debates about Women and National Socialism," *Gender & History* 3, no. 3 (Autumn 1991): 350–358.

24. Compare Heinz Niggemann, *Emanzipation zwischen Sozialismus und Feminismus: Die sozialdemokratsiche Frauenbewegung im Kaiserreich* (Wuppertal, 1981); Florence Hervé, ed., *Geschichte der deutschen Frauenbewegung* (Cologne, 1982); Sabine Richebächer, *Uns fehlt nur eine Kleinigkeit: Deutsche proletarische Frauenbewegung 1890–1914* (Frankfurt/M., 1982); Rosemarie Nave-Herz, *Die Geschichte der Frauenbewegung in Deutschland* (Hannover, 1982); Ingeborg Drewitz, ed., *Die Deutsche Frauenbewegung: Die soziale Rolle der Frau im 19. Jahrhundert und die Emanzipationsbewegung in Deutschland* (Bonn, 1983); Ilse Reicke, *Die großen Frauen der Weimarer Republik: Erlebnisse im "Berliner Frühling"* (Freiburg, 1984); Christl Wickert, *Unsere Erwählten: Sozialdemokratische Frauen im Deutschen Reichstag und im Preußischen Landtag 1919 bis 1933* (Göttingen, 1986); Doris Kaufmann, *Frauen zwischen Aufbruch und Reaktion: protestantische Frauenbewegung in der ersten Hälfte des 20. Jahrhunderts* (Munich, 1988); and exceptionally Petra Kellermann-Haaf, *Frau und Politik im Mittelalter: Untersuchungen zur politischen Rolle der Frau in den höfischen Romanen des 12., 13. und 14. Jahrhunderts* (Göppingen, 1986).

25. Barbara Greven-Achoff, *Die bürgerliche Frauenbewegung in Deutschland, 1894–1933* (Göttingen, 1981); Wobbe, *Gleichheit und Differenz*; Bärbel Clemens, *Menschenrechte haben kein*

Geschlecht: Zum Politikverständnis der bürgerlichen Frauenbewegung (Pfaffenweiler, 1988). Compare American perspectives that challenged the distinctions: Joan Scott, "Deconstructing Equality-Versus-Difference: Or, the Uses of Post-structuralist Theory for Feminism," *Feminist Studies* 14 (1988): 33–50; Karen Offen, "Defining Feminism: A Comparative Historical Approach," *Signs* 14 (1988), 119–157.

26. Christoph Sachße, *Mütterlichkeit als Beruf: Sozialarbeit, Sozialreform und Frauenbewegung, 1871–1929* (Frankfurt/M., 1986); Irene Stoehr, "'Organisierte Mütterlichkeit': Zur Politik der deutschen Frauenbewegung um 1900," in *Frauen suchen Ihre Geschichte*, ed. Karin Hausen (Munich, 1983), 221–249; Dietlinde Peters, *Mütterlichkeit im Kaiserreich: Die bürgerliche Frauenbewegung und der soziale Beruf der Frau* (Bielefeld, 1984).

27. Herrad-Ulrike Bussemer, *Frauenemanzipation und Bildungsbürgertum: Sozialgeschichte der Frauenbewegung in der Reichsgründungzeit* (Weinheim, 1985).

28. Carola Lipp, "Frauen und Öffentlichkeit: Möglichkeiten und Grenzen politischer Partizipation im Vormärz und in der Revolution," in *Schimpfende Weiber und patriotische Jungfrauen im Vormärz und in der Revolution 1848/49*, ed. Carola Lipp (Elster, 1986), 270–307.

29. Anna A. Bergmann, "Frauen, Männer, Sexualität und Geburtenkontrolle: Zur 'Gebärstreikdebatte' der SPD 1913," in Hausen, *Frauen Suchen*, 83–111. Compare also Atina Grossmann's piece in this volume.

30. Ute Frevert, *Frauen-Geschichte zwischen bürgerlicher Verbesserung und neuer Weiblichkeit* (Frankfurt/M., 1986).

31. Karen Hagemann, *Frauenalltag und Männerpolitik: Alltagsleben und gesellschaftliches Handeln von Arbeiterfrauen in der Weimarer Republik* (Bonn, 1990).

32. See also Karen Hagemann, "Men's Demonstrations and Women's Protest: Gender in Collective Action in the Urban Working-Class Milieu During the Weimar Republic," in *Gender and History* 5, no. 1 (1993): 101–119.

33. Compare Lipp, *Schimpfende Weiber*; Christiane Eifert and Susanne Rouette, eds., *Unter allen Umständen: Frauengeschichte(n) in Berlin* (Berlin, 1986); and, among nonhistorians, Jutta Dalhoff et al., eds., *Frauenmacht in der Geschichte* (Düsseldorf, 1986).

34. This was published ultimately as Jürgen Reulecke, *"Ich möchte einer werden so wie die": Männerbünde im 20. Jahrhundert* (Frankfurt/M., 2001). Also, Hagemann, *Frauenalltag*, as well as subsequent work; Ute Frevert, *"Mann und Weib und Weib und Mann": Geschlechter-Differenzen in der Moderne* (Munich, 1986); Peter Assion, ed., *Tranformationen der Arbeiterkultur* (Marburg, 1986).

35. Konto, *Die Partei kämpft wie ein Mann*.

36. Dagmar Herzog, *Intimacy and Exclusion: Religious Politics in Pre-revolutionary Baden* (Princeton, 1996). Clearly discussion of multiple identities marked this literature from the outset. Compare Ann T. Allen in this volume.

37. Ann Taylor Allen, *Feminism and Motherhood in Germany, 1800–1914*, (New Brunswick, 1991); her forthcoming comparative volume continues to de-emphasize German "peculiarities." Compare Clemens, *Menschenrechte*; Christiane Eifert, *Frauenpolitik und Wohlfahrtpflege: Zur Geschichte der sozialdemokratischen Arbeiterwohlfahrt* (Frankfurt/M., 1993); Iris Schröder, *Arbeiten für eine bessere Welt: Frauenbewegung und Sozialreform, 1890–1914* (Frankfurt/M., 2001); Young-Sun Hong, *Welfare, Modernity, and the Weimar State* (Princeton, 1998); Kevin Repp, *Reformers, Critics, and the Paths of German Modernity: Anti-politics and the Search for Alternatives, 1890–1914* (Cambridge, Mass., 2001); Andrew Lees, *Cities, Sin, and Social Reform in Imperial Germany* (Ann Arbor, 2002); also Elizabeth Harvey, "The Failure of Feminism? Young Women and the Bourgeois Feminist Movement in Weimar Germany 1918–1933," *Central European History* (1995): 1–28.

38. Compare Anna Bergmann, *Die verhütete Sexualität: Die Anfänge der modernen Geburtenkontrolle* (Hamburg, 1992); Cornelie Usborne, *The Politics of the Body in Weimar Germany:*

Women's Reproductive Rights and Duties (Ann Arbor, 1992); Atina Grossmann, *Reforming Sex: The German Movement for Birth Control and Abortion Reform, 1920–1950* (New York, 1995); Anette Herlitzius, *Frauenbefreiung und Rassenideologie: Rassenhygiene und Eugenik im politischen Programm der "radikalen Frauenbewegung" (1900–1933)* (Wiesbaden, 1995).

39. See for example Julia Sneeringer, *Winning Women's Votes: Propaganda and Politics in Weimar Germany* (Chapel Hill, 2002); Belinda Davis, *Home Fires Burning: Food, Politics, and Everyday Life in World War I Berlin* (Chapel Hill, 2000).

40. Nancy Reagin, *A German Women's Movement: Class and Gender in Hanover, 1880–1933* (Chapel Hill, 1995); Jean Quataert, *Staging Philanthropy: Patriotic Women and the National Imagination in Dynastic Germany, 1813–1916* (Ann Arbor, 2001); Raffael Scheck, *Mothers of the Nation: Right-Wing Women in Weimar Germany* (Oxford, 2004); also Ute Frevert, "Nation, Krieg und Geschlecht im 19. Jahrhundert," in *Nation und Gesellschaft in Deutschland: Historische Essays,* ed. Manfred Hettling and Paul Nolte (Munich, 1996), 151–170; and Ute Planert, ed., *Nation, Politik und Geschlecht: Frauenbewegung und Nationalismus in der Moderne* (Frankfurt/M., 2000).

41. As a broad sampling, Ursula Baumann, *Protestantismus und Frauenemanzipation in Deutschland, 1850 bis 1920* (Frankfurt/M., 1992); Christiane Berneike, *Die Frauenfrage ist Rechtsfrage: Die Juristinnen der deutschen Frauenbewegung und das Bürgerliche Gesetzbuch* (Baden-Baden, 1995); Irmgard Maya Fassmann, *Jüdinnen in der deutschen Frauenbewegung, 1865–1919* (Hildesheim, 1996); Gerhard, *Unerhört;* Sabine Hering, *Und das war erst der Anfang: Geschichte und Geschichten bewegter Frauen* (Zurich, 1994); Christl Wickert, ed., *Frauen gegen Diktatur: Widerstand und Verfolgung im nationalsozialistischen Deutschland* (Berlin, 1995); Gisela Breuer, *Frauenbewegung im Katholizismus: der Katholische Frauenbund 1903–1918* (Frankfurt/M., 1998); Dirk Reder, *Frauenbewegung und Nation: Patriotische Frauenvereine im frühen 19. Jahrhundert (1813–1830)* (Cologne, 1998).

42. Compare Thomas Kühne, ed., *Männergeschichte—Geschlechtergeschichte: Männlichkeit im Wandel der Moderne* (Frankfurt/M., 1996); Stefan Dudink et al., eds., *Masculinities in Politics and War: Gendering Modern History* (Manchester, 2004); Christiane Eifert et al., eds., *Was sind Frauen? Was sind Männer? Geschlechterkonstruktionen im historischen Wandel* (Frankfurt/M., 1996); Ute Planert, *Antifeminismus im Kaiserreich: Diskurs, soziale Formation und politische Mentalität* (Göttingen, 1998); also Thomas Lindenberger, *Straßenpolitik. Zur Sozialgeschichte der öffentlichen Ordnung in Berlin 1900 bis 1914* (Bonn, 1995); among usually Anglophone authors: Eve Rosenhaft, "Links gleich rechts?: Militante Straßengewalt um 1930," in *Physische Gewalt: Studien zur Geschichte der Neuzeit,* ed. Thomas Lindenberger and Alf Lüdtke (Frankfurt/M., 1995), 238–275; Uta Poiger, *Jazz, Rock and Rebels* (Berkeley, 2000); Sneeringer, *Winning Women's Votes.* As an overview, Thomas Kühne, "Staatspolitik, Frauenpolitik, Männerpolitik: Politikgeschichte als Geschlechtergeschichte," in *Geschlechtergeschichte und Allgemeine Geschichte. Herausforderungen und Perspektiven,* ed. Hans Medick and Anne-Charlotte Trepp (Göttingen, 1998).

43. Compare Ingaburgh Klatt, *"Wir wollen lieber fliegen als kriechen": historische Frauenportraits* (Lübeck, 1997); Barbara Böttger, *Das Recht auf Gleichheit und Differenz: Elisabeth Selbert und der Kampf der Frauen um Artikel 2.3 des Grundgesetzes* (Münster, 1990); Angelika Epple, *Henriette Fürth und die Frauenbewegung im deutschen Kaiserreich: Eine Sozialbiographie* (Pfaffenweiler, 1996); Elke Schuller, *Wer stimmt bestimmt? Elisabeth Selbert und die Frauenpolitik der Nachkriegszeit* (Wiesbaden, 199); Gabriele Hoffmann, *Frauen machen Geschichte: berühmte Frauen—von Kaiserin Theophanu bis Rosa Luxemburg* (Weyarn, 1999); Baschka Mika, *Alice Schwarzer: Eine kritische Biographie* (Reinbek, 1998); Schöck-Quinteros "Else Lüders (1872–1948)," in 1999. *Zeitschrirt für die Sozialgeschichte des 20. und 21. Jahrhunderts* 12, 1 (1997): 49–67; Marianne Brentzel, *Anna O., Bertha Pappenheim: Biographie* (Göttingen, 2002); Christiane Henke, *Anita Augspurg* (Reinbek, 2000).

44. Christl Wickert, *Helene Stöcker, 1869–1943: Frauenrechtlerin, Sexualreformerin und Pazifistin* (Bonn, 1991). It should be noted that Wickert produced a substantial range of publications about this period.

45. Angelika Schaser, *Helene Lange und Gertrud Bäumer: Eine politische Lebensgemeinschaft* (Cologne, 2000).

46. Anne Dünnebier and Ursula Scheu, *Die Rebellion ist eine Frau: Anita Augspurg and Lida G. Heymann: das schillerndste Paar der Frauenbewegung* (Kreuzlingen, 2002).

47. Compare Ute Gerhard, "Westdeutsche Frauenbewegung: Zwischen Autonomie und dem Recht auf Gleichheit," *Feministische Studien* 2 (1992): 35–55.

48. Ingrid Miethe, *Frauen in der DDR-Opposition: Lebens- und kollektivgeschichtliche Verläufe in einer Frauenfriedensgruppe* (Opladen, 1999). See also Myra Marx Ferree, "'The Time of Chaos Was the Best': Feminist Mobilization and Demobilization in East Germany," *Gender and Society* 6, no. 8 (1994): 597–623; Dorothy Rosenberg, "Women's Issues, Women's Politics, and Women's Studies in the Former German Democratic Republic," *Radical History Review* 54 (1992): 110–126; Lynn Kamenitsa, "East German Feminists in the New German Democracy: Opportunities, Obstacles, and Adaptation," *Women in Politics* 17, no. 3 (1997): 41–68; Andrea Wuerth, "National Politics/Local Identities: Abortion Rights Activists in Post-wall Berlin," *Feminist Studies* 25, no. 3 (1999): 601–631; also Donna Harsch, "Approach/Avoidance: Communists and Women in East Germany, 1945–9," *Social History* 25, no. 2 (2000): 156–182. Compare Hagemann, *Frauenalltag* as a seminal precedent.

49. See Fantifa Marburg, ed., *Kameradinnen: Frauen stricken am Braunen Netz* (Münster, 2002); Petra Wlecklik, *Frauen und Rechtsextremismus* (Göttingen, 2002); Christiane Tillner, ed., *Frauen: Rechtsextremismus, Rassismus, Gewalt. Feministische Beiträge* (Münster, 2002); also the substantial new literature on ethnicity, gender, and activism in postwar West Germany/Germany.

50. Compare Ute Gerhard, *Atempause*.

51. See for example the issue of the *Journal of Women's History* devoted to German women leaders in the historic peace movement, including Jennifer Davy's defense of the biographical approach: Jennifer Davy, "Pacifist Thought and Gender Ideology in the Political Biographies of Women Peace Activists in Germany, 1899–1970," *Journal of Women's History*, 13, no. 3 (2001): 34–46. Compare Belinda Davis, "'Women's Strength against Their Crazy Male Power?' Gendered Language in the West German Peace Movement of the 1980s," in *Frieden-Gewalt-Geschlecht: Friedens- und Konfliktforschung als Geschlechtforschung*, ed. Jennifer A. Davy et al. (Essen, 2005), 224–265. Peace history is an area in which for the first time women's leadership role has been increasingly acknowledged in the mainstream.

52. Compare Kristina Schulz, *Der lange Atem der Provokation: Die Frauenbewegung in der Bundesrepublik und in Frankreich* (Frankfurt/M., 2002); Macdougall, "Councils of Women"; see also Dagmar Herzog, *Sex after Fascism: Memory and Morality in Twentieth-Century Germany* (Princeton, 2005). Memoirs, even edited group memoirs, are not historiography, of course, but are also useful: see Ute Kätzel, *Die 68erinnen* (Berlin, 2002) and Ursula G. T. Müller, *Die Wahrheit über die lila Latzhosen* (Frankfurt, 2004). My own work in progress treats gender as one key element in understanding the range of extraparliamentary politics in West Germany, 1962–1983.

53. Compare Gabriele Boukrif et al., eds., *Geschlechtergeschichte des Politischen: Entwürfen von Geschlecht und Gemeinschaft im 19. und 20. Jahrhundert* (Münster, 2002); Ortrun Niethammer, ed., *Frauen und Nationalsozialismus: Historische kulturgeschichtliche Positionen* (Osnabrück, 1996); also Barbara Holland-Cunz, ed., *Die Alte Neue Frauenfrage* (Frankfurt/M., 2003).

54. Compare for example *German Politics and Society* special issue on women and politics in 1991–1992, and fairly regularly throughout its issues.

6

THE ORDER OF TERMS

Class, Citizenship, and Welfare State in German Gender History

Kathleen Canning

The keywords of class, citizenship, and welfare state signify three distinct but contingent sociopolitical categories in modern German history. Certain assumptions seem to underpin the very order of these terms—class, citizenship, welfare state—which seem to flow so easily into one another (and which formed the original title of the conference session for which I wrote this paper). Does this order of terms imply a hierarchy or an implicit chronology, whereby class figures as the definitive concept—the genuine megaconcept of the three perhaps—in the history of Germany and Europe during the nineteenth and twentieth centuries? Other questions, more specific to gender history, also frame my query: for example, how have definitions of class *changed* in the wake of its confrontation with the differences of gender? Citizenship, which has yet to gain the status of a keyword in German history, has also been redefined and expanded through the turn(s) to culture, language, and gender. To what extent have these critiques proceeded in similar or different terms? Has historical research on gender and the welfare state propelled new and more explicitly gendered conceptions of citizenship? How are these three concepts related or imbricated in one another in German history and more specifically in German gender history? Finally, has feminist historical study of these terms fostered a process of "mainstreaming" German gender history? Is this a desirable or attainable goal for a historical approach that has distinguished itself from the outset by a critical, even subversive impulse?

Assumptions about a temporal relationship among and between these terms would also seem to underlie their ordering. In mainstream German histories class seems situated in a historical time period that predates or inflects that of citizenship. Class figures as a far more definitive term for the study of the period from 1848 to 1933, in which the emergence of a German labor movement and socialism were shaped by languages of class. It is thus plausible to view class as informing the research domain of social history, while citizenship, until the 1990s, was more likely to be theorized by sociologists and political scientists than studied empirically by historians.[1] Citizenship served as a kind of partner concept to class in studies of the French Revolution, British Chartism, and suffrage reform campaigns, that is, in studies in which class consciousness was expressed in the demands for new or expanded citizenship rights. Yet citizenship, in the sense of participatory rights and claims rather than mere national belonging, has been far less tangible than class in the history of Imperial Germany, with the important exception of studies of voting or electoral behavior as one aspect of this participation. Citizenship is also curiously absent in the abundant historiography on the democratic experiment of Weimar.[2] If class has thus far dominated the history of Germany's long nineteenth century, citizenship appears to serve as a crucial historical category for the history of the Federal Republic since 1949, when democracy was sustained over a longer historical time span.

Also noteworthy is citizenship's close affinity with the welfare state, especially in German history. Did the German welfare state, perhaps from its earliest Bismarckian conception, serve as a site at which the hopes of class were refashioned into the rights of citizenship, whether in their Social Democratic or Social Catholic guise? Did the very efficacy of the welfare system depend upon its ability to produce citizenship rights as it gained the capacity to mediate or displace "class" struggle? Finally, does the welfare state constitute the very site at which citizenship appears to transcend or displace class, particularly for the period after the Second World War when consumption and social welfare combined to create the veneer of a *nivellierte Gesellschaft* (an equalized society), in which social equalities were no longer easily signified or defined?

In addition to this implicit temporal positioning, each of these terms carries a certain amount of structuralist baggage, in the sense of invoking processes of structural transformation—of economies (the transition from agrarian to industrial production, for example) and geographies (urbanization), of populations (migrations), social relations (class formation), bureaucratization, and modernization of the state (social welfare, social citizenship). So class and citizenship have mainly been understood as embedded in economic or juridical structures and have only relatively recently been examined as cultural constructs. In this article I will explore the place of these terms in epistemological debates of the last decades, comparing how each was recast and probing their significance in the development of German and European gender history. The fact that so many studies in German gender history contend with one or more of these keywords—on both sides of the Atlantic divide—prompts the question as to whether these concepts can viably serve as stepping stones to the "mainstreaming" of gender history, a fantasy of legitimation that seems particularly pronounced in the field of German history.

Engendering Class

It is no exaggeration to assert that class has been the definitive term in several waves of historical scholarship, from the new social history of the 1960s to the "linguistic turn" of the late 1980s and early 1990s. The concept of class forms an axis in histories of "the social," of labor, women, and gender, around which many different epistemological debates have turned. Also indisputable is the fact that class, since the linguistic turn, no longer serves as a unitary category designating a lived social experience, definitive social identity or line of social demarcation. As Geoff Eley and Keith Nield argued some years ago in their article, "Farewell to the Working Class?" this transformation does not mark the "death of class," rather the passing of one particular meaning of class, "one particular *type* of class society."[3] Yet class remains present, even ubiquitous, in our historical vocabulary, as a looser descriptive term of social belonging (working class, middle class). Class, according to Joan Scott, has become "one way of naming, understanding, and organizing certain forms of social inequality,"[4] that coincides or jostles against race, gender, nationality, ethnicity, and sexuality, depending upon the object of study. Our reluctance to dismiss class altogether may have more to do more with politics than with history, for even if class is no longer taken as a social fact, global capitalism continues to thrive and reproduce inequalities in new forms for which class remains an important shorthand.[5] Furthermore, there is nothing universal about class—either its salience, its crisis, or its recasting. Because the political and historical resonances of class clearly vary across regional, national and colonial spaces, this exploration is meant to apply to the field of European, particularly German history, where class enjoyed an incomparable dominance, at least until the (North American) linguistic or (German) culturalist turn. Let us backtrack to see how gender history helped chart the path to this present moment.

For most of the 1960s and 1970s, even into the 1980s, histories of class were informed by disparate methodologies. It is fair to generalize that British and

American histories of class, inspired by E. P. Thompson's definitive *The Making of the English Working Class* (1963), tended to be more culturalist than structuralist, in the sense of pursuing "the authentic voices and authentic experiences of working people" that underlay the metahistories of class formations and class conflicts.[6] In Germany, by contrast, studies of labor, industrialization, urbanization, and social movements drove the rise of social-science history, the hallmark of which was the analysis of structures and processes of social transformation. The "authentic experiences" and everyday lives of German workers came to figure in German labor history mainly as an oppositional narrative of historians of everyday life (*Alltagshistoriker*), whose anthropologically informed critiques and conceptual innovations were widely heralded in the English-speaking academy, but which were subjected to scathing criticism and subsequent marginalization by mainstream German historians.[7]

It is safe to say that the early labor history, whether structuralist or culturalist, seldom included women or tended to rely upon gendered prisms and paradigms that "highlighted their differences from men."[8] Yet I would contend that the attention to workers' cultures and collective actions, sociability and leisure, everyday negotiations and self-perceptions in English language labor history of the 1960s and 1970s left more openings for a history of women than did the more structurally oriented German labor histories. Proletarianization, for one, stood for a quintessentially male experience of industrialization, while work had "sexual" meanings and characteristics only for women. The separation of home and work, in turn, could figure as a dramatic rupture only because of presumptions about women's natural location in the home. One outcome of the history of women's work in the 1970s and early 1980s was the powerful evidence it delivered for "the centrality of sex as well as class to women workers' experiences" of workplace, neighborhood, and home.[9] Feminist history managed to force labor history to concede a place to sex next to class, but for long years the recognition of the importance of sex did not fundamentally *change* the meanings of class. Awkward schemata arose by which historians and theorists worked to fit women into existing models of class, proposed that women formed a separate or parallel class of their own, or concluded that sex presented an inherent obstacle to the formation of cohesive and conscious classes. Joan Kelly's formulation of a "doubled vision of society" in the late 1970s pointed the way toward a resolution of this theoretical impasse, postulating that sex and class were inextricably linked in shaping social identities of men and women and making clear that models, master narratives, and chronologies would require disruption and redefinition in order to account for this dynamic.[10]

Kelly's postulation of a doubled vision of society also marks the point at which the concept of gender came into currency in English-language historiography. Feminist scholarship of the next decade began to devote more attention to the ideologies, norms, and symbolic systems that shaped identities, social institutions, and relations between the sexes. By 1983, with the publication of the pioneering collection of essays, *Sex and Class in Women's History*, the category of "gender" had come to denote the systematic ways in which sex differences cut through society and culture and conferred inequality upon women.[11] First sex, then gender, began to destabilize key terms like class, as some Anglo-Saxon feminists even sought to emancipate feminist history from class as "privileged signifier of social relations and their political representations."[12]

Class was thus at the heart of the wider epistemological crisis that began during the mid to late 1980s in the social sciences, which over the next decade saw the gradual displacement of notions of socioeconomic causality as scholarly interest was reoriented toward representations, languages, and ideologies.[13] Unitary subjects and social identities, including class, were undermined not only by the linguistic turn, but also, perhaps more powerfully, by the interventions of scholars of race and empire whose work made clear the inflection of class through race. At the same time real-life transformations of technologies, relations and locations of production, the feminization and visible racialization of European labor markets, and the collapse of socialist governments and ideologies in the late 1980s seemed to eclipse the vocabulary of class, to cut it loose from its "materialist common sense," as William H. Sewell, Jr. noted in a 1993 essay.[14] The combined effect of these transformations in social and scholarly arenas was the erosion of a catalog of oppositional categories, from structure-agency, material-cultural, production-reproduction, and public-private, which had formed the conceptual foundation of labor history. The degree to which labor and class had a crucial place in the linguistic turn, and the extent to which feminist scholarship prepared the way for the fundamental rethinking of these keywords, has been overlooked in many of the retrospectives on this methodological turning point.[15]

German labor history, by contrast, remained quite impervious to this epistemological crisis surrounding labor and class, as orderly models of class formation, broken into stages and levels, remained largely intact. The fact that women and gender could not be made to fit these models easily led to the conclusion that gender belonged to a category of "non-class" distinctions, which included race, ethnicity, nationality, and religion.[16] The impetus to rethink key categories such as class was perhaps weaker in Germany because labor history had already been declared practically passé by the early 1990s, at least for the periods of the Kaiserreich, Weimar, and Nazi Germany.[17] Indeed, the turn from labor to other social formations, such as the *Bürgertum*, coincided, perhaps not by chance, with an unusually vital moment in the production of feminist labor history in Germany.[18] The practitioners of German labor history had already closed up shop, so to speak, and had already penned their synthetic volumes showcasing the field's accomplishments, before a critical mass of scholarship on women/gender and labor could be incorporated or "mainstreamed," before its critical concepts could be interrogated or redefined.[19] Also noteworthy is the crucial role of crisis in prompting the renovation of concepts and methodologies. On a comparative note, this German turn away from labor toward other historical topics and social strata, such as the *Bürgertum*, and the subsequent embrace of cultural history took place in the absence of the kind of epistemological crisis that shook the foundations of social history in North America.

By the early 1990s, then, labor history was widely viewed as in decline and the keyword of class had been significantly dethroned, even if for different reasons, on either side of the Atlantic divide. A positive rendering of this development portrayed it as a benign shift to new historical terrain: histories of work and class had enjoyed a long and hallowed career in the annals of social history but had fulfilled their historical and political mission. A more negative view emphasized the onslaught of culture, language, discourse, or deconstruction, which figured as destructive forces aimed at the bedrock of real, lived histories of workers and class formations. Regardless of which narrative was favored, in North America graduate seminars on work, where the epistemological debates of this decade had been most lively, emptied in the 1990s, as the new and exciting thematics of race, colonialism and empire, popular culture and consumption, and bodies and sexualities appeared to displace these more worn histories.

Yet the narratives of labor history's decline overlooked the genuine reinvigoration of this field that took place during the early to mid 1990s as a generation of scholars who entered the profession on the eve of the "linguistic turn" set out to dissolve oppositions that had arisen in the course of the "linguistic turn" between material and discursive transformations.[20] In taking representations and discourses seriously, new studies of gender and labor helped to map the connections between and among arenas that had thus far been viewed as separate or distinct. The project of "rewriting" labor history from the perspective of gender demonstrated the relevance of work and class for the arenas of welfare states and social reform, citizenship and consumption, empires and diasporas, and thus enlarged rather than narrowed the scope of labor history. The study of labor and class became, then, a less bounded inquiry as it expanded well beyond the factory shops, spilling over into new studies of states; public and civic spheres; arenas of social, medical, and hygienic reform; of social and individual bodies. The gendering of labor history pushed open the boundaries of the field in other respects as well, effectively dissolving the dichotomy of production and consumption that underpinned most European social and labor history. While histories of middle-class formation, such as

Leonore Davidoff and Catherine Hall's classic, *Family Fortunes*, highlighted the significance of women's labor as consumers in fashioning the proper middle-class household, feminist labor histories analyzed both wage-earning and frugal consumption as forms of female labor.[21]

The process by which the study of labor and class has become less bounded has not produced one dominant paradigm or epistemology, culturalist or discursive. Exploration of citizenship and welfare states revived inquiry into the relationship between law and social practices, while the history of consumption linked the symbolic and the social in its pursuit of the processes of "commodification, spectatorship, and commercial exchanges."[22] Nor did the willingness of "culturalist" labor historians to grapple with new concepts and methodologies, like discourses and narratives, mean the wholesale neglect of the "material," or of experience and agency. The breakdown of class as an unitary category and the dispersion of labor across other thematic arenas coincided with world historical changes, such as the collapse of state socialism in the Soviet Union and Eastern Europe, which imbued citizenship with a new relevance. Yet the process by which class was revised and expanded did not provide a road map for redefinitions of *citizenship*, which instead took place in quite historically specific terms that were cast by the powerful presence of the welfare state, especially in the German field.

Citizenship beyond the Welfare State?

Citizenship gained new currency as the concept of class became more porous and labor history less bounded, but this was far from a straightforward path. Citizenship emerged as a thematic within labor history as historians probed how state social policy shaped divisions of labor and gendered ideologies of work. In the German field the differential provisions of the welfare state—social insurance for fully employed male workers, protective labor laws for working women—form the historical foundation for the rights and claims of male and female citizens.[23] In some historiographies, citizenship was more contingent and less embedded from its inception in the state. Most of the examples of a fluid boundary between class and citizenship stem from English language historiography, while in the German case citizenship rights in the realm of the social have appeared to mitigate against their relevance for politics, as suggested, for example, by the notion of the "negative integration" of German workers into the state. German peculiarities—Bismarckian social policy, the discrepant suffrage policies of nation and province in Imperial Germany, and the political development of German Social Democracy, including its formative phase as an "outlawed party," meant that class politics were seldom conducted in rhetorics of citizenship.[24]

These specificities of German history, along with the fact that citizenship translates only awkwardly into German (its meaning in English is captured neither by *Staatsangehörigkeit* nor *Staatsbürgerschaft*) may explain the relative absence of the term in most German historiography. One of the most porous concepts in contemporary academic parlance, citizenship can be understood as a political status assigned to individuals by states, as a relation of belonging to specific communities, or as a set of social practices that define the relationships between peoples and states and among peoples within communities.[25] As a legal status bestowed upon a people by the state, citizenship is "bounded and exclusive," demarcating territories and borders: "Every state claims to be the state of, and for, a particular, bounded citizenry, usually conceived as a nation," posits Rogers Brubaker in the preface to his *Citizenship and Nationhood in France and Germany*.[26] *Staatsangehörigkeit*, that is, the status of belonging to a territorially defined state or national formation, has received considerable attention in German historiography since the publication of Brubaker's book. Citizenship in the sense of *Staatsangehörigkeit* had a spatial dimension as well, in that the place of permanent residence conferred citizenship, so elaborate sets of rules applied to those emigrating and immigrating across the boundaries of the various German states.[27] The legal framework of this variation of citizenship changed very little with national unification, as citizenship remained localized in a specific German state. Only with the passage of the 1913 citizenship law did the principle of citizenship as a "community of descent" became primary, thus facilitating that which Brubaker terms an "ethnicization of citizenship." At the height of German imperial desire and competition, then, citizenship law prescribed the closing of national borders to (Polish and Jewish) immigration from the East and opened the way for émigrés and German minorities living in the Eastern borderlands to reclaim lost citizenship status.[28]

While studies of *Staatsangehörigkeit* have at least been revitalized by the new cultural study of nationalism and nation-formation, *Staatsbürgerschaft* has scarcely been creatively rethought. In fact, it has remained a far more static, juridically fixed, and generally unproblematized notion than either civil society or public sphere in the historiography of nineteenth and twentieth-century Germany. While the dual concepts of Staatsangehörigkeit and Staatsbürgerschaft provide the indisputable starting points for the study of German citizenships, their very confinement to the realms of law and state have inhibited exploration of the experiential, subjective level of citizenship that has informed Anglo-Saxon study of colonial, cultural, or sexual citizenships.[29] Recent attention to suffrage and the practices of voting in Imperial Germany has circled around but not explicitly addressed the issue of participatory citizenship.[30] In modern German history, then, citizenship has most frequently studied in its guise as *social citizenship* in the context of the welfare state.

Although social citizenship has been the most visible citizenship in German history, it represents only one rubric of citizenship rights, if we take T. H. Marshall's typology of modern Western citizenship as a grid for this discussion.[31] Marshall's schema, which charts the progressive development of citizenship rights in Western societies, has served more as a point of departure for studies of citizenship than as an actual paradigm. Following its trajectory, white men first became citizens with civil rights in the eighteenth century (in the sense of individual rights within the state and civil society); then they gained the rights of political citizenship (suffrage, representation, participation in the exercise of political power) in the mid to late nineteenth century; and, third, they acquired expanded rights of social citizenship—state protection and provision of the basic means of social reproduction—with the rise of welfare states in the twentieth century.[32] This evolutionary model has come under frequent, even relentless critique, by scholars of gender, race, empires, and ethnicities who have emphasized the impossibility of fitting the citizenship struggles of minorities, women, or colonized peoples into these progressive stages.[33]

A second point about social citizenship is that its imbrication in the welfare state has meant the implicit or explicit presence of family and women in histories of social citizenship. Social citizenship has thus been understood from the outset in more gendered terms than, say, class or the labor movement, which enjoyed a long life before studies of women and gender began to question their terms. In fact, social citizenship constituted a quasi-feminized realm of research into maternalism, social work, and welfare policies. Collections of essays, like Seth Koven and Sonya Michel's *Mothers of a New World*, Gisela Bock and Pat Thane's *Maternity and Gender Policies*, and Linda Gordon's *Women, the State and Welfare* defined this inquiry, offering convincing comparative analysis of the divergent patterns of relations among and between gender, welfare-state formation, ideologies of motherhood, and social citizenship across different national settings.[34]

Citizenship has also been a key concept in feminist theory, if not history, for the last quarter-century. Certainly Catherine MacKinnon's writings on women and the state, Jean Bethke Elstain's *Public Man, Private Woman*, and Carole Pateman's analysis in *The Sexual Contract*, in theorizing the purported "public-private" divide, laid the critical groundwork for theorizing women's citizenship in the 1980s. A second round of theorizing about gender and citizenship involving Nancy Fraser, Iris Marion Young, Seyla Benhabib, and Chantal Mouffe took place in the context of debates about the public sphere, democracy, and difference.[35] Feminist scholars have also had a leading role in conceptualizing global transformations in terms of their implications for the citizenship rights of women and minorities.[36] Citizenship garnered increasing attention in feminist *history* only in the last decade, after the linguistic turn was well underway. Indeed, the critical interventions of feminist theorists on the subject of citizenship have remained notably separate from feminist *historical* study of citizenship, certainly in German history.[37] Nor has the previous critical engagement of feminist theorists and historians with the concept of class appeared to lay the groundwork for a similarly critical approach to citizenship.[38]

Social citizenship represents a vital area of feminist historical inquiry in the German field, not least because it was a variation of citizenship that women *actually possessed*, by contrast with the civic and political citizenship they strove to achieve before 1918 and were forced to defend after the founding of Weimar democracy. Interestingly, studies of the campaigns of bourgeois and Social Democratic women for suffrage rights, of their mobilizations on behalf of civic equality during the revision of the Civil Code in the late 1890s, have seldom been cast in terms of campaigns for *citizenship*, even if this is a fair characterization of their goals.[39] Perhaps the absence of the concept of citizenship in this historiography reflects the ambivalence of the bourgeois women's movement itself toward political citizenship, which led many of its activists to eschew suffrage or civil rights in favor of the rights and duties of maternalist social citizenship. Certainly these older studies of German women's suffrage campaigns, often linked to analyses of the limitations of women's participatory rights by the Prussian law of association, deliver important evidence of how female activists envisioned political citizenship. Yet modernizationist trajectories have cast decisive turning points—the repeal of the Prussian law in 1908 and the granting of women's suffrage in 1918—as short-lived gains that were ultimately overwhelmed by tenacious reassertions of patriarchal power in their aftermath.

While the significance of political citizenship has seemed difficult to document, recent histories of the German welfare state have illustrated the importance of gender in shaping the rights the state dispensed and in sparking mobilizations of the public around and in the milieu of "the social" that impinged upon these rights. Histories of gender, social citizenship, and the welfare state have provided the basis for a fundamental revision of the relationship between state and public, delivering convincing evidence of a far more reciprocal relationship than had previously been conceded, and thus fostering perhaps a kind of "mainstreaming" in this arena of historical research.[40] The exploration of social citizenship as the site of women's most meaningful citizenship rights has had the effect of neglecting or suppressing the fact that social citizenship usually constitutes a de facto "secondary citizenship" reserved for those deprived of political and civil rights.[41] A relational approach to these differential citizenships explicates how, for example, the counterpart to the "feminization of protective labor legislation"—a crucial facet of late nineteenth century social citizenship in Germany—was the "extreme masculinization of political identities."[42] Feminist scholarship on social citizenship has been abundant and impressive, but it also seems to have implicitly accepted the gendered boundaries that divide male and female realms of citizenship and distinguish civic and political from social citizenship. Moreover, studies of social citizenship have been constrained by the equality/difference debate, which by now represents a figurative spinning of the wheels of feminist history in the sand. It is thus important to investigate the work that a term like social citizenship has *not* performed or to pursue the questions it has inhibited or left unanswered.

Advancing the study of citizenship beyond the realm of the welfare state requires thinking beyond some of our own most familiar categories. The critiques of feminist social theorists of the concept of citizenship form one starting point; innovative scholarship from adjacent disciplines, particularly cultural studies, offers another. The most recent feminist theory on citizenship has embraced the dualities, contingencies, and contradictions it encompasses, rendering it "a site of intense struggle," both theoretical and political.[43] British sociologist Ruth Lister's conception of citizenship as *both* (rather than *either*) status and practice underlines the distinction between the legally prescribed and subjectively lived realms of citizenship and cites the complex situation of those contemporary women who possess legal citizenship status but who are unable able to "fulfill the full potential of that status" by practicing or acting as citizens because of the constraints of caregiving and child rearing.[44] American historian Nancy Cott has postulated a similarly fluid notion of women's citizenship in the United States as "not a definitive either/or proposal—you are or you are not—but a compromisable one" that is consistent with the status/practice spectrum Lister proposes.[45]

Sociologists Pnina Werbner and Nira Yuval-Davis define citizenship as a relationship "inflected by identity, social positioning, cultural assumptions, institutional practices, and a sense of belonging." A multidimensional discursive framework, in their rendering, citizenship consists of the languages, rhetorics, and formal categories of claims-making that are accessed and deployed not only by those who are endowed with formal citizenship rights, but also by those excluded from them. The emphasis I place here on claims-making posits an intentional link between the experiential and discursive dimensions of citizenship in order to understand the ways in which they diverged from or were dissonant with one another.[46] The discrepancies between legal prescriptions of citizenship and the historical meanings or experiences of citizenship (or its absence) reveal the importance of the intervening and acting subject in historicizing citizenship. Lauren Berlant's conception of citizenship as a means of viewing the self as public, as "an important definitional frame for the ways people see themselves as public, when they do," implies that citizenship is one of "an ensemble of subject positions."[47] Yet this formulation is not as flexible, porous, or impossible to historicize as it may seem. In proposing

citizenship = flexible, porous

an understanding of citizenship as subjectivity, my intention is not to eschew the importance of the realms of law or the policies of states in designating the margins of inclusion/exclusion or in defining the formal rights and obligations of citizens, active or passive.

My main preoccupation here is rather the meanings historical actors assigned to these prescriptions and delineations of citizenship; that is, how they became subjects in their encounters with citizenship laws, rhetorics, and practices. I understand the process of subject formation as an inherently meditative one, encompassing both legal and discursive prescriptions as well as the interventions and interpretations of those who encounter, embrace, or contest them. This approach thus considers the realms of state and law as crucial frameworks for citizenship, but also probes the realms of popular culture, consumption, media, and visual arts as definitive of the parameters and promises of citizenship.[48] Attention to the assignment of meaning beyond the juridical or prescriptive definitions of citizenship rights and duties emphasizes the historicity and mutability of citizenship rights (even where they remain fixed in law). It is thus important to differentiate between moments in history, when, as Chantal Mouffe has noted, citizenship was "just one identity among others," and those moments when it was "the dominant identity that overrides all others," when it operated as the "articulating principle that affects the different subject positions of the social agent."[49] Mouffe argues, for example, that citizenship in a regime of liberalism may figure as "just one identity among others," while in "Civic Republicanism" it becomes "the dominant identity that overrides all others." Mouffe's schema prompts consideration of those historical moments in which citizenship may have served as that "articulating principle that affects the different subject positions of the social agent,"[50] such as in the founding years of the Weimar Republic.

This interpretive framework seems pertinent as well for the years after the First World War when republicans, socialists, and Catholics fashioned a democracy and new visions of citizenship for women from the standpoints of their disparate traditions. For a time in the history of the Weimar Republic citizenship may have had the capacity to cohere the social identities and affinities that were broken down by the devastation of war and collapse of nation. The women who became citizens in the aftermath of the First World War wielded a recognizable language of claims we might call "citizenship" to articulate a "plurality of specific allegiances."[51] At the outset of the Republic the advances in political citizenship (suffrage) and the anchoring of social citizenship rights (as mothers and workers) in the welfare state stood in stark contrast to the loss of the right to work and the reinforcement of women's civil subordination to men in the realms of marriage and family. The consideration of this subjective, experiential dimension of citizenship allows for the possibility that political citizenship *was* meaningful for women after 1918, even as they seemed to vanish from the arenas of formal politics by 1920.

Attention to both the discursive and experiential moments of this period of upheaval provides an analytical framework for grasping both the apparent "return to normal" of gender and family relations during the 1920s and the deeper-running ruptures in families and gender ideologies that occurred in the course of defeat, demobilization, revolution, and the founding of democracy. The gulf between the official pronunciations of citizenship and women's own interpretation or experience of its contradictory catalog of rights and duties designates the very space for their citizenship claims in the early Republic. Even after it had come under assault, not least as the symbol of women's "emancipation," citizenship formed the one common ground for the articulation of distinct subject positions of women in Weimar—as demobilized workers, widowed mothers, newly endowed voters, consumers of popular culture, and sexually independent negotiators of their private lives. Citizenship not only became a site at which these contradictions were named and contested, but also a new language for the assertion of women's claims upon the state and fellow citizens that resonated across the realms of party politics and the welfare state and into the increasingly politicized domains of sexuality, reproduction, and consumption.

for some people . . .

Conclusion

In this essay I have suggested that the unmooring of class and citizenship from their so-called structural confines is a productive process, one that may be a necessary outcome, even the fulfillment of the project of gender history, as Joan Kelly outlined it some twenty-five years ago. In the case of neither concept—class or citizenship—have I proposed that these terms be wholly detached from economies, geographies, laws, or state power. Instead such structural formations constitute an important starting point, beyond which histories of meaning and experience remain crucial. Rather than using historical concepts like class or citizenship to seek the kind of closure necessitated by the project termed "mainstreaming," I propose that a more open-ended understanding of these terms will contribute considerably more to revising or fundamentally recasting historical narratives and chronologies. Instead of seeking to fit the analysis of gender and citizenship into the political history of Weimar, we might consider the ways in which the acquisition of citizenship rights thoroughly altered the perception of women by others in the newly expanded public of Weimar, as well as transformed women's own views and displays of themselves in this arena. A reconsideration of citizenship in these terms may render 1918 a different kind of turning point for gender history than for political history.

While my own work pursues a quite specific historicization of the meanings, experiences, and subject positions of citizenship, it appears that a decade of intensive interdisciplinary conversation, encounter, and debate has, in fact, changed the meaning of historicization itself, at least as it is understood in the American academy. So the goal of historicizing citizenship for the Weimar period may not be exhausted by a close reading of constitutions and laws, but might productively turn to analysis of women's novels, visual arts, theater, and popular culture in order to gain a fuller sense of the arenas in which citizenship rights were made meaningful or engendered conflict. This point brings me, in closing, to the question of mainstreaming, which seems like it can only flourish as a stringently *disciplinary* exercise. The more interdisciplinary our queries and research projects become, the less likely they are to fit back into the narratives, chronologies, and concepts that were once conceived without the history of women or gender. Yet the outlook for a more generalized mainstreaming of gender history remains uncertain. While it is surely desirable that the kind of metanarratives represented by textbooks or synthetic histories of "high politics" incorporate scholarship on gender, this in itself does little to redefine key concepts or chronological frameworks. Yet it is worth considering whether the drive for acceptance into the mainstream might inhibit the potential of gender history to reconceive more fundamentally the terms and temporalities upon which prevalent historical narratives have relied. In fact, a premature embrace of the project of mainstreaming gender history may obscure from view the ways in which feminist history has accepted the limitations of its most productive terms, including—for purposes of this discussion—the concept of citizenship.

Notes

Author's note: This is a substantially revised and shortened version of the essay, "Class vs. Citizenship: Keywords in German Gender History," *Central European History* 37, no. 2: 225–244 (2004), a special issue honoring Prof. Vernon L. Lidtke. I thank Kenneth F. Ledford, editor of *Central European History*, for allowing me to publish this revised version here. An amended version of this essay also appears in my book, *Gender History in Practice: Historical Perspectives on Bodies, Class and Citizenship* (Cornell University Press, 2005). I would also like to express my appreciation to the editors of the special issue of *Central*

European History, Gary Stark and Lawrence Stokes, for their input on this essay. I also thank Christine von Oertzen, who commented on the first version of this paper, which I presented to the conference, "Gendering Modern German History: Rewriting the Mainstream," held in March 2003 at the University of Toronto. Finally, I thank the editors of this volume, Karen Hagemann and Jean Quataert, for their comments and suggestions.

1. See, for example, Margaret R. Somers, "Citizenship and the Place of the Public Sphere, Law, Community and Political Culture in the Transition to Democracy," in *American Sociological Review* 58 (1993): 587–620.

2. Important exceptions are: Julia Sneeringer, *Winning Women's Votes: Propaganda and Politics in Weimar Germany* (Chapel Hill, 2002); and Heidemarie Lauterer, *Parliamentarierinnen in Deutschland 1918/19–1949* (Königstein, 2002).

3. Geoff Eley and Keith Nield, "Farewell to the Working Class?" *International Labor and Working Class History* 57 (Spring 2000): 1–30. Respondents to this article include: Stephen Kotkin, Judith Stein, Barbara Weinstein, Don Kalb, Frederick Cooper, and Joan W. Scott.

4. Joan W. Scott, "The 'Class' We Have Lost," *International Labor and Working Class History* 57 (Spring 2000): 69–75.

5. See Frederick Cooper's response to Eley and Nield: "Farewell to the Category-Producing Class?" and Barbara Weinstein, "Where Do New Ideas (About Class) Come From?" *International Labor and Working Class History* 57 (Spring 2000): 53–59, 60–68, respectively.

6. See Lenard R. Berlanstein, ed., *Rethinking Labor History: Essays on Discourse and Class Analysis* (Urbana, 1993), especially "Introduction," 1.

7. For some of the early debates on *Alltagsgeschichte*, see Hans Medick, "'Missionäre im Ruderboot?' Ethnologische Erkenntnisweisen als Herausforderung an die Sozialgeschichte," *Geschichte und Gesellschaft* 10, no. 3 (1984): 295–319; and the responses in the same issue by Jürgen Kocka, "Zurück zur Erzählung? Plädoyer für historische Argumentation," 395–408; and Klaus Tenfelde, "Schwierigkeiten mit dem Alltag," 376–394. Alf Lüdtke's essay, "Organizational Order or *Eigensinn?*: Workers' Privacy and Workers' Politics in Imperial Germany," in *Rites of Power: Symbolism, Ritual and Politics since the Middle Ages*, Sean Wilentz, ed. (Philadelphia, 1985), 303–334, played an important role in the U.S. reception of Alltagsgeschichte. For incisive overviews see David F. Crew, "*Alltagsgeschichte*: A New Social History from Below?" *Central European History* 22, nos. 3–4 (1989): 394–407; and Geoff Eley, "Labor History, Social History, *Alltagsgeschichte*: Experience, Culture and the Politics of the Everyday—A New Direction for German Social History?" *Journal of Modern History* 61, no. 2 (1989): 297–343.

8. Laura L. Frader and Sonya O. Rose, eds., *Gender and Class in Modern Europe* (Ithaca, 1996), "Introduction," 4.

9. Ibid., 19.

10. Joan Kelly-Gadol, "The Social Relation of the Sexes: Methodological Implications of Women's History," in *Signs* 1, no. 4 (1976): 809–823. Also see her essay collection, *Women, History, and Theory: The Essays of Joan Kelly* (Chicago, 1984).

11. Judith L. Newton et al., eds., *Sex and Class in Women's History* (London, 1983).

12. Sally Alexander, "Women, Class and Sexual Differences in the 1830s and 1840s: Some Reflections on the Writing of a Feminist History," *History Workshop* 17 (1984): 125–154.

13. Kathleen Canning, "Feminist History after the Linguistic Turn: Historicizing Discourse and Experience," *Signs* 19, no. 2 (Winter 1994): 368–404.

14. William H. Sewell, Jr., "Toward a Post-materialist Rhetoric for Labor History," in Berlanstein, *Rethinking Labor History*, 17; Eley and Nield, "Farewell," 3.

15. See John Toews, "Intellectual History after the Linguistic Turn: The Autonomy of Meaning and the Irreducibility of Experience," *American Historical Review* 92 (October 1987): 879–907. Labor was a central focus of Joan W. Scott's *Gender and the Politics of History* (New York, 1988).

16. I elaborated this argument in my essay, "Gender and the Politics of Class Formation: Rethinking German Labor History," *American Historical Review* 97, no. 3 (June 1992): 745–748.

17. Labor history of the post-World War II period was still in its infancy at this time and has since had a significant presence in the newer studies of both the Federal Republic and the former German Democratic Republic. Two excellent examples include Christine von Oertzen, *Teilzeit und die Lust am Zuverdienen: Geschlechterpolitik und gesellschaftlicher Wandel in Westdeutschland, 1948–1969* (Göttingen, 1999); and Annegret Schüle, *"Die Spinne": Die Erfahrungsgeschichte weiblicher Industriearbeit im VEB Leipziger Baumwollspinnerei* (Leipzig, 2001).

18. See, for example, Karen Hagemann, *Frauenalltag und Männerpolitik: Alltagsleben und gesellschaftliches Handeln von Arbeiterfrauen in der Weimarer Republik* (Bonn, 1990); Marlene Ellerkamp, *Industriearbeit, Krankheit und Geschlecht* (Göttingen, 1991); Karin Hausen, ed., *Geschlechterhierarchie und Arbeitsteilung: Zur Geschichte ungleicher Erwerbschancen von Männern und Frauen* (Göttingen, 1993); Brigitte Kerchner, *Beruf und Geschlecht: Frauenberufsverbände in Deutschland 1848–1908* (Göttingen, 1992); Susanne Rouette, *Sozialpolitik als Geschlechterpolitik: Die Regulierung der Frauenarbeit nach dem Ersten Weltkrieg* (Frankfurt/M., 1993); and Sabine Schmitt, *Der Arbeiterinnenschutz im deutschen Kaiserreich: Zur Konstruktion der schutzbedürftigen Arbeiterin* (Stuttgart, 1995).

19. For additional Anglo-Saxon debates, see "What Next for Labor and Working-Class History?" special issue, *International Labor and Working-Class History* (Fall 1994). The synthetic volumes appeared in a series edited by Gerhard A. Ritter entitled *Geschichte der Arbeiter und der Arbeiterbewegung in Deutschland seit dem Ende des 18. Jahrhundert.* See especially Jürgen Kocka, *Weder Stand noch Klasse* and *Arbeitsverhältnisse und Arbeiterexistenzen;* as well as Gerhard A. Ritter and Klaus Tenfelde, eds., *Arbeiter im deutschen Kaiserreich, 1871 bis 1914* (Bonn, 1992).

20. A partial list of these books includes: Sonya O. Rose, *Limited Livelihoods: Gender and Class in Nineteenth-Century England* (Berkeley, 1992); Anna Clark, *The Struggle for the Breeches: Gender and the Making of the British Working Class* (Berkeley, 1994); Tessie Liu, *The Weaver's Knot: The Contradictions of Class Struggle and Family Solidarity in Western France, 1750–1914* (Ithaca, 1994); Laura Tabili, *"We Ask for British Justice': Workers and Racial Difference in Late Imperial Britain* (Ithaca, 1994); Deborah Valenze, *The First Industrial Woman* (New York, 1995); Laura Lee Downs, *Manufacturing Inequality: Gender Division in the French and British Metalworking Industries, 1914–1939* (Ithaca, 1995); Judith G. Coffin, *The Politics of Women's Work: The Paris Garment Trades, 1750–1915* (Princeton, 1996); Kathleen Canning, *Languages of Labor and Gender* (Ithaca, 1996); Leora Auslander, *Taste and Power: Furnishing Modern France* (Berkeley, 1997); and Nancy L. Green, *Ready-to-Wear and Ready-to-Work: A Century of Industry and Immigrants in Paris and New York* (Durham, 1997).

21. See, for example, Leonore Davidoff and Catherine Hall, *Family Fortunes: Men and Women of the English Middle Class, 1780–1850* (Chicago, 1987); Jane Lewis, ed., *Labour and Love: Women's Experience of Home and Family 1850–1940* (London, 1986); Ellen Ross, *Love and Toil: Motherhood in Outcast London, 1870–1918* (Oxford, 1993); Leora Auslander, "The Gendering of Consumer Practices in Nineteenth-Century France," in *The Sex of Things: Gender and Consumption in Historical Perspective*, eds. Victoria de Grazia and Ellen Furlough (Berkeley, 1996), 79–112; see especially de Grazia's essay, "Empowering Women as Citizen-Consumers," in de Grazia and Furlough, *The Sex of Things*, 275–286.

22. de Grazia and Furlough, "Introduction," in *The Sex of Things*, 4–5.

23. See, for example, the forum on "Women, Work and Citizenship," *International Labor and Work-ing-Class History* 52 (Fall 1997): 1–71. Contributors include Louise Tilly, Chiara Saraceno, Ann Shola Orloff, Roderick Phillips, and W. Robert Lee. On social insurance see Greg Eghi-gian, *Making Security Social: Disability, Insurance, and the Birth of the Social Entitlement State in Germany* (Ann Arbor, 2000).

24. Vernon L. Lidtke, *The Outlawed Party: Social Democracy in Germany 1878–1890* (Princeton, 1966). On suffrage, see Thomas Kühne, *Dreiklassenwahlrecht und Wahlkultur in Preussen 1867–1914* (Düsseldorf, 1994); and Margaret Anderson, *Practicing Democracy: Elections and Political Culture in Imperial Germany* (Princeton, 2000).

25. See Christoph Conrad and Jürgen Kocka, eds., *Staatsbürgerschaft in Europa: Historische Erfahrungen und akutelle Debatten* (Hamburg, 2001), especially "Einführung," 9–26; Bryan S. Turner, "Contemporary Problems in the Theory of Citizenship," in *Citizen-ship and Social Theory*, ed. Bryan S. Turner (London, 1993): 2–3; Bryan S. Turner, Peter Hamilton, eds., *Citizenship: Critical Concepts* (London, 1994); and Geoff Andrews, ed., *Citizenship* (London, 1991). On the dual nature of citizenship as a status and a practice, see Ruth Lister, "Citizenship: Towards a Feminist Synthesis," in "Citizenship: Pushing the Boundaries," eds. Pnina Werbner and Nira Yuval-Davis, special issue, *Feminist Re-view* 57 (1997): 29–33.

26. Rogers Brubaker, *Citizenship and Nationhood in France and Germany* (Cambridge, Mass., 1992), x.

27. For histories of Staatsangehörigkeit in Germany, see Andreas K. Fahrmeier, "Nineteenth-Century German Citizenships: A Reconsideration," *The Historical Journal* 40, no. 3 (1997): 721–752; idem, *Citizens and Aliens: Foreigners and the Law in Britain and the German States 1789–1870* (New York, 2000). Also see Dieter Gosewinkel, *Einbürgern und Ausschließen: Die Nationalisierung der Staatsangehörigkeit vom Deutschen Bund bis zur Bundesrepublik Deutsch-land* (Göttingen, 2001); and Wolfgang J. Mommsen, "Nationalität im Zeichen offensiver Weltpolitik: Das Reichs- und Staatsangehörigkeitsgesetz des Deutschen Reiches vom 22. Juni 1913," in *Nation und Gesellschaft in Deutschland: Historische Essays*, eds. Manfred Het-tling and Paul Nolte, (Munich, 1998), 128–141.

28. Brubaker, *Citizenship and Nationhood*, 114–115. Also see Brubaker's essay, "Homeland Na-tionalism in Weimar Germany and 'Weimar Russia,'" in idem, *Nationalism Reframed: Na-tionhood and the National Question in the New Europe* (Cambridge, 1996): 107–147. Brubak-er's schema has been criticized on a number of fronts. See, for example, Lora Wildenthal, "Race, Gender, and Citizenship in the German Colonial Empire," in *Tensions of Empire: Colonial Cultures in a Bourgeois World*, eds. Frederick Cooper and Ann L. Stoler (Berke-ley, 1997); and more recently: Dieter Gosewinkel's "Citizenship in Germany and France at the Turn of the Twentieth Century: Some New Observations on an Old Comparison," in *Citizenship and National Identity in Twentieth-Century Germany*, eds. Geoff Eley and Jan Palmowski (Stanford, Fall 2007).

29. See among others Gershon Safir, ed., *The Citizenship Debates: A Reader* (Minneapolis, 1998); Aihwa Ong, "Cultural Citizenship as Subject Making: Immigrants Negotiate Racial and Cultural Boundaries in the United States," in *Race, Identity, and Citizenship: A Reader*, ed. Rodolfo D. Torres et al. (Oxford, 1999); and Aihwa Ong, *Flexible Citizenship: The Cultural Logics of Transnationality* (Durham, 1999); Evelyn Nakano Glenn, *Unequal Freedoms: How Race and Gender Shaped American Citizenship and Labor* (Cambridge, Mass., 2004); Mae Ngai, *Impossible Subjects: Illegal Aliens and the Making of American Politics* (Princeton, 2003); Elizabeth Thompson, *Colonial Citizens: Republican Rights, Paternal Privilege, and Gender in French Syria and Lebanon* (New York, 2000); and David T. Evans, *Sexual Citizenship: The Material Construction of Sexualities* (London, 1993).

30. Anderson, *Practicing Democracy*; and Kühne, *Dreiklassenwahlrecht*.

31. See, for example, the discussion of Marshall's schema in Bryan Turner, ed., *Citizenship and Social Theory* (London, 1993).

32. T. H. Marshall, "Citizenship and Social Class," in T. H. Marshall and Tom Bottomore, *Citizenship and Social Class* (London, 1992). Also see Sylvia Walby, "Is Citizenship Gendered," *Sociology* 28, no. 2 (May 1994): 379–395.

33. See, for example, Linda Gordon, ed. *Women, the State and Welfare* (Madison, 1990), 18; Ruth Lister, *Citizenship: Feminist Perspectives* (New York, 1997); and Ong, "Cultural Citizenship," 263.

34. Seth Koven and Sonya Michel, eds., *Mothers of a New World: Maternalist Politics and the Origins of Welfare States* (New York, 1993), especially "Introduction: 'Mother Worlds.'" Also see Gisela Bock and Pat Thane, eds., *Maternity and Gender Policies:. Women and the Rise of the European Welfare State* (London, 1991); Gordon, *Women, the State and Welfare*, especially the introductory essay on "The New Feminist Scholarship on the Welfare State;" Susan Pedersen, *Family, Dependence and the Origins of the Welfare State: Britain and France, 1914–1945* (Cambridge, 1993); Theda Skocpol, *Protecting Soldiers and Mothers: The Political Origins of Social Policy in the United States* (Cambridge, 1992); and Ulla Wikander et al., eds., *Protecting Women. Labor Legislation in Europe, the United States and Australia, 1880–1920* (Urbana, 1995).

35. Catherine MacKinnon, *Toward a Feminist Theory of the State* (Cambridge, 1989); Jean Bethke Elstain, *Public Man, Private Woman* (Princeton, 1981); Carole Pateman, *The Sexual Contract* (Stanford, 1988); Nancy Fraser, "Rethinking the Public Sphere: A Contribution to the Critique of Actually Existing Democracy" in *Habermas and the Public Sphere*, ed. Craig Calhoun (Cambridge, Mass., 1992); and "Sex, Lies, and the Public Sphere: Reflections on the Confirmation of Clarence Thomas," in *Feminism, the Public and the Private*, ed. Joan Landes (Oxford, 1998); Iris Marion Young, "Polity and Group Difference: A Critique of the Ideal of Universal Citizenship," in *The Citizenship Debates: A Reader*, ed. Gershon Shafir; and Chantal Mouffe, "Feminism, Citizenship and Radical Democratic Politics," in *Feminists Theorize the Political*, eds. Judith Butler and Joan W. Scott (New York, 1992).

36. Sonya O. Rose and I made this point in our essay, "Gender, Citizenship and Subjectivity: Some Historical and Theoretical Considerations," in *Gender, Citizenships and Subjectivities*, ed. Kathleen Canning and Sonya O. Rose (London, 2002), 1.

37. An important and exemplary exception here are some of the articles in Calhoun, *Habermas and the Public Sphere*, most notably those by Mary P. Ryan and Geoff Eley.

38. See, for example, the scholarly controversy on "Women, Work and Citizenship," 1–71.

39. Richard J. Evans, *The Feminist Movement in Germany 1894–1933* (London, 1976); Barbara Greven-Aschoff, *Die bürgerliche Frauenbewegung in Deutschland 1894–1933* (Göttingen, 1981); Ute Frevert, *Women in German History: from Bourgeois Emancipation to Sexual Liberation*, trans. Stuart McKinnon-Evans (Oxford, 1989); and Ute Gerhard, *Unerhört. Die Geschichte der deutschen Frauenbewegung*, Reinbek, 1990. Other important older studies include: Christel Wickert, *Unsere Erwählten: Sozialdemokratische Frauen im Deutschen Reichstag und im Preussischen Landtag 1919 bis 1933*, vols. 1–2 (Göttingen, 1986); and Helen Boak, "Women in Weimar Germany: The 'Frauenfrage' and the Female Vote," in *Social Change and Political Development in the Weimar Republic*, ed. Richard Bessel, E. J. Feuchtwanger (London, 1981):155–173.

40. Seth Koven and Sonya Michel, "Gender and the Origins of the Welfare State," *Radical History Review* 43 (1989): 112–119.

41. Geoff Eley and Atina Grossmann pose useful questions about the "connections and overlaps between social and political citizenship" in their essay, "Maternalism and Citizenship in Weimar Germany: The Gendered Politics of Welfare," *Central European History* 30, no. 1 (1997): 72. Chantal Mouffe makes a similar point in her critique of Jean Elstain and Carole

Pateman's critiques of liberal citizenship. See Mouffe, "Feminism and Radical Politics," 374–375.

42. Teresa Kulawik, *Wohlfahrtsstaat und Mutterschaft: Schweden und Deutschland 1870–1912* (Frankfurt am Main, 1999), Introduction.

43. Werbner and Yuval-Davis, *Citizenship.* See especially, "Introduction: Women and the New Discourse of Citizenship," 2. See also Erna Appelt, ed., *Citizenship*, special issue, *L'Homme: Zeitschrift für Feministische Geschichtswissenschaft* 10, no. 1 (1999).

44. Werbner and Yuval-Davis, "Women and the New Discourse of Citizenship," 4.

45. Nancy Cott, "Marriage and Women's Citizenship in the United States, 1830–1934," *American Historical Review* 103, no. 5 (1998): 1442. For an innovative and important discussion of women's citizenship that works creatively with Cott's suggestions, see Maureen Healy, "Becoming Austrian: Women, the State, and Citizenship in World War I," *Central European History* 35, no. 1 (2002): 1–35.

46. For a fuller discussion of this point, see Canning and Rose, "Gender, Citizenship and Subjectivity," 1–17.

47. Lauren Berlant, *The Queen of America Goes to Washington City: Essays on Sex and Citizenship* (Durham, 1997), 10; see also Mouffe, "Feminism and Radical Politics," 372–373.

48. Nick Mansfield, *Subjectivity: Theories of the Self from Freud to Haraway* (New York, 2000): 3–4.

49. Mouffe, "Feminism, Citizenship and Radical Democratic Politics," 372, 378–379.

50. Ibid.

51. For a more general discussion of this topic, see Canning and Rose, "Gender, Citizenship and Subjectivities."

23 sources in Germ.

7

A Tributary and a Mainstream

Gender, Public Memory, and the Historiography of Nazi Germany

Claudia Koonz

In the 1980s, feminist historians often claimed that including women and gender in history would force a rewriting of its master narrative. However, as it turned out, feminist theorists' epistemological skepticism has obviated the possibility of a single narrative and contributed to the dismantling of accounts anchored in politics, class, and race. Women's history and gender as an analytic category have challenged conventional wisdom and enriched mainstream research on National Socialist Germany, and to a lesser extent, the Holocaust.[1] Scholarship on women and gender has entered such mainstream venues as scholarly journals, professional conferences, and the H-Net.[2] Most textbooks and anthologies on Nazi Germany incorporate information about women that has been produced by a veritable avalanche of new research. For three decades before 1990, roughly seventy-five scholarly books and articles on women in National Socialist Germany were published, excluding scholarship on the Holocaust, literature, psychology, and education. Between 1991 and mid 2005, more than two hundred books and articles on the history of women in Nazi Germany appeared.

Faced with a staggering amount of new scholarship and the space constraints of this collection, I will focus on recent cultural, political, and social histories of ordinary women. Carola Sachse's fine interpretative overview of the field before 1997 provides a more complete guide to that scholarship than I can give here.[3] Readers interested in research on sexuality can turn to Atina Grossmann's essay in this collection and Elizabeth Heineman's review article.[4] For an overview of women victims, readers may consult *Women in the Holocaust* and *Different Voices*.[5]

In terms of sheer quantity alone, it is evident that a once-marginal subfield has become an important tributary that has contributed fresh archival discoveries and challenged conventional interpretations of Nazi Germany. In this essay I explore the course of this tributary as it has entered particular areas of mainstream history. Although historiographical transformations are typically examined within the context of an academic habitus, in this essay, I begin by suggesting that a changing public culture also affected trends that made gender and women crucial to historical research. Next I identify the end of cold war culture as a turning point, or *Wende*, that accelerated trends begun in the 1980s. In the last part of this essay, I survey particular subfields that have been enriched by research on women and gender.

Cold War Orthodoxies

From the late 1940s, historians investigated the Nazi period within the parameters of largely unexamined assumptions about causality and periodization that rendered research on women and thinking about gender irrelevant. Despite fractious disputes among themselves, the historians who dominated the field had more in common than was usually realized.[6] Some, labeled "intentionalists," took a "great man" approach and studied Hitler and his deputies. Others shared a statist (or, in the German Democratic Republic, economist) perspective called both "functionalist" and "structuralist" that derived from Weberian (or Marxist) social science. Believing history should and could be objective, both groups stressed the primacy of politics and collected facts from government and organization archives. Most saw the period from 1933 to 1945 as a rupture in historical continuity, although some traced its origins in distinctive German or Prussian traditions. With their research eye trained on the *Herrschaftsstruktur* (literally "structure of mastery"), historians dismissed the experiences of ordinary women and men as irrelevant. Not surprisingly, victims, bystanders, and all but a few powerful perpetrators had no place in the historical canon. Nicolas Berg connected historians' enthusiasm for "faceless" hegemonic interpretations to the founding fathers of postwar history who wished to obscure their own complicity with National Socialism. Cold war culture also facilitated this elision.

In the 1950s, with one "evil empire" in ruins and another rising on the Eastern horizon, academics in the "free world" saw "mass man" as a threat to humane values. In *The Origins of Totalitarianism*, Hannah Arendt wrote memorably about the forces that drained human beings of their individuality. In her narrative, Nazi rule had coerced Germans with an "iron band of terror" (four mentions in two pages) and subjected them to propaganda that ground them down into a monolithic "One Self" (capitalization in the original). For her, Adolf Eichmann epitomized the human product of a bureaucratized totalitarianism that made men into "functionaries and mere cogs in the administrative machinery."[7]

In the Jerusalem courtroom, Arendt saw an utterly obedient Eichmann who thought in clichés and denied responsibility for his crimes. Her portrait fixed "the perpetrator" in the historical imaginary in part because it resonated with the popular culture of cold war Western Europe and North America. The conformists in David Riesman's *The Lonely Crowd* (1950), William H. Whyte, Jr.'s *The Organization Man* (1956), and Sloan Wilson's best-selling novel *The Man in the Gray Flannel Suit* (1956) quietly pervaded historical thinking about Germans under Nazi rule. From liberals like psychologist Erich Fromm and writer George Orwell to ex-Nazi social scientists like Arnold Gehlen and Helmut Schelsky, intellectuals castigated the "massification" of modern society that had produced willing perpetrators who applied instrumental reason to whatever tasks were assigned to them. Former concentration camp prisoner Hermann Langbein recalled his tormentors as "small cogs in an omnipotent machine." Psychiatrist G. M. Gilbert, who mindlessly examined the twenty-two German leaders on trial at Nuremberg, entitled his study, "The Mentality of the SS Murderous Robots."[8] The fact that the obedient cog was "Aryan" and masculine seemed too obvious to require investigation. With the "mass man" of social science and social criticism standing in the limelight, the woman at his side disappeared.

At the Margins, the History of Women Evolves

In an era when policy makers agonized about the de-masculinized German men who had suffered crushing defeat, historians did not think of manhood as a cultural construction or doubt the universality of homemaker wives. To open up this inquiry would have acknowledged the instability of the very roles that formed the bedrock of postwar normalization. Nevertheless, historians of women in Nazi Germany created a vibrant field of their own, thanks to the small presses that published their books and the readers who purchased them; universities that created positions; and the foundations that offered stipends. In the 1970s, Gerda Zorn, Hannah Elling, and others documented women's opposition to Nazi rule. As Dorothea Schmidt noted, many early overviews of women's role in the Third Reich (by Dorothee Klinsiek, Margaret Lück, Georg Tidl, Jürgen Kuczinski, and Rita Thalmann) tended toward general overviews (*pauschalisirenden Darstellungen*) that emphasized the Nazis' instrumentalization of women.[9] Reading these works, it sometimes appears that while women resisters exercised agency, ordinary women did not.

Changes in thinking about women began to appear outside the profession, notably in Christa Wolf's *Kindheitsmuster* (1977), which challenged canonical accounts of the Third Reich as a "man's world." Leila Rupp, Jill Stephenson, Michael Kater, and Karin Berger exposed the contradictions between Nazi policy and women's activities. Gabriele Bremme analyzed women voters' choices before and after Nazi rule. In the next decade, Richard Evans, Godele v. d. Decken, Doris Kampmann, Annette Kuhn, Ursula Aumüller-Roske, Georg Kaiser, Michael Phayer, Dagmar Reese, Carola Sachse, and Tilla Sigel, among others, chronicled women's political associations, religious organizations, and Nazi Party formations. Much of the new research suggested that women had exerted more influence than ordinarily assumed. When historians grappled with the meaning of their discoveries, some turned to Silvia Bovenschen's concept of "imagined femininity" or Klaus Theweleit's "masculine fantasies." These psychological frameworks diverted research away from the major issues addressed by established scholars in the universities.

Social history during these years opened up a conceptual space for studies of women as wives, white-collar and factory workers, political activists, students, labor organizers, party members, and mothers. Works by Stephan Bajor, Tim Mason, Dörthe Winkler, David Schonbaum, Ingrid Schupetta and others attest to social historians' early recognition of women's vital contributions to the labor force and to organized labor, grassroots activism, and social reproduction. Editors of social history anthologies (among them David Crew, Geoff Eley, Alf Ludtke, Adelheid von Saldern, and Winfried Schulze) included articles on women. Yet, despite debates about the television series *The Holocaust* (1978–1979) and Jeanine Meerapfel's 1983 film about her parents' lives in Nazi Germany, most social historians ignored racial persecution as a research topic.[10] In the 1980s, amateurs (nicknamed "barefoot historians") and professionals mounted oral history and archival projects that investigated the history of daily life (*Alltagsgeschichte*) under Nazi rule, which sometimes included Jewish subjects.[11] Carola Sachse and Susanne Dammer were among the first historians to call attention to the crucial importance of race in the construction of gender in Nazi Germany.[12]

Historians' Disputes in the Late Cold War

Since the emergence of history as a discipline in the eighteenth century, *querelles* have affirmed their centrality in public culture. Three debates about Nazi Germany provide a litmus test for the status of women and gender relative to mainstream history: Did German history follow a unique path (*Sonderweg*) that predisposed it to authoritarian rule? Did "structuralist" or "intention-alist," "totalitarian" or "fascist" theories offer the best analytic framework? Did comparisons between Hitler's Germany and Stalin's Russia relativize Nazi evil? In these altercations, the litmus did not change color. Research on women and gender played no role.

Nevertheless, historians of women discussed the first two questions amongst themselves. The exchanges in the third mainstream debate grew so acrimonious that it became known as the male historians' debate (*Historiker-streit*), and women launched their own *HistorikerInnenstreit* (female historians' dispute).[13] Its origins dated from fractious debates that had divided feminists in the 1970s on the question of women's responsibility for their own oppression. Disputes about women's voluntary subjugation (*freiwillige Unterwerfung*) came to a head in 1980 during a public debate among feminists about whether women in patriarchies were victims or perpetrators.[14] In German, the former term (*Opfer*) conveys overtones of "sacrificial offering." The latter (*Täter*) means "perpetrator." Since German has no word for "agent" (although *die Agentur* and *das handelnde Subjekt* come close), the conceptual issues at stake are not immediately apparent in English.

On the Anglo-American side of what Kathleen Canning called "the Atlantic Divide," few historians perceived ordinary women simply as victims of Nazism. But in the context of polemics among German-speaking scholars, a stark *Opfer-Täter* binary framed many histories of women in Nazi Germany during the 1980s. Two psychologists established the terms of the debate. Margaret Mitscherlich diagnosed antisemitism as a "masculine disease" and perceived women as victims of Nazi power. Christina Thürmer-Rohr retorted that women had never been only victims and could not base their demands for equality on a false history of their own passivity. Following Mitscherlich, in her history of forced sterilization, Gisela Bock referred to the one percent death rate among sterilized women, not as an unintended consequence of the operation, but as "planned and intentional mass murder." In a review of my *Mothers in the Fatherland*, Bock insisted that because ethnic German women had been sterilized and otherwise abused by a sexist regime, and because wives and mothers had preserved humane values within their homes, they had exercised no significant agency in racial crimes.[15] But psychologist Karin Windaus-Walser accused Bock, Mitscherlich, and others of blinding themselves to historical facts that demonstrated women's agency in National Socialist Germany.[16] Although it may seem illogical to assert that Nazi policies deformed private, "feminine" spheres and simultaneously allowed the women who operated within those spheres to exert agency, in fact, that is precisely how oppression functions. Ordinary women could be victims of misogyny as well as beneficiaries (and sometimes facilitators) of racial persecution.

Angelika Ebbinghaus captured the ambiguities inherent in thinking about women, historical agency, and periodization in her anthology, *Opfer und Täterinnen*, which documented women's roles in state-sanctioned killing and identified continuities that linked Weimar, Nazi, and West German history. In other anthologies, notably *Daughters' Questions*, feminists subjected women's participation in National Socialism to new understandings of agency and complicity.[17] Particularly in Anglo-American contexts, many historians found poststructural approaches useful for examining identity formation and subjectivity as well as for analyzing the subtle gradations in power across ethnic, age, and gender (as well as class) lines that had been obscured by *Opfer-Täter* polemics as well as by hegemonic history and its focus on large-scale state and economic structures.[18]

During the 1980s, these disputes caused barely a ripple on the surface of the academic mainstream. Nevertheless, the interpretative and methodological questions about agency, chronology, and the extent of ordinary Germans' participation in persecution that were raised in the women historians' (*HistorikerInnen*) debate prefigured the emphasis on ordinary Germans that dominated mainstream research agendas during the coming decade.

The Historical *Wende*

The end of the Cold War accelerated the demise of explanatory paradigms based on powerful men and impersonal structures as historians explored contradictions and learned to live with ambiguity. Although 1989–1990 represented a turning point, I do not imply that historians began anew from a kind of Zero Hour or that mainstream scholars suddenly embraced novel approaches, but rather I want to call attention to a methodological openness that inspired greater appreciation of pioneering work from earlier years.[19] To take one example, for three decades George Mosse had been writing a new kind of cultural history in his studies of commemoration antisemitism, sexuality, and masculinity, and in the 1990s more journal editors, conference organizers, departmental search committees, and funding institutions prioritized these approaches. Besides new theoretical understandings of history, four features of public culture contributed to shifts in the academic mainstream. The first change democratized the scholarly infrastructure via electronic communication and cheaper air travel, both of which facilitated international networking.

Commemorative culture occasioned by the fiftieth anniversaries of turning points in World War II provided a second catalyst. Exhibitions, scholarly conferences, ceremonies, mass-market publications, films, and media specials depicted Jewish victims, ordinary soldiers, and civilians, as well as previously ignored minorities, including homosexuals, Sinti, Roma, social misfits, victims of forced sterilization, and people with disabilities.[20] Many exhibits unleashed bitter debates that made the historian's craft visible to general audiences. Feminists also raised troubling questions about male lust when they read news of demands for an apology by Korean "comfort women" for their enslavement in Japanese wartime brothels and of mass rapes in Bosnia. During the height of "Holocaust awareness" in the 1980s, it had been considered unseemly to dwell on Germans' suffering, but Helke Sander's film *BeFreier und Befreite* (1992) shattered the silence about German women raped by Soviet soldiers. In another film, *Das Grosse Schweigen* (1995), Caroline von der Tann and Maren Niemeyer documented the forced prostitution organized by the German military. Commemorations of civilians who died as the result of Allied bombing raids culminated in mass protests against the newly erected statue of Sir Arthur "Bomber" Harris in England. In Michael Verhoven's *Nasty Girl* (which was acclaimed at the 1990 Berlin festival), a young woman exposes the Nazi past of her hometown. Annette Neumann's film about Ravensbrück, *Frauenkonzentrationslager* (1996), and Thomas Hausner's two-part television documentary, "Hitler's Women" and "Women and Hitler" (2000), indicated that women as historical figures had arrived in the public memory of Nazism.

Another ingredient of the new confrontation with the past, (*Vergangenheitsbewältigung*), was a veritable explosion of primary sources. Historians perused previously ignored diaries and letters and scoured newly opened Eastern European archives for evidence about genocidal processes within particular offices, camps, military units, ghettos, and towns under German occupation. Banks and corporations opened up their archives to scrutiny. Ulrich Herbert signaled the advent of a new era when he challenged researchers to "leave behind the stale and rigid terms of Holocaust scholarship" and "plunge afresh into the archives."[21] Herbert's own research reminds us, however, that this new empiricism did not necessarily emphasize women or gender.

In addition to shifts in scholarly infrastructures, public memory, and evidence, an ephemeral quality of the *Wende* subtly undercut cold war shibboleths. Feature films, like Stephen Spielberg's *Schindler's List* (1993), Max Färberböck's *Aimée and Jaguar* (1999), and Roman Polanski's *The Pianist* (2002), accustomed audiences to the coexistence of dissent and collaboration, sometimes within a single individual. On the eve of the sixtieth anniversary of the German defeat/liberation, audiences viewed the ordinary facets of the formerly demonized Third Reich in André Heller's *The Blind Spot* (2003), Lutz Hachmeister's *Hitler's Hit Parade* (2004), Oliver Hirschbiegel's *Downfall* (2004), and in the television series *Adolf Hitler and Alfred Speer* (2005).

The stark black-or-white categories of the cold war mainstream dissolved into post-*Wende* shades of gray. In his Nobel speech, Günter Grass commented that Germans who had been born just before the war "who had our fingers burned, we were the ones to repudiate the absolutes, the ideological black or white. Doubt and skepticism were our god-parents and the multitude of gray values their present to us."[22] Grass captured the extremes of the Third Reich in *Crabwalk* (*Im Krebsgang*), his account of a glorious Nazi cruise ship and its calamitous sinking at the end of the war.

Agency, Gender, and Experience

"Structures do not kill. Individuals do."[23] This simple statement encapsulated the interpretative *Wende* of the 1990s. The macro-level constructs once admired as elegant came to seem simplistic. Historians discovered dozens of mid-level Nazis as well as dissenters and produced a change so dramatic that the German Historical Institute (London) in 2004 sponsored a conference on the "biographical turn." In dozens of international conferences, historians asked what differentiated Nazi rule from other patriarchal dictatorships and how women's experiences differed from those of their male counterparts.

In preparing to write this review essay, I noted three conceptual changes in the ways historians frame their research. First, as the years 1933 through1945 settle into *la longue durée*, periodization based on this time period recedes. 1929, 1934, 1939, 1942 and 1948 emerge as chronological markers. For example, Lora Wildenthal and Martha Mamozai continue the history of women and colonialism into the Third Reich. In *The Heimat Abroad*, the contributors follow the ethnic German (*Volksdeutsche*) diaspora across time and space. Christine Eckelmann's study of women in health care, Geraldine Horan's account of the feminine in Nazi discourse, and Raffael Scheck's study of politically conservative women all make (dis)continuities with Weimar a central theme. The authors of *Hidden Traditions*, compare images of women in Weimar, Nazi, and Federal Republic of Germany. In her magisterial *Warriors' Wives*, Birthe Kundrus makes World War I fundamental to her interpretation of World War II.

The second trend, a proliferation of specialized studies, means that historians conduct research on topics that would have been dismissed by conventional scholars as trivial two decades ago. Close readings of visual and verbal texts enable historians of gender to discern the workings of power in relationship to identity and popular culture. Concentrating on a single town or organization allows oral historians to view history and memory as mutually constitutive. Collaboration among archivists, civic leaders, and historians has produced a wealth of information about individual memory, as suggested by titles based on informants' words, such as, *"Finally I Have a Place to Put My Memory"* and *"Did Something Actually Happen Back Then?"* Working within a tight focus allows authors to capture nuance and vivid detail in books that range from a study of women composers in Nazi Germany to a history of women in the Nazi Party before 1933.[24]

Third, much recent scholarship explores the formation of collective gender and ethnic identities in opposition to the "racially unwanted." Instead of taking hierarchies for granted, historians explore the ways "Aryan" arrogance deepened phobic racism and ask how both shaped ethnic Germans' as well as persecuted minorities' experiences of sexuality and violence. Rather than searching for contradictions between Nazi doctrine and a stable "reality," historians are more concerned with understanding how gender-specific social norms and cultural expectations constructed identity and experience.

Much recent scholarship occurs at points where the history of women and gender addresses questions that also engage mainstream scholars. Two major lines of inquiry call attention to women and gender. The first asks to what extent Germans participated in a transnational modernity that was characterized by secularism, mass consumption, social welfare, and leisure. The second inquires into ordinary Germans' participation in the persecution and, ultimately, extermination of "outsiders."

Gender and Modernity

According to canonical cold war history, Nazism was barbaric—part of what Norbert Elias called a "de-civilizing" process. In the late 1980s, however, a counter narrative revived an older tradition that traced the Holocaust to the ravages of a rationality that began with Enlightenment thinkers' hubris about the perfectibility of human society.[25] National Socialist modernity, in this account, took the form of utopian schemes to cleanse the *Volkskörper*, which, as a gendered lens shows, had different outcomes for males and females. Research on two very different subjects falls under this rubric: (1) programs to improve the health, reproduction, and welfare of the *Volksgemeinschaft* (ethnic community) and (2) programs to maintain levels of consumption that would gratify ethnic Germans' expectations for "the good life."

Investigating what Michel Foucault termed "biopower," historians identify the operations of gender within state-directed health care, data collection, behavioral regulation, and surveillance operations.[26] As Nazi rule stabilized, Germans' vulnerability to intrusive state policies varied according to gender, ethnicity, and generation, and it becomes clear how porous the "private" sphere was. Gabriele Czarnowsky documents the ways that laws, state surveillance, and public scrutiny affected ordinary citizens as well as people designated as "dangerous." Using records of public health campaigns against venereal disease, Annette Timm identifies the mechanisms that constrained women's and men's personal choices in the name of collective good.[27] Claudia Schoppmann and Günther Grau trace the impact of sexual repression on lesbians and homosexuals. Petra Fuchs analyzes the fates of physically handicapped people under policy guidelines of Weimar and Nazi regimes. Petra Kannappel's and Bettina Bab's histories of individual women who had been sterilized add to our understandings of individual Aryans classed as "unworthy."[28]

Social histories of gender reconstruct cultural milieus and document broad structural trends. Kundrus interprets the records of the women accused of having forbidden sexual relationships in the context of prescriptive literature that exhorted soldiers' wives to chastity. Alexandra Przyrembel follows the cases of the two thousand Jewish men convicted of having sexual relations with non-Jewish women (who were not punished) and also examines the Nazi media campaign that capitalized on these relatively few cases to spread panic about "racial treason." Besides documenting Gestapo officials' obsessive investigations of *Rassenschande*, Patricia Szobar analyzes the media coverage of supposedly hyper-sexualized male and female Jews that shaped the "modes of perception and legitimization" among average Germans.[29]

As Susanne Heim, Henry Friedlander, and others have noted, the extermination facilities constructed during World War II employed personnel from prior eugenic programs that targeted "unproductive elements" in the *Volksgemeinschaft*. Women in the helping professions made a vital contribution by reporting potentially "defective" students and clients to public health authorities, caring for them, and (after 1939) administering the lethal injections that most physicians preferred to avoid. Through biographies of individual women, Lilo Haag traces social workers' responses to Nazism within specific institutions. In *Women in a Dark Time*, an authors' collective portrays the variety of responses to Nazi goals among women social workers in the Confessing Church. In the archives of two "euthanasia" centers, Bronwyn McFarland-Icke chronicles nurses' "moral realignment" as they accommodated themselves to a daily routine of quiet murder. She also observes that the few women who dissented were simply transferred. Official rebuke, McFarland-Icke suggests, could have made their opposition a question of conscience. By not calling attention to dissent, authorities framed civil courage as a personal failing.[30]

In the second focus of the modernity debates, gender plays a key role in histories of consumer society. Although historians of other nations explored the topic during the 1980s, historians of Nazi Germany studied leisure and sports but neglected consumption—perhaps because the concept of a totalitarian consumer society seemed oxymoronic. According to cold war thinking, Nazi propaganda deprived individuals of choice, which was a precondition of a consumer society. As Arendt put it, "The aim of totalitarian education has never been to instill convictions but to destroy the capacity to form any."

Where earlier studies equated Nazi propaganda with brainwashing (a cold war concept), scholars in the 1990s depict the Nazis as consummate marketers. Disputing images of an austere anti-consumer Nazi culture, Hartmut Berghoff contends that "official regulation and the inherent dynamics of consumerism" were evenly balanced. Advertisers enhanced consumerist desires, despite official admonitions to live frugally.[31] Nancy Reagin and Renate Harter-Meyer examine the impact of housewife education and consumer culture in guiding shopping patterns that facilitated the first Four Year plan.[32] Innovative studies of working-class life barely mention police terror and the decline in real wages, but instead explore topics like family consumption patterns and leisure activities. New research dispels other stereotypes. Hitler's charisma, long treated as if it were innate, comes under the scrutiny of feminists who analyze its production. The word "Kitsch" vanishes as historians take seriously the gendered and racialized cultural practices of National Socialist Realism. Christina von Braun draws on Otto Weiniger in exploring the affinities between misogyny and anti-Semitism. Alelheid von Saldern shows how cultural feminism could reinforce the masculinity of Nazi art forms (particularly sculpture).[33] Uli Linke juxtaposes "the feminine" against "the Jew" and examines the operations of collective representation in the "feminization of the racial subaltern" in the aesthetic of the *Volksgemeinschaft*.[34]

Building on Walter Benjamin's concept of the "aestheticization of politics," historians of material culture describe the aestheticization of everyday life. What Peter Reichel called the "beautiful glow" (*schöne Schein*) of the Third Reich was not merely a simulacrum of well-being that masked a grim reality, but a reflection of most "Aryan" Germans' experience. Shelley Baranowski, Kristin Semmens, and Christine Keitz describe workers' gratitude for the first paid vacation of their lives.[35] In histories of cabaret, jazz, sports, and the 1936 Olympics, German women and men behaved like other ordinary Europeans. Barbara Schrödl and Angela Vaupel analyze gender in feature films that appeared to be devoid of ideology. Gloria Sultano integrates her own family history into a nuanced account of the expulsion of Jews from the clothing industry, and the discursive strategies that both rationalized theft of Jews' property and also celebrated Nazi style. Refusing an either/or paradigm, Irene Guenther highlights the ways in which prudery and sexual enticement functioned in tandem in women's fashion.[36] In these works, the gendered, "Aryan" consumer displaces "mass man" as an icon of modernity.

Perhaps because of the attention to the role of gender and generation in shaping women's subjectivity, new studies provide a complex view of growing up in Nazi Germany. Two collections of documents, one by Sabine Hering and Kurt Schilde and one by Gisela Miller-Kipp, give readers direct access to a wealth of primary sources. Specialized studies abound, among which are Angela Vogel's and Susanne Watzke-Otte's histories of work programs,

Alexander Shuck's analysis of school books, and Haidi Manns's history of university women.[37]

As historians escape from the chronological straightjacket of 1933–1945, many notice unsettling continuities. For example, Johanna Gehmacher, Katharina von Kellenbach, Ljiljana Radonic, Ilse Korotin, and Charlotte Kohn-Ley discover a tradition of anti-Semitism in women's rights organizations. Alison Owings' oral history reveals women's fond memories of their lives as young women in Nazi Germany. Under Angelika Schaser's gaze, women's rights campaigner Gertrud Bäumer becomes at best an ambivalent role model.[38] Generation-based comparisons raise gender-specific issues. In comparing mothers past childbearing age to younger mothers with children at home, Elizabeth Heineman contrasted mothers' and soldiers' gender-specific entitlements in wartime. Dorothee Wierling's description of postwar public memory in the Federal Republic explores the interaction between gender and generation.[39] These studies testify to the dynamism that can result when histories of gender and modernity converge.

The Demise of the Genderless Perpetrator

Perpetrator research (*Täterforschung*) comprises the second historiographical line of inquiry that expanded after the *Wende*. What role did average Germans play in persecuting Jews and stigmatizing "unwanted" people? A neglected subject during the Cold War, perpetrator research galvanizes immense scholarly energy today Although several underappreciated historical works had already exposed chilling details about the extent of ordinary Germans' participation in genocide, the renewed interest in perpetrators coincided with a public culture convulsed by the memory wars of the 1990s. After years of quarrelling about the agency of either ideology or social structures, researchers share a "new consensus" that genocidal killers had been neither cogs nor sadists, but "opportunistic idealists" who maximized their own self-interest in the name of collectivist goals—with considerably more autonomy (*Spielraum*) than previously suspected.[40]

Troubling questions emerge. If participation in mass murder had not been coerced, why had so few dissented? Although most perpetrator researchers see themselves as empiricists, the few who theorize their findings turn to social science, particularly to the obedience and conformity experiments of the cold war that generalized about human behavior on the basis of male subjects' responses. A few historians paid attention to gender in histories written for general readers in the 1980s. Writer Gitta Sereny, journalist Tom Segev, and geneticist Benno Müller-Hill understood the role of wives and women relatives of perpetrators in stabilizing their murderous husbands.

Peter Chroust and Ernst Klee edited primary sources by perpetrators that revealed the coexistence of sentimentality about their families with cruelty toward their victims.

Statistics aggregated by sex that had been overlooked previously provided new insights into perpetrators' weltanschauung. When, for example, in the late summer of 1941, *Einsatzkommando* units began to murder, not only Jewish men (described as "bandits" being punished for crimes) but also women and children (labeled simply "Jews"), the shift marked a new stage in soldiers' moral hardening. Nazi leaders' reluctance to conscript most categories of German women into the wartime labor force indicated the power of polarized gender stereotypes. In Hungary, Miklós Horthy's decision to send Jewish males to slave labor brigades instead of deporting them to death camps, underscored the contrast between his pragmatic anti-Semitism and Nazi commanders' exterminatory zeal.[41]

Unlike most historians of genocide, some researchers realized, as Ann Taylor Allen put it in 1997, that we "can no longer treat women as symbols or subjects in a female realm outside of history, but as active agents with moral responsibility for history."[42] Gudrun Schwarz's meticulous archival research provides a wealth of information about SS men's wives and mistresses who lived (usually sumptuously) near killing sites and also about the dense social world of the SS "tribal community" (*Sippengemeinschaft*). Karin Orth explains how assumptions about "natural" differences between men and women contributed to the sham respectability extolled by Heinrich Himmler.[43] Yaacov Lozowick observes that women's presence could make the offices in which extermination was organized seem like ordinary workplaces. Even historians of all-male organizations mentioned women. Michael Kater's history of the Hitler Youth, Michael Wildt's analysis of SS functionaries in the RSHA, and Michael Mann's profile of genocidal soldiers include information about females that contests conventional images of the ideal Nazi woman.[44]

Earlier histories had ignored the five hundred bordello barracks near military encampments on the Eastern Front and the special (*sonder*) comfort stations on concentration camp grounds. But recent historians of women refuse to accept men's sexual crimes as a natural byproduct of war. Birgit Beck examines what amounted to institutionalized mass rape in officially sanctioned army bordellos. Far from being sex workers, many (perhaps most) inmates of these camps had been arrested for petty crimes, black marketeering, or suspicion. Many had "volunteered" in exchange for promises their family would be safe. Christa Schulz and Cristl Wickert call attention to a gender-specific dimension of male labor camps in the practice of rewarding not only guards but also "privileged" male slave laborers with brothel visits.[45] Ingrid Schmidt Harzbach, Norman Naimark, Atina Grossmann, Andrea Pető, Regina Mühlhäuser, and others investigate Soviet soldiers' rape of German women at the end of the war. Paralleling this research, histories of aerial bombing include German civilians (disproportionately women and children) as victims.[46]

Personal letters and diaries by soldiers and their families provide a wealth of data about gendered subjectivities during the war years. Researchers who mine this material do not search for overarching narratives or metatheories because, as Anne Sattler phrases it, the contradictions in family interviews, letters, and newspapers form the core of her research. In her interviews with German women who had grown up in the Third Reich, Birgit Rommelspacher examines complex attitudes toward Jews and memories of Nazi atrocities that resist simplification.[47]

In conducting research on soldiers' morale, unit cohesion, and cultural expectations of heroism, scholars observed the dependence of masculine identity on an imagined feminine, in ways that build on Karin Hausen's concept of gendered spheres. Hannes Heer, for example, notes that soldiers' visions of their wives and families enhanced their self-image as "quiet heroes," which in turn facilitated the "moralization of crime."[48] In soldiers' letters, Inge Marssolek discovers a doubled moral self that cordoned off a "feminine" home front from a brutal "masculine" eastern front. As Thomas Kühne puts it, "constructs of femininity made this world tolerable for both men and women." In her study of frontline soldiers, Susanne zur Nieden hypothesized that soldiers' motivation shifted from racial conquest of inferior peoples early in the war to defense of virtuous wives and families when defeat became inevitable. In her study of Auschwitz, Sybille Steinbacher describes the role of domesticity in sustaining the mental stability of the SS personnel at Auschwitz. "Mass murder and domesticity were not, therefore, the poles of an opposition but instead tightly interwoven."[49]

Far from being a natural byproduct of war, heroism was formed according to specifically Nazi ideals, as Jay Baird and René Schilling have noted. Examining male bonding, Christoph Rass finds a surprising degree of unit cohesion even in the chaos of retreat. In *Home/Front*, contributors examine role of gender in such commonplace aspects of military life as *Manneszucht*, disability, sexuality, and comradeship.[50] Doris Bergen discovered that military chaplains, who ought to have exerted a humane influence, actually eased killers' consciences by adopting a "tough guy" swagger to ward off ridicule as "sissies." Polarized gender expectations were far from "natural," however, as Todd Ettelson demonstrates in his analysis of the interplay of sexuality and discipline, chaos and order, in the elite cultures of the SS and SA.[51]

Most anthologies on women and the Holocaust, like those edited by Barbara Distel and Claus Füllberg-Stollberg, include only a few studies of direct perpetrators. Given the immense disproportion between male and female perpetrators, the paucity of research on women is not surprising. Until Gudrun Schwarz's work, historians barely noticed the roughly ten thousand women employed by the SS and the three thousand women who served in labor and extermination camps. This oversight originated in part because only a handful of the thousands of individuals tried for war crimes were women. In addition, as Insa Eschebach observes, because survival for Jewish prisoners depended on avoiding contact with guards, they remembered little, and non-Jewish former prisoners may not have admitted to knowing much about their guards because that would suggest that they had collaborated in order to survive. Even when evidence exists, it is difficult to interpret the acts of women victims of misogyny who supply vital support to men who oppress other women. Perhaps, as Susannah Heschel put it, it's easier to think women are "innocent by nature."[52]

Anyone who studies female perpetrators does so in the context of a culture that has sensationalized Nazism by locating evil in eroticized women (from Lina Wertmuller's 1975 film *Seven Beauties* through Bernard Schlink's 2001 novel *The Reader*). Historians of gender make this context central to their research. Approaching the eroticization of Nazi brutality from very different standpoints, Silke Wenk and Carolyn Dean historicize the ways particular narratives of masculine/feminine and perpetrator/victim stabilize our knowledge about unspeakable atrocity.[53] The strength of much new research lies in its careful attention not only to the accuracy of memory, but also to its construction (*Gedächtniskonstruktion*).

Recent scholarship on war crimes trials compares the sentences of women and men defendants. In her article in *Memory and Gender*, Julia Düsterberg attributes women's higher conviction rates to West German prosecutors' representations of female concentration camp guards as "monsters." Contributors to Ulrike Weckel and Edgar Wolfrum's *'Bestien' und 'Befehlsempfänger'* take an additional step by examining the fluid discursive frames within which binary gender oppositions played out in trials, the media, and public memory. Eschebach, for example, discovers that immediately after German defeat, judges in the Soviet zone sentenced women camp personnel lightly because they perceived them as naïve, working-class girls who had been led astray. But in the 1950s when GDR leaders used similar trials for didactic purposes, prosecutors represented defendants as masculine bitches (*Mannweiber*), beasts, shrews (*Megäre*), and girl gun slingers (*Flintenweiber*)—akin to representations of guards Irma Grese, Ilsa Koch, and Dorothea Binz in earlier trials in the West.[54]

New biographies of key women in Nazi Germany contest earlier stereotypes. In addition to Massimiliano Livi's study of Gertrud Scholtz-Klink, chief of Nazi Women's organizations, other biographers depict mid-level women leaders, film stars, social workers, leaders' wives, and unique personalities like Gestapo agent Carmen Mory, pilot Hannah Reitch, theologian Meta Eyl, and film director Leni Riefenstahl. Less flamboyant figures also attract attention, among them the gynecologist and racial scientist Agnes Bluhm, Hitler's secretary Gertraud Junge, the chief of the "protective" youth camp at Uckermark Johanna Braach, and the director of a Ravensbrück satellite camp Hermine Braunsteiner. Other women facilitators of Nazi power operated quietly at the grass roots. Vandana Joshi's and Rita Wolters's examinations of police archives make it clear that large numbers of women denounced neighbors and friends to the Gestapo, although Katrin Dördelmann reminds us that women were slightly underrepresented among denouncers and that their motivations were often more family-centered and less political than men's.[55]

The seemingly clear-cut cases of women camp guards defy categorical judgments because so many of them had been deceived by recruiters who promised them ordinary war-related employment. When they discovered the deception, most did their duty. Recent accounts of women concentration camp personnel elucidate multiple strata of privilege and oppression.[56] In an exemplary monograph on so-called asocial women in Ravensbrück, Christa Schikorra supplements her archival research with oral histories that reveal complex webs of complicity, shame, and opposition. Typologies based on perpetrators' motivation impose an order on this complexity, but these ideal types have limited heuristic value because it is impossible to account for any individual's motives for collaboration or dissent.[57]

New empirical research dispels the notion that race war was exclusively men's work. From the first laws in 1933, the effectiveness of racial persecution depended on women's willingness to enforce what Orlando Patterson calls social death by, for example, betraying friends, ostracizing "undesirables," and boycotting proscribed businesses. War intensified the pressure to maintain spatial and emotional frontiers against the forced laborers who toiled in the midst of "Aryan" society. Annekatrein Mendel's interviews with "employers" and "their" *Fremdarbeiter* (foreign workers) recall master and slave narratives, in which the former recall happy times and the latter bleak oppression. In a study of one labor camp in the Harz Mountains, Bernhild Vogel weaves together documents, interviews of Ukrainian former inmates, photographs, and her own thoughtful comments. In addition to statistically demonstrating the dependence of the war economy on non-German women workers, Pia Gerber describes the brutal methods that drew "volunteers" to German factories and also carefully reads the figurative language in which Nazi administrators expressed their instrumental rationality.[58]

Zealous female Nazis also maintained racial borders in occupied nations. Elizabeth Harvey describes Nazi women who created a sense of racial order behind the front while soldiers faced the chaos of conquest in the "wild East." Their morale-building activities included preparing expropriated houses for German settlers, keeping ethnic Germans as well as Polish "natives" under surveillance, and selecting "Aryan-looking" infants born to Polish mothers for adoption by Germans. Although they must have witnessed cruelty, as one woman told Harvey, they worked so hard, they simply "forgot all Jews and Poles." Gudrun Brockhaus, in her outstanding cultural study, however, suspects that the forgetting happened after German defeat. She quoted the wife of a Polish teacher in Chelmo, who presumably had not been aware of a need to censor herself when she told Claude Lanzmann, "When the Jews arrived and were herded into the church or the castle . . . The screaming, oh, it was so terrible . . . Fearful screams!"[59]

The Challenge of Post-Cold War History

Since the *Wende*, it appears that the "Atlantic divide" is closing. Most recent histories of women and gender written in German and English attest to authors' willingness to acknowledge the contingency of their conclusions. Whether or not they explicitly engage theoretical concepts, they accept the fluidity of the categories they use when interpreting archival evidence. Historians writing in German have expanded social science methodology and conducted meticulous research on topics that once would have been regarded as marginal. To a greater extent than among Anglophone scholars, German historians assume that "gender" encompasses masculinity as well as femininity. On both sides of the erstwhile divide, historians shun grand narratives and instead investigate the representations that structured their subjects' experiences. In place of coherent truth claims, most historians of women and gender accept the conceptual fuzziness of their sources and undermine stable notions of periodization, agency, and subjectivity.

New scholarship on women and gender has entered the mainstream in textbooks, anthologies, journals, and conferences. Anthologies and surveys of women's history no longer pass lightly over the Nazi period. As historians of women and gender situate their research within an expanding historiographical mainstream, it would seem that a once-marginal subfield has "arrived."

In 1989 Isabel Hull noticed how easily mainstream historians may think they "know" women's history on the basis of reading a few monographs—as if they "have just acquired some tinsel they can hang on their old tree." Most recent "old tree" *Gesamtdarstellungen* include bits of tinsel but remain unchanged.[60] Recent scholarship on women finds a niche without affecting larger metanarratives. For example, perhaps because Hans-Ulrich Wehler disdains what he calls "the fashionable trends in the United States," his grand synthesis includes scholarship on women as subjects without attributing agency either to them or to constructions of gender.[61] Rather than perceiving this situation as an impasse, I suggest we see it as a threshold. Grappling with the revisionist interpretations and meticulous research of recent scholarship, the *Gesamtdarstellungen* of the next decade will shift. Although gender and women may not illuminate all research questions or provide the structure of a new metanarrative, historians of women and gender will expand this swiftly moving tributary. Historians in the mainstream will understand that without including women and accounting for the force of gender in Nazi Germany, no account of this catastrophic era can be satisfying.

Notes

1. Atina Grossmann, "Women and the Holocaust," *Holocaust and Genocide Studies* 16, no. 1 (2002): 94–105; Dalia Ofer and Lenore Weitzman, "Introduction," in *Women in the Holocaust* (New Haven, 1998), 12–16; and Joan Ringelheim, "The Split between Gender and the Holocaust," in ibid., 340–350.
2. The basis for my generalization about the mainstream is the inclusion of research on women and gender in journals of general history such as *Geschichte und Gesellschaft* (GG), the *Vierteljahrshefte für Zeitgeschichte* (VfZ), *German Studies Review* (GerSR), *Central European History* (CEH), and *German History* (GH) as well as in specialized journals such as the *Révue d'histoire de la Shoah, Dachauer Hefte* (DH), *Leo Baeck Yearbook*, (LBY), *Yad Vashem Studies* (*YVS*) and *Holocaust and Genocide Studies* (HGS).
3. Carola Sachse, "Frauenforschung zum Nationalsozialismus," *Mittelweg 36* 6 (April–May 1997): 24–42.
4. Elizabeth D. Heineman, "Sexuality and Nazism: The Doubly Unspeakable?" in *Sexuality and German Fascism*, ed. Dagmar Herzog (New York, 2002), 22–67.
5. Ofer and Weitzman, *Women;* and Carol Ann Rittner and John Roth, eds., *Different Voices* (New York, 1993).
6. Richard Bessel, "Functionalists vs Intentionalists," *German Studies Review* 26, no. 1 (2003): 15–20; Mark Roseman, "Ideas, Context, and the Pursuit of Genocide," *Bulletin of the German Historical Institute* (London) 25, no. 3 (2003): 64–87; and Michael Geyer, "Germany," *South Atlantic Quarterly* 96, no. 4 (1997): 663–702.
7. Hannah Arendt, *The Origins of Totalitarianism* (Cleveland, 1958), 465–468; and Stephen Miller, "A Note on the Banality of Evil," *The Wilson Quarterly* 22, no. 4 (1998): 54–56.
8. Hermann Langbein, *Menschen in Auschwitz* (Vienna, 1972), 320; G. M. Gilbert, "The Mentality of the SS Murderous Robots," *Yad Vashem Studies* 5 (1963); and Michael Allen, *The Business of Genocide* (Chapel Hill, 2002), 8–15, 78–92. Max Weber wrote, "It is horrible to think that the world could one day be filled with nothing but those little cogs, little men clinging to little jobs and striving toward bigger ones." in *Sociological Theory*, eds L.A. Coser and B. Rosenberg New York, 1976, 361–362.
9. Dorothea Schmidt, "Die peinlichen Verwandtschaften—Frauenforschung zum Nationalsozialismus," in *Normalität oder Normalisierung?* ed. Heide Gerstenberger and Dorothea Schmidt (Münster, 1987), 51–55.
10. Mary Nolan, "Work, Gender and Everyday Life," in *Stalinism and Nazism*, ed. Ian Kershaw and Moshe Lewin (Cambridge, 1997), 311–315, 329, 334.

11. Martin Broszat et al., eds., *Bayern in der NS-Zeit* (Munich, 1977–1983); Lutz Niethammer, *'Die Jahre weiss man nicht'* (Berlin, 1983); Thomas Lindenberger, "Everyday History," in *The Divided Past*, ed. Christoph Klessmann (Oxford, 2001), 46–53; and Geoff Eley, "Hitler's Silent Majority?" *Michigan Quarterly Review* 42, nos. 2–3 (2003): 389–425, 550–583.

12. Suzanne Dammer and Carola Sachse, "Nationalsozialistische Frauenpolitik," *Beiträge zur feministischen Theorie und Praxis* 5, no. 5 (1981): 108, 117.

13. See also Ute Frevert, "Klasse und Geschlecht—ein deutscher Sonderweg?" in *Nichts als Unterdrückung?* ed. Logie Barrow et al. (Münster, 1991); and Kathleen Canning, "German Particularities," *Journal of Women's History* 5, no. 1 (1993): 102–113.

14. Frigga Haug, "Frauen—Opfer oder Täter," *Argument Studienhefte* 46 (1982): 3, 37.

15. Margarete Mitscherlich, *Die friedfertige Frau*. Frankfurt a.M., 1985, 151–152; Gisela Bock, *Zwangssterilisation im Nationalsozialismus*, Opladen, 1986, 380; idem., "Die Frauen und der Nationalsozialismus," *GG*, 15, no. 4 (1989): 563–79; Christine Thürmer-Rohr, "Aus der Täuschung in die Ent-Täuschung," *Beiträge zur feministischen Theorie und Praxis*. 8 (1983): 11–26. P. 11.

16. Karin Windaus-Walser, „'Gnade der weiblichen Geburt?'" *Feministische Studien*, 1988, no. 1, 102–115. See also Helga Schubert, *Judasfrauen*, Frankfurt a.M.,1990; Atina Grossmann, "Feminist Debates," *Gender & History*, 3, no. 3 (1991): 350–58; Adelheid von Saldern, "Victims or Perpetrators? in *Nazism and German Society*, ed David Crew, London, 1994, 141–66; Joyce Mushaben, "Collective Memory Divided: and Reunited," *History & Memory* 11.1 (1999) 7–40; R.M. Leck, "Conservative Empowerment," *Journal of Women's History* 12 no. 2 (2000): 147–169.

17. Angelika Ebbinghaus, ed., *Opfer und Täterinnen* (Nördlingen, 1987); Lerke Gravenhors and Carmen Tatschmurat, eds., *Töchter-Fragen* (Freiburg i.Br., 1990); and Uta Schmidt, "Wohin mit unserer gemeinsamen Betroffenheit?" in *Weiblichkeit in geschichtler Perspektive*, ed. Ursula Becher and Jörn Büsen (Frankfurt/M., 1988), 502–516.

18. Jane Caplan, "Post Modernism, Poststructuralism," and Isabel V. Hull, "Feminist and Gender History," *Central European History* 22, no. 3–4 (1989): 260–301; Hannah Schissler, *Geschlechterverhältnisse im historischen Wandel* (Frankfurt/M., 1993); and Ute Daniel, "Clio unter Kulturschock," *Geschichte in Wissenschaft und Unterricht* 48 (1997): 195–217.

19. Hans-Ulrich Wehler is among the doubtful. See Andreas Daum, "German History in Historical Perspective: Interview with Hans-Ulrich Wehler," at http://www.ghi-dc.org/bulletin26S00/b26wehler.html, (accessed 15 March 2005).

20. Jürgen Müller, Wolfgang Berude, eds., *Das sind Volksfeinde!* (Cologne, 1998); and Mary Nolan, "Air Wars," *Central European History* 38, no. 1 (2005): 7–40.

21. "Foreword," in *National Socialist Extermination Policies*, ed. Ulrich Herbert (New York, 2000), vii.

22. The full text is found at http://nobelprize.org/nobel_prizes/literature/laureates/1999/lecture-e.html (April 10, 2005).

23. Klaus-Michael Mallmann, "Die Sicherheitspolizei," in *Täter der Shoah*, ed. Gerhard Paul (Göttingen, 2002), 125.

24. Bea Dörr et al., eds., *"Endlich habe ich einen Platz für meine Erinnerungen gefunden"* (Herbolzheim, 2000); Ursula Bernhold et al., *"Ist denn da was gewesen?"* (Oldenbourg, 1996); Claudia Friedel, *Komponierende Frauen* (Hamburg, 1995); Hans-Jürgen Arendt et al., eds., *Nationalsozialistische Frauenpolitik* (Frankfurt/M., 1995); and Andrew Bergerson, *Ordinary Germans* (Bloomington, 2004).

25. Enzo Traverso, *Origins of Nazi Violence* (New York, 2003), 35–45.

26. Edward Ross Dickinson, "Biopolitics, Fascism, Democracy," *Central European History* 37, no. 1 (2004): 1–48; Kathleen Canning, "The Body as Method?" *Gender & History* 11, no. 3 (1999): 499–513.

27. Gabriele Czarnowski, *Das kontrollierte Paar* (Weinheim, 1991); and Annette F. Timm, "Sex with a Purpose," in Herzog, *Sexuality*, 23–255.

28. Claudia Schoppma and Günther Grau, eds., *Hidden Holocaust?* (Chicago, 1995); Petra Fuchs, *"Körperbehinderte" zwischen Selbstaufgabe und Emanzipation* (Neuwied, 2001); Petra Kannappel, *Die Behandlung von Frauen im nationalsozialistischen Familienrecht* (Darmstadt, 1999); and Bettina Bab, "Im falschen Moment laut gelacht," *BfTP* 18 (1995): 33–42.

29. Miriam Enzweiler, *Fremdarbeiterinnen und Fremdarbeiter* (Krefeld, 1994); Birthe Kundrus, "Forbidden Company," in Herzog, *Sexuality*, 142; Patricia Szobar, "Race Defilement in Germany," in idem, 201–222; Kundrus, "'Die Unmoral deutscher Soldatenfrauen,'" in *Zwischen Karriere und Verfolgung*, ed. Kirsten Heinsohn et al. (Frankfurt/M., 1997), 96–110; Alexandra Przyrembel, *Rassenschande* (Göttingen, 2003); Doris Bergen, "Sex, Blood, and Vulnerability," and Annette Timm, "The Ambivalent Outsider," in *Social Outsiders*, eds. Robert Gellately and Nathan Stoltzfuss (Princeton, 2001), 192–211.

30. Lilo Haag, *Berufsbiographische Erinnerungen von Fürsorgerinnen* (Freiburg i.Br., 2000); Bronwyn McFarland-Icke, *Nurses in Nazi Germany* (Princeton, 1999), 248; Uta Cornelia Schmatzler, *Verstrickung, Mitverantwortung und Täterschaft* (Kiel, 1994). 241–287; and Susi Hausammann et al., eds., *Frauen in dunkler Zeit* (Cologne, 1996).

31. Hartmut Berghoff, "Enticement and Deprivation," in *The Politics of Consumption*, ed. Martin Daunton and Matthew Hilton (Oxford, 2001), 166–177; Pamela Swett et al., eds., *Selling Modernity* (Durham, 2006); Alon Confino and Rudy Koshar, "Régimes of Consumer Culture," *German History* 19,no. 2 (2001): 135–161; and Paul Betts, *The Authority of Everyday Objects* (Berkeley, 2004), 21–34. See also Ulrich Heinemann, "Krieg und Frieden an der 'inneren Front,'" in *Nicht nur Hitlers Krieg*, ed. Christoph Klessmann and Ute Frevert (Düsseldorf, 1989).

32. Nancy Reagin, *"Marktordnung* and Autarkic Housekeeping," *German History* 19, no. 2 (2001): 162–184; Renate Harter-Meyer, *Der Kochlöffel ist unsere Waffe* (Baltmannsweiler, 1999); 74–81, 84–107.

33. Uta Gerhardt, "Charismatische Herrschaft," *Geschichte und Gesellschaft* 24, no. 4 (1998): 503–538; Cristina von Braun, "'Der Jude' und 'Das Weib,'" *Metis* 1, no. 2 (1992): 6–28; Adelheid von Saldern, *The Challenge of Modernity* (Ann Arbor, 2002), 313–315, 337. Other works on popular culture include Barbara Determann et al., eds., *Verdeckte Überlieferungen* (Frankfurt/M., 1991); Andrew Bergerson, "Listening to the Radio," *German Studies Review* 24, no. 1 (2001): 83–113; Kate Lacey, *Feminine Frequencies* (Ann Arbor, 1996); and Inge Marssolek et al., eds., *Radio im Nationalsozialismus* (Tübingen, 1998).

34. Uli Linke, "The Violence of Difference," in *Sacrifice and National Belonging*, ed. Marcus Funck, et al. (College Station, TX, 2002), 156, 179–187.

35. Shelley Baranowski, *Strength through Joy* (Cambridge, 2004); Christine Keitz, *Reisen als Leitbild* (Munich, 1997); and Kristin Semmens, *Seeing Hitler's Germany* (Houndmills, 2005).

36. Barbara Schrödl, *Das Bild des Künstlers und seiner Frauen* (Marburg, 2004); Angela Vaupel, *Frauen im NS-Film* (Hamburg, 2002); Jo Fox, *Filming Women in the Third Reich* (Oxford, 2000); Gloria Sultano, *Wie Geistiges Kokain* (Vienna, 1995); and Irene Guenther, *Nazi chic?* (Oxford, 2004).

37. Sabine Hering and Kurt Schilde, *Das BDM Werk "Glaube und Schönheit"* (Berlin, 2000); Elisabeth Perchinig, *Zur Einübung von Weiblichkeit* (Munich, 1998); Gisela Miller-Kipp, *Auch Du gehörst dem Führer* (Weinheim, 2001); Angela Vogel, *Das Pflichtjahr für Mädchen* (Frankfurt/M., 1997); and Haide Manns, *Frauen für den Nationalsozialismus* (Opladen, 1997).

38. Johanna Gehmacher, *Völkische Frauenbewegung* (Vienna, 1998); Charlotte Kohn-Ley et al., eds., *Der feministische "Sundenfall"?* (Vienna, 1994); Ilse Korotin et al., eds., *Gebrochene Kontinuitäten* (Vienna, 2000); Katharina von Kellenbach, *Anti-Judaism in Feminist Religious Writings* (Atlanta, 1994); Susanne Omran, *Frauenbewegung und 'Judenfrage,'* (Frankfurt/M.,

2000), 405–435; Ljiljana Radoni, *Die friedfertige Antisemitin?* (Frankfurt/M., 2004); and Angelika Schaser, "Gertrud Bäumer," in *Zwischen Karriere*, Heinsohn et al eds., 24–43.

39. Elizabeth Heineman, "Age and Generation," *JWH* 12, no. 4 (2001): 139–164; Dorothee Wierling, "Generations," in Klessmann, *Divided Past*, 69–90; Mark Roseman, ed., *Generations in Conflict* (Cambridge, 1995).

40. George Browder, "Perpetrator Character and Motivation,"*Holocaust and Genocide Studies* 17, no. 3 (2003): 480–497; Peter Lieb, "Täter aus Überzeugung?" *Vierteljahrshefte für Zeitgeschichte* 50, no. 4 (2002): 523–558; and Wolf Kaiser, ed., *Täter im Vernichtungskrieg* (Berlin, 2002).

41. Herbert, ed. *Extermination*, 31, 87, 231, 261, 270 n., 48; Ute Frevert, "Frauen an der Heimatfront," in Klessmann, *Nicht Nur*, 50–73; Kundrus, *Kriegerfrauen*, 318–351; Tim Cole, "A Gendered Holocaust?" in *The Holocaust in Hungary*, ed. Randolph Braham (New York, 2005–2006).

42. Ann Taylor Allen, "The Holocaust and the Modernization of Gender," *Central European History* 30, no. 1 (1997): 349–364.

43. Gudrun Schwarz, *Eine Frau an seiner Seite* (Hamburg, 1997); Karin Orth, "Concentration Camp SS," in Herbert, *Extermination*, 306–334; and Yaacov Lozowick, *Hitler's Bureaucrats* (London, 2002), 55, 128–130, 164, 189.

44. For *Täterforschung* that mentions women in passing, see Klaus-Michael Mallmann et al., eds., *Karrieren der Gewalt* (Darmstadt, 2004); and Paul, *Täter*, 15, 55, 97, 105, 122–123, 182, 238, 262; Michael Kater, *Hitler Youth* (Cambridge Mass., 2004), 70–112; Michael Wildt, *Generation des Unbedingten* (Hamburg, 2002), 46–49, 190–203; and Michael Mann, "Were the Perpetrators of Genocide 'Ordinary Men' or 'Real Nazis'?" *Holocaust and Genocide Studies* 14, no. 3 (2000): 331–355.

45. Christa Schulz, "Weibliche Häftlinge aus Ravensbrück in Bordellen," in Fullberg-Stollberg, *Frauen*, 135–146; Birgit Beck, *Wehrmacht und sexuelle Gewalt* (Paderborn, 2004); Christl Wickert, "Tabu Lagerbordell," in Eschebach, *Gedächtnis*, 41–57; Christa Paul, *Zwangsprostitution* (Berlin, 1994).

46. Ingrid Schmidt Harzbach, "Eine Woche in April," in *Befreier und Befreite*, ed. Helke Sander et al. (Munich, 1992); Atina Grossmann, "A Question of Silence?" in *West Germany under Construction*, ed. Robert Moeller (Ann Arbor, 1997), 33–52; Angela Martin et al., *Ich fürchte die Menschen* (Berlin, 1996); Lothar Kettenacker, *Ein Volk von Opfern?* (Berlin, 2003); Regina Mühlhäuser, "Massenvergewaltigung," *Geschlecht hat Method*, ed. Veronika Aegeter et al. (Zurich, 1999); and Andrea Pető, "Stimmen des Schweigens," *Zeitschrift für Geschichtswissenschaft* 47 (1999): 892–913.

47. Anne Sattler, *Und was erfuhr des Soldaten Weib?* (Münster, 1994); and Birgit Rommelspacher, *Schuldlos—schuldig?* (Hamburg, 1995).

48. Klara Löffler, *Aufgehoben: Soldatenbriefe* (Bamberg, 1992), 87–116, 125–148; Wolfram Wette, ed., *Der Krieg des kleinen Mannes* (Munich, 1992); Ingrid Hammer et al., eds., *"Sehr selten habe ich geweint"* (Zurich, 1992); and Detlef Bald et al., eds., *Zivilcourage* (Frankfurt/M., 2004).

49. Karin Hausen, "Frauenräume," in Hausen, *Frauengeschichte*, 21–23; Hans Heer, "Bittere Pflicht, Der Rassenkrieg," in *Die Wehrmacht im Rassenkrieg*, eds Walter Manoschek et al., (Vienna, 1996), 116–136; Inge Marssolek, 'Ich möchte Dich zu gern mal in Uniform sehen,' *Werkstattgeschichte* 22 (1999): 41–59; Thomas Kühne, "Comradeship: Gender Confusion and Gender Order in the German Military," in *Home/Front: The Military, War and Gender in Twentieth-Century Germany*, eds Karen Hagemann and Stefanie Schüler-Springorum (Oxford, 2002), 233–254; Susanne zur Nieden, "Erotic Fraternization," in ibid., 303–306; Claudia Koonz, *Mothers in the Fatherland* (New York, 1987), 408–418; Sybille Steinbacher, *"Musterstadt" Auschwitz: Germanisierungspolitik und Judenmord in Ostoberschlesien* (Munich, 2000), 187.

50. Jay Baird, *To Die for Germany* (Bloomington, 1990); René Schilling, *"Kriegshelden"* (Paderborn, 2002); Christoph Rass, *"Menschenmaterial,"* (Paderborn, 2003); Hagemann et al. eds *Home/Front;* Stephen R. Haynes, "Ordinary Masculinity," *Journal of Men's Studies* 10, no. 2 (2002): 143–164.

51. Doris L. Bergen, "German Military Chaplains," *Church History* 70, no. 2 (2001): 232–248; Mario Zeck, *Das Schwarze Korps* (Tübingen, 2002); Todd Ettelson, "The Nazi 'New Man,'" Ph.D. diss., University of Michigan, 2002; Gudrun Schwarz, "During Total War," in *Crimes of War,* eds Omer Bartov et al. (New York, 2002), 121–137.

52. Claudia Card, "Women, Evil, and Grey Zones,"*Metaphilosophy* 31, no. 5 (2000): 517; Susannah Heschel, "Does Atrocity Have a Gender?" in *New Currents in Holocaust Research,* ed. Jeffrey Diefendorf, (Evanston, 2004), 293; Doris L. Bergen, "Pandora's Box," *JWH* 9, no. 1 (1997): 164–174.

53. Silke Wenk, "Rhetoriken der Pornografisierung," in Eschebach, *Gedächtnis,* 285–290; and Carolyn Dean, "Empathy, Pornography, and Suffering," *Differences* (Spring 2003): 88–125.

54. Julia Düsterberg, "Von der 'Umkehr aller Weiblichkeit,'" in Eschebach, *Gedächtnis,* 227–242; Insa Eschebach, "Gespaltene Frauenbilder," Isabel Richter, "Das *‚Andere'* hat kein Geschlecht," and Sabine Horn, "' . . . ich fühlte mich damals als Soldat,'" in *"Bestien" und "Befehlsempfänger": Frauen und Männer in NS-Prozessen nach 1945,* eds UlrikeWeckel and Edgar Wolfrum (Göttingen, 2003), 83–115, 175–193, 222–245; Anna Przyrembel, "Transfixed by an Image," *German History* 19, no. 3 (2001): 369; Ingrid Müller-Münch, *Die Frauen von Majdanek* (Hamburg, 1982); Daniel Patrick Brown, *The Beautiful Beast* (Ventura, Calif., 1996); Cate Haste, ed., *Nazi Women* (London, 2001); and Brown, *The Camp Women* (Atglen, Pa., 2002).

55. Vandana Joshi, *Gender and Power* (New York, 2003); Katrin Dördelmann, "Denunziationen im Nationalsozialismus," in Jerouschek et al. eds *Denunziation* (Tübingen, 1997), 157–167; idem, "'Aus einer gewissen Empörung,'" in Heinsohn, *Zwischen Karriere,* 189–205; Rita Wolters, *Verrat für die Volkswirtschaft* (Pfaffenweiler, 1996); Schmatzler, *Verstrickung,* 186–315; and Stephanie Abke, *Sichtbare Zeichen unsichtbarer Kräfte* (Tübingen, 2003), 101ff.

56. Bernhard Strebel, "Die 'Lagergesellschaft,'" in *Frauen in Konzentrationslagern,* ed. Claus Füllberg-Stollberg et al., (Bremen, 1994), 13–79, 241; Jack G. Morrison, *Everyday Life* (Princeton, 2000); Markus Kienle, *Gotteszell—das frühe Konzentrationslager für Frauen* (Ulm, 2002); Insa Eschebach, "SS-Aufseherinnen der Frauenkonzentrationslagers Ravensbrück," *Werkstatt Geschichte* 5, no 13 (1996): 39–48.

57. Christa Schikorra, *Kontinuitäten der Ausgrenzung,* (Berlin, 2001); Astrid von Chamier et al., eds., *Das Frauenkonzentrationslager Ravensbrück* (Berlin, 1997); and Bernard Strebel, *Das KZ Ravensbrück* (Paderborn, 2003); Gisela Bock, "Ganz normale Frauen," and Dagmar Reese, "Verstrickung und Verantwortung," in Heinsohn, *Zwischen Karriere,* 206–222 and 245–247, respectively.

58. Bernhild Vogel, *"Wir waren fast noch Kinder,"* Goslar, 2003; Annekatrein Mendel, *Zwangsarbeit im Kinderzimmer,* Frankfurt/M., 1994; and Pia Gerber, *Erwerbsbeteiligung von deutschen und ausländischen Frauen,* Frankfurt/M., 1996.

59. Elizabeth Harvey, *Women and the Nazi East* (New Haven, 2003), 137–146, 177–190; and Gudrun Brockhaus, *Schauder und Idylle* (Munich, 1997), 28.

60. Major histories, like the six reviewed by Eley, "Hitler's Silent Majority," and those discussed by Dickinson, "Biopolitics," overlook gender entirely, while others mention gender only in passing, as in, for example, Confino and Koshar, "Régimes." Among the surveys lacking references to gender or women are: Götz Aly's *Volksstaat,* Michael Burleigh's *Third Reich,* Ian Kershaw's *Hitler,* and Pierre Ayçoberry's *Social History.*

61. Hans-Ulrich Wehler, "Frauen im 'Dritten Reich,'" in *Deutsche Gesellschaftsgeschichte:Vom Beginn des Ersten Weltkriegs bis zur Gründung der beiden deutschen Staaten 1914–1949,* vol. 4 (Munich, 2003), 752–760, 1118–1119. Daum, "Interview with Hans-Ulrich Wehler."

8

JEWS, WOMEN, AND GERMANS
Jewish and German Historiographies in a Transatlantic Perspective

Benjamin Maria Baader

In this volume, German-Jewish history figures as one of ten fields of German history for which scholars evaluate the achievements of gender and women's history. This is remarkable, and it constitutes a rewriting of German history in itself. Thus, in this chapter, I explore the process in which German-Jewish history became a field of German history, and I argue that the integration of German-Jewish history into German history, on one hand, and women's and gender history having entered and altered the mainstream of German history, on the other hand, are two related and intersecting developments. Women's and gender history and German-Jewish history have much in common and have benefitted from each other significantly. They promise to continue doing so in the future.

Like women and like men, the collective "Jews" and individual Jewish identities are not self-evident, natural categories. Manhood, womanhood, and Jewishness are social and cultural configurations of outstanding flexibility and fluidity, and yet of a vitality that has kept each of them operating as a recognizable entity for millennia. Depending on context, time, and place, Jews have been defined by religion or identified as an ethnic group, a race, a nation, or a people. Jewishness and forms of Jewish communal life have been constituted through a web of social, political, and cultural practices, analogue to how we conceive of the construction of gender. Like gendered selves, Jews and Jewish identities are mapped on bodies, and like maleness and femaleness, it is useful to understand Jewishness "not as a ground of politics but as its effect."[1] Moreover, for centuries, women as well as Jews have figured as the marginal and often invisible—though conceptually indispensable—other in societies in which the norm and its "mainstream" history were male and gentile. Thus, women's and gender history and Jewish history have been driven by similar sets of questions. As they have established themselves against the backdrop of the shifting grounds of a mainstream German history, German women's and gender history and German-Jewish history have navigated their way through competing and often contradicting claims of equality and difference, universalism and particularism, belonging and otherness. In the process, these histories have challenged the master narrative of a normative German history.[2]

The historicization of the Jewish experience, of Judaism, and of Jewishness, however, has been the object of a Jewish historiographical tradition beyond the realm of German history. German-Jewish history is located at the intersection between German history and Jewish history. Thus, German-Jewish history is not only the history of the Jews in Germany, but it also forms a segment of the history of Jewish civilizations and cultures across the ages and continents. Conceiving of Jews only as Germans leaves half of the conceptual framework of German-Jewish history in the dark. This is also the case for German-Jewish women's and gender history. In fact, in Jewish historiographical texts, composed by Jews in German lands since the Middle Ages, gender politics have played an important role. Therefore, in this essay I start by discussing the premodern textual traditions of Jewish historiography, without an understanding of which, I contend, significant dimensions of modern German-Jewish historiography remain unintelligible. After having paid attention to these premises, I shall lay out how female German Jewish scholars of the early twentieth century such as Hanna Arendt and Selma Stern expanded and commented on this existing body of texts created by male Jews. Then, I will move to the German-Jewish historiography after the attempted destruction of German Jewry and of German Jewish culture by Nazi Germany. I shall discuss postwar historiographical trends and compare the development of German-Jewish history and German-Jewish women's and gender history in Germany to that in North America. Subsequently, I shall examine the ways in which German-Jewish women's and gender history has integrated into the mainstream of German-Jewish history and into the mainstream of German history and has challenged and changed both mainstream narratives. Finally, I shall argue that despite the important achievements of German-Jewish history and German-Jewish women's and gender history, a gender-sensitive German-Jewish historiography that takes the double axes of Jewish history and German history fully into account is still lacking.

Premodern and Modern Jewish Historiographies

Like the history of German non-Jewish women, the history of German-Jewish and other Jewish women has been understudied and neglected for centuries.[3] Yet Jewish historical texts, broadly defined, also include writings in which the Jewish experience and women were linked in significant ways. In the writings of the premodern era, Jewish men addressed existential questions of loyalty and belonging by assigning women an important function in representing the condition of the Jewish collective. Thus, modern German-Jewish women's and gender history and modern German-Jewish history on women and gender build on a historiographical legacy in which women embody the vulnerability as well as the vivacity of the Jewish people. In Germany, this historiography first found expression in texts commonly known as the Hebrew Crusade chronicles, in which the authors report on the attacks that the Jewish communities of Germany had suffered during the First Crusade, in 1096. The accounts describe the crusaders' assaults on the Jewish communities, the efforts made by gentile authorities to protect the Jewish communities, Jewish acts of self-defense, the murder of Jews by the hands of crusaders, and Jews who chose baptism rather than martyrdom. The most salient and disturbing feature of these chronicles are descriptions of how entire families, poor and rich, young and old, men and women, slaughtered each other and themselves before the crusaders could reach them. The reports culminate in the account of Rachel of Mainz who sacrificed her four children as an act of *Kiddush Ha-Shem* (sanctification of the name of God).[4]

Scholars are divided about the facticity of these accounts. While Robert Chazan holds that the data related in the descriptions is overall reliable, others have contested such a reading. The descriptions of Jewish martyrdom in the Crusade chronicles rework Biblical themes; the narrative of Rachel of Mainz mirrors that of a woman's acts of heroic self-sacrifice in the Maccabees account; and almost identical incidents were later retold about the Chmielnitzky massacres in 1648 Ukraine. Whatever their factual core, the Crusade chronicles were clearly religious texts in which Jews expressed and explored their relationship to the Divine. In fact, Yosef Hayim Yerushalmi has argued that medieval Jewish authors textualized communal memories primarily in liturgical writings. In the same vein, what may or may not be historical records of collisions with non-Jewish populations were to a significant degree vehicles for an almost ahistorical mode of collective memorization and Jewish self-examination within religious parameters.[5]

In the twentieth century, Hannah Arendt also used events of a recent past and the figure of a female protagonist as a way to explore her own condition as a Jew, the condition of the Jewish collective in Germany, and the Jews' relationship to their non-Jewish neighbors. In *Rahel Varnhagen*, a biography of a Jewish woman who had been prominent in the salon culture of Berlin in the late eighteenth century and who converted to Christianity, Arendt reflected on Judaism, womanhood, and on the possibilities and limits of Jewish integration into German society.[6] Even though *Rahel Varnhagen* first appeared in 1957 in London, Arendt had completed the manuscript in 1933 in Germany, and the book is a document of Jewish life in the late years of the Weimar Republic.[7] Moreover, as the work of a well-educated, middle-class, twentieth-century woman, *Rahel Varnhagen* is also an expression of the female experience in the cultural and political setting of interwar Germany. Thus, Arendt's work certainly forms part of the wider German history. It also needs to be read, however, as a Jewish history text, in which Arendt, like the authors of the Crusade chronicles, examined issues of conversion and explored the relationship of the Jews to their religion, to their people, and to their place in German society. Yet unlike the conceptual framework in which the medieval chroniclers gave meaning to their predicaments, for Arendt the place of Jews in non-Jewish society was no longer mediated by how the people of Israel related to their God. In *Rahel Varnhagen*, modern concepts of Jewishness and Germanness had replaced the religiously defined parameters in which Jews had made sense of their existence for centuries.

This secularization of Jewish historiography occurred in the nineteenth century, when the Jewish men who founded the scholarship of the *Wissenschaft des Judentums* (Scholarly Study of Judaism) began to interpret the Jewish experience according to contemporary scholarly methods. As subsequently Arendt, Isaac Marcus Jost, Heinrich Graetz, and the other nineteenth-century German-Jewish historians no longer most importantly examined the Jews' relationship to their God. Rather, they explored the question of whether and how Jews belonged into German society, as an existential issue in its own right.[8] In the realm of the *Wissenschaft des Judentums*, this conversation took place almost exclusively among men, who talked about men. Secular scholarship and the academic method formed markers of fitness for civic participation as well as of male identity and of a rational masculinity. However, in the religious sphere across the spectrum from Reform to modern Orthodoxy, nineteenth-century German Jewry embraced a more women- and family-centered approach. In an array of publications, rabbis and preachers discussed issues of Jewish womanhood and of the Jewish family and praised the virtues of women in Jewish history.[9] Thus in 1879, the rabbi Meyer Kayserling authored the first Jewish women's history in the German language, a book on Jewish women's contributions to history, literature, and art from the Talmudic period to the present. Thirteen years later, a woman and convert to Judaism, Nahida Remy, eventually Nahida Ruth Lazarus, published *Das Jüdische Weib* (The Jewish Woman), a Jewish women's history.[10]

Yet not before the 1920s did a woman establish herself truly as a scholar of German-Jewish history. In 1925, Selma Stern published the first volume of a multivolume study on the history of the German court Jews, entitled *Der Preußische Staat und die Juden* (The Prussian State and the Jews).[11] In this work, Stern embedded the legal, economic, and social history of the Jews of Prussia from the mid-seventeenth through the eighteenth century into a narrative of German state formation. Thus, Stern broke new ground by presenting Jewish history as a constitutive element of German history and thereby forcefully argued that German Jews were Germans. She went beyond the program of the nineteenth-century *Wissenschaft des Judentums*, whose scholars had aimed at convincing the non-Jewish world that Jewish texts belonged to the canon of world literature. Stern was a twentieth-century university-trained German historian, and in *Der Preußische Staat und die Juden* she addressed the general German public. However, Stern also contributed to the age-old conversation that Jews had among themselves. She added another chapter to the well-established story of the Jews' vulnerability to the moods of the gentile populace and to the caprices of their royal protectors, and she raised questions of power, belonging, and loyalty. Now, however, this Jewish introspection affirmed the Germanness of the German-Jewish collective, and it emphasized the contribution of Jews to German culture and German history. Nevertheless, like her forebears, Stern took pride in the Jewish cultural heritage and created narratives in which Jewish women stood out as women and as Jews. In a series of articles on the history of the achievements of Jewish women from the Middle Ages to the present, Stern lauded fifteenth-century Jewish women physicians and oculists, and she asserted that even the apostate Rahel Varnhagen drew her deepest strength from Judaism.[12]

The second volume of *Der Preußische Staat und die Juden* was still printed by the publisher Schocken in Berlin in 1938, but it was immediately destroyed by the Nazis.[13] In the 1960s and 1970s, when the multivolume work was published in its final form, Stern's study had become a historical document of Jewish life in Weimar Germany as much as it was a study of court Jews. Most German Jews had been killed or had left Germany, and with the refugees, German-Jewish historiography as a Jewish enterprise had gone into exile. In the dispersion, in 1955, German-Jewish emigrants founded the Leo Baeck Institute (LBI) for the study of the history and culture of German-speaking Jewry and established three branches of the Institute in Jerusalem, London, and New York. The LBI in New York came to house the archive of the Institute, the central repository for historical documents pertaining to German Jewry, and all branches together have now for five decades played a leading role in promoting and facilitating German-Jewish historical research worldwide. Hannah Arendt's *Rahel Varnhagen* was one of the first publications of the Leo Baeck Institute.[14] After a disaster as devastating as the Crusades or the expulsion from Spain, German-Jewish survivors regrouped outside of Germany and initiated a new era of (German-)Jewish historiography. A multifaceted politics of memory and commemoration, metaphysical quests, and interrogations of identity and loyalty characterize this historiography, as it has generations of Jewish historical writings before. However, in the former homeland of German Jews, an unprecedented development occurred that has added an additional dimension to the hitherto already complex dynamics of Jewish historiography.

After World War II in Germany

In the 1970s, an important change set in in German-Jewish historiography that constituted as much a break in the history of Jewish historiography as the secularization of Jewish historiography in the nineteenth century: Non-Jews, more precisely, non-Jewish Germans entered the field. In Germany, German-Jewish history ceased to be a self-reflective conversation in which Jews talked to Jews and sometimes addressed non-Jews. As a new generation of German historians engaged in labor history, social history, the history of minorities and outsiders, and indeed women's history, the history of German Jews became part of German history. Non-Jewish Germans began to converse with other non-Jewish Germans about Jews as Germans. After the Shoah or the Holocaust, German-Jewish history became also a German project rather than an almost exclusively Jewish project. In Germany, in the 1970s, a generation of non-Jewish Germans who had grown up in the shadow of their parents,' teachers,' and political leaders' murderous involvement in Nazi politics created a new school of German-Jewish historiography, as they searched for meaningful and morally sustainable forms of a postwar German identity.[15] Yet this scholarship on Jews in modern German history stands out by its dispassionate and sober tone.

Scholars such as Reinhard Rürup and Stefi Jersch-Wenzel began publishing works on the legal and political history of the Jews in Germany and on the history of anti-Semitism.[16] The first modern social history of German Jews, however, was an international cooperation between a German scholar and the LBI in New York. On the initiative of the LBI and with funds from the Deutsche Forschungsgemeinschaft, Monika Richarz selected excerpts from memoirs written by German-Jewish men and women and held at the LBI archives in New York. Richarz edited the autobiographical testimonies, which covered the period from 1780 to 1945, and the LBI published them in three volumes under the title *Jüdisches Leben in Deutschland* (Jewish Life in Germany). A decade later, in 1991, an abridged one-volume English edition appeared.[17] The work is not a history of Jewish women. However, it includes a significant number of memoirs by female authors and, more importantly, as a modern social history, Richarz's work focuses on family history and on men and women alike as historical agents. *Jüdisches Leben in Deutschland* is gender-sensitive in the spirit of the feminist historiography of the 1970s. Moreover, it is a work of German social history that treats Jews as a group of the German population, and the original three-volume edition addressed primarily German (non-Jewish) readers.

A Feminist School of German-Jewish Historiography in the United States

In the meantime, Jewish women in the United States, some of them descendants of emigrants from Germany, developed a full-fledged feminist German-Jewish historiography, a true modern Jewish women's history. First, in 1979, Marion Kaplan published her study on the Jewish feminist movement in Germany.[18] With this work, Kaplan pursued the goals of the first generation of feminist historians to record women's own history and achievements, and in the wake of Kaplan's publication, female scholars in Germany created an entire body of scholarship on the first German women's movement.[19] In concert with her feminist colleagues, Kaplan discussed the Jewish feminist movement in Germany as German history. Thereby, Kaplan asserted the Germanness of German Jews. Yet, in this study on the Jüdischer Frauenbund in Germany and its leader Bertha Pappenheim, Kaplan also portrayed her feminist German-Jewish predecessors as distinctly Jewish and explored in some depth how Pappenheim and other German-Jewish feminists at the time negotiated being women, being Jews, and being Germans. By way of women's history, Kaplan successfully integrated Jewish history into German history. The other study on German-Jewish women's history in this period of German-Jewish feminist historical writings, Deborah Hertz's *Jewish High Society in Old Regime Berlin*, likewise combined Jewish history and modern feminist historiography in innovative ways. In this book on the Berlin salon women of the late eighteenth and early nineteenth centuries, and in a host of other articles, Hertz has applied a rigorous social-history methodology, while asking Jewish questions about loyalty, belonging, and identity anew.[20] Recently, Harriet Freidenreich has added a third monograph to this genre of German-Jewish women's history. In *Female, Jewish, and Educated*, a collective biography of Jewish university women in Germany and Austria, Freidenreich has explored how these women of the late nineteenth and the early twentieth centuries pursued their university education and thereafter often strove to balance careers and family responsibilities.[21] Within the framework of a feminist historiography, Freidenreich has examined these women's integration in the surrounding non-Jewish society and has inquired into their affiliation and identification as Jews. Thus, the book not only notes the achievements of these university women as Jews, but as a study of Jewish history it also investigates modes of Jewishness in a certain social and cultural setting. Moreover, *Female, Jewish, and Educated* addresses issues relevant to women's history, social history, and family history far beyond the concerns of Jewish history. It constitutes a significant contribution to the study of the "New Woman" in Europe and North America.

Along similar lines, Marion Kaplan has in her work *The Making of the Jewish Middle Class* as well as in her more recent publication on Jewish life in Nazi Germany succeeded in writing a Jewish history that fully qualifies as German history.[22] Kaplan's studies indeed have contributed vitally to central fields of German historiography: the history of the German middle class and the social history of Nazi Germany. Furthermore, the two publications by Kaplan are not merely women's history anymore, but also family history and gender history. Yet before discussing this in more detail, let me point out that beyond their status as scholarship of German history, Kaplan's publications, like Hertz's and Freidenreich's, also possess time-honored Jewish history dimensions. The authors raise the ongoing questions about the state of the universe and the Jews' place in it, about hostility, violence, and loyalty, about redemption and destruction. In fact, we could very well consider Kaplan's study on Jews in Nazi Germany, *Between Dignity and Despair*, her Crusade chronicle.

The younger scholars of German-Jewish women's and gender history in North America who have followed Kaplan and Hertz have fully embraced gender history approaches as opposed to women's history methodologies. Sharon Gillerman's work on the Jewish family in Weimar Germany, and Alison Rose's studies on Jewish gender politics in fin-de-siècle Vienna stand for this new scholarship which is in the process of appearing in print. In these publications, the authors pay attention to social policies and investigate the material and the discursive boundaries of communities and individuals. Gender and Jewishness figure as interrelated and interdependent categories of investigating belonging and identity, Jewishness and Germanness.[23]

Jewish Women's and Gender History in Germany

In present-day Germany, feminist Jewish historiography possesses a very different character, as it is being written overwhelmingly by non-Jews. A German equivalent of the community of American Jewish women historians who could create a synthesis of the new feminist historiography and the traditions of Jewish history does not exist. The works that the few German-Jewish feminist scholars have produced in the past two decades tend to lack the innovative force and the conceptual breadth of their American counterparts. Claudia Ulbrich's outstanding social history on "power, gender, and religion" in the overlapping Christian and Jewish communities of eighteenth-century Alsace forms an exception.[24] Conversely, the much-noted study by Rachel Monika Herweg from 1995, a history of the Jewish mother from the Bible to the present, includes little new research and offers a heavily idealized account of Jewish womanhood.[25] The same is the case for Pnina Navè Levinson's *Was wurde aus Saras Töchtern?* (What Became of Sarah's Daughters?) and the slightly more original Gerda Hoffer's *Zeit der Heldinnen* (Time of Heroines), collections with biographical sketches of Jewish women from the Biblical Eve to Golda Me'ir.[26] Furthermore, Navè Levinson and Hoffer both live in Israel, even though their publications were written in German and appeared in Germany.

As a study of Jewish women's history in Germany, Irmgard Maya Fassmann's *Jüdinnen in der deutschen Frauenbewegung 1865–1919* (Jewish Women in the German Women's Movement, 1865–1919) from 1996 is noteworthy.[27] The work is a feminist version of a type of German-Jewish historiography that is not uncommon in Germany. In works whose titles begin with the words "The Jews in . . . ," scholars have explored the contributions of Jews to particular areas of German society, and have described the integration of Jews into more or less significant sections of German politics, arts, or economics. These studies add to Jewish history and sometimes also improve our understanding of the German institutions, professions, or social, cultural, and political arenas they discuss. For example, Barbara Strenge's relatively recent work, *Juden im Preußischen Justizdienst 1812–1918* (Jews in the Prussian Judiciary System, 1812–1918) explores the integration of German Jews in the law profession as a function of their "social emancipation."[28] Yet, beyond the specific interests of Jewish history, Strenge's work also contributes to the study of privilege, power, and state control in Prussia and Germany.

This integration of Jewish history and German history is particularly well developed in the study of the German *Bürgertum* (middle class), a field in which German-Jewish women's and gender history also plays a substantial role. However, there are several other excellent studies of German-Jewish women's history, issued in the past decade in the German language, that deserve attention in their own right. In 1995, Sibylle Quack published an outstanding social history of the German-Jewish female emigrants from Nazi Germany to the United States, and more recently Gudrun Maierhof presented us with a detailed and nuanced account of women's extraordinary achievements in the Jewish self-help organizations of Nazi Germany.[29] In the same vein though for an earlier period and for Austria rather than Germany, Elisabeth Malleier chronicled the history of Jewish women's voluntary associations in Vienna from 1816 to 1938, and thereby pioneered in recovering Jewish women's history as the history of a working-class as well as a middle-class population. Malleier located Jewish women's associational life at the intersection between the quest for education and improvement, the social politics of the Austrian labor movement, and Jewish strategies of philanthropy. Malleier has added significantly to our understanding of the social, economic, and cultural history of Viennese Jewry.[30]

Malleier's, Maierhof's, and Quack's works document both the successful integration of women's history and social history into German-Jewish history and a sustained interest by German scholars in the history of the German and Austrian Jews. Thereby, these studies form the counterpart of North American scholarship on German-Jewish history. Yet the German and Austrian contributions to German-Jewish historiography also significantly differ from the studies of American-born scholars such as Marion Kaplan, Deborah Hertz, and Sharon Gillerman and are distinct from the works by Selma Stern and Hannah Arendt. Studies on the histories of German and Austrian Jews such as the ones by Elisabeth Malleier, Gudrun Maierhof, and Sibylle Quack belong to the new school of German-Jewish historiography launched by non-Jewish German scholars such as Monika Richarz and Reinhard Rürup. Here, historiography does not form part of the Jewish quest for meaning and belonging, and arguably, these German-language texts do not constitute Jewish history at all. In fact, they are strictly concerned with German Jews as Germans. They fail to interpret the history of German Jews in the perspective of the history of a people and a culture beyond Germany (or Austria) and Germanness. However, this post-Shoah German historiography on Jewish Germans has played a path-breaking role in moving Jews as objects of historical interest onto the screen of mainstream German historical scholarship.

From the Margins to the Mainstream of Jewish History?

Thus, I now turn to the question that stands at the center of inquiry in this volume: has Jewish women's and gender history entered and altered the mainstream writings of German-Jewish history as well as of the mainstream of German history? For German-Jewish history the answer is a conditional yes. Mainstream Jewish history—as it was conceived in the nineteenth century, with its focus on intellectual history, religious history, and political history—is still an overwhelmingly male affair, where men talk to men about men without paying much attention to how gendered the field is. In German-Jewish religious history, Bettina Kratz-Ritter's work on Jewish women's prayer books, my own study on gender and nineteenth-century bourgeois Judaism, and Ruth Abusch-Magder's scholarship on food, religion, gender, the politics of Jewishness, and the boundaries of the Jewish community form exceptions.[31] Abusch-Magder and myself challenge established notions of the modernization of Judaism, and our works constitute interventions into what defines the mainstream of Jewish history as the history of Jewish culture. Nineteenth-century Jewish religious history, we claim, is insufficiently described by the existing accounts of Jewish denominationalism and Jewish intellectual history. Yet gender analyses bring the shift of Jewish religious culture from male-centered practices of Talmud Torah, Hebrew prayer, and halakhic observance to new forms of bourgeois religiosity and modern understandings of ritual and religious authority into focus.

The field in which women and gender studies has already changed the mainstream of German-Jewish history is social history. In Steven Lowenstein's marvelous social history on the Jewish community of Berlin between 1770 and 1830, published in 1994, Lowenstein included a chapter with the title "Was the Experience of Women Different from Men's Experience?"[32] In the early 1990s, this was still a perplexing and daring question for most Jewish studies scholars. Today, cutting-edge research on issues of Judaism and gender has reached Jewish studies fields such as Biblical and rabbinic scholarship. This is less so in Jewish philosophy and modern Jewish thought. Yet even in Jewish studies, the number of those who admit the necessity of including women or a female perspective or even a gender analysis in Jewish studies and Jewish history works has increased, and in new Jewish cultural studies, gender operates as an essential category.[33]

Considering this state of affairs in Jewish studies, German-Jewish women's and gender history has fared relatively well. At least in the past decade, the leading periodical of German-Jewish history, the *Leo Baeck Institute Year Book*, has welcomed work on women and gender and has published it together with masculinist, gender-blind contributions and with gender-aware articles that include but do not focus on issues of women or gender. Likewise, the four-volume *German-Jewish History in Modern Times*, published in English between 1996 and 1998 under the auspices of the LBI, reflects the inroads that women's and gender history has made in German-Jewish history as well as the lacunae.[34] Overall, the shift away from a German-Jewish history that is overwhelmingly a political, intellectual, religious, and economic history towards the inclusion of a social history perspective is impressive. The social history sections of *German-Jewish History in Modern Times* invite and include discussions of community, family, and daily life, and the trend towards a gender-sensitive Jewish social history has also found expression in a publication on German-Jewish *Alltagsgeschichte* (everyday history) which supplements the four-volume work.[35] Yet of the volumes of *German-Jewish History in Modern Times*, only volume three, which covers the era of Imperial Germany, includes a fuller discussion of particular women's issues such as Jewish women's involvement in the feminist movement and their occupational patterns.

Whatever its shortcomings, the four-volume scholarly work on the history of German Jewry from 1600 to 1945 represents a great achievement of German-Jewish historiography and in fact constitutes a milestone of German-Jewish history itself. Half a century before the work appeared, German Jews had been persecuted in Germany and many of them had been deported and killed. Others had fled, and some had established the LBI in order to preserve the German-Jewish legacy that then had seemed doomed to extinction. And now the LBI was able to publish the fruits of decades of research on the history of German Jewry in an international and cross-cultural effort. *German-Jewish History in Modern Times* was published in English and German simultaneously. It was written and edited by a team of North American, Israeli, British, and German scholars, many—but not all of them—German Jews or descendants of German Jews.[36] Non-Jewish Germans contributed too and Jürgen Kocka—an important scholar of German rather than of Jewish history—served on the advisory committee. This was not an insular or parochial affair. Pride and satisfaction over this achievement would have filled the young men who, in 1819, had established the Verein für Cultur und Wissenschaft der Juden (Association for Culture and the Scholarly Study of the Jews) in Berlin and thereby founded the *Wissenschaft des Judentums* and modern Jewish scholarship. As the nineteenth-century Jewish scholars had aspired to, with this multivolume work of the 1990s and with the previous LBI publications, German Jews have asserted their place in German society. In fact, ironically, Jewish scholarship in Germany has achieved a type of integration that remains unmatched in North America. In the United States and in Canada, Jewish studies and Jewish history publications largely cater to scholarly and lay communities of Jews. A German-language publication, on the contrary, addresses today overwhelmingly non-Jewish Germans. The intense interest in things Jewish in contemporary Germany of course stems to a significant degree from non-Jewish Germans' own specifically German investment in the Shoah or the Holocaust. Yet whatever the motivation, the fact is that in no other country do a comparable number of non-Jewish scholars work in Jewish studies or Jewish history. Scholarly as well as popular publications on German-Jewish history have an audience in present-day Germany.

From the Margins to the Mainstream of German History?

Can we therefore conclude that German-Jewish history indeed forms part of German history? Has it entered and changed mainstream German historiography beyond a popular engagement with Jews and Judaism? And has the history of Jews and other Germans or German-Jewish history from a gendered perspective become part of German history? It seems to me that Jewish women's and gender history has been particularly successful in penetrating the field of German history. In contrast, the topics that, from the nineteenth century on, have been at the center of Jewish history as a modern enterprise, such as intellectual and religious Jewish history, have hardly had an impact on German historiography. As I have mentioned above, studies on Jews in particular segments of German society, such as Jews in the legal professions or in the women's movement, have increased our knowledge of German history. In German social history, however, the history of German Jews has become an indispensable part. In particular in the area of the *Bürgertumsforschung* (research on the middle classes), German scholarship has greatly profited from the examination of the Jewish process of embourgeoisement, and German-Jewish women's and gender history has played a pioneering role in the field of German middle-class history.[37]

Kaplan's *The Making of the Jewish Middle Class* was the first and still is one of the most important full-fledged studies on the German middle-class family and the gendered dynamics of middle-class life. Publications by Anne-Charlott Trepp and Rebbekka Habermas followed Kaplan's work and, together, they hold a vital place in the historiography on the German middle classes.[38] Thus, social history created openings for or even called for the integration of Jewish history as well as for the integration of women's and gender history and family history into mainstream German history. A glance at the social history of Nazi Germany leads to the same conclusion. In this field as well, Kaplan's book on Jewish life in Nazi Germany is a central work. As it documents the life of the social and racial other in a fascist society, in its *Alltagsgeschichte* approach, *Between Dignity and Despair* raises fundamental questions about agency and about gender in Nazi Germany. In fact, Kaplan's work has changed and shaped the social history of Nazi Germany independent from German, Jewish, or German-Jewish investment in the history of German Jewry. Unquestionably, any social history on Nazi Germany needs to include the history of the German-Jewish population to meet its own promises and claims.

Thus, on the one hand, the works of Marion Kaplan, a North American scholar of German-Jewish women's, gender, and family history, have become an integral part of German social history. On the other hand, a German scholar, Till van Rahden, succeeded in writing a history of the Jews of Breslau between 1860 and 1925, which is more than a work of Jewish history and in which gender plays a significant role. Van Rahden situated Breslau Jewry in the context of the multiethnic make-up of the Silesian capital, explored the fault lines of Jewish integration in relation to Catholic and Protestant populations from a German-history perspective, and investigated the connection between the rise of the New Woman and changing patterns of Jewish-Christian intermarriage. Van Rahden wrote a work of social history in which Jewish history, women's and gender history, and German history are integrated into each other.[39]

In a similar vein, Dagmar Herzog has shown in her work *Intimacy and Exclusion: Religious Politics in Pre-Revolutionary Baden* that interconnecting the examinations of politics that relate to Jews with those that relate to gender can open new windows into German history. Herzog's publication is not a study of Jewish history. However, a gender analysis and an analysis of the "Jewish question" in the political landscape of Baden stand at the core of the book. Herzog's investigation of sexuality, philo-Semitism, and anti-Semitism offers fresh insights into religious politics, gendered notions of Germanness, and liberalism in Germany in the first half of the nineteenth century. Herzog significantly deepens our understanding of mainstream history (in this case the politics of Christian men) by exploring how Jews and women came to figure as others in relation to Christian men and by relating the othernesses of Jews and women to each other.[40]

This leads me to an entire field of great significance and innovative potential that will here not receive the attention which it deserves. Namely, combining gender studies and Jewish studies has led to an examination of masculinity in relation to questions of German nationhood and German identity, a topic touched on in the chapter on war and nationalism. The scholar who has established this field is the German-Jewish emigrant George Mosse. As a historian, he published both on German-Jewish history and on German nationalism, masculinity, and sexuality in the nineteenth and twentieth centuries.[41] Yet Mosse did not create a full synthesis of these two areas of scholarship. It was the literature scholar Sander Gilman who, in an array of publications, put gendered conceptions of Jewish men, anti-Semitism, and issues of Germanness in relation to each other.[42] Importantly, however a history of Jewish masculinity as a part of the history of German masculinity is still missing in the literature.

In her recent book, *Die kasernierte Nation* (The Nation in Barracks), Ute Frevert took an important step towards such a history. Frevert explored the connections between German nation building and citizenship, German concepts of masculinity, and the role of the military in German society. As a part of her investigation, she discussed Jewish men's inclusion into these arenas and their exclusion from them.[43] Along similar lines, Karen Hagemann included a section on anti-Semitism into her study on military, nationalism, and gender in Prussia's anti-Napoleonic wars. Interestingly, Hagemann did not find explicit attacks on German-Jewish men as overly feminine, which are so typical for the discourse on manly Germanness in the later nineteenth century.[44] Indeed, my own work on early nineteenth-century Jewish culture makes the point that, at least in the religious and domestic realm, German-Jewish men advocated a gentle masculinity.[45] Stefanie Schüler-Springorum documented such an approach still for a Jewish man in the early twentieth century, and Daniel Wildmann's study reveals that even Jewish gymnasts and athletes of that period, who had adopted elements of a Zionist ideology, embraced decidedly complex concepts of a Jewish masculinity. By no means did they endorse a strictly martial or combative ideal of Jewish manhood.[46]

Conclusion

German-Jewish women's and gender history has made important contributions to German history and has the potential for making more inroads in the future. First, Jewish history and German history truly intersect in the history of the gendered concepts of "German" and "Jewish" that lay at the root of German nation and identity building. Inquiries into German and Jewish notions of womanhood and manliness are central to this area of scholarship. In this field, some interesting work has been completed, more is in progress, but much is still to be done. In particular, the challenge to integrate the German history dimensions of this gender history with its Jewish history dimensions is largely unmet. Jewish history scholars have just begun to examine intra-Jewish perspectives and inter-Jewish traditions of gender organization and to inquire into whether a Jewish gender order contributed to the construction and the maintenance of Jewish distinctiveness throughout the ages, as has been suggested.[47] The results of this research then need to be related to investigations of how non-Jewish Germans constructed their sense of Germanness by "othering" Jewish men and women in highly gendered ways.

Another field in which German-Jewish women's and gender history has a rightful place in German history is social history, in particular the history of the German middle classes. As a part of German social history, women's and gender history and German-Jewish history appeared on the stage together, when historians set out to examine the history of "minorities" or of groups that had not been represented adequately in the dominant historical accounts. Here, as I have shown, the works of German-Jewish women's and gender history, such as those of Marion Kaplan, have significantly contributed to enriching the field of German history. Moreover, novel social history methodologies that scholars such as Till van Rahden are developing not only take gender and socioreligious variables such as Jewishness into account but have the potential to revolutionize our understanding of German history and of German culture. Van Rahden recently called for a new German history in which women and Jews cease to figure as marginal others. He questioned the concept of German-Jewish history as a minority history and suggested that nineteenth- and twentieth-century Germany did not possess a universal majority culture, but was inhabited by individuals and groups with multiple,

constantly evolving identities that together shaped "a public space of common culture."[48] This program of a decentered, multivalent German history
as part of which German-Jewish history and German women's and gender
history would be fully realized waits to be put into practice.

Despite the achievements of German-Jewish women's and gender history
of the past decades, the field is still marked by significant research gaps. Most
glaringly, perhaps, any work on the early part of the nineteenth century suf-
fers from our only vague grasp of Jewish social, religious, and family life in
the early modern period. It is difficult and at times impossible, for instance,
to evaluate changes in patterns of female piety, in domestic arrangements,
and in educational habits in the process of nineteenth-century Jewish embourgeoisement on a background that tends to be sketchy. In order to explore
these aspects of eighteenth-century Jewish life, we need scholars or teams of
researchers who are able to master the challenging Hebrew-language texts
of early modern Jewry, who are competent in Jewish history as well as in
German history, and who are conversant with the theory and the practice of
gender studies.[49] Filling the research gaps of later periods will be slightly less
demanding, but also requires an understanding of how the distinct strands
of Jewish history and of German history intersect in the gendered sphere of
German-Jewish history. Did Jewish women in Weimar Germany have a cultural renaissance and if so, how did it look?[50] What happens if we examine the
politics and sensitivities of the Jewish men who participated in the masculinist
circles around Martin Heidegger and Stefan George as part of the history
of the exclusivist male culture of Jewish learning and male Jewish homoso-
ciability? We need to pose these and other Jewish history questions in order
to take into account both of the historiographical dimensions of German-
Jewish history. German-Jewish history is German *Jewish* history as well as a
part of German history. In fact, a dialogue between German-Jewish history
as German history and German-Jewish history as Jewish history is called for,
now that the history of Jewish Germans is moving towards the center of a
redefined German history and that German-Jewish history no longer belongs
exclusively to Jews.

Before the nineteenth century, Jewish historical writings served Jews as a
means to express their relationship to God, to explore the status of the universe in a religious framework, and to cultivate a rather static form of collective
memorization. In a secularized and more dynamic mode, this still holds true
for contemporary Jewish and German-Jewish historiography. Yet today, more
than half a century after their parents' and grandparents' generation killed
much of European Jewry, non-Jewish Germans use the history of Jews in Germany as a vehicle for gaining insights into the dynamics of redemption in their
own history, and German historical texts give witness to a past that refuses
to pass. In present German-Jewish and German non-Jewish historiographies,

two distinct quests for meaning and fulfillment in history interconnect. On this level, too, scholarship on Jews in Germany has become part of the German historiographical enterprise. Nevertheless, we have to bear in mind that German-Jewish history is more than the history of Jewish Germans. It is also a field of Jewish history, and German-Jewish women's and gender history needs to be honored and continually evaluated in each of its multiple perspectives and contexts, as women's or men's history, gender history, Jewish history, and German history.

Notes

1. Judith Butler, "Gender Trouble, Feminist Theory, and Psychoanalytical Discourse," in *Feminism/Postmodernism*, ed. Linda J. Nicholson (New York, 1990), 339.
2. Here I borrow heavily from the comments that Till van Rahden delivered at the conference "Gendering Modern German History" in Toronto in March 2003 in response to an earlier version of this chapter. See also Dagmar Herzog, "Telling Ethnic and Gender History Together: A Comment," *Leo Baeck Institute Year Book* 46 (2001): 150–158, esp. 155; Till van Rahden, "Germans of the Jewish 'Stamm': Visions of Community and Particularism, 1850–1933," in *German History from the Margins, 1800 to the Present*, ed. Neil Gregor et al. (Bloomington IN, 2006): 27–48; Till van Rahden, "Jews and the Ambivalences of Civil Society in Germany, 1800 to 1933: Assessment and Reassessment," *Journal of Modern History* 77, no. 4 (2005): 1024–1047. I am likewise indebted to insights that Harriet Freidenreich shared with me, and I am grateful for Karen Hagemann's, Jean Quataert's, and Stefanie Schüler-Springorum's suggestions. However, all errors and shortcomings of the essay remain my own.
3. Marion Kaplan, "Where We Have Come From and Where We Have Come To," *Leo Baeck Institute Year Book* 45 (2000): 215–218, esp. 215.
4. On the Crusade chronicles and Rachel of Mainz, see for instance Robert Chazan, *European Jewry and the First Crusade* (Berkeley, 1987), 111–113.
5. Robert Chazan, *God, Humanity, and History: The Hebrew First Crusade Narratives* (Berkeley, 2000); Jeremy Cohen, *Sanctifying the Name of God: Jewish Martyrs and Jewish Memories of the First Crusade* (Philadelphia, 2004), 117; Yosef Hayim Yerushalmi, *Zakhor: Jewish History and Jewish Memory* (Seattle, 1982), 47–52, 73–75. For an account of the historiographical debate, see Cohen, *Sanctifying the Name*, 31–47.
6. Hannah Arendt, *Rahel Varnhagen: The Life of a Jewess* (London, 1957).
7. Liliane Weissberg, "Introduction," in Hannah Arendt, *Rahel Varnhagen: The Life of a Jewess* (Baltimore, 1997), 5, 42.
8. Nils Roemer, *Jewish Scholarship and Culture in Nineteenth-Century Germany: Between History and Faith* (Madison, 2005); Ismar Schorsch, *From Text to Context: The Turn to History in Modern Judaism* (Hanover, 1994).
9. Benjamin Maria Baader, *Gender, Judaism, and Bourgeois Culture in Germany, 1800–1870* (Bloomington, 2006).

10. Meyer Kayserling, *Die jüdischen Frauen in der Geschichte, Literatur und Kunst* (Leipzig, 1879); Nahida Ruth Lazarus (Nahida Remy), *Das jüdische Weib: Mit einer Vorrede von M. Lazarus*, 3rd ed. (Berlin, 1896); Isidore Singer and Frederick T. Haneman, "Lazarus, Nahida Ruth," in Isidor Singer, ed., *The Jewish Encyclopedia: A Descriptive Record of the History, Religion, Literature, and Customs of the Jewish People from the Earliest Times to the Present Day*, vol. 7 (New York, 1904), 654.

11. Selma Stern, *Der Preußische Staat und die Juden*, 8 vols. (Tübingen, 1962–1975). See also Selma Stern, *The Court Jew: A Contribution to the History of the Period of Absolutism in Central Europe* (Philadelphia, 1950).

12. Selma Stern, "Die Entwicklung des jüdischen Frauentypus seit dem Mittelalter," *Der Morgen* 1 (1925): 324–337, 496–516, 648–657; here 333 and 502. On Stern, see also Marina Sassenberg, *Das Eigene in der Geschichte: Selbstentwürfe und Geschichtsentwürfe der deutschjüdischen Historikerin Selma Stern (1890–1981)* (Tübingen, 2004).

13. On the destruction of almost the entire edition, see Stern, *Der Preußische Staat*, vol. 1 (1962), xiv.

14. Christhard Hoffmann, ed., *Preserving the Legacy of German Jewry: A History of the Leo Baeck Institute, 1955–2005* (Tübingen, 2005); Frank Mecklenburg, "Deutsch-jüdische Archive in New York und Berlin: Drei Generationen nach dem Holocaust," *Menora* 12 (2001): 311–323; Weissberg, "Introduction," 42.

15. See Beate Meyer, "Statt einer Laudatio: Monika Richarz—Zum Lebensweg einer Pionierin der deutsch-jüdischen Geschichtsschreibung," in *Jüdische Welten: Juden in Deutschland vom 18. Jahrhundert bis in die Gegenwart*, ed. Marion Kaplan and Beate Meyer (Göttingen, 2005), 9–28; Stefanie Schüler-Springorum, "The 'German Question': The Leo Baeck Institute in Germany," in *Preserving the Legacy of German Jewry: A History of the Leo Baeck Institute, 1955–2005*, ed. Christhard Hoffmann (Tübingen, 2005), 201–236.

16. Stefi Jersch-Wenzel, *Juden und "Franzosen" in der Wirtschaft des Raumes Berlin/Brandenburg zur Zeit des Merkantilismus* (Berlin, 1978); Stefi Jersch-Wenzel, *Jüdische Bürger und kommunale Selbstverwaltung in preußischen Städten 1808–1848* (Berlin, 1967); Reinhard Rürup, *Emanzipation und Antisemitismus: Studien zur "Judenfrage" der bürgerlichen Gesellschaft* (Göttingen, 1975); idem, "Judenemanzipation und bürgerliche Gesellschaft in Deutschland," in *Gedenkschrift Martin Göhring: Studien zur europäischen Geschichte*, ed. Ernst Schulin (Wiesbaden, 1968), 174–199.

17. Monika Richarz, ed., *Jüdisches Leben in Deutschland: Selbstzeugnisse zur Sozialgeschichte*, 3 vols. (Stuttgart, 1976–1982); idem, ed., *Jewish Life in Germany: Memoirs from Three Centuries* (Bloomington, 1991). See also Meyer, "Statt einer Laudatio," 15–18.

18. Marion Kaplan, *The Jewish Feminist Movement in Germany: The Campaigns of the Jüdischer Frauenbund, 1904–1938* (Westport, Conn., 1979).

19. Some of the most important German publications in the 1980s are: Herrad-Ulrike Bussemer, *Frauenemanzipation und Bildungsbürgertum: Sozialgeschichte der Frauenbewegung in der Reichsgründungszeit* (Weinheim, 1985); Bärbel Clemens, *"Menschenrechte haben kein Geschlecht": Zum Politikverständnis der bürgerlichen Frauenbewegung* (Pfaffenweiler, 1988); Doris Kaufmann, *Frauen zwischen Aufbruch und Reaktion: Protestantische Frauenbewegung in der ersten Hälfte des 20. Jahrhunderts* (Munich, 1988); Elisabeth Meyer-Renschhausen, *Weibliche Kultur und soziale Arbeit: Eine Geschichte der Frauenbewegung am Beispiel Bremens 1810–1927* (Cologne, 1989); Dietlinde Peters, *Mütterlichkeit im Kaiserreich: Die bürgerliche Frauenbewegung und der soziale Beruf der Frau* (Bielefeld, 1984); Theresa Wobbe, *Gleichheit und Differenz: Politische Strategien von Frauenrechtlerinnen um die Jahrhundertwende* (Frankfurt/M., 1989). For an American publication, see Catherine Prelinger, *Charity, Challenge, and Change: Religious Dimensions of the Mid-Nineteenth-Century Women's Movement in Germany* (New York, 1987); and for an influential early study on the German women's movement

by male scholar who was primarily interested in German political culture rather than in women's experiences and agency, see Richard Evans, *The Feminist Movement in Germany, 1894–1933* (London, 1976).

20. Deborah Hertz, "Emancipation through Intermarriage? Wealthy Jewish Salon Women in Old Berlin," in *Jewish Women in Historical Perspective*, ed. Judith R. Baskin, 2nd ed. (Detroit, 1991), 193–207; idem, *Jewish High Society in Old Regime Berlin*, (New Haven, 1988); idem, "Leaving Judaism for a Man: Female Conversion and Intermarriage in Germany 1812–1819," in *Zur Geschichte der jüdischen Frau in Deutschland*, ed. Julius Carlebach (Berlin, 1993), 97–112; idem, "Mischehen in den Berliner Salons," *Bulletin des Leo Baeck Instituts* 79 (1988): 37–74; idem, "The Troubling Dialectic Between Reform and Conversion in Biedermeier Berlin," in *Towards Normality? Acculturation and Modern German Jewry*, ed. Rainer Liedtke and David Rechter (Tübingen, 2003), 103–126.

21. Harriet Freidenreich, *Female, Jewish, and Educated: The Lives of Central European University Women* (Bloomington, 2002).

22. Marion A. Kaplan, *Between Dignity and Despair: Jewish Life in Nazi Germany* (New York, 1998); idem, *The Making of the Jewish Middle Class: Women, Family, and Identity in Imperial Germany* (New York, 1991).

23. Sharon Gillerman, "The Crisis of the Jewish Family in Weimar Germany: Social Conditions and Cultural Representations," in *In Search of Jewish Community: Jewish Identities in Germany and Austria, 1918–1933*, ed. Michael Brenner and Derek J. Penslar (Bloomington, 1998), 176–199; idem, *Germans into Jews: Remaking the Jewish Social Body in the Weimar Republic* (Stanford, forthcoming); idem, "Samson in Vienna: The Theatrics of Jewish Masculinity," *Jewish Social Studies* n.s. 9, no. 2 (2003): 65–98; Alison Rose, "Imagining the 'New Jewish Family': Gender and Nation in Early Zionism," in *Families of a New World: Gender, Politics, and State Development in Global Context*, ed. Lynne Haney and Lisa Pollard (New York, 2003), 64–82; Alison Rose, "The Jewish Woman as 'Other': The Development of Stereotypes in Vienna, 1890–1914," Ph.D. diss., Hebrew University, 1997. See also Robin Judd, "Circumcision and Modern Jewish Life: A German Case Study, 1843–1914," in *The Covenant of Circumcision: New Perspectives on an Ancient Jewish Rite*, ed. Elizabeth Wyner Mark (Hanover, NH, 2003), 142–155; Robin Judd, Cutting Identities: Jewish Rituals and German Politics (Ithaca, N.Y., forthcoming).

24. Claudia Ulbrich, *Shulamit und Margarete: Power, Gender, and Religion in a Rural Society in Eighteenth-Century Europe* (Boston, 2004).

25. Rachel Monika Herweg, *Die jüdische Mutter: Das verborgene Matriarchat* (Darmstadt, 1995).

26. These publications are updated renderings of a Jewish women's history in the style of Meyer Kayserling's or Nahida Ruth Lazarus's works. See note 10. Gerda Hoffer, *Zeit der Heldinnen: Lebensbilder außergewöhnlicher jüdischer Frauen* (Munich, 1999); Pnina Navè Levinson, *Was wurde aus Saras Töchtern? Frauen im Judentum* (Gütersloh, 1989). For articles by a Jewish man who already in the 1970s asked original questions on Jewish women's and gender history, see Julius Carlebach, "Family Structure and the Position of Jewish Women," in *Revolution and Evolution: 1848 in German-Jewish History*, ed. Werner Mosse et al. (Tübingen, 1981), 157–187; Julius Carlebach, "The Forgotten Connection—Women and Jews in the Conflict between Enlightenment and Romanticism," *Leo Baeck Institute Year Book* 24 (1979): 107–136. Also note the quite specific but excellent book on the first woman rabbi in Germany. Elisa Klapheck, *Fräulein Rabbiner Jonas: The Story of the First Woman Rabbi* (San Francisco, 2004).

27. Irmgard Maya Fassmann, *Jüdinnen in der deutschen Frauenbewegung 1865–1919* (Hildesheim, 1996).

28. See subtitle of the study. Barbara Strenge, *Juden im Preussischen Justizdienst 1812–1918: Der Zugang zu den juristischen Berufen als Indikator der gesellschaftlichen Emanzipation* (Munich, 1996).

For other works of this genre, see Ernest Hamburger, *Juden im öffentlichen Leben Deutschlands: Regierungsmitglieder, Beamte und Parlamentarier in der monarchischen Zeit 1848–1918* (Tübingen, 1968); Arthur Prinz, *Juden im deutschen Wirtschaftsleben: Soziale und wirtschaftliche Struktur im Wandel, 1850–1914* (Tübingen, 1984).

29. Gudrun Maierhof, *Selbstbehauptung im Chaos: Frauen in der jüdischen Selbsthilfe 1933–1943* (Frankfurt, 2002); Sibylle Quack, *Zuflucht Amerika: Zur Sozialgeschichte der Emigration deutsch-jüdischer Frauen in die USA, 1933–1945* (Bonn, 1995).

30. Elisabeth Malleier, *Jüdische Frauen in Wien, 1816–1938: Wohlfahrt—Mädchenbildung—Frauenarbeit* (Vienna, 2003).

31. Ruth Abusch-Magder, "'Eating Out': Food and the Boundaries of Jewish Community and Home in Germany and the United States," *Nashim: A Journal of Jewish Women's Studies and Gender Issues* 5 (2002): 53–82; idem, "Kulinarische Bildung: Jüdische Kochbücher als Medien der Verbürgerlichung," in *Jüdische Geschichte als Geschlechtergeschichte: Studien zum und 20. Jahrhundert*, ed. Kirsten Heinsohn and Stefanie Schüler-Springorum (Göttingen, 2005); idem, "Home-Made Judaism: Food and Domestic Jewish Life in Germany and the United States, 1850–1914," Ph.D. diss., Yale University, 2006; Baader, *Gender, Judaism, and Bourgeois Culture*; Baader, "When Judaism Turned Bourgeois: Gender in Jewish Associational Life and in the Synagogue, 1750–1850," *Leo Baeck Institute Year Book* 46 (2001): 113–123, 164–170; Bettina Kratz-Ritter, *Für "fromme Zionstöchter" und "gebildete Frauenzimmer": Andachtsliteratur für deutsch-jüdische Frauen im 19. und frühen 20. Jahrhundert* (Hildesheim, 1995).

32. Steven M. Lowenstein, *The Berlin Jewish Community: Enlightenment, Family, and Crisis, 1770–1830* (New York, 1994), 162–176.

33. On the "slower progress in theory and methodology" in Jewish history and studies, see Beth S. Wenger, "Notes from the Second Generation," in *Judaism Since Gender*, ed. Miriam Peskowitz and Laura Levitt (New York, 1997), 113–119. Otherwise, see Matti Bunzl, "Jews, Queers, and Other Symptoms: Recent Work in Jewish Cultural Studies," in *GLQ: A Journal of Lesbian and Gay Studies* 6, no. 2 (2000): 321–341; Bryan Cheyette and Laura Marcus, eds., *Modernity, Culture, and "the Jew"* (Stanford, 1998); Jonathan Frankel, ed., *Jews and Gender: The Challenge to Hierarchy* (New York, 2000); T. M. Rudavsky, ed., *Gender and Judaism: The Transformation of Tradition* (New York, 1995).

34. Michael A. Meyer and Michael Brenner, eds., *German-Jewish History in Modern Times*, 4 vols. (New York, 1996–1998).

35. Marion Kaplan, ed., *Jewish Daily Life in Germany, 1618–1945* (Oxford, 2005).

36. Michael A. Meyer and Michael Brenner, eds, *Deutsch-jüdische Geschichte in der Neuzeit*, 4 vols. (Munich, 1996–1997).

37. For contributions to the German *Bürgertumsforschung* that started to flourish in the 1980s, see for instance George L. Mosse, "Das deutsch-jüdische Bildungsbürgertum," in *Bildungsbürgertum im 19. Jahrhundert*, vol. 2, *Bildungsgüter und Bildungswissen*, ed. Reinhart Koselleck (Stuttgart, 1990), 168–180; Shulamit Volkov, "The 'Verbürgerlichung' of the Jews as Paradigm," in *Bourgeois Society in Nineteenth-Century Europe*, ed. Jürgen Kocka and Allan Mitchell (Oxford, 1993), 367–391 (published in German in 1988). On the hesitant reception of German-Jewish history within the field of *Bürgertumsforschung*, see Rahden, "Jews and the Ambivalences." Of crucial significance for German-Jewish history as well as for the history of German middle-class formation is also the recent Simone Lässig, *Jüdische Wege ins Bürgertum: Kulturelles Kapital und sozialer Aufstieg im 19. Jahrhundert* (Göttingen, 2004).

38. Rebekka Habermas, *Frauen und Männer des Bürgertums: Eine Familiengeschichte (1750–1850)* (Göttingen, 2000); Anne-Charlott Trepp, *Sanfte Männlichkeit und selbständige Weiblichkeit: Frauen und Männer im Hamburger Bürgertum 1770–1840* (Göttingen, 1996).

39. Till van Rahden, *Juden und andere Breslauer: Die Beziehungen zwischen Juden, Protestanten und Katholiken in einer deutschen Großstadt von 1860 bis 1925* (Göttingen, 2000).

40. Dagmar Herzog, *Intimacy and Exclusion: Religious Politics in Pre-Revolutionary Baden* (Princeton, 1996).

41. See in particular, George L. Mosse, *German Jews Beyond Judaism* (Bloomington, 1983); idem, *Nationalism and Sexuality: Respectability and Abnormal Sexuality in Modern Europe* (New York, 1985); idem, *The Image of Man: The Creation of Modern Masculinity* (New York, 1996). On Mosse's work in general, see Stanley G. Payne et al., eds., *What History Tells: George L. Mosse and the Culture of Modern Europe* (Madison, 2004).

42. See most importantly perhaps Sander Gilman, *The Jew's Body* (New York, 1991); idem, *Jewish Self-Hatred: Anti-Semitism and the Hidden Language of the Jews* (Baltimore, 1986); idem, *Freud, Race, and Gender* (Princeton, 1993).

43. Ute Frevert, *A Nation in Barracks: Modern Germany, Military Conscription and Civil Society* (Oxford, 2004).

44. Karen Hagemann, *"Männlicher Muth und Teutsche Ehre": Nation, Militär und Geschlecht in Preußen zur Zeit der Antinapoleonischen Kriege* (Paderborn, 2002), 255–270.

45. Baader, *Gender, Judaism, and Bourgeois Culture*, 78–80, 90.

46. Stefanie Schüler-Springorum, "'Denken, Wirken, Schaffen': Das erfolgreiche Leben des Aron Liebeck," in *Juden, Bürger, Deutsche: Zur Geschichte von Vielfalt und Differenz, 1800–1933*, ed. Andreas Gotzmann et al. (Tübingen, 2001), 369–393, esp. 387; Daniel Wildmann, "Nationaljüdische Turner—Zugehörigkeit, Körperlichkeit, Männlichkeit: Jüdische Körperinszenierungen in Deutschland zwischen 1895 und 1921," Ph.D. diss., University of Basel, forthcoming.

47. This has been proposed most prominently in Daniel Boyarin, *Unheroic Conduct: The Rise of Heterosexuality and the Invention of the Jewish Man* (Berkeley, 1997).

48. Rahden, "Jews and the Ambivalences," 1043.

49. Chava Weissler's path-breaking work on the Jewish women's culture of prayer focuses on East European rather than on German Jewry. Yet the volume on the life world of Glikl of Hameln by Monika Richarz, Claudia Ulbrich's book, and Robert Liberles's work are promising beginnings in early modern German-Jewish gender history. Robert Liberles, "On the Threshold of Modernity: 1618–1780," in *Jewish Daily Life in Germany, 1618–1945*, ed. Marion Kaplan (Oxford, 2005), see esp. 19, 24–51, 59–61, 76–79; Monika Richarz, ed., *Die Hamburger Kauffrau Glikl: Jüdische Existenz in der Frühen Neuzeit* (Hamburg, 2001); Ulbrich, *Shulamit und Margarete*; Chava Weissler, *Voices of the Matriarchs: Listening to the Prayers of Early Modern Jewish Women* (Boston, 1998).

50. Michael Brenner, *The Renaissance of Jewish Culture in Weimar Germany* (New Haven, 1996); Joan Kelly-Gadol, "Did Women Have a Renaissance?" in *Becoming Visible: Women in European History*, ed. Renate Bridenthal and Claudia Koonz (Boston, 1977), 137–163.

9

Religion and Gender in Modern German History
A Historiographical Perspective

Ann Taylor Allen

Religion as the bulwark of patriarchy has become a feminist cliché. In 1896, the American Elizabeth Cady Stanton charged that the Christian Church had "steadily used its influence against progress, science, the education of the masses and freedom for women."[1] The French philosopher Simone de Beauvoir likewise affirmed in 1949 that "Christian ideology has contributed no little to the oppression of the female sex."[2] Starting in the 1970s, a new generation of feminist scholars—including theologians such as Mary Daly, author of *The Church and the Second Sex*—insisted that the rejection of traditional religious beliefs was an essential step toward emancipation.[3] But these claims are not borne out by the historical record. In fact, most of the period in which women made progress toward emancipation—the nineteenth and first half of the twentieth centuries—was marked by a considerable increase in their activity and influence in both Christian and Jewish religious life. And this was a highly gender-specific trend, for although the clergy of most religious bodies continued to be entirely male, the religious involvement of lay men declined as that of lay women increased.

Clearly the "feminization of religion" is a key aspect of gender history in the modern era. But though its importance is acknowledged by historians of women and gender in the English-speaking world, it has received less attention in German-speaking countries. This essay will look at recent historical research on three important topics: religion and modernization, feminism and women's religious practices, and the relationship of religion, gender, and nationalism, particularly in the National Socialist period. It will conclude by suggesting some directions for future research.

Religion, Gender, and Modernization

The history of gender and religion from 1800 to the present is usually seen in the context of a general theory of modernization. As Jonathan Sperber points out, until recently Max Weber's theory has been very influential among historians of Germany. In Weber's view, the modernization process was marked by a transition from a religious to a secular worldview. Faith gave way to scientific rationality, religious practice to a secular work ethic (or "worldly asceticism"), and the belief in the supernatural to a bleak disenchantment (*Entzauberung*). Following Weber, historians often assumed that in the modern West religious belief was a mere vestige of a bygone age, and hardly needed to be taken seriously except as a reactionary obstacle to modernity.[4]

Feminist historians added a corollary that Weber never intended. Though himself a liberal feminist, Weber did not associate modernity with the emancipation of women. For him, the rise of modern society was also the rise of patriarchy and thus the marginalization of women. As his biographer Arthur Mitzman points out, Weber regarded rationality chiefly as a male trait and attributed to women an emotional and intuitive way of thinking which harked back to an archaic age and to "the long-suppressed deities of the libido, femininity, Eros, and community, of blind passion as well as compassion."[5] But upon this pessimistic theory feminist historians have often superimposed what the historian Jean Quataert calls an "emancipatory teleology" based on the assumption—stated or implied—that the direction of modern history was or should be toward gender equality.[6] As two aspects of the same process of modernization, emancipation and secularization were often assumed to have gone together.

Therefore historians of women and religion have usually identified as "feminist" only those groups that made the transition from religious belief to secularism. Marion Kaplan, the author of some of the earliest and best-known histories of German-Jewish women in the late nineteenth and early twentieth centuries, explains that these women remained "more traditional, more Jewish-centered" than their husbands and worked to keep Jewish traditions alive.[7] But she also shows that religion became steadily less relevant to these women's "modern status aspirations" toward a secular identity based on German nationality, middle-class status, and humanistic education, and that they defined their Jewishness more through community and ethnic ties rather than through religious observance.[8] Kaplan's history of the Jewish Women's

League (*Jüdischer Frauenbund*), an "umbrella" organization that included many civic and charitable groups, concludes that the energy that had previously been invested in religious life was transferred to secular social activism, often with a feminist emphasis.

Another example of the same transition—from religious belief to feminism and secularism—is the so-called "German Catholic" movement (also known as the Free Congregations or *freie Gemeinde*), which flourished for a very short period from its founding in about 1840 until its suppression after the 1848 revolutions. Led by men who rejected Christian orthodoxy and promoted a utopian agenda that included the reform of marriage, education, and politics, this movement attracted many unconventional and courageous women. Among the earliest histories of these women was a book by an American historian, Catherine Prelinger, entitled *Charity, Challenge, and Change: Religious Dimensions of the Mid-Nineteenth-Century Women's Movement in Germany*. The book focuses on several groups that worked in Hamburg in the years between 1830 and 1852. Prelinger treats the religious beliefs of these women with sympathy. Nonetheless, she presents religion chiefly as a framework for the development of positions on various secular issues, including marriage, the family, and politics.[9] The German historian Sylvia Paletschek is likewise most interested in the secular activities of the German Catholic activists, to whom she refers as the "chief pillars of the early phase of the German women's movement." She regards their decision to withdraw from both Christian denominations after their reform movement was suppressed as an essential stage in the development of German feminism.[10]

As the American historian Dagmar Herzog points out, this tendency to equate anticlericalism and secularism with emancipation is anachronistic. In *Intimacy and Exclusion: Religious Politics in Pre-Revolutionary Baden*, Herzog shows that the dissenting groups were led chiefly by men whose attack on religious (and particularly on Catholic) belief was often intended less to emancipate women than to subject them to a tighter control within the family.[11] In some households the priest was the confidant, friend, and ally of the wife against the husband.[12] Campaigns to free women from superstition and priestly wiles may have been motivated more by husbands' jealousy than by feminism.[13] Nonetheless, German Catholic women were able to appropriate these anticlerical arguments and turn them to their own purposes.

But to a larger number of women, the years between 1850 and 1950 brought an increase in religious commitment rather than secularization. Historians have often written these women off as enemies of both feminism and modernity. The German scholar Irmtraud Götz von Olenhusen dismisses the entire history of women's religious activities in the years from 1850 until 1945 by insisting that the emancipatory potential of the German Christian churches was crushed by the suppression of the dissenting sects after 1848.[14]

She and other feminist historians often equate emancipatory potential with late-twentieth-century notions of sexual freedom and gender equality.

An early and still influential historian of German women's movements, Richard J. Evans, classifies his subjects—women who were active during the era from 1890 to 1933—according to a definition of feminism that was current in the 1970s. A true feminist, according to Evans, must profess individualistic values and understand "equality" as a denial of most gender differences. The German Protestant Women's League (*Deutsch-Evangelischer Frauenbund,* or DEF), a large organization founded in 1898, serves Evans only as a negative example. "It seems reasonable to say that the German-Evangelical Women's League was not feminist," he declares. "If on some criteria it has to be accounted feminist, then those criteria must be wrong."[15]

In her study of Protestant women's religious movements from the 1890s until 1914, Ursula Baumann starts from a Weberian definition of modernity as "the rationalization of attitudes and norms, that culminates in the dissolution of religious world-views."[16] It follows that the movements that she describes, which encouraged women to become more committed and active believers, must simply have been regressive. In Baumann's rather condescending view, these Protestant women were vulnerable people who needed religion in order to deal with "the universal human experiences of sickness and death."[17] Presumably they were incapable of living up to Weber's bracing exhortation to "bear the fate of the times like a man."[18] While Baumann concedes that Protestant women sympathized with some feminist causes and criticized the hidebound conservatism of their pastors, she nonetheless condemns them as reactionary opponents of emancipation.

For Baumann, Evans, and Barbara Greven-Aschoff, the author of another early and widely read book on the history of German feminism from the 1890s until 1933, the DEF figures chiefly as the prime mover of a sinister rightward shift in a national "umbrella" organization, the League of German Women's Associations (*Bund Deutscher Frauenvereine,* or BDF), to which the Protestant organization was admitted in 1908.[19] Baumann sums up the effects of the admission of the DEF to the BDF as "the triumph of a Judaeo-Christian tradition that confined women primarily to the role of wife and mother and refused them the right to control their own bodies."[20] It is true that the votes of the new Protestant members helped to defeat some resolutions proposed in 1908 by the BDF's most radical faction, who among other changes favored the complete legalization of abortion. But opposition to these resolutions was in no way peculiar to religious or conservative women—at this time, most feminists in Germany and elsewhere would have rejected them. Baumann concludes that the mobilization of Protestant women worked against modernization by stabilizing "conservative ideologies and interests," and that German Protestantism overcame its "conservative-national" past only in the 1960s.[21]

Nancy Reagin's excellent book on DEF activists in Hanover during the early twentieth century passes a similar judgment. Although these women must have been at least partly motivated by religious beliefs, Reagin hardly mentions religion. Instead, her almost Marxist approach attributes most of their actions to their membership in the middle class and their opposition to socialism and other movements toward democracy and working-class empowerment. All of these women's attitudes, from their positive views of domesticity to their opposition to the employment of married women, are interpreted as expressions of religious conservatism. In fact these were mainstream attitudes that were by no means peculiar to conservatives or to religious believers—they were almost as common on the left as on the right. According to Reagin, the Hanover women impeded progress and modernization by strengthening the power of conservative male elites.[22]

These and other historical assessments of middle-class feminism exhibit a distinctively German tendency to draw a bright ideological line between so-called "bourgeois feminism" and the socialist (or "proletarian") women's movement. Almost regardless of content, the ideas and activities of middle-class women are often identified as politically right-wing and thus as reactionary. Even liberal feminists such as Helene Lange and Gertrud Bäumer, who were deeply influenced by progressive Protestant ethics and theology, are often included among the snobbish and ineffectual *bourgeoisie*. The feminist leaders' secular Protestant ethic, writes Irmtraud von Olenhusen, produced only the ideology of "spiritual motherhood." Ignoring the immense importance of this ideology to many areas of women's education, professional development, and political culture, Olenhusen dismisses it as a sentimental fantasy that lost whatever influence it had ever had after the First World War.[23]

The problem with these interpretations, as with the Weberian theory on which they are based, is that by equating modernity with secularization they also associate it with maleness. Women who did not follow men in their flight from the churches are often written off, at best as old-fashioned, at worst as antifeminist. A theory that leaves out so many women cannot help us to understand women's and gender history. Obviously, men and women experienced the modernization process differently.

Feminism and Religion: A Comparative Perspective

Judgments that stereotype religious women as opponents of emancipation are often based on criteria derived from late twentieth-century feminism. Karen Offen, a historian of European feminist movements from 1700 to 1950, proposes a more historical definition: feminists are people (male and female) who recognize "the value of women's own interpretations of their lived experience and needs and acknowledge the values women claim publicly as their own. . . . They exhibit consciousness of, discomfort at, or even anger over institutionalized injustice (or inequity) toward women as a group by men as a group in a given society; and they advocate the elimination of that injustice by challenging, through efforts to alter prevailing ideas and/or social institutions and practices, the coercive power, force, or authority that upholds male prerogatives in that particular culture."[24] This is a definition that encompasses a wide variety of ideas and movements, both religious and secular.

By contrast to the works on German women mentioned above, historical accounts of English-speaking women often identify religion as a major component of feminist consciousness. This difference may be due to the lesser influence of Weber and Marx in the English-speaking cultures, as well as to these countries' greater religious diversity. Unlike their German counterparts who often view religion as a form of false consciousness, even left-wing British historians such as E. P. Thompson and Eric Hobsbawm portray the evangelical conscience as a progressive political force.[25] According to the British historian Hugh McLeod, the Christian zeal of British and American women was no fearful retreat from modernity, but an upsurge of self-confidence, transformative energy, and feminist conviction.[26] Olive Banks's *Faces of Feminism* and Jane Lewis's *Women and Social Action in Victorian and Edwardian England* are two early works of British women's history that trace the rise of modern feminism to women's religious movements.[27]

In their approach to the relationship of religion and feminism, English-speaking feminists emphasize complexity and ambiguity rather than antagonism. "The most important task facing the historian of women's spirituality," remarks the historian Gail Malmgreen, "is to keep alive the central paradox, the complex tension between religion as an 'opiate' and as an embodiment of ideological and institutional sexism, and religion as transcendent and liberating force."[28] In her essay on Protestant deaconesses in nineteenth- and early-twentieth-century Britain, Martha Vicinus paints a "complicated picture of institutional subordination and self-determination." While she concedes that the deaconesses were subject to male authority and to a highly patriarchal theology, she nonetheless emphasizes that the religious life enabled many women to live independently of marriage and the family in a supportive female community. Religion, she concludes, both "opened and closed doors for single women."[29]

The most complex picture emerges from the United States. In a country where the majority of the population is still religiously observant, Weber's picture of religion as a relic of a bygone age is obviously much less convincing than in post-Christian societies such as Germany. American religious history is in many ways a *Sonderweg* (special path) that was produced by the distinctively American separation of church and state. Unlike European established

churches, American churches depended for their existence on the commitment of their congregations, in which women were often in the majority.
The historian Ann Douglas pointed out in 1977 that the alliance of female
congregants and pastors changed the character of American Protestantism, in
which severe Calvinist doctrines were superseded by a more comforting faith
in God's mercy and human perfectibility. Douglas herself calls this feminized
theology sentimental.[30]

But the American women activists of the Abolitionist movement, whose
toughness and controversial brilliance made them effective advocates of the
rights of women as well as slaves, hardly deserved that reproach. Resisting the
common tendency to portray these women chiefly as secular reformers, Anna
Speicher shows that they were resolved "to maintain and strengthen the religious aspect of everyday life in the face of societal attempts to partition the
sacred and the secular into separate spheres."[31]

Certainly, the activities and beliefs of religious women of the nineteenth
century do not always fit into today's notions of feminism or social justice.
For example, the largest of all women's organizations of this era, the Women's
Christian Temperance Union (WCTU), was founded in 1874. The group
gained a vast membership among female members of Protestant churches
who cited scriptural authority to justify a vociferous and aggressive campaign
against the sale of alcohol. The WCTU soon expanded its work into countless
areas, including philanthropy, social reform, and politics. Unlike male-dominated European and British temperance societies, the American movement
was led by women who channeled their group's enormous energy into the
suffrage movement and other feminist causes.[32] Largely due to the WCTU,
the American woman suffrage movement became a mass movement earlier
than similar movements in Europe. Composed chiefly of white, native-born
women, the WCTU associated the evils of drink with immigrant groups,
thus heightening ethnic tensions and creating damaging stereotypes. Though
they do not exemplify today's feminist ideals, the WCTU leaders cannot be
dismissed as reactionary or backward looking. Their populist religiosity, their
bustling civic activism, and not least their ethnic prejudices mark them as
thoroughly modern Americans.[33]

Gender and Religious Practice

Partly due to the influence of English-language scholarship, many historians
of Germany have recently turned away from Weber's view of religion as a
mere vestige of an earlier age. They recognize that nineteenth-century religious culture was not static—on the contrary, it showed a considerable capacity to adapt its message to the changing times. As Rudolf Schlögl points out,

traditional Catholic doctrines had denounced women as vessels of sin whose weakness disqualified them for the religious life, except perhaps as cloistered nuns. And Protestants, too, had traditionally assigned responsibility for family devotions and the religious education of children to fathers. But when the secularizing impact of the Enlightenment cut back on men's religious participation and industrialization removed fathers from the home, both churches quickly revised their theology to encourage a more active role for women in both church and household. Among the most striking changes was in the Catholic cult of Mary, which tempered its traditional exaltation of virginity with a new emphasis on the importance of the housewife and mother.[34]

That the churches supported the era's cult of domesticity has often been taken as a sign of their conservatism. But some historians point out correctly that this cult was not entirely conservative, but contained many modern elements. Rebekka Habermas explains that the role of the middle-class (*bürgerlich*) woman was new, for she presided over a home that was no longer a center of economic production but rather of emotional intimacy, nurture, and individualized child rearing. In these homes religion, which had traditionally been expressed through public rituals, became a private practice of familial devotion and personal spirituality. In a conclusion that is influenced by the American anthropologist Clifford Geertz, Habermas asserts that this religious ideology promoted neither "emancipation" nor "patriarchal authority" but rather provided women with a framework with which to make sense of their lives.[35] In Austria, Edith Saurer notes that prayer books, which had originally been designed for use in church, were adapted in the nineteenth century for private or family devotions. Religious tracts that were printed in millions exhorted women to combat the evils of the modern world, which included the era's popular literature and the new temptations of urban life.[36]

Jewish religious practice also evolved to create a modern, middle-class identity for women. According to Benjamin Baader, Jewish rituals had traditionally privileged men and the Jewish learning to which men alone had access. These rituals were adapted in the nineteenth century to appeal to "bourgeois sensibility" through the inclusion of music and sermons in the vernacular—changes that made services more welcoming and accessible to women. Baader adds to Kaplan's picture of Jewish women by placing them in the synagogue as well as in the home and the workplace.[37]

These changes in religious culture did not usually encourage feminism—in fact, as Lucian Hölscher observes, the protective authority of male figures such as the priest, pastor, or Jesus himself may actually have enhanced the appeal of religion to some women.[38] But female religiosity was not always submissive; it could also assume active, even rebellious forms. A telling example is provided by David Blackbourn in his study of the uproar produced in 1876 by the alleged appearance of the Virgin to three little girls in the village of Marpingen.

The enthusiastic response of local Catholics, who rushed to Marpingen in huge numbers, has often been dismissed as an outburst of primitive superstition and a protest against the modern world. But Blackbourn points out that the villagers' religious sensibility was distinctively modern in its focus on a powerful female figure—the Virgin—whom nineteenth-century culture endowed with the traits that it considered distinctively female. This religious culture bolstered the self-confidence of women and provided them with a "respite from powerlessness."[39] By appearing to children, the Virgin affirmed another attitude that was distinctive to the nineteenth century—the idealization of children as innocent creatures who had a direct connection to the Divine. Blackbourn's sympathy for the pious villagers is matched by his contempt for the Prussian government officials who used scientific arguments to discredit the Marpingen apparitions and police power to disperse the pilgrims. Though ostensibly defending rationality against superstition, these men in fact defended gender and class privilege against a populist movement that was led by workers, women, and children.[40]

Lay women's participation changed nineteenth-century Catholicism in many ways. In the closing years of the nineteenth century, the cult of the Sacred Heart of Jesus transformed the image of Jesus. No longer the stern judge, he appeared as an empathetic and sensitive confidant—an image that appealed powerfully to women. As Norbert Busch has shown, clerics responded ambivalently to this cult, fearing that its lurid emotionalism would further alienate men from Catholicism. Male worshippers, some priests complained, had to elbow their way through crowds of women to get to the confessional![41]

The feminization of religion created new options not only for lay women but also for nuns. A little-studied aspect of nineteenth-century German history is the upsurge in the founding of female religious orders between 1840 and 1860. As Relinde Meiwes points out, this was a distinctively female trend—male orders lost membership during the same period. Why were Catholic women more attracted to the religious life than their male co-religionists? Meiwes explains this as a response to urbanization and industrialization, which by disrupting the family economy had left many single women, especially in rural areas, without a means of livelihood. By joining a religious order, such women gained not only a community but also vocational opportunities that were not yet available to them in the secular world. Among these were nursing, social work, and teaching.[42] Rather than a retreat into the past, the religious vocation was a context in which many women were enabled to make the transition from traditional to modern ways of life.

Jonathan Sperber reproaches Meiwes for what he considers her excessive emphasis on the independence of these religious orders, which were in fact guided by male theologians and controlled by the Church hierarchy.[43] But Meiwes does not commit the anachronism of associating Catholic nuns with feminist notions of autonomy—in fact, she stresses their devout submission to the all-male Catholic hierarchy.[44] These nuns nonetheless helped to transform their church, in which a new emphasis on charitable work and social outreach was made possible by a vast increase in female participation, both by lay women and by those in religious orders.[45]

Influenced by these and other works, some recent accounts reinterpret the entire history of church-state relations in nineteenth-century Germany using gender as a category of analysis. Michael Gross depicts the *Kulturkampf* as an assertion of masculinity as well as secularism. "As liberals coded public life and the state as masculine," he concludes, "they coded the domestic sphere and Catholicism as feminine . . . if the Catholic Church was an aging lady, then liberalism was a young man, assertive and in the prime of life."[46] Manuel Borutta's colorful story of the anticlerical propaganda that fueled the *Kulturkampf* likewise emphasizes gender relations. Lurid exposés of convent life—of rampant sexuality and of the physical abuse of nuns—expressed masculine resentment of religious orders and the opportunity they afforded women to live a single life free of family responsibilities. Borutta suggests that the *Kulturkampf* reduced the Catholic Church to a role that was symbolically feminine: "While the state laid claim to primacy in the 'masculine' sphere of politics and public life, the church withdrew, at least provisionally, into domains like the care of the sick whose connotation was predominantly female."[47] However, we must remember that some women were firmly in the secular and anticlerical camp. Hedwig Dohm, a well-known feminist, was the wife of Ernst Dohm, who was the editor of the very anticlerical satirical sheet *Kladderadatsch*. She hotly denied that women were more religious by nature than men. "To this day, women have not invented a religion," she wrote in 1873, "Men have driven women into the churches by excluding them from all other areas of spiritual life. The clerical influence will diminish in proportion to women being permitted to participate in higher duties."[48]

Gender, Church, and Nation

At the turn of the twentieth century, the doctrine of separate spheres began to make way for a new gender order that integrated women (albeit at a subordinate level) into politics, the labor market, and civil society. And religious culture changed accordingly. As church attendance among lay men declined, both churches looked to women for political support. Catholic and Protestant clerics whose predecessors had forbidden women to engage in politics now encouraged their female congregants to defend their religious beliefs in the public forum. The result was the founding of lay women's groups which eventually far surpassed secular feminist organizations in numbers and political influence.

The Protestant DEF (mentioned above) was founded in 1898 and its Catholic counterpart, the Catholic Women's League (*Katholische Frauenbund*, or KFB) in 1903.

Gisela Breuer, who has written the history of the latter group, emphasizes the Catholic women's assertiveness and ambition. Unlike previous Catholic women's organizations, which had been led by male clerics, the KFB insisted on female leadership and allied itself with a wider women's movement that included secular organizations. The Marian cult was once again updated, this time to vindicate the dignity and worth of the single life that was lived by many professional women. The Catholic Church continued to insist on the subordination of women, but Catholic women modified this doctrine by giving it a functional rather than an intrinsic meaning, claiming that it defined some female roles but not women's value as human beings. The KFB showed considerable independence, resisting domination by Catholic clerics and by secular feminist organizations. The group refused to join the BDF and opposed woman suffrage until the Weimar Republic made it a fait accompli.[49]

In other European countries, too, religion provided a major avenue for the emergence of women into the public sphere. In her history of the huge and influential Catholic women's movement that developed in France between 1900 and 1940, the French historian Anne Cova shows that French Catholic women, like their German counterparts, opposed many cherished goals and values of secular feminists. However, she does not write off the Catholic movement as reactionary and patriarchal—and, indeed, it championed reforms that many contemporaries considered progressive, such as family allowances (state subsidies for children) and other forms of aid to mothers. Cova portrays this movement as a vast field for the development of women's ideas, organizational skills, and political agency.[50]

Only recently have historians of German feminism looked at the early-twentieth-century women's movement in its full diversity—a task that requires them to distance themselves from their own notions of what feminism "should" be. Two newly published dissertations examine the culture of activist women in German cities at the turn of the twentieth century. Christina Klausmann's *Politik und Kultur der Frauenbewegung im Kaiserreich: Das Beispiel Frankfurt am Main* (*Politics and Culture of the Women's Movement in the German Empire: The Example of Frankfurt am Main*), gives an overview of the women's organizations in Frankfurt, the activities that they sponsored, and the social composition of their membership at the turn of the twentieth century. Klausmann demonstrates that cooperation was sometimes possible despite differences in religion, social background, and political ideology.[51] In *Arbeiten für eine bessere Welt: Frauenbewegung und Sozialreform, 1890–1914* (*Working for a Better World: The Women's Movement and Social Reform, 1890–1914*), Iris Schröder observes that religious belief of some sort was common to almost all activists across the political spectrum of women's groups. Not all of these activists were conservative—in fact, religious belief could sometimes provide a basis for very progressive views of the role of women in social reform. Schröder, who takes religious belief seriously, explains how the differing beliefs of Protestant, Catholic, and Jewish women shaped their approach to social activism.[52] She concludes that feminist culture encouraged religious tolerance and commitment to common goals—a conclusion that is confirmed by my own works on the kindergarten movement, the League for the Protection of Mothers, and the BDF.[53]

Another work that broadens our picture of German gender politics by including conservative and religious women is Jean Quataert's *Staging Philanthropy: Patriotic Women and the National Imagination in Dynastic Germany, 1813–1916*, a study of women's associations, philanthropic organizations, and religious orders during the period from the Napoleonic wars to the First World War.[54] Patriotism and militarism appealed to women as well as men, and mobilized women's talents and energies as effectively as progressive reform movements. Feminism was not the only, or even the predominant, catalyst for women's organizing. Distancing herself from "emancipatory teleology," Quataert demonstrates the many ways that patriotic organizations helped to shape the German state and to construct national identity.[55]

The most controversial questions about the relationship of religious and gender identity are raised by the National Socialist period. Recent historical works have presented two views of Nazi religious culture that seem, at first glance, to be antithetical. Claudia Koonz claims that Nazi ideology emphasized gender difference, and idealized domesticity and motherhood. Because this ideology had a great deal in common with that of Catholic and Protestant women's organizations and of middle-class feminist groups, Koonz assigns to these groups much of the responsibility for popularizing National Socialism among German women.[56]

However, Doris Bergen's study of the German Christians—a group that modified Christian theology to accord with Nazi ideology—portrays the Nazis as misogynists who had nothing but contempt for motherliness or any other stereotypically "feminine" quality. Even biological motherhood was not understood as a female, but rather as a racial function to be performed only by an elite. The German Christians compensated for what they considered the excessive influence of women in Protestant churches by creating a "manly church" that rejected the female-identified ethic of compassion and emphasized patriotism and the warlike virtues.[57] Irmtraud Götz von Olenhusen reminds us that the cult of the "manly church" was not confined to Protestants, but also promoted by Catholic youth movements that warned their male members against sentimentality and encouraged a more tough-minded approach to religion.[58]

But these two readings of Nazi religious culture—one centered on motherly and the other on masculinist values—are not so contradictory as they at first appear, for religion can be interpreted in many different ways. The German Christians appealed only to a minority of churchgoers, and their efforts to transform Christianity failed. As Koonz points out, many women tried to reconcile the new political ideology with their more familiar roles as Christians and as mothers.

For women as well as men, the relationship between Nazism and religion could be problematic. Though they made short-term concessions to the churches, the Nazis were a highly secular group whose long-term objective was to destroy religion—Christianity as well as Judaism—and to replace it with a cult of the leader and the state.[59] In a few cases, religious belief inspired dissent or resistance. In her study of Protestant religious women in the era of the Weimar Republic, Doris Kaufmann presents a revised view of organized Protestant women, who are so often presented merely as conservatives. In the Weimar period, the Protestant religious organizations were brought together in the Union of German Protestant Women's Associations (*Vereinigung evangelischer Frauenvereine Deutschlands*) under the leadership of the educator and theologian Magdalene von Tiling. Von Tiling was a devout Lutheran who opposed many feminist aspirations, aligned her organization with the conservative German National People's Party (*Deutsch-nationale Volkspartei*, or DNVP), and hailed the Nazi takeover as a hopeful new beginning.[60] However, her Lutheran belief in the separation of religious and secular authority soon distanced her from the new regime. "State, nation, blood and race are not the ultimate values," she protested, "the Lord is the first and the last aim of our struggle."[61] Von Tiling tried to preserve her group's independence of the totalitarian state, but was soon overruled by the Nazi leader Gertrud Scholz-Klink, who integrated the Protestant women into the Party's women's organization.[62]

Historical judgments are always contextual, and in this context forms of piety that might otherwise be dismissed as reactionary take on a positive significance. The historians Laura Gellott and Michael Phayer show how some Austrian Catholic women's organizations protested against totalitarianism in both its German and Italian forms. The German Catholic Women's League (*Katholische Deutsche Frauenbund)* and the Catholic Women's Organization (*Katholische Frauenorganisation*), both of which included many working and professional women, cited religious doctrine to discredit Fascist policies that ruthlessly exploited women in the service of population growth and eugenic improvement. Catholic women, they argued, revered the Virgin Mary as a role model for the single life. Not only did they oppose measures that dismissed married women from their jobs, but they also refused to cooperate with Nazi-inspired social policies that supported unmarried motherhood.[63]

Marian apparitions, too, could inspire resistance to totalitarianism. In 1937, pilgrims to the village of Heede, where the Virgin had been sighted by four young girls, responded so rebelliously to an official prohibition of their gatherings that they had to be put down forcibly by the Gestapo.[64] However, cases of religiously motivated resistance remained few and far between. In general, the Christian churches cooperated with the regime, and even reinforced some elements of Nazi ideology, including anti-Semitism.

Conclusion: Directions for Future Research

Since the 1970s, when a new generation of mostly female historians aspired to create a "usable past" to guide to their own struggle for equality, feminist historians have focused chiefly on the history of women. But recently this focus has been broadened to include gender itself as an aspect of culture and individual identity—a change that brings men as well as women within the scope of the historian's analysis. Though most of the studies cited here are centered on women, many raise intriguing questions about gender relationships. The years between 1800 and 1950 saw a divergence between the religious cultures of men and women, the former group tending toward secularization, and the latter toward increased religious activism. This development must have had major consequences for gender relations in many areas. How were marital relationships, child-rearing practices, educational institutions, and religious reform movements shaped by conflicts between female religiosity and male skepticism? Was the feminization of religion a cause or an effect of the general decline in male religious belief and practice? Were the churches' positions on such issues as the ordination of women, reproduction and sexuality, and the family motivated in part by an attempt to win men back to the fold?

The question also remains whether religion will continue to shape the gender identities of both men and women. Weber's claim that modernization results inevitably in the decline and eventually in the disappearance of religion has not stood the test of time. Church attendance by both sexes has declined drastically in Germany and in other Western European countries since the 1960s. The Christian churches, however, have not disappeared but have adapted to a changing culture. In Germany, their chief role is now to dispense various forms of social assistance and to champion weak and vulnerable members of society—a role that lay women and female religious orders helped to create.[65] And the United States presents an alternative model of modernization in which religion flourishes rather than declines. Today, the feminization of religion has entered a new stage as women throughout the Western world directly challenge male hierarchies and aspire to leadership positions as priests, ministers, theologians, and administrators. If they succeed, they will continue to transform the churches; if they fail, the forces of patriarchal conservatism and fundamentalism will win another victory.

Meanwhile European societies have become more diverse and now include substantial Muslim communities. The struggle between religious and secular worldviews often centers on issues concerning gender, sexuality, and the status of women. The accession to the European Union of Eastern European countries, which since the fall of communism have experienced a religious revival, may raise other controversial issues. At such a time, it is more important than ever to understand religious belief, not as a vestige of the past, but as an important force in the present.

Notes

1. Elizabeth Cady Stanton, *Bible and Church Degrade Woman* (Chicago, 1896), 11.
2. Simone de Beauvoir, *The Second Sex*, trans. and ed. H. M. Parshley (New York, 1989), 971.
3. Mary Daly, *The Church and the Second Sex* (New York, 1975).
4. See Jonathan Sperber, "*Kirchengeschichte* or the Social and Cultural History of Religion?" *Neue politische Literatur* 43 (1995): 13–35. This review article by one of the best-known specialists in the history of German Catholicism provides a useful overview of the theoretical foundations and current status of the historical study of religion in Germany. For one statement of Weber's theory, see Max Weber, "Science as a Vocation," in *Essays in Sociology*, trans. and ed. H. H. Gerth and C. Wright Mills (New York, 1946), 129–156.
5. Arthur Mitzman, *The Iron Cage: A Historical Interpretation of Max Weber* (New Brunswick, 1985), 302–306, quotation 304; see also Terry R. Kandal, *The Woman Question in Classical Sociological Theory* (Miami, 1988), 89–185.
6. Jean H. Quataert, *Staging Philanthropy: Patriotic Women and the National Imagination in Dynastic Germany* (Ann Arbor, 2001), 295.
7. Marion A. Kaplan, *The Jewish Feminist Movement in Germany: The Campaigns of the Jüdischer Frauenbund* (Westport, Conn., 1979), 20.
8. Marion A. Kaplan, *The Making of the Jewish Middle Class: Women, Family and Identity in Imperial Germany* (New York, 1991), 84; idem, *Jewish Feminist Movement*, 234.
9. Catherine M. Prelinger, *Charity, Challenge and Change: Religious Dimensions of the Mid-Nineteenth-Century Women's Movement in Germany* (New York, 1987), xiii.
10. Sylvia Paletschek, *Frauen und Dissens: Frauen im Deutschkatholizismus und in den freien Gemeinden* (Göttingen, 1990), 233.
11. Dagmar Herzog, *Intimacy and Exclusion: Religious Politics in Pre-Revolutionary Baden* (Princeton, 1996).
12. Thomas Mergel, "Die subtile Macht der Liebe: Geschlecht, Erziehung und Frömmigkeit in katholischen rheinischen Bürgerfamilien 1830–1910," in *Frauen unter dem Patriarchat der Kirchen: Katholikinnen und Protestantinnen im 19. und 20. Jahrhundert, Mit Beiträgen von Irmtraud Götz von Olenhusen, Thomas Mergel, Sylvia Paletschek, RelindeMeiwes, Ursula Baumann, Birgit Sack, Martin König, Antonia Leugers, Jochen-Christoph Kaiser* (Stuttgart, 1995), 22–47;

David Blackbourn, "'Die von der Gottheit überaus bevorzugten Mägdlein': Marienerscheinungen im Bismarckreich," in *Wunderbare Erscheinungen: Frauen und katholische Frömmigkeit im 19. und 20. Jahrhundert*, ed. Irmtraud Götz von Olenhusen (Paderborn, 1995), 22–47.

13. Thomas Mergel, "Die subtile Macht der Liebe."

14. Irmtraud Götz von Olenhusen, "Die Feminisierung von Religion und Kirche im 19. und 20. Jahrhundert: Forschungsstand und Forschungsperspektiven," in *Frauen unter dem Patriarchat der Kirchen*, 9–21.

15. Richard J. Evans, "The Concept of Feminism: Notes for Practicing Historians," in *German Women in the Eighteenth and Nineteenth Centuries: A Social and Literary History*, ed. Ruth Ellen Joeres and Mary Jo Maynes (Bloomington, 1986), 247–258, quotation 251.

16. Ursula Baumann, *Protestantismus und Frauen-Emanzipation in Deutschland, 1850 bis 1920* (Frankfurt/M., 1992), 22.

17. Ibid., 36.

18. Weber, "Science as a Vocation," 155.

19. Richard J. Evans, *The Feminist Movement in Germany, 1894–1933* (London, 1976), 145–174; Barbara Greven-Aschoff, *Die Bürgerliche Frauenbewegung in Deutschland, 1894–1933* (Göttingen, 1981), 87–124.

20. Baumann, *Protestantismus und Frauen-Emanzipation*, 166.

21. Ibid., 275–276.

22. Nancy R. Reagin, *A German Women's Movement: Class and Gender in Hanover,* (Chapel Hill, 1995), 221–257.

23. Von Olenhusen, "Die Feminisierung von Religion und Kirche."

24. Karen M. Offen, "Defining Feminism: A Comparative Historical Approach," *Signs* 14 (1988): 119–157, quotation 152.

25. E. P. Thompson, *The Making of the English Working Class* (New York, 1964); E. J. Hobsbawm, *Primitive Rebels: Studies in Archaic Forms of Social Movements in the 19th and 20th Centuries* (New York, 1965).

26. Hugh McLeod, "Weibliche Frömmigkeit —männlicher Unglaube?: Religion und Kirche im bürgerlichen 19. Jahrhundert," in *Bürgerinnen und Bürger: Geschlechterverhältnisse im 19. Jahrhundert, zwölf Beiträge*, ed. Ute Frevert (Göttingen, 1988), 134–156.

27. Olive Banks, *Faces of Feminism: A Study of Feminism as a Social Movement* (New York, 1981); Jane E. Lewis, *Women and Social Action in Victorian and Edwardian England* (Stanford, 1991).

28. Gail Malmgreen, "Introduction," in *Religion in the Lives of English Women, 1760–1930*, ed. Gail Malmgreen (Bloomington, 1986), 1–10, quotation 6–7.

29. Martha Vicinus, *Independent Women: Work and Community for Single Women, 1850–1920* (Chicago, 1985), 48.

30. Ann Douglas, *The Feminization of American Culture* (New York, 1977).

31. Anna M. Speicher, *The Religious World of Anti-Slavery Women: Spirituality in the Lives of Five Abolitionist Lecturers* (Syracuse, 2002), 7; see also McLeod, "Weibliche Frömmigkeit."

32. See for example Lilian Lewis Shiman, "'Changes are Dangerous': Women and Temperance in Victorian England," in Malmgreen, *Religion in the Lives of English Women*, 193–215; and Elisabeth Meyer-Renschhausen, *Weibliche Kultur und soziale Arbeit: Eine Geschichte der Frauenbewegung am Beispiel Bremens*, 1810–1927, Cologne,1989, 171–270.

33. For example, see a textbook that is widely used in women's history courses: Sarah M. Evans, *Born for Liberty: A History of Women in America* (New York, 1997????), 125–130.

34. Rudolf Schlögl, "Sünderin, Heilige oder Hausfrau?: Katholische Kirche und weibliche Frömmingkeit um 1800," in von Olenhusen, *Wunderbare Erscheinungen*, 13–50.

35. Rebekka Habermas, "Weibliche Religiosität—oder: von der Fragilität bürgerlicher Identitäten," in *Wege zur Geschichte des Bürgertums: Vierzehn Beiträge*, ed. Klaus Tenfelde, Hans-Ulrich Wehler, Göttingen, 1994, 125–148.

36. Edith Saurer, "Bewahrerinnen der Zucht und Sittlichkeit: Gebetbücher für Frauen—Frauen in Gebetbüchern," *L'Homme* 1 (1990): 37–58.

37. Benjamin Maria Baader, "When Judaism Turned Bourgeois: Gender in Jewish Associational Life and in the Synagogue, 1750–1850," *Leo Baeck Institute Yearbook* 46 (2001): 113–123.

38. Lucian Hölscher, "Weibliche Religiosität?: Der Einfluss von Religion und Kirche auf die Religiosität von Frauen im 19. Jahrhundert," in *Erziehung der Menschengeschlechter: Studien zur Religion, Sozialisation, und Bildung in Europa seit der Aufklärung*, ed. Margret Kraul and Christoph Luth (Weinheim, 1996), 45–62.

39. David Blackbourn, *Marpingen: Apparitions of the Virgin Mary in Nineteenth-Century Germany* (New York, 1994), 31.

40. Ibid., 256–270, 360–374.

41. Norbert Busch, "Die Feminisierung der ultramontanen Frömmigkeit," in von Olenhusen, *Wunderbare Erscheinungen*, 203–220.

42. Relinde Meiwes, *Arbeiterinnen des Herrn: Katholische Frauenkongregationen im 19. Jahrhundert* (Frankfurt/M., 2000).

43. Sperber, "Kirchengeschichte," 18–19.

44. Meiwes, *Arbeiterinnen des Herrn*, 288–309.

45. Ibid., 310–312. Women became Protestant deaconesses for many of the same reasons; see Inke Wegener, *Zwischen Mut und Demut: Die weibliche Diakonie am Beispiel Elise Averdiecks* (Göttingen, 2004).

46. Michael B. Gross, *The War against Catholicism: Liberalism and the Anti-Catholic Imagination in Nineteenth-Century Germany* (Ann Arbor, 2004), 201–202.

47. Manuel Borutta, "Enemies at the Gate: the Moabit *Klostersturm* and the *Kulturkampf*: Germany," in *Culture Wars: Secular-Catholic Conflict in Nineteenth-Century Europe*, ed. Christopher Clark and Wolfram Kaiser (Cambridge, 2003), 227–254, quotation 252.

48. Hedwig Dohm, *Der Jesuitismus im Hausstande* [1873], excerpted in *Women, the Family, and Freedom: The Debate in Documents*, vol. 1., ed. Susan Groag Bell and Karen Offen (Stanford, 1983), 508.

49. Gisela Breuer, *Frauenbewegung im Katholizismus: Der Katholische Frauenbund 1903–1918* (Frankfurt/M., 1998). A new volume of essays on many aspects of Catholic women's organizational life celebrates the one-hundredth anniversary of the founding of the *Katholische Frauenbund*: see Gisela Muschiol, ed., *Katholikinnen und Moderne: Katholische Frauenbewegung zwischen Tradition und Emanzipation* (Münster, 2003).

50. Anne Cova, *Au Service de l'Église, de la Patrie, et de la Famille: Femmes Catholiques et maternité sous la III République* (Paris, 2000); see also Karen Offen, "Body Politics: Women, Work, and the Politics of Motherhood in France, 1920–1950," in *Maternity and Gender Policies: Women and the Rise of European Welfare States, 1880s–1950s*, ed. Gisela Bock and Pat Thane (London, 1991),138–159.

51. Christina Klausmann, *Politik und Kultur der Frauenbewegung in Kaiserreich: Das Beispiel Frankfurt a. M.* (Frankfurt/M., 1997).

52. Iris Schröder, *Arbeiten für eine bessere Welt: Frauenbewegung und Sozialreform, 1890–1914* (Frankfurt/M., 2001).

53. Ann Taylor Allen, *Feminism and Motherhood in Germany, 1800–1914* (New Brunswick, 1991).

54. Quataert, *Staging Philanthropy*, 293–304.

55. Ibid., 295.

56. Claudia Koonz, *Mothers in the Fatherland: Women, the Family, and Nazi Politics* (New York, 1987), 13–17 and passim.

57. Doris L. Bergen, *Twisted Cross: The German Christian Movement in the Third Reich* (Chapel Hill, 1996).

58. Irmtraud Götz von Olenhusen, "Geschlechterrollen, Jugend, und Religion: Deutschland 1900–1933," in Kraul and Luth, *Erziehung der Menschengeschlechter*, 239–258.

59. Compare Zygmunt Bauman, *Modernity and the Holocaust* (Ithaca, 1989); and Ann Taylor Allen, "The Holocaust and the Modernization of Gender," *Central European History* 30 (1997): 349–364.

60. Doris Kaufmann, *Frauen zwischen Aufbruch und Reaktion: Protestantische Frauenbewegung in der ersten Hälfte des 20 Jahrhunderts* (Zurich, 1988), 86; see also Gury Schneider-Ludorff, "Positionen und Handlungsspielräume von Frauen des konservativen Protestantismus in der Weimarer Republik am Beispiel Magdalene von Tilings," in *Starke fromme Frauen?: Eine Zwischenbilanz konfessioneller Frauenforschung heute*, ed. Ute Gause et al. (Hofgeismar, 2000), 71–92. On the role of women in Nazi religious organizations, see also Heike Köhler, *Deutsch—Evangelisch—Frau: Meta Eyl—eine Theologin im Spannungsfeld zwischen nationalsozialistischer Reichskirche und evangelischer Frauenbewegung* (Neukirchen-Vluyn, 2003).

61. Kaufmann, *Frauen zwischen Aufbruch und Reaktion*, 96.

62. Ibid., 97.

63. Ibid.

64. Anna Marie Zumholz, "Die Resistenz des katholischen Milieus: Seherinnen und Stigmatisierte in der ersten Hälfte des 20. Jahrhunderts," in von Olenhusen, *Wunderbare Erscheinungen*, 221–251.

65. Ursula Baumann, "Religion und Emanzipation: Konfessionelle Frauenbewegung in Deutschland 1900–1933," in *Frauen unter dem Patriarchat der Kirchen*, 89–118.

10

CONTINUITIES AND RUPTURES
Sexuality in Twentieth-Century Germany:
Historiography and Its Discontents

Atina Grossmann

In the introduction to the Spring 2002 special issue on sexuality and German fascism of the *Journal of the History of Sexuality*, Dagmar Herzog lays out the beginnings of a research agenda for a surprisingly under-researched and under-theorized topic in modern German history: "What is the relationship between sexual and other kinds of politics? How should we periodize transformations in the history of sexuality in Germany?"[1] It is not an accident surely that a volume devoted to identifying "major theoretical and methodological problems" in the history of sexuality is focused on the Nazi period, its origins and its aftermath. Like everything we touch as historians of modern Germany, the history of sexuality cannot be read outside of the shadow and echo of National Socialism. Questions of continuity and rupture, singularity and comparability, are central to all of our inquiries, whether they are directed before or after the Third Reich. The history of sexuality is inseparable from the history of population policy, race hygiene, and eugenics on the one hand, and the history of women and gender on the other. As recent scholarship in history and literature has shown, it should also be read in the context of German colonialism and the imperial racist legacy.[2]

Population and sexual politics—the notion of *When Biology Became Destiny*—were from the beginning at the center of feminist interpretations of modern German history. Those interpretations, however, have shifted quite substantially, often in tandem with the political, personal, and scholarly trajectory of the first generation of second-wave feminist historians.[3] When women's studies emerged from the 1960s student movement and New Left, both in Germany and the United States, we thought we knew the story. Nazism and its call to return women to *Kinder, Küche, Kirche* was the repressive reaction to the freewheeling sexuality of Weimar; a clampdown on the New Woman who had materialized in the wake of World War I, revolution, and the Weimar Constitution. It is worth recalling those beginnings, both for those of us who might have forgotten as we moved into more strictly academic ways of apprehending the past, and for those of us for whom the 1960s as well as the beginning of second-wave feminism in the United States and Germany already began as a memory. Pirated editions of Wilhelm Reich's *Mass Psychology of Fascism* and *Sex Pol*, passed around among the '68ers and peddled from book stalls in front of university meeting halls, announced that sexual repression led to fascism (as well as Stalinism), and gave political justification to a heady search for pleasure and efforts to combine the struggle for social change with individual rebellion. The sense that true sexual liberation was central to genuine political freedom was reinforced in its early feminist version by Kate Millet's pioneering *Sexual Politics*, which (heavily influenced by Reich) chronicled the Nazi "counterrevolution" against women and unproblematically assumed that a large part of the fascist agenda was the resubordination of women and a women's movement that had been unleashed after the First World War.[4] For many young left intellectuals and activists in the United States and Germany, in the 1960s and early 1970s, the fantasy of a free and explosively innovative Weimar culture that was then destroyed and exiled became a touchstone for dreams of sexual equality and freedom.[5]

Already by the mid 1970s, however, along with disillusionment with the promise of sexual liberation among the male "heavies" of the New Left, came a reconsideration of Weimar and its progressive visions. Renate Bridenthal and Claudia Koonz, in their germinal 1976 article "Beyond *Kinder, Küche, Kirche*: Weimar Women in Politics and Work," cautioned that German women may not have been so much corralled and repressed by National Socialism as responsive to the failed emancipation of Weimar; in some ways Nazism was the revolution against a republic that had offered the vote but little else. "German women," they concluded, "had come a long way—in the wrong direction."[6] Following on this Marxist-feminist revision of rosy views of Weimar came a much more critical and darker view of Weimar's "laboratory of modernity" and its commitment to social welfare and innovative culture. This revision was inspired less by Marx and more by an (in some ways) overly rigid reading of Foucault's portrayal of sexuality as a "regime of power-knowledge-pleasure." This analysis rejected the "hydraulic" model offered by Reich and the leftist sexual liberationists in which the lid of sexual repression could be snapped off and on, and saw sexuality rather as a dense grid of power relations that could work in multiple and ambiguous ways. The new distrust of Weimar was later solidified by Detlev Peukert's provocative argument about the "pathologies of modernity" in his "The Genesis of the 'Final Solution' from the Spirit of Science."[7]

This turn in the view of Weimar modernity and its welfare state did not, however, lead to much work directly focused on sexuality. It did produce significant studies of Weimar social and population policy and rationalization experiments by scholars on both sides of the Atlantic, often working in international teams. Indeed, our extensive examinations of the discourses and practices of interwar rationalization, and the related interplay of body and machine so characteristic of Weimar, in all areas ranging from industry to housework to sexuality, would be well worth revisiting.[8] But for the most part, we left sexuality and the related examination of the "new woman" to the domain of cultural history and cultural studies (especially literature and film, and to a lesser degree, art history), which focused on gender in the modern metropolis, notably Berlin, rather than specifically on issues of sexuality.[9] Curiously, there has been no twentieth century equivalent to Isabel Hull's complex study of eighteenth and early nineteenth century "sexual system[s]" as "the patterned ways in which sexual behavior is shaped and given meaning through institutions." Conversely, standard English language histories of sexuality have treated Germany only glancingly and mostly in relation to the history of sexology and the homosexual rights movement.[10] For the turn of the century and interwar period, George Mosse's analysis in *Nationalism and Sexuality*, produced quite outside of the context of burgeoning feminist historiography in the 1980s, of how gendered prescriptions for sexual normality and abnormality defined bourgeois respectability in modern Germany, remains groundbreaking and challenging.[11] In some ways, moreover, our disappointment with Weimar allowed us to focus more extensively on National Socialism; we moved from worrying about what went wrong in Weimar to confronting the monster itself.

In the 1980s, a younger generation of German social historians (both female and male, German and Anglo-American) moved from a focus on the "Hitler State," the class and gender aspects of the *Volksgemeinschaft*, to biological politics and the nature of the *Volkskörper*. Our studies of the origins and workings of what came to be called the "Racial State" focused increasingly on the "body" and its regulation.[12] This critical shift brought its own set of complicated problems. In my 1995 book on sex reform, I worried that social as well as medical and women's historians had become increasingly "fixed on 'biomedical' politics and a particularly 'modern' scientific and technocratic arrogance as explanatory models for the triumphant and relatively straightforward progress of National Socialism from 'Weimar to Auschwitz'" and cautioned that this sweeping indictment did not account for the drastic ruptures in the "motherhood-eugenics-consensus" achieved by the regime change from Weimar to National Socialism. But to make my case I wrote about sex reform and eugenics, about varieties of rationalization of reproduction and the body, and did not pursue my earlier work on the "new woman," sex, and sexuality.[13]

The focus on population policy and racial hygiene privileged questions about the regulation of the body and reproduction, overwhelming earlier fascinations with Weimar's cultural and sexual innovativeness, both its promise and its failures. To have remained on that topic would have been interpreted as a romanticization of a sexual liberation that we had come to question in our own lives, and perhaps even as a misplaced attachment to radical dreams that had become suspect in the wake of our "linguistic turn" toward postmodernity and our post-New Left suspicion of planned utopias.[14] How then do we now build on and escape beyond a scholarly context that has for some thirty years embedded sexuality in studies of what Ute Planert has called the "'threefold body' of the nation: the individual body, the reproductive body (*Gattungskörper*) and the national body (*Volkskörper*)?"[15] In this essay I will address three areas ripe both for looking back at work already begun and for plunging ahead into new territory. My review is organized chronologically, starting with a look at the Weimar Republic and concluding with a discussion of postwar Germany.

Weimar: Recuperating Sexual Modernism

My first *Desideratum* for further research would be a revisiting of the Weimar years. An open and unsentimental approach to sexual activity and representation was after all a crucial marker of modern identity in the Weimar Republic, particularly for women. A certain kind of performative sexuality—taking lovers, a language of sexual banter, a vogue for bisexuality and triangular love affairs—was integral to Weimar's pervasive discourse of the "new."[16] We are still struck and slightly bewildered by the apparent *Sachlichkeit* or matter-of-fact lack of sentimentality, even cynicism, with which Weimar "new women" approached their romantic and sex lives. The sexual shamelessness of the "new woman," her willingness not only to separate sex from procreation, but also to separate sex from love, her supposed embrace of Alexandra Kollontai's (also putative) "glass of water" take on sexuality as a natural physiological process, appeared as among the more shocking effects of a technologized rationalized age; all the more so because as numerous sociological surveys and journalistic reports attested, such attitudes were by no means limited to a bourgeois elite.[17]

Young working women's pursuit of sexual pleasure and their cynical awareness that they could not depend on men to take care of them economically or emotionally has certainly been investigated in the context of its many (horrified, fascinated, and bemused) contemporary literary, theatrical, and cinematic representations. Literary and film studies scholars write about the fragmented dissociation between head and body in Hannah Höch's collages, the streamlined serialization in Lubitsch's spectacles, or the chopped-up prose of Irmgard Keun and Marie-Luise Fleisser, as expressions of the rationalization of sexuality, the body, and everyday life.[18] They have taken seriously these portrayals in which "new women" embraced (or accepted) sex but resisted love because it might threaten the precarious negotiations between work and family, independence and protection, that structured their lives. Photo and document collections or exhibition catalogs, often produced by the "barefoot" amateur or student researchers and local historians who generated West Germany's turn to *Alltagsgeschichte* in the 1980s, tried to retrieve memories of a Weimar culture of sexual experimentation and female (including lesbian) independence that they sensed had been lost to Nazism and exile.[19] So far, however, the linguistic turn notwithstanding, professional social historians have been much better at exposing the bleaker or at least less exciting "reality" behind the "images" than in examining how and why so many young women insisted that when it came to love and sex, "*Sachlichkeit* was the magic word."[20]

Most academic texts about sexuality in Weimar turn out to be about the politics of reproduction; that is, the constraints, such as economic crisis or restrictions on birth control and abortion, that limited emancipation and made sexual freedom dangerous, or, alternatively, about so-called "deviance" or life on the sexual "margins," especially homosexuality, prostitution, and venereal disease.[21] Precisely those areas of Weimar culture that intrigued or titillated popular audiences remained largely unexamined, whether it was the adventures of prominent women in politics, entertainment, or the professions (many of whom did leave us engaging memoirs), or the wide spectrum of post-World War I women, single and married, working and middle class, who led the Marxist psychologist Manes Sperber to declare women "the avant garde of a radical emancipation, of a sexual revolution" in the "aftermath" of the "social earthquake of World War I."[22] Astonishingly, given the ubiquity of sports and athletic displays of both the male and female body in Weimar culture, Erik Jensen's recent dissertation is the first history to examine seriously the role of sexuality and female athletes in constructing a modern culture of celebrity in Germany.[23] We have done little to complement the contemporary sociological studies of the ordinary working girls who, with their pert hats, chopped-off hair, and newly shaven legs visible under shorter skirts marked modern asphalt culture. We do not even have good contextualized studies of glamorous and sexy screen stars, such as Pola Negri or Asta Nielsen (not to mention Marlene Dietrich and Greta Garbo), or of the saucy molls (*kesse Bolle*) of Berlin's stage and cabaret, like Claire Waldorff, Trude Hesterberg, and Fritzi Massary, who were free with both their bodies and their mordant wit. [24]

After decades of scholarly fascination with critical theory and the Frankfurt School, the Institute for Social Research's pioneering survey of women's sexual behavior, conducted as part of its investigation of "Authority and the Family" and distributed to (mostly male) physicians, has not been systematically analyzed; nor do we seem to know where and whether the original questionnaires have been preserved. What and whose social/sexual experiences were actually referenced when doctors complained that, "Emancipated women adopt more readily the bad habits of men than their good ones"? Rationalization and modernity brought with it, it seemed, independent and "cool conduct" which threatened to subvert women's nurturing and comforting social tasks but no longer mandated celibacy. As the befuddled and disturbed doctors reported, "Almost all women seem to have been seized by an amorous flurry . . . and this in circles where such things were formerly unheard of, or at least practiced less openly."[25]

What all this hectic activity and insistence on sexual freedom as a hallmark of emancipation and indeed of modernity, as such, had to do with actual experiences of genital sexuality, not to mention desire and pleasure, is still very much open to question (and research). Clearly, sex reformers devoted much anxious attention to combating female "coldness," but while we have comprehensively documented their efforts, we know much less about their actual effect.[26] Indeed, one of my very favorite "new women" stories comes from the redoubtable Claire Goll, who in a memoir aptly entitled *Ich verzeihe keinem* (I Forgive No One) remarks (more in revenge than embarrassment) at the beginning of a story replete with many lovers and sexual exploits, that, "I have loved a few men and many more have loved me, but only at age seventy-six did I have my first orgasm. All my adventures and love affairs notwithstanding, I had to reach that age to learn from a twenty-year-old boy that a woman could also experience sex (*Liebesakt*) in something other than a subordinate (*unterwürfige*) manner." And then hastened to add, in best *Neue Frau* matter-of-fact manner, "but I'm not complaining" (*aber ich beklage mich nicht*). Her life had been interesting none the less.[27] Sex was not necessarily about pleasure or orgasms—that demand would indeed wait for second-wave feminism despite the best efforts of Van de Velde and the other 1920s sex reformers—but about being modern, avant garde, up-to-date, anti-bourgeois. Sex in Weimar, it would seem, was a great passion, but not necessarily about sex.

We still have surprisingly little analysis of this modernist sexual culture, and how it was experienced and represented by women and men. Sexuality was undeniably a key reference in all arenas of popular and consumer culture, in advertising, fashion, cinema, photography (certainly a "new woman" genre) as well as in the youth movement, sports, body culture and expressionist dance, the proliferation of erotic art, pornography and "enlightenment" literature (such as Magnus Hirschfeld's *Sittengeschichte*), and the prominence of prostitution and sex crimes in especially expressionist art and literature.[28] Indeed, Hirschfeld himself, and his (much mentioned but actually relatively little studied) Institute of Sexual Science needs to be analyzed in the context, not only of the history of sexology and Weimar decadence, but as part of the world that produced "new women" and "new men," writers, journalists, artists, and political activists whose passionate and painful attempts to ban prudery and jealousy, and entirely non-nostalgic openness to the new and experimental defined so much of how Weimar was perceived and remembered. It is perhaps surprising but hardly coincidental that one of the—to this day—very few biographies of Hirschfeld was written by Charlotte Wolff, late in her life in exile and as a kind of "labor of love." She too had been a sex reformer, a physician in the Berlin birth control and sex counseling centers, an out lesbian and denizen of Berlin's gay subculture, a quintessential "new woman" and then also, like Hirschfeld, a Jewish refugee from National Socialism.[29]

We often think Weimar culture has been "overdone" by scholars, but it may in fact be the period of modern German history most in need of critical reexamination. We still need to unravel what a woman like Charlotte Wolff remembered when she reported years later, about her youth in pre-1933 Berlin, "In the atmosphere of the twenties one breathed the 'permissiveness' of freedom. One's sensuous and emotional needs, whatever they were, could be satisfied . . . Heaven was not somewhere above us, but on earth, in the German metropolis." What did she really mean when she asked 1970s feminists, "Who were we and all those other young women of the twenties who seemed to know so well what we wanted?" and insisted that, "We never thought of ourselves as being second-class citizens. We simply were ourselves, which is the only liberation which counts anyway"?[30]

Remarkably, the story of the "new woman" remains to be told by historians. It is still the case, over twenty-five years after Bridenthal and Koonz's first article, that German women's, gender, and social historians have been so busy debunking the myth of the emancipated woman of the Golden Twenties or conversely, correcting the notion of women in Nazi Germany confined to *Kinder, Küche, Kirche*, that we have not paid sufficient attention to the ways in which sexuality expressed and reflected both the radical ruptures and the stubborn continuities in modern German history. Weimar, profoundly shaped by the shocks of World War I, was after all, as Peter Fritzsche has argued, a laboratory of modernity, "less a failure than a series of bold experiments that did not come to an end with the year 1933."[31] Kathleen Canning has recently reminded us that "stories of indisputable rupture" accompany its history. We should examine further, in terms of sexuality and gender, as Dagmar Herzog has begun to do in her provocative book, *Sex after Fascism*, which ruptures

were indeed irrevocable and which institutions and sensibilities survived into
and were reworked in the Third Reich and the postwar period.[32]

National Socialism:
Normality and Terror, Entitlement and Repression

Newer work on art and culture in the Third Reich, such as Terri Gordon's
studies of dance and Irene Guenther's book *Nazi Chic?* confirms that, despite
a drastically different political, social, and cultural context, and despite the
radical purging of Jewish "decadence," the "new woman" and certain kinds
of sexual radicalism (including the kinky and the deviant) did not disappear
in 1933. The continued popularity of girl troupes such as the Hiller Girls,
expressionist dance, and the cult of the body speak to the appropriation of
Girlkultur. Guenther insists that for all the efforts to create a docile and clean
German domesticity in "dirndls" and "uniforms," Nazism also had "another
countenance, one that was intensely modern, technologically advanced, su-
premely stylized, and fashionably stylish." [33] Herzog's work traces the many
ways in which National Socialism and war served as incitements to sexual
expression; Elizabeth Heineman's review essay suggests that by now the links
between "Sexuality and Nazism" are no longer "The Doubly Unspeakable."
But Herzog is careful to note also that sexuality in the Third Reich was not
only about incitements to Aryan heterosexuality and the *frisson* of the forbidden, but about "the invasion and control and destruction of human beings."
She insists on "the need to make sense of the inextricability of anti-Semitism from both anti- *and* prosexual Nazi efforts, as well as the inseparability
of homophobia from injunctions to happy heterosexuality." Patricia Szobar
and Geoffrey Giles argue that the graphic intimate details recorded in Nazi
prosecutions of homosexuality or miscegenation provided titillating pornographic narratives, but they also keep in mind the terrorizing circumstances
in which those narratives were constructed and their consequences. Yet, as
Giles and Stefan Micheler show, there was great unevenness in the persecution of homosexuality. Himmler may have been obsessed with sexual deviance
but there was no "Gay Holocaust." In a crucial leap from earlier studies of
Nazi racial policies, the research presented in *Sexuality and German Fascism*
recognizes the centrality of an anti-Semitism suffused with sexual references
and sanctions, and the ways in which repression of, and incitement to, sexuality relied on those anti-Semitic referents.[34]

Part of Nazi modernity—and its capacity to hijack much of Weimar sensibility—(including certainly aspects of the "new woman" and sex reform)
was its contempt for conservative Christian prudery, a fact that the churches
knew to use to their advantage in the postwar period, when they fashioned

themselves as the restorers of moral values. As we uncover the compatibility of National Socialism with certain forms of sexual radicalism, we are reminded of familiar tropes: Communist Party critiques of Nazi decadence, the jokes about BDM girls as *Bedarfsartikel* (useful objects) *deutscher Männer*, as well as Susan Sontag's revelatory 1976 piece "Fascinating Fascism," which recognized the simultaneously "asexual" and "pornographic" aspects of Nazi aesthetics and appeal.[35] At the same time, as Julia Roos demonstrates, "propaganda about" prostitution and venereal disease fused anti-Semitism with conservative fears about "moral decay" and "sexual Bolshevism." Let us not, in our constant process of historical reexamination, forget Nazism's ability to align itself with conventional conservative morality and gain support from the churches and women's associations concerned with such issues.[36] Roos's research on Center Party support for the Enabling Act as the result of the backlash against the 1927 Venereal Disease Law's liberalized treatment of prostitutes and prostitution supports a less censorious view of Weimar reform that gives due credit to its emancipatory as well as disciplinary goals.

War and Holocaust: Sex, Violence, and Survival

As has now been amply noted, the discovery of the National Socialist regime as a racial state did not until recently, and still uneasily, manage to integrate histories of Jews, anti-Semitism, and the Holocaust. The memory boom of the 1990s and our turn of the millennium preoccupation with the traumas of the Holocaust—as well as their apparent echoes in places like Bosnia and Rwanda—led to a new interest not only in the racial and population politics of the Nazi regime but in the workings of sexuality and population policy during war and genocide.

Sexual violence perpetrated on German women by especially the Soviet victors has been highlighted in rather different ways by German and American feminists, and also by Germans and Jews. We might recall the varied approaches taken by Elizabeth Heineman, Gertrud Koch, and myself on the one hand, and by Helke Sander on the other, to the rapes of German women by Red Army soldiers. In debates on the supposedly "taboo-breaking" depictions in Sander's 1992 film *BeFreier und Befreite*, we saw not only transatlantic, but also German/Jewish divides. Some of these differences are still reflected, although in less predictable ways, in the current discussions about the revival of German war victimization narratives.[37] If the discussions of the early 1990s erupted in the shadow of the mid-1980s *Historikerstreit* about the uniqueness of Nazi atrocities and the subsequent *Historikerinnenstreit* about women's complicity and mobilization, the most recent (re)discovery of Red Army violence against German women has occurred in the context of lively and contentious general reporting about German civilian suffering under Allied bombs and Red Army invasion. These debates have been propelled by Antony Beevor's highlighting of brutal Red Army rapes in his grand narrative of the *Fall of Berlin 1945* and by Hans Magnus Enzensberger's best-selling reprint in the summer of 2003 of *Eine Frau in Berlin*, a rape narrative of war's end by an anonymous but very articulate diarist. The subsequent controversies about the legitimacy of "outing" Anonyma's name and identity as a kind of Nazi "new woman," a journalist who had worked for Goebbels's Propaganda Ministry before the war, were enacted, as they virtually always are in Germany, on the *Feuilleton* pages of major newspapers amongst male scholars and journalists. They were blissfully ignorant of the substantial and sometimes bitter arguments among German and American feminist scholars over a decade earlier, about how to contextualize German women's experiences as victims of mass rape, bombings, and flight from the East. [38]

German feminist scholars, after years of debates about the usefulness of *Opfer/Täter(innen)* (victim/perpetrator) dichotomies in analyzing women's place in the Third Reich, have recently also scrutinized the gendered "performativity" of Nazi war crimes trials and the sexualization of female perpetrators as a kind of excess assignment of guilt. Christina von Braun and others have noted the eroticization accompanying the demonization of Nazi women, in contrast to the emphasis, for example, by Gisela Bock, on the masculinized nature of female perpetrators. German feminist historians have argued that unlike male perpetrators (*Befehlsempfänger*), to whom the "banality" of "ordinary men" was often attributed, women perpetrators such as Ilse Koch, the *Kommandeuse* of Buchenwald, were bestialized and pathologized, precisely made "unordinary" and unwomanly by way of being sexualized.[39]

When it comes to the Holocaust per se, researchers were long inhibited by the sense that sexuality or gender could and should not be a major category in a situation where "race" so clearly seemed to determine fate. But feminist demands (sometimes impatient and insensitive, but laudably insistent) for survivors to provide us with gendered memories and our own retrained research eye have indeed revealed "delayed narratives," as Japanese historian Ueno Chizuko has termed them, generated in the interplay between memory and later research.[40] Notwithstanding the conventional wisdom that racial laws inhibited German rapes of Jewish women, it has become clear that sexual violation and fear of rape were integral to Nazi terror and torture. Survivors have spoken more—or we are beginning to notice the stories that were always present—about their terror and humiliation when ordered to undress, or when their pubic hair was shaved along with the hair on their head; about prostitution and rape, about sexual abuse by tormentors, rescuers, or fellow victims; but also about genuine love affairs, and all the "gray zone" situations in between that required the use of those crucial currencies of survival: money and sex.[41]

Because feminist, human rights, and therapeutic discourse now offers an available language, because rape has finally been recognized in international law not only as a war crime but as a crime against humanity, and perhaps because the passage of time frees older women, especially widows, to tell hidden stories, the assumption that "sexual violation paled in comparison to the other dehumanizing crimes being committed," is being interrogated and stories of "gender-based harm" have emerged more clearly.[42] When the topic is raised in survivor memoirs or diaries, it is usually about the complexities of sexual instrumentality and exploitation in the ghettos, resistance, and hiding, and sometimes the threat from Soviet troops during and after liberation. At the same time, new work on intermarriage and miscegenation, and on the importance of intimate and marital ties for providing protection, incorporates sexuality (not sexual violence) into our studies of relations between Germans and other gentiles and Jews. Surely there is much more to be learned about wartime sexual violations by Germans of "inferior" groups, about both regulated and "wild" sexual exploitation within the military and the camp system, about brothels and rape in death and labor camps, as well as Wehrmacht rapes (and fraternization) in occupied territory and on the battlefront.[43] Indeed, there may be a reciprocal relationship between the new willingness to engage "gray zones" of complicity and persecution during the war and Holocaust and the attention to issues of sexuality and gender. Still, at this point, and in contrast for example to studies of Japanese war guilt, issues of sexual violence and coercion remain marginal to discussions of German atrocities.

Postwar Sexualities: Germans and "Others"

Historians have repeatedly shown that the postwar period—certainly not the immediate occupation years, but also not the miserable conformist (*Nierentisch*) 1950s—was hardly a time of silence and repression (either for memory or sex). This postwar history, moreover, was also inextricably linked to the presence of "others," occupiers, black as well as white, and displaced persons, Jewish and not. Maria Höhn has investigated the triangular relationship between American GIs, German women, and Polish-Jewish bar owners; Heide Fehrenbach's new book discusses interracial "occupation babies."[44] The disintegration of bourgeois morality that had alarmed cultural conservatives at least since World War I and the Weimar *Systemszeit* clearly continued during and after the Second World War. Annemarie Tröger's still provocative (and largely forgotten) 1986 article on rape and fraternization in postwar Berlin reminded us that the women who marked the apocalyptic landscape of destroyed Germany, especially in the rubble of Berlin, were in many cases the same women who had participated in the "ferment" of Weimar. They had also, as Birthe Kundrus' new research is documenting, fraternized with foreign forced laborers during a war that had inevitably and paradoxically led to a loosening of domestic bonds and an eroticization "of public life," and was unevenly prosecuted, sometimes denounced and sometimes accepted by the populace. Tröger, herself a woman of the 1960s, suggested that the disassociative endurance with which women survived their rapes and sometimes also their instrumental fraternizing affairs bore an uncanny resemblance to the *sachliche* romances delineated in the Weimar novels of Irmgard Keun or Marieluise Fleisser. German women, she argued, had been trained into a sexual cynicism "freed *from* love" that served them well during the war and its aftermath.[45] In that regard, we could follow further the common American occupier conviction that German women were so much more sexually available and sophisticated than the girls they had left behind (Billy Wilder's *Foreign Affair* has to work very hard to resignify the prim and repressed American woman as desirable). As Petra Goedde notes, fraternizing relationships between male occupiers and German women—who functioned as interpreters and secretaries as well as sex partners and girlfriends—went a long way towards transforming the image of Germans from ruthless aggressor to sympathetic victim, a mediating process that worked well in tandem with the changing allegiances of the Cold War.[46]

This pragmatic sexuality, a result perhaps not only of Weimar loosening and wartime dislocations but also, as Dagmar Herzog insists, of Nazi incitements to "Aryan" pleasures, was frequently described in postwar reports and novels. In fact, the plots and language of such relatively lurid postwar novels as *The Big Rape* by J. W. Burke, published in the United States in 1951, or even Thomas Berger's remarkable *Crazy in Berlin* are peculiarly similar to that of Anonyma's *Eine Frau in Berlin*. The generally enthusiastic reception of the current edition of *Anonyma* (one recent review likened it to such "classics" as the diaries of Anne Frank and Victor Klemperer) should provoke further and careful research into its particular provenance as well as into the different ways in which wartime and postwar sexuality and sexual violence was remembered and recorded in the following decades.

My own current research has pointed to the importance of sexuality as well as reproduction in negotiating the fraught relationships between defeated Germans and surviving Jews after 1945. Relations between Jewish men and German women remained a painful contentious issue long after the allied military had given up on trying to enforce regulations banning fraternization with *Fräuleins*. Their encounters serve as good examples of the ambivalent complexities of sexuality as a social and cultural historical category, and we are a long way from acknowledging and understanding their significance.[47]

Conclusion: Gender, Feminism and the Mainstream

We have become more sophisticated about integrating rather than segregating our studies of anti-Semitism and racial/population policy. We have established gender as a significant historical category; we have made the study of sexuality respectable in the academy. But we have done so mostly for ourselves and our students, parallel, rather than really subordinate to, the "mainstream." Indeed, an unintended consequence of the determined dismantling of master-narratives has been that there is no clearly established unilateral mainstream history left for us to gender. [48]

Moreover, we have done this work on gender and sexuality still mostly by thinking about women rather than men (studies of homosexuality are a somewhat different case). We haven't quite figured out how to gender men, except in particular instances such as Frank Biess's, Robert Moeller's, or Thomas Kühne's work on soldiers and POWs, which usually involve a focus on men's "bodies" (their wounding, their trauma, their camaraderie) rather than sexuality per se. [49] German scholars have been more interested in masculinity as an important category for militarism and nationalism, leading some American feminist historians to suspect that in what remains a more closed and conservative historical *Zunft*, gender studies are more likely to be legitimated when they come in male form. [50] But at the same time, with all due allowance for differences in approach, also to do with different subject positions as the children and grandchildren of—to use those inadequate and much problematized terms—Jewish victims or German perpetrators (or at least bystanders/beneficiaries), the notion of an "Atlantic divide" in feminist historiography has obscured the multiple scholarly, professional, and personal connections that existed and exist between German and American feminist historians of modern Germany. Dialogs and debates very clearly criss-cross national lines and we are in constant contact.

Feminist historians have become more elegant and inventive in the use of theory since the linguistic turn, mining both postmodernist and to a lesser extent, postcolonial discourse. The payoff has been huge. It is hard to imagine our work without Foucault and those who followed. We have also mined the archives, especially the new troves that opened up after 1989. But our romance with theory and our zeal for uncovering archival sources has sometimes led us to us to neglect available printed sources and texts produced either at the time or by scholars from previous generations; we are always in danger of neglecting our own historiographic legacy and we do entirely too much reinventing the wheel. Just as gender still tends to be about women, sexuality still tends to be about the margins, or about reproduction and population. We need to think more about the ways in which everyday vanilla sex, its experience and its representation, regulation, and marketing does its work in political and social life. Elizabeth Heineman's new project on Beate Uhse, which reads Germany's most successful sex entrepreneur as a template for changing German self-perceptions and interpretations of its own Nazi and postwar history and integrates a history of sexuality with analysis of emerging consumer culture, promises to move us in that direction.

Almost twenty years ago, Ute Frevert's vanguard effort at producing a comprehensive history of *Women in Modern Germany* from the late eighteenth century through the 1980s, originally published in German with the appropriate subtitle "Between Bourgeois Reform and New Femininity" was issued in English with a more whiggish interpretation on the right side of the title colon, "From Bourgeois Emancipation to Sexual Liberation." The latter phrase seems to reflect the astonishing declaration at the very end of the story that the "availability of reliable forms of contraception has allowed women to satisfy their sexual desires with the same carefree passion as men have since time immemorial." Such brief and almost surreal optimism notwithstanding, however, the book emphasizes the fragility of Weimar emancipation, notes the Nazis' success at mobilizing German women, and casts a highly skeptical eye on the pressures of the postwar period and the continuing restrictions on women's lives and work, even after the "second" women's movement of the 1970s. It also barely discusses sexuality.[51] And in 2002, many of the papers presented at a conference on "Sexuality in Modern German History" at the German Historical Institute in Washington, DC, dealt with reproduction, homosexuality or some form of "deviance." Remarkably, given the acknowledged centrality of biological and body politics in modern German history and Germany's status, from the late 1800s until 1933, as a central site for both sexual experimentation and the scientific study of sexuality, we have, as yet, no major studies bridging the long gap between Isabel Hull's book on the late eighteenth and early nineteenth century and Dagmar Herzog's recent book on sexual patterns and discourse in the Third Reich and its traces in postwar sex talk *and* behavior.[52]

In her introduction to the *History of Sexuality* special issue, Herzog acknowledges both "the value and the recalcitrance" of sexuality as a focus of historical inquiry. When it comes to studying a subject that is simultaneously so intimate, universal, and ill-defined, and so subject to both regulation and fantasy, we may, she suggests, need concepts more refined even than our by now familiar tools of race, class, gender, and sexual orientation; we will probably have to borrow more from queer theory, psychoanalysis, and even sexology itself.[53] We will, I would add in conclusion, need to range more widely in other ways as well. The study of sexuality, like all German history, is still too self-enclosed, both in its definition of "German" and national focus. We require more comparative and interdisciplinary work: on the everyday postwar impact of occupiers, foreign displaced persons, and millions of ethnic German refugees, and certainly also increased attention to the decades after 1960; not only the upheavals of 1968 and the new social movements of the 1970s, but the impact of "guest workers," unification, the European Union, and new immigration in a global context.[54] In other words, when it comes to sexuality, the gendering of German history will benefit from more "sex" and less "German."

Notes

1. Dagmar Herzog, "Hubris and Hypocrisy, Incitement and Disavowel: Sexuality and German Facism," special issue, *Journal of the History of Sexuality* 11, no. 1–2 (January/April 2002): 1; this issue was reissued as Dagmar Herzog, ed., *Sexuality and German Fascism* (New York, 2005).
2. See Lora Wildenthal, *German Women for Empire, 1884–1945* (Durham, NC, 2001); and Sara Friedrichsmeyer et al., eds., *The Imperialist Imagination: German Colonialism and its Legacy* (Ann Arbor, 1999).
3. For reflections, see Renate Bridenthal et al., forum on "When Biology Became Destiny: Women in Weimar and Nazi Germany—Twentieth Anniversary Retrospective," *German History* 22, no. 4 (2004): 600–612.
4. Kate Millett, *Sexual Politics* (New York, 1969), especially "The Counterrevolution: 1930–1960," 215–239, on Nazi Germany and Stalinist Russia. In retrospect, Millett's research on German feminism and Nazi policy—at a time when German historians were oblivious—is remarkable. Among her sources were Clifford Kirkpatrick's pioneering *Nazi Germany: Its Women and Family Life* (Indianapolis, 1938); and Katherine Thomas, *Women in Nazi Germany* (London, 1943). She also references, as did 1960s radicals and 1970s feminists, Wilhelm Reich, *Mass Psychology of Fascism* (New York, 1970), first translation 1946; and Reich, *The Sexual Revolution* (New York, 1969), first published in English in 1945. See also Reich, *Sex-Pol Essays, 1929–1934*, ed. Lee Baxandall (New York, 1966), Hans-Peter Gente, ed., *Marxismus Psychoanalyse Sexpol*, vol. 1 (Frankfurt/M., 1970).
5. At the same time, political groups, communes (*Wohngemeinschaften*), and "anti-authoritarian" child-care centers argued about Herbert Marcuse's Weimar-infused notion of "nonrepressive sublimation" and struggled to balance his warnings, drawn from the fascist experience, that market- or ideology-driven "repressive de-sublimation" could lead to "totalitarianism," with delight in popular culture and sexual freedom. See Herbert Marcuse, *Eros and Civilization: A Philosophical Inquiry into Freud* (New York, 1955, rpt. 1962). On the contradictions of these "anti-authoritarian" projects in Germany, see Dagmar Herzog, "'Pleasure, Sex and Politics Belong Together': Post-Holocaust Memory and the Sexual Revolutions in West Germany," *Critical Inquiry* 24 (Winter 1998): 393–444.
6. Renate Bridenthal and Claudia Koonz, "Beyond *Kinder, Küche, Kirche:* Weimar Women in Politics and Work," in *Liberating Women's History: Theoretical and Critical Essays*, ed. Berenice A. Carroll (Chicago, 1976), 320; revised in *When Biology Became Destiny: Women in Weimar and Nazi Germany*, ed. Bridenthal et al. (New York, 1984), 33–65.
7. Detlev J. K. Peukert, "The Genesis of the 'Final Solution' from the Spirit of Science," in *Reevaluating the Third Reich*, ed. Thomas Childers and Jane Caplan (New York, 1993), 234–252. See Michel Foucault, *History of Sexuality, Vol. 1: An Introduction* (New York, 1978).

8. See the many projects on "rationalization" in the interwar years, including work by Mary Nolan, Carola Sachse, Tilla Siegel, and myself. See especially the excellent review essay by Carola Sachse, "Rationalizing Family Life—Stabilizing German Society: The 'Golden Twenties' and the 'Economic Miracle' in Comparison," in *Three Postwar Eras in Comparison: Western Europe 1918–1945–1989*, ed. Carl Levy and Mark Roseman (New York, 2002), 257–276; Dagmar Reese et al., eds, *Rationale Beziehungen? Geschlechterverhältnisse im Rationalisierungsprozess* (Frankfurt/M, 1993); Mary Nolan, *Visions of Modernity: American Business and the Modernization of Germany* (New York, 1994); and Atina Grossmann, "Gender and Rationalization: Questions about the German-American Comparison," in *Gender and Rationalization in Comparative Historical Perspective—Germany and the United* States, ed. Karen Hagemann and Molly Ladd-Taylor, special issue, *Social Politics* 4, no. 1 (1997), 6–18.

9. See Katharina von Ankum, ed., *Women in the Metropolis: Gender and Modernity in Weimar Culture* (Berkeley, 1997); also Maria Tatar, *Lustmord: Sexual Murder in Weimar Germany* (Princeton, 1995); Patrice Petro, *Joyless Streets: Women and Melodramatic Representation in Weimar Germany* (Princeton, 1989); Kerstin Barndt, *Sentiment und Sachlichkeit: Der Roman der neuen Frau in der Weimarer Republik* (Cologne, 2003); Richard W. McCormick, *Gender and Sexuality in Weimar Modernity: Film, Literature, and "New Objectivity"* (New York, 2001); Maud Lavin, *Cut with the Kitchen Knife: The Weimar Photomontages of Hannah Höch* (New Haven, 1993); and essays in Katharina Sykora et al., eds., *Die Neue Frau: Herausforderung für die Bildmedien der Zwanziger Jahre* (Marburg, 1993); and Sigrun Anselm and Barbara Beck, eds., *Triumph und Scheitern in der Metropole: Zur Rolle der Weiblichkeit in der Geschichte Berlins* (Berlin, 1987).

10. Isabel V. Hull, *Sexuality, State, and Civil Society in Germany 1700–1815* (Ithaca, 1996), 1. Jeffrey Weeks's excellent *Sex, Politics and Society: The Regulation of Sexuality since 1800* (London, 1981), focused on Britain, barely mentions Germany and then only in reference to international homosexual rights or sex reform movements.

11. George L. Mosse, *Nationalism and Sexuality: Respectability and Abnormal Sexuality in Modern Europe* (New York, 1985).

12. Martin Broszat, *The Hitler State: The Foundation and Development of the Internal Structure of the Third Reich*, trans. John W. Hiden (New York, 1981 [in German: 1969]); Michael Burleigh and Wolfgang Wippermann, *The Racial State: Germany 1933–1945* (Cambridge, 1991). Key to this shift for feminist historians was Gisela Bock, *Zwangssterilisation im Nationalsozialismus: Studien zur Rassenpolitik und Frauenpolitik* (Opladen, 1986). For another perspective, see Gabrielle Czarnowski, *Das kontrollierte Paar: Ehe- und Sexualpolitik im Nationalsozialismus* (Weinheim, 1991). Absolutely central to discussions of Nazism and the body was Klaus Theweleit's *Männerphantasien*, 2 vols. (Frankfurt/M, 1977, 1978 [in English: Minneapolis, 1987]), essentially a literary and psychoanalytic, not historical, study.

13. Atina Grossmann, *Reforming Sex: The German Movement for Birth Control and Abortion Reform 1920–1950* (New York, 1995), vi–vii; Edward Ross Dickinson, "Biopolitics, Fascism, Democracy: Some Reflections on Our Discourse about 'Modernity,'" *Central European History* 37, no. 1 (2004): 1–48 has more recently criticized the preoccupation with the totalitarian aspects of "biopolitics" for ignoring its democratic potential. On birth control see also Cornelie Usborne, *Politics of the Body in Weimar Germany: Women's Reproductive Rights and Duties* (Ann Arbor, 1992); and Karen Hagemann, *Frauenalltag und Männerpolitik: Alltagsleben und gesellschaftliches Handeln von Arbeiterfrauen in der Weimarer Republik* (Bonn, 1990). For a fresh look at Central European interwar sex reform and social hygiene, see Britta McEwen, "Viennese Sexual Knowledge as Science and Social Reform Movement, 1900–1934," Ph.D. diss., University of California, Los Angeles, 2003.

14. See Kathleen Canning's article, "Feminist History after the Linguistic Turn: Historicizing History and Experience," *Signs* 19, no. 2 (1994): 368–404; also Jane Caplan, "Notes on

Postmodernism, Poststructuralism, and Deconstruction," and Isabel V. Hull, "Feminist and Gender History: Through the Literary Looking Glass—German Historiography in Postmodern Times," *Central European History* 22, no. 3–4 (1991): 141–161, 319–354.

15. Ute Planert, "Der dreifache Körper des Volkes: Sexualität, Biopolitik und die Wissenschaften vom Leben," in *Geschichte und Gesellschaft* 26, no. 4 (2000): 539–576; see Dickinson's discussion in "Biopolitics, Fascism, Democracy."

16. Think of Charlotte Wolff's descriptions of the triangular affairs of Franz and Helen Hessel and Pierre Roche, the basis for François Truffaut's 1962 film, *Jules et Jim*, in *Hindsight*, (Charlestown, Mass., 1980), 107–108. Hannah Tillich's entirely unembarrassed memoir, *From Time to Time* (New York, 1973) also recounts bisexuality and a Weimar love/sex triangle (and reflects on continuations and permutations after emigration to the United States). Much discussion of Weimar eroticism has been left to slightly (or not so) risqué publications. See Hanna Vollmer-Heitman, *Wir sind von Kopf bis Fuss auf Liebe eingestellt: Die Zwanziger Jahre* (Hamburg, 1993); and Birgit Haustedt, *Die Wilden Jahre in Berlin: Eine Klatsch und Kulturgeschichte der Frauen* (Berlin, 2002); or in a more directly pornographic vein (with illustrations), Barbara Ulrich, *The Hot Girls of Weimar Berlin* (New York, 2002); and Mel Gordon, *Voluptuous Panic: The Erotic World of Weimar Berlin* (New York, 2000); see also Adele Meyer, ed., *Lila Nächte: Die Damenclubs der Zwanziger Jahre* (Cologne, 1981), which reprinted Ruth Roellig's 1928 collection, *Berlins Lesbische Frauen*.

17. See Atina Grossmann, *"Girlkultur* or Thoroughly Rationalized Female: A New Woman in Weimar Germany?" in *Women in Culture and Politics: A Century of Change*, ed. Judith Friedlander et al., (Bloomington, 1986), 62–80. This volume was part of an innovative series of conferences and publications developed out of a "New Family and New Woman Research Planning Group" which had met in France in 1979 and 1980 and in the United States in 1982 and included feminist scholars working on and/or from France, Great Britain, the Netherlands, Spain, the Soviet Union, Japan, China, and Latin America. The 1987 conference on "Women in Dark Times: Private Life and Public Policy under Five Nationalist Dictatorships in Europe and Asia, 1930–1950" at the Rockefeller Foundation Study Center at Bellagio, Italy, was another such generative moment, influencing a host of books, including Robert G. Moeller, *Protecting Motherhood: Women and the Family in the Politics of Postwar West Germany* (Berkeley, 1993); Marion A. Kaplan, *Between Dignity and Despair: Jewish Women in Nazi Germany* (New York, 1998); Mary Nolan, *Visions of Modernity*; Victoria de Grazia, *How Fascism Ruled Women: Italy 1922–1945* (Berkeley, 1992); Mary Nash, *Defying Male Civilization: Women in the Spanish Civil War* (Denver, 1995); and my own *Reforming Sex*. A later transatlantic collaboration was published in Helmut Gruber and Pamela Graves, eds., *Women and Socialism/Socialism and Women: Europe Between the Two World Wars* (Providence, 1998).

18. See also Rachel Epp Buller, "Fractured Identities: Photomontage Production by Women in the Weimar Republic," Ph.D diss., University of Kansas, 2003.

19. Many such volumes and catalogs were published from the 1970s through the early 1990s. Motivated by feminist activism, filled with images and painstakingly researched vignettes of local history, they focused on the *Frauenbewegung*, "new women" and lesbian culture. See Petra Zwaka et al., eds., *"Ich bin meine eigene Frauenbewegung": Frauen-Ansichten aus der Geschichte einer Grossstadt* (Berlin, 1991); *Hart und Zart: Frauenleben 1930–1970* (Berlin, 1990); and *Fräulein vom Amt* (Frankfurt/M., 1994).

20. Margarete Buber-Neumann, *Von Potsdam nach Moskau: Stationen eines Irrweges* (Stuttgart, 1957), 53. For a marvelously funny description of this *Neue Sachlichkeit*, see Max Fürst's account of his youth movement wedding in *Talisman Scheherezade: Die schwierigen zwanziger Jahre* (Munich, 1976), 267–270.

21. Marielouise Janssen-Jurreit's useful document collection, *Frauen und Sexualmoral* (Frankfurt/M, 1986), addressed sex reform, feminism, and particularly Paragraph 218 and prostitution,

rather than sexuality. Karin Hausen's early edited collection, *Frauen suchen ihre Geschichte* (Munich, 1983), a kind of German *Becoming Visible*, included articles by Anneliese Bergmann on the 1913 SPD (Social Democratic Party of Germany) birth strike debate and Gudrun Schwarz on the treatment of lesbianism in sexology; see also Ilse Kokula, *Die weibliche Homosexualität um 1900: In Zeitgenössischen Dokumenten* (Munich, 1981).

22. Manes Sperber, *Die Vergebliche Warnung: All das Vergangene . . .* (Vienna, 1975), 213.

23. Erik N. Jensen, "Images of the Ideal: Sports, Gender, and the Emergence of the Modern Body in Weimar Germany," Ph.D. diss., University of Wisconsin-Madison, 2003.

24. See Walter Ruttmann's 1927 film *Symphony of a City* and the stories and feuilletons in Anna Rheinsberg, ed., *Bubikopf: Aufbruch in den Zwanzigern: Texte von Frauen* (Darmstadt, 1988). See "star" memoirs (listed in bibliography) by Elisabeth Bergner, Vicki Baum, Tilla Durieux, Valeska Gert, Pola Negri, and Steffie Spira, and political or literary memoirs (sometimes presented as biographies by "wives") by Karola Bloch, Margarete Buber-Neumann, Marta Feuchtwanger, Käte Frankenthal, Ruth von Mayenburg, Rosa Meyer-Leviné, Gabriele Tergit, Hannah Tillich, and Salka Viertel, as well as Klaus Mann. Many of these tales are also about exile and flight from National Socialism and postwar reinvention.

25. "Erhebung über Sexualmoral," in *Studien über Autorität und Familie*, ed. Max Horkheimer (Paris, 1936), 277, 280. For a by now "classic" version of this sexual and romantic *Sachlichkeit*, see Irmgard Keun's novel, *Gilgi—eine von uns* (1931 [reprinted in Düsseldorf, 1979]); also Erich Kästner, *Fabian. Die Geschichte eines Moralisten* (1931 [reprinted in Zurich, 1973]). See Helmut Lethen, *Cool Conduct: The Culture of Distance in Weimar Germany* (Berkeley, 2002). There is no German history equivalent to Marie Louise Roberts, *Civilization Without Sexes: Reconstructing Gender in Postwar France, 1917–1927* (Chicago, 1994).

26. See Grossmann, *Reforming Sex*, and "The New Woman and the Rationalization of Sexuality in Weimar Germany" in *Powers of Desire: The Politics of Sexuality*, ed. Ann Snitow et al. (New York, 1983), 153–176; also in idem, *Die Politik des Begehrens: Sexualität, Pornographie und neuer Puritanismus in den USA* (Berlin, 1985), 38–62.

27. Claire Goll, *Ich verzeihe keinem: Eine literarische Chronique Scandaleuse Unserer Zeit* (Munich, 1976), 5.

28. See Tatar, *Lustmord*; see also Atina Grossmann, "Magnus Hirschfeld, Sexualreform und die Neue Frau: Das Institut für Sexualwissenschaft und Weimar Berlin," in *Magnus Hirschfeld: Ein Leben im Spannungsfeld von Wissenschaft, Politik und Gesellschaft*, ed. Elke-Vera Kotowski and Julius H. Schoeps (Berlin, 2004), 201–216.

29. Charlotte Wolff, *Magnus Hirschfeld: A Portrait of a Pioneer in Sexology* (London, 1986). For a critical assessment of Hirschfeld, see John Fout, "Sexual Politics in Wilhelmine Germany: The Male Gender Crisis, Moral Purity and Homophobia," *Journal of the History of Sexuality* nos. 2, 3 (1992): 388–421.

30. Charlotte Wolff, *Hindsight: An Autobiography* (London, 1980), 65–66, 106. Surprisingly, film critic B. Ruby Rich's almost 25-year-old essay, "Mädchen in Uniform: From Repressive Tolerance to Erotic Liberation," *Jump Cut* 24, no. 25 (1981): 44–50, remains one of the most suggestive considerations of lesbian subculture in Weimar Berlin.

31. Peter Fritzsche, "Did Weimar Fail?" *Journal of Modern History* 68, no. 3 (1996): 629–656.

32. See Kathleen Canning "Claiming Citizenship: Suffrage and Subjectivity in Germany after the First World War," in Canning, *Gender History in Practice: Historical Perspectives on Bodies, Class and Citizenship* (Ithaca, N.Y., 2006): 212–38. See also Elizabeth Heineman's excellent review essay, "Gender, Sexuality, and Coming to Terms with the Nazi Past," *Central European History* 38, no. 1 (2005): 41–74.

33. Terri J. Gordon, "Fascism and the Female Form: Performance Art in the Third Reich," in *Sexuality and German Fascism*, 164–200; also Irene Guenther, *Nazi Chic? Fashioning Women in the Third Reich* (Oxford, 2004), 265.

34. Dagmar Herzog, "Hubris and Hyprocrisy, Incitement and Disavowal: Sexuality and German Fascism," *Journal of History of Sexuality* 11, nos. 1–2 (2002), 3–21; Elizabeth D. Heineman, "Sexuality and Nazism: The Doubly Unspeakable?"; Patricia Szobar, "Telling Sexual Stories in the Nazi Courts of Law: Race Defilement in Germany, 1933–1945"; Geoffrey J. Giles, "The Denial of Homosexuality: Same Sex Incidents in Himmler's SS and Police"; Stefan Micheler, "Homophobic Propaganda and the Denunciation of Same-Sex Desiring Men under National Socialism," all in *Sexuality and German Fascism*, 22–66, 131–163, 256–291, 95–130, respectively. See also Claudia Schoppmann, *Days of Masquerade: Life Stories of Lesbians During the Third Reich* (New York, 1996).

35. Susan Sontag, "Fascinating Fascism," *New York Review of Books*, 6 February 1975.

36. See Claudia Koonz, *Mothers in the Fatherland: Women, The Family and Nazi Politics* New York, 1987).

37. See especially Helke Sander and Barbara Johr, eds., *BeFreier und Befreite: Krieg, Vergewaltigung, Kinder* (Berlin, 1992); and the special issue of *October* 72 (Spring 1995), which highlighted many of the debates about relative victimization and its particularly gendered and sexualized quality that are being rolled out again—with even more emphasis on German suffering—during the sixtieth anniversary year. For an even earlier feminist consideration of sexual violence in World War II, including Red Army rapes, see Susan Brownmiller, *Against Our Will: Men, Women, and Rape* (New York, 1975), 48–79.

38. Anonyma, *"Eine Frau in Berlin" Tagebuch Aufzeichnungen vom 20 April bis zum 22 Juni 1945* (Frankfurt/M, 2004). First published in English as Anonymous, *A Woman in Berlin*, trans. James Stern (New York, 1954), and then as *Eine Frau in Berlin. Tagebuchaufzeichnungen* (Geneva, 1959). See Jens Bisky, *Süddeutsche Zeitung*, (24 September 2003), for Anonyma's "outing" as the journalist (*Kleinpropagandistin*) Marta Hiller, who had written propaganda texts for the NSDAP. See English language republication: Anonymous, *A Woman in Berlin: Eight Weeks in the Conquered City*, trans. Philip Boehm, with introduction by Antony Beevor (New York: Metropolitan Books 2005).

39. See Ulricke Weckel and Edgar Wolfram, eds., *"Bestien" und "Befehlsempfänger": Frauen und Männer in NS-Prozessen nach 1945* (Göttingen, 2003). On the sexualized representations of war and Holocaust, see Insa Eshebach et al., eds., *Gedächtnis und Geschlecht: Deutungsmuster in Darstellungen der Nationalsozialistischen Genozids* (Frankfurt/M, 2002).

40. Chizuko Ueno, "The Politics of Memory, Nation, Individual and Self," *History and Memory* 11, no. 2 (1999): 129–152.

41. See Nechama Tec, *Courage and Resilience: Women, Men, and the Holocaust* (New Haven, 2004); also Fanya Gottesfeld Heller, *Strange and Unexpected Love: A Teenage Girl's Holocaust Memoirs* (Hoboken, NJ, 1993); and Edith Hahn Beer, *The Nazi Officer's Wife: How One Jewish Woman Survived the Holocaust* (New York, 1999).

42. Fionnuala Ni Aolain, "Sex-Based Violence and the Holocaust—A Reevaluation of Harms and Rights in International Law," *Yale Journal of Law and Feminism* 12, no. 1 (2000): 46–47. See also Sara R. Horowitz, "Engendering Jewish Trauma Memory," in *Women and the Holocaust*, eds. Dalia Ofer and Lenore Weitzman (New Haven, 1998), 364–378.

43. See Wendy Jo Gertjejanssen, "Victims, Heroes, Surviviors: Sexual Violence on the Eastern Front During World War II," Ph.D. diss., University of Minnesota, 2004; also Annette Timm, "Sex with a Purpose: Prostitution, Venereal Disease, and Militarized Masculinity in the Third Reich," *Sexuality and German Fascism*, 223–255.

44. Heide Fehrenbach, *Race After Hitler: Black Occupation Children in Postwar Germany and America* (Princeton, 2005).

45. Annemarie Tröger, "'Between Rape and Prostitution': Survival Strategies and Chances of Emancipation for Berlin Women after World War II," in Friedlander et al., *Women in Culture and Politics*, 13; and Birthe Kundrus, "Forbidden Company: Romantic Relationships between

Germans and Foreigners, 1939 to 1945," in *Sexuality and German Fascism*, 201–222. See also Atina Grossmann, "A Question of Silence: The Rape of German Women by Occupation Soldiers," in *October* 72 (1995): 43–63.

46. Petra Goedde, *GIs and Germans: Culture, Gender, and Foreign Relations 1945–1949* (New Haven, 2003). Semi-lurid novels like J. W. Burke's *The Big Rape* (Frankfurt/M, 1951); or William G. Smith's *Last of the Conquerors* (New York, 1948) about African American soldiers' adventures in Germany; and Thomas Berger, *Crazy in Berlin* (New York, 1958) tell much the same story. See also Maria Höhn, *GIs and Fräuleins: The German-American Encounter in 1950s West Germany* (Chapel Hill, 2002); and Fehrenbach, *Race After Hitler.*

47. Atina Grossmann, *Jews, Germans, and Allies: Close Encounters in Occupied Germany* (Princeton, 2007); also idem, "Victims, Villains and Survivors: Gendered Perceptions and Self-Perceptions of Jewish Displaced Persons in Occupied Postwar Germany," in *Sexuality and German Fascism*, 291–318.

48. See for example Konrad Jarausch and Michael Geyer, *Shattered Pasts: Reconstructing German Histories* (Princeton, 2003).

49. Frank Biess, "Survivors of Totalitarianism: Returning POWs and the Reconstruction of Masculine Citizenship in West Germany, 1945–1955," in *The Miracle Years: A Cultural History of West Germany 1949–1968,* ed. Hanna Schissler (Princeton, 2001); Robert G. Moeller, "The Last Soldiers of the 'Great War' and Tales of Family Reunions in the Federal Republic of Germany," *Signs* 24, no. 1 (1998): 126–146; and Moeller, *War Stories: The Search for a Usable Past in the Federal Republic of Germany* (Berkeley, 2001); and Thomas Kühne, ed., *Männergeschichte-Geschlechtergeschichte: Männlichkeit im Wandel der Moderne* (Frankfurt/M., 1996). In an indication of transatlantic conversation, Klaus Naumann, ed., *Nachkrieg in Deutschland* (Hamburg, 2001), reprints in German translation articles by Moeller, Biess, Heineman, Fehrenbach, Poiger, from Schissler's volume as well as articles by Dagmar Herzog.

50. This is a point already addressed by Isabel Hull in her 1991 *Central European History* article on the lack of distinction between sex and gender in the German word *Geschlecht* and the ways in which a focus on gender might lead to men's history. See also Kühne, *Männergeschichte-Geschlechtergeschichte*, and the articles in *Home/Front: The Military, War, and Gender in Twentieth Century Germany*, eds. Karen Hagemann and Stefanie Schüler-Springorum (Oxford, 2002).

51. Ute Frevert, *Women in German History: From Bourgeois Emancipation to Sexual Liberation* (Oxford, 1988), 318–321 (in German: 1986).

52. Dagmar Herzog, *Sex After Fascism: Memory and Morality in Twentieth Century Germany* (Princeton, 2005), has much to say also about the 1960s through the post-unification period in both East and West.

53. Herzog, "Hubris and Hypocrisy," in *Sexuality and German Fascism*, 19, 2–3.

54. For example, I have found ethnographic studies of sex and birth among Palestinian or Rwandan refugees very helpful in my own work on Jewish survivors in occupied Germany. See John Borneman, "Reconciliation after Ethnic Cleansing: Listening, Retribution, Affiliation," *Public Culture* 14, no. 2: 281–304; Rhoda Ann Kanaaneh, *Birthing the Nation: Strategies of Palestinian Women in Israel* (Berkeley, 2002); Lisa Malkii, *Purity and Exile: Violence, Memory and National Cosmology among Hutu Refugees in Tanzania* (Chicago, 1995).

THE ELEPHANT IN THE LIVING ROOM
Or Why the History of Twentieth-Century Germany Should Be a Family Affair

Robert G. Moeller

In a book of eleven essays, the family comes last. Sexuality and bodies appear near the end, but this placement doubtless reflects that the editors have followed the example of clever conference organizers: put the jazziest panel late in the day, and maybe you will keep your audience. But the family appears as something of an afterthought. As I prepared this essay—which focuses primarily on the twentieth century, the period I know well enough to say something with any confidence—I began to think that maybe this was appropriate. Perhaps for feminist historians, family history is a topic whose time came and went.

Some thirty or so years ago, when historians of women—not yet gender—began to write *her*stories, the family was a good place to begin. Take for example *Women, Work, and the Family*, a 1978 book written by Joan Scott—in her pre-linguistic-turn persona—and Louise Tilly. Here the family is the structure that determines how labor is deployed—either unpaid in the home or outside of it for wages—over the course of the nineteenth and twentieth centuries.[1] The economy evolves, and the family evolves with it. The arrival of social history in West Germany in the 1970s was characterized by a similar interest in the family as the place to study fertility, marriage patterns, social mobility, the transition from households to "modern" nuclear families, and historical shifts in the sexual division of labor. And when historians—drawing on socialist feminist approaches that could trace their origins back not only to Marx but also to Engels' *The Origin of the*

Family, Private Property and the State—noted that families were often arenas of conflict, they illuminated how family structures relegated women to a primary identity as wife and mother and left them uncomfortably straddling the divide between home and work.

For the most part, the twentieth century was not on this agenda.[2] The one exception to this rule was a substantial literature on the Third Reich. Beginning with important studies by Jill Stephenson and Tim Mason in the 1970s, historians illuminated Nazi population policy and the tensions between the competing priorities of encouraging women to produce more "Aryan" babies and enticing women into a hothoused economy headed for war.[3] In the mid eighties Claudia Koonz's *Mothers in the Fatherland* put forward the powerful thesis that "Nazi leaders relied on the sheltering family (or on its myth) to keep alive an ersatz sense of decency in the men who would work most closely with mass murder."[4] Koonz's depiction of mothers as accomplices—however unwitting—in mass murder collided head on with the scholarship of Gisela Bock who argued that the Nazis' goal was to prevent births of the *wrong* sorts of Germans, not prop up Aryan motherhood. The ensuing debate between Koonz and Bock raised important questions about how to understand female agency and responsibility for Nazi policy, and it highlighted the difference between a feminism that emphasized equality as the sine qua non for emancipation and a feminism that saw difference as a key source of empowerment.[5] But no other part of twentieth-century family history received such careful scholarly scrutiny.

In the meantime, feminist historians concluded that in order to make clear the centrality of gender as a category of analysis, they needed to look beyond the family, and they illuminated how gender structured politics, society, and culture. The other essays in this book leave no doubt about what feminist historians accomplished in these areas. They indicate not that gender history has been mainstreamed but rather that it has shifted the course of the river, challenging key master narratives of modern German history.

So did the family cease to be important as an object for feminist historical analysis? To get an answer, I took one crude measure, the database that creates a virtual library joining all nine University of California campuses and a search engine that allowed me to browse the subject headings created by the Library of Congress in Washington, DC, one classificatory framework for organizing knowledge. I began with the post–World War II period. When I tried "Germany (East) Family," it appeared that the field had been all but completely abandoned to sociologists. "Germany (West)" yielded little more. When I substituted time for space and stuck in "20th Century," the results were only slightly better. Perhaps, I thought, it was the arbitrary nature of the classifications, but when I opted instead for keywords—"German Family," "*deutsche Familie*"—the results did not significantly improve.

Where had the family gone? In this paper, I argue that it has not disappeared; rather, it has migrated into other keywords. Finding it requires retracing some of the steps that other authors have taken in this volume, because where the twentieth-century family resides is in some of the thematic clusters others have addressed. A bit of excavation—which can only be illustrative, given the space constraints we confront in the volume—reveals that the family is inescapable, the elephant in the living room of twentieth-century German history, always present but apparently something that we seem reluctant to put in book titles and subject headings. My argument in this chapter is that its study is a crucial part of any attempt to "rewrite the mainstream." Perhaps it is time to "bring the family back in," and in the final section of the paper, I'll suggest one possible agenda for how that might be accomplished.

One final introductory note: When I use the word family in this chapter, I will not tuck it safely between quotation marks, but I also do not mean to suggest that it represents an unchanging social reality. In uncovering its modern history, we should explore it on multiple levels. Thus, I understand the family as an ideological and legal construct; a metaphor used to organize our thought about social, political, and even economic interactions; a space where generation, gender, and relations of power play themselves out; a bundle of emotional, physical, and sexual relationships that can be the source of pleasure and pain; and a structure that is thought to mediate between individuals and the state. Part of exploring its twentieth-century history must involve analyzing how it has been understood—historicizing the category—not assuming that we already know what it is.

Keywords: Social Policy, Welfare State, Labor Law

Feminist historians have done much to illuminate the ways in which states have attempted to regulate what goes on in families, making public ostensibly private spaces. The historiography on Germany in the twentieth century provides no exception to this rule. Particularly since the late nineteenth century, in ways suggested in this volume by Kathleen Canning, the German state—through the regulation of the labor market, the provision of social services, and the legal definition of familial relationships—has circumscribed women's claims to citizenship by emphasizing women's reproductive capacities and identities as mothers. Social welfare policy was founded on the assumption that the world was made up of families that included male worker wage-earners and their dependents who worked for wages only when the breadwinner's wage packet was too light. The German welfare state assumed households made up of wage-earning *Familienväter* (family fathers), who worked outside the home in production, and mothers whose unpaid workplace was the household and whose responsibility was *re*production.[6]

Concerns about population size and its relationship to where women worked intensified in the First World War as real and potential fathers donned uniforms and were killed in ever greater numbers. In studies on the war and Weimar, discussed in this volume by Canning, the family is never far from view. Young Sun Hong quotes the liberal feminist Marie Elisabeth Lüders, who asserted that "the entire sphere of women's private life became a matter of concern for war politics. . . . Military policy and social policy entered the battlefield hand in hand." The state's attempts to centralize social welfare services aimed at women and children were part of what Hong describes as the "collapse of the boundary between the public and the private . . . the militarization of both the national economy and familial life."[7]

Whatever their differences, Koonz and Bock agreed that gender was as central as race to defining the Nazi state, and it was in families that race was reproduced. Nazi policy drew on the biomedical discourse of eugenics that had been around at least since the end of the nineteenth century and also continued to loom large in debates over the welfare state during the Weimar Republic, but after 1933 ruptures outnumbered continuities; the Nazis drove into exile or underground most Weimar sex reformers on the political left, eliminated Jewish doctors from discussions of maternal politics altogether, closed birth control clinics, enforced the prohibition of abortion, and made reproducing the *Volk* an obligation of all Germans deemed racially fit.[8]

Moving past the Second World War, a number of books—including one that I wrote—analyze the state's continued preoccupation with the family as it reformulated welfare policies and note the high priority placed on "reconstructing the family in reconstruction [West] Germany" and resolving the "crisis of the family" brought on by the disruption of the war and the massive loss of adult male life. By no means solely the preoccupation of the conservative coalition of the Christian Democratic Union and the Christian Social Union, in the Federal Republic Social Democrats also supported policy solutions that emphasized women's dependent status as wives and mothers. Politicians reasoned that it was the state's responsibility to overcome the postwar legacy of a "surplus of women" (*Frauenüberschuss*) and a "scarcity of men" (*Männermangel*) and combat the phenomenon of "wild marriages" and "uncle marriages" (Onkelehen)—unions sanctioned by neither church or state—by creating jobs that gave "family fathers" adequate wages, allowing mothers to work where they worked best—at home raising the next generation. Restoring the "normal family"—a married heterosexual couple with children—marked a return to normalcy after the trauma and devastation of war. These political objectives were widely shared by postwar West Germans. Based on interviews conducted with women three decades after the war's end in an oral history project that he headed, Lutz Niethammer concludes that after 1945, the family emerged for women as "an obligation, a phantom, and a project" that promised "warmth, understanding and help, simplicity, fairness, and protection." It was, as Niethammer emphasizes, "the project of fantasy," a "concrete utopia," but in the years after 1945 it was difficult for German women to fantasize in other directions, to envision other "concrete utopia."[9]

Taking this story farther, Merith Niehuss suggests that in the Federal Republic, behind the ideological smoke and mirrors of family policies, heavily influenced by conservative Catholic beliefs, was often little concrete support for women and children. And she also provides a careful analysis of state efforts to rebuild housing stock leveled by Allied bombers in the war following a blueprint that incorporated conceptions of how families should look. Pushing into the 1960s, Sybille Buske's research into the reform of laws governing the rights of illegitimate children concludes that by the end of that decade, the courts recognized "unmarried mothers and their children as families," testifying to a "fundamental change in the idea of the family." Buske's work represents a rare foray into the 1960s, and it indicates how much we still *don't* know about changing conceptions of what constituted a family in the former Federal Republic.[10]

Much work on the postwar period also describes how women negotiated the competing demands of home and work. Elisabeth Heineman asks *What Difference Does a Husband Make?* and determines that the answer is not the same in East and West Germany. In the East, the combination of labor shortages and socialist theory resulted in policies that sought to draw all adult women into the labor force. In the West, beginning in the mid 1950s, the recruitment of foreign "guestworkers" was consciously adopted as an alternative to labor market policies that would aim at mobilization of the "silent reserve" of female labor; but as Christine von Oertzen's study of women's part-time work in West Germany demonstrates, there too women with children worked in growing numbers. In the Federal Republic, however, women could claim that they worked because they *chose* to, not because they were *forced* to as members of a "workers' and peasants'" state. Concerns over how best to allow women to work both in and outside the home made "dirty laundry a public and political affair," in the words of Carola Sachse, who focuses on the "housework day" given to employed women who also had domestic responsibilities in East and West. Her research confirms Donna Harsch's conclusion that in the East, "[r]eproduction ran a close second to production when it came to policy towards women."[11] In both Germanies, mothers and fathers bore responsibility not only for bringing babies into the world but also for ensuring that they became the right kinds of young women and men. Studies by Uta Poiger and Dorothee Wierling illuminate how policy makers in the East and West sought to negotiate the private/public divide, implicating parents in their attempts to socialize the next generation.[12]

The family defined a major battlefield of the Cold War. The socialist system that East Germans celebrated because it freed women to work was excoriated in the West as a form of "forced emancipation" for women who would rather rock cradles than break rocks in uranium mines. And while West German parliamentarians extolled the virtues of women's unpaid domestic labor in the *Lebensraum* (living space) of the family, official East German pronouncements expressed scorn for a system that relegated women to the status of unpaid servants of their husbands. However, historians have also made clear what the Germanies had in common: in neither state were policy makers willing to discuss a sexual division of labor that left women responsible for children and maintaining households whether they worked outside the home or not.

The historical trail that winds through the twentieth-century history of the state's attempts to regulate families disappears into a forest dominated by social scientists once we move beyond the mid 1960s.[13] We can learn much from what our colleagues have done, but we are now almost as far removed from the 1970s as Mason and Stephenson were from the Nazi years when they began to study family policy in the Third Reich. It is high time that we make the more recent past into history. This is easier for historians of East Germany—where the end of the Cold War brought with it virtually unrestricted access to many archival sources—but historians of the West can also gain access to more and more materials and would do well to assess the masses of information collected and published by the state, political parties, and trade unions, and generated by sociologists.[14]

There are some signposts in place that might guide the direction of historical research: By the 1970s, the East German state became even more concerned about the declining birthrate and promoted maternity even as divorce rates continued to soar. By the 1980s, the divorce rate in the East was fully a third higher than in the West. In the East, the elimination of alimony, the ease of divorce, and subsidies for single parents, almost all of whom were female, made existence as a single mother quite possible. By 1989 almost one-third of live births—three times more than in the Federal Republic—were to women who were not married. Read against other data that reveal that of twenty-year-olds polled in 1990, 90 percent of women and 75 percent of men believed in the significance of the family, we are left with an interesting *historical* question about what meanings the category of family bore and how—in the previous forty years—state policy had framed answers.[15]

In both Germanies, the ready availability of birth control methods that women could regulate led to continued trends in family size reduction, paralleling the move of ever-greater numbers of mothers into wage labor. Yet the continued high rates of endogamy among "Ossies" and "Wessies" in the present and the greater instability of marriages that mix East and West suggest the lasting impact of the different ways in which these common changes were processed socially and culturally.[16] Historians should start to fill in these general outlines, and once they begin, they may well color outside the lines, telling a messier and more nuanced story than social scientists have offered, and focusing less on snapshots of a moment than on how conceptions of the family changed over time.

Keyword: Politics

The literature on state social policy offers a window onto conceptions of gender relations precisely because debates about the family engage such a variety of witnesses and experts; employers, trade unionists, party politicians, religious ministers, organized women's groups, lawyers and judges, medical practitioners, and civil servants all become part of the story. But the family appears here largely as an *object* of social policy. There is also much recent scholarship that illuminates how the sexual division of labor lodged in familial structures and conceptions of families allowed women to become political subjects, offering them languages to make demands, protest, and resist.

As many studies of middle class women's political mobilization demonstrate, bourgeois feminists promoted forms of maternalist politics that used the state's emphasis on the family as the basis for making demands on the state. If society required women to be mothers, mothers should be given what they needed to do their job; middle class feminists called on the state to meet the needs of families and acknowledge the economic significance of women's unpaid domestic labor. These topics are addressed in this volume in the contribution of Belinda Davis.

The political valence of middle class feminism, organized around conceptions of motherhood, was not self-evident. Nancy Reagin's important study of *A German Women's Movement* reminds us that a "politics of motherhood" could clearly articulate class interests and might just as readily solidify relations between middle class women and men as between bourgeois and working-class women. In her study of "'Professional' Housewives" in the 1920s, Renate Bridenthal also demonstrates that women who organized to control the labor market for domestic servants sought tractable subordinates, not sisters.[17] But whether on the left or the right or somewhere in between, it takes only a couple of steps to get from conceptions of maternal responsibilities to forms of women's organized political activity.

After 1945, organized women continued to claim identity as mothers in forms of political activism that extended from demands to reform family law to campaigns to bring world peace.[18] We could push this agenda further to consider what motivated women to participate in the "citizens' initiatives" of the 1970s and 1980s or the campaigns against the placement of U.S. nuclear weapons on West German soil. Strains of maternalist politics could also be heard after 1945 in East Germany, where in 1957, a leader of the Democratic Women's Federation could address her comrades in Weimar, "home of German classicists and humanists," reminding them that "every woman . . . at the bottom of her heart is a true humanist, she, who gives a child life." How did maternal politics survive in Communist Germany where the proclamation of complete gender equality had banished bourgeois feminism's insistence on separate spheres?[19]

We should also continue to explore forms of women's collective action that defy easy categorization on a conventional political spectrum. Consider, for example, Marion Kaplan's rich description of how mothers in German-Jewish families in the 1930s allowed German Jews to survive in a world where both the law and the unwritten law of social ritual had been violated by their non-Jewish fellow citizens. Kaplan describes communal institutions—the Central Organization of German Jews, the synagogue—that affirmed families, but in acts like lighting the Sabbath candles and preparing food in accord with religious dietary laws, German-Jewish women engaged in a "politics of daily life" that affirmed the community. And Atina Grossman's discussion of "Trauma, Memory, and Motherhood" among Jewish displaced persons (DPs) and Germans at the end of the Second World War leads her to conclude that in the "'steady rush of weddings' in DP camps" it was possible to see "a conscious affirmation of Jewish life . . . a possible reconstruction of collective, national, and individual identity." Under these circumstances, should we not consider survival and self-affirmation as expressions of the political?[20] These studies also suggest the importance of what connects religious identity, the particular conceptions of the family, and political action, an area in which there is room for much more research, even in an increasingly secularized twentieth century.

And what of the maternal politics that consist of shopping, cooking, and keeping children alive? When women in Berlin took to the streets in the First World War to protest inadequate provisioning, they acted not as autonomous individuals but as women responsible for maintaining households.[21] This was something the Nazis clearly understood. What Tim Mason described as "The Legacy of 1918 for National Socialism" included Nazi fears of male workers, striking and protesting against the state, but Belinda Davis demonstrates that it also involved fears of wives and mothers who were fully capable of participating in violent collective action.[22]

Davis's work offers an approach to the "politics of daily life" that could be usefully applied to many other moments in the twentieth century.[23] What motivated women's protests around food and provisioning at the end of World

War II and how does it compare with the protests at the end of World War I? And what of the bases for collective resistance to state regulation of markets on the other side of the urban-rural divide? After all, the farms overrun by urban women in the First World War and the period immediately following the Second were maintained by other wives, daughters, and mothers whose husbands, sons, and brothers were often absent. Or in the East German case, how should we understand the politics of women's protests over food short-ages in the spring of 1953—on the eve of the violent revolt in June of that year?[24] Or consider other forms of the "politics of daily life" in which women were instrumental, such as forbidding a child to participate in Communist youth organizations or securing the boundaries of the fabled East German "niche society" (*Nischengesellschaft*), a point of retreat beyond the grasp of the state. In what ways were women's participation in such forms of politics in-formed by their self-identification as wives and mothers?[25]

Politics that begin around the kitchen table do not always affirm family ties, and generational conflicts that originate in families also deserve our at-tention. Consider some post-1945 examples. In Uta Poiger's work, young people rejected parental authority to the rhythms of rock n' roll, actions that were interpreted in West Germany in depoliticized psychological categories that shifted responsibility for aberrant behavior to families. According to East German officials, in contrast, the siren call of U.S. imperialism, not the fam-ily, was to blame for an Americanized youth culture. By the late 1960s, the political import of West German youth protest was less easily explained away when Gudrun Ensslin proclaimed that "you can't argue with the people who made Auschwitz," indicting an entire generation, and the counterculture de-nounced the family as a fundamentally repressive institution.[26] In turn, critics of radical politics demonized the left because it violated family values. Alan Rosenfeld describes how the conservative Springer press denounced Ulrike Meinhof not only as a bomb-throwing terrorist, but also as an unnatural mother who abandoned her two children to pursue her delusions.[27]

The story of parents and children in East Germany, presented in fascinat-ing detail by Wierling, was quite different. There the "parental state" con-tinued to fulminate against Western cultural influences so vehemently that it alienated *real* parents, bolstering the barrier between families and the state.[28] Wierling also suggests how we might approach a missing part of the West German story, and it would be illuminating to move from the West German counterculture's critique of the family to the particular family histories of stu-dent radicals, exploring whether at least some of them learned their progres-sive politics from Mutti and Vati.[29]

If we seek the sources of women's political activity only in historically spe-cific forms of family values, we will fail to understand the multiple ways in which women act as political subjects. The brief review offered here, however, indicates that by analyzing how politics begins at home, we gain important insights into what has frequently formed the bases for collective action, and we can begin to interrogate the very boundaries of what we want to call politics.[30]

Keyword: Nationalism and Citizenship

In all of the political regimes in Germany's long twentieth century, families have been seen as one of the key institutions charged with mediating between individuals and the nation. In addition, until the beginning of the twenty-first century, the principle of *jus sanguinis*—parental descent—defined citizenship in Germany.[31] In approaching these themes, there is an obvious overlap with the contributions of Angelika Schaser and Kathleen Canning in this book, but it is worth underscoring how centrally the family figured as a locus of definitions of citizenship. In the categories of eugenics and racial hygiene, the family was charged with reproducing the nation. When mothers became mothers of the *Volk*, they gave birth not only to sons and daughters but also to Germany, a political obligation that was hardly personal.

When we move beyond research into a biomedicalized welfare state and the "racial state" of the Nazis, however, the literature that describes the intersection of families and the nation is far thinner for the twentieth century than it is for the nineteenth.[32] But there are good examples of the direction that future research might take. Lora Wildenthal moves back into the Kaiserreich to explore how race and claims to citizenship collided in German Southwest Africa, East Africa, and Samoa, where some white male settlers contested miscegenation laws that would have barred their mixed-race offspring from citizenship.[33] In her analysis of the literature on household management in the late nineteenth and early twentieth centuries, Nancy Reagin describes how the nation was produced not only in the bedroom but also at the business end of a broomstick. The discourse of a specifically German domesticity distinguished Germans from the frivolous French and the British, too reliant on domestic servants. Translated into colonial settings, German domesticity could sweep the way clear for civilization.[34]

Moving to the post-1945 period, I have argued that in the wake of fascism's defeat, the family was no less important in defining Germanness. Particularly in the Federal Republic, at a moment when a political language of "nation" and "nationalism" was highly problematic, an idealized conception of the family took on enormous significance as a repository of quintessentially German values that had survived the Third Reich. The family became a placeholder for values that could no longer be easily located in any other *Gemeinschaft*.[35] The political priority of reconstituting a private family sphere embodied a critique of the ideological alternatives presented by National

Socialism and East German communism. By positioning an idealized family as a "noncommercialized nucleus" in a commercial society, social commentators and politicians could also present the family as the defense against the threat of an Americanized consumer culture.

Taken one step further, drawing on Thomas Lindenberger's work, the attack on this "re-established gender order" in the 1960s "by the very generation that had been raised under its seemingly unrestricted rule," can be read as an attack on fundamental understandings of the nation. Lindenberger calls for comparing West German "family-centered citizenship" with the East German state-citizen alternative, where "party and state posed and acted as 'parents' taking care of their 'children' thus undermining the symbolic and material autonomy of 'real families.'"[36] The contrast Lindenberger outlines might be revised by considering the reformulation of the East German family law of 1965, which, Donna Harsch argues, "made much of 'parental' responsibility for producing good citizens"[37] and Annegret Schüle's emphasis on the ways in which the "work collective" in East German firms drew on "typical family structures and modes of behavior," suggesting that the relationship of work and home was one of complementarity, not competition.[38] But Lindenberger's proposal of a German-German comparison that focuses on the relationship of citizenship to conceptions of the family is extremely promising. Pursuing this agenda might also usefully involve a more careful look at family and kinship relations in a divided Germany and the ways in which visions of East and West were communicated through "East packages" of delicacies sent from the West, and particularly after the "basic treaty" of 1972, the visits paid by West Germans to their East German relatives.

If the nation is defined by the *right* sorts of families, then the *wrong* sorts of families are left without full access to citizen rights. The Nuremberg Laws provide the most jarring, but by no means the only, example. In her work on middle-class German-Jewish families at the turn of the twentieth century, Marion Kaplan describes how German Jews focused on elimination of dirt and smell from their households not only because these represented class markers, but also to emphasize their distinction from those who stood outside the nation—their Eastern European coreligionists. Maria Höhn describes the scorn heaped on mixed-race relationships between African American forces of occupation after the Second World War and their German "soldier's brides," unions that transgressed racial and national boundaries.[39] And in the *post*-postwar years, as difference was defined more in cultural than racial terms, the popular press implied that "guestworkers" would remain forever guests—not fit for inclusion in the nation—at least in part because of how their families were organized. By the 1970s, against the background of an emergent feminist movement and greater labor force participation rates for married German women, reporters argued that constraints on

Turkish women's freedom impeded their successful integration into West German society. These examples suggest a twentieth-century history that could expand to include the relationship between conceptions of the family and conceptions of national belonging at other moments in Germans' uneven record of acknowledging that theirs is a nation of immigrants, from the arrival of Polish families in the Ruhr in the late nineteenth century to the arrival of Turkish families in Kreuzberg in the 1970s.[40]

Finally, it is worth considering how the language of family has frequently been used to describe political authority. A few examples: What significance does it have that in the early 1950s, the near-octogenarian Konrad Adenauer was positioned as the "good father of Germany"? Why did the Christian Democratic Union and the popular press so carefully craft his public persona as loving husband and adoring grandfather—implicitly comparing him with the childless *Führer* who ruled Germany until May 1945?[41] What meanings were intended when a popular biography of the East German leader Walter Ulbricht described him a "son of the working class"?[42] How can we explain the use of the metaphor of marriage to describe the unification of a dominant male West Germany with a needy, dependent female East?[43] And how have conceptions of gender and the family intersected with the language of *international relations*? Consider, for example, the history of post-1945 American attitudes toward the vanquished foe. Petra Goedde describes a defeated Germany—characterized by a population in which women outnumbered men—in which U.S. soldiers become real and symbolic protectors of German women in a "feminized" Germany.[44] More careful consideration of the gendered language of politics will invariably bring us back to metaphors of the family—as fantasy, utopia, vision of community, and a gendered space that defines relations of authority.[45]

Keyword: Consumption

In the burgeoning literature on consumer practices, historians have stressed that consumption makes possible individual expression, but it is also worth remembering that for much of the twentieth century, the consumption that concerned most Germans ended up on the dinner table, in the pots, pans, and appliances used to prepare food and keep clothes clean, and in household furnishings. Surveying consumption in the twentieth century, Michael Geyer reminds us that many Germans' attitudes toward consumer society were shaped not by memories of excess but rather by memories of intensive deprivation from 1915–1923 and again from 1944–1953.[46] It was women as housewives and mothers—positioned culturally and socially as those responsible for organizing consumption—who were charged with managing scarcity, and as we have already seen, these responsibilities could translate into claims for rights and entitlements.

Families remained the central site of consumption well into the 1960s. In her investigation *How German Is She? Postwar West German Reconstruction and the Consuming Woman*, Erica Carter's answer to her question is "very," if the she was a housewife and mother in West Germany. Carter studies how the emerging "social market economy" gave housewives "an important part in the restitution of cultural order for the postwar nation, through their work as cultural producers of consumer lifestyles in the family home."[47] Standing at the intersection of the pronatalist exhortation to demonstrate a "*Wille zum Kind*" (wish for a child) and Economics Minister Ludwig Erhard's encouragement to develop a "*Wille zum Verbrauch*" (wish to consume), they were also charged to police the border between need and desire, ensuring that a "craving for pleasure and the striving for exaggerated security" did not lead them to go out to work or worse yet, to pursue the "auto, the television set, the luxury dog, which have become the indirect means of contraception."[48]

As Jennifer Loehlin and Michael Wildt have shown, when incomes began to rise in the late 1950s, families first spent their extra money on washing machines and refrigerators, the appliances that would make easier the work of housewives and mothers—thus freeing them to focus more attention on their children and orchestrate the increased leisure time and weekends of husbands whose workweeks were getting shorter as the 1950s progressed.[49] In his work on post-Second World War design, Paul Betts adds that modernizing the home signaled a move away from National Socialism, a self-distancing from the Communist present, and an affirmation of cultural progress. Modern home furnishings implied a self-conscious acknowledgment of the Third Reich—understood as what West Germany was *not*—and a form of confronting the past in which housewives were instrumental.[50] The evening meal could also become the vehicle for cosmopolitan fantasies—that did not involve aggressive imperialism—when a housewife whipped up "Nasi Goreng," a rice dish from an imaginary Indonesia.[51] Oertzen's work demonstrates that by the 1960s, increased consumption was made possible in part by the entry of growing numbers of housewives into part-time work. When a pickle and sauerkraut business could advertise for part-time employees by asking potential women workers, "What would you think of a fur coat?"[52] it was also clear that the range of legitimate consumer desires was expanding. Greater amounts of disposable income also paid for the family vacation, which became a priority for more and more Germans.[53]

Legitimate for one generation might, however, be illegitimate for another, and Carter provides suggestive evidence of the ways in which generational conflict within families played itself out around the pair of nylon stockings that the 1950s teenage daughter wore, gleeful in her knowledge that they would run and be tossed away, annoying her parsimonious mother. And Poiger describes forms of youth consumption—rock n' roll, blue jeans, leather jackets—of which parents little approved. Once again, consumption leads us back to the family, the struggle over resources, and the meanings of what it meant to be a postwar German. Once again, we know little of how any of these stories end, as they continue on past the 1960s.[54]

The pathbreaking work of Ina Merkel and Katherine Pence has done much to illuminate post-1945 consumer culture in East Germany. There the ruling Socialist Unity Party constantly repeated that among its top priorities was to meet its citizens' consumer demands, especially those that emanated from families. As Merkel persuasively demonstrates, as a point of reference the West never vanished from the East German imaginary or, for that matter, from East German TV screens, whose increasing numbers in the 1960s became yet another source for the transmission of desires that the East German economy could not fulfill. The East German state's involvement in decisions about everything from spring fashions to the price of basic consumer goods suggests how fundamentally important consumption was to the self-definition of the East German regime.[55] Its unwillingness to take up directly the sexual division of labor within the family while tacitly underwriting the status quo, with its emphasis on producing those consumer goods that the (female) socialist citizen needed to fill her multiple roles, ensured that wives consumed 40 percent less of one good—leisure—than their husbands.[56]

Getting and spending are not only about sustaining life, the evening meal, and clean clothes, and as much of the literature on consumption makes clear, they are also about fantasy, desire, and self-fashioning. Still, much consumption—like much of politics—is mediated through families.

Keyword: Sexuality

Sexuality is another keyword that leads us back to families not least because well into the 1970s most Germans endorsed the view that sex was something that should be contained within marriage. The very terminology of "unmarried sex" (*unehelicher Geschlechtsverkehr*) as a term of opprobrium indicated where sex was supposed to take place. In this volume, I will leave it to Atina Grossmann to review the key parts of the history of sexuality in twentieth-century Germany that have already been written, but it is worth emphasizing that the twentieth-century discourse on sex was invariably tied to the twentieth-century discourse on the family.[57]

It is also worth underscoring that any history of *hetero*sexuality, particularly the uneven history of the ideological, political, and legal attempts to contain it within families, also requires a history of *homo*sexuality, parts of which constitute a parallel story of social, emotional, and sexual unions that until the most recent past have been persecuted, not protected, by the state. By the 1960s, in both German states there were moves toward revision of Paragraph 175, the criminal statute prohibiting same-sex sexual activity among men, leading to the end to prosecution of sexual activity between consenting adults, and in 1994, the law was wiped completely from the books when the age of consent was made uniform for all Germans, whatever their sexual preference.

The interrelated themes of changing attitudes toward homosexuality, conceptions of families, and the relationship between sex and reproduction have yet to be told as parts of one twentieth-century German history,[58] and it is a past that pushes into the present. In July 2002, with a five-to-three majority, the justices of the Bundesverfassungsgericht, the highest constitutional court in Germany, threw out claims of states ruled by CDU/CSU governments arguing that the legal protection of the status of gay and lesbian partnerships, on the books for only about a year, threatened the constitutional guarantee of the family's protection. The decision affected some 150,000 couples, and, as news accounts reported, in one in seven gay and lesbian households, there were children. The court's decision was thus another part of the gradual move toward the recognition that Germany is populated by many different sorts of *post*-modern families.[59] Explaining this long-term development should be high on any agenda of the history of the family in twentieth-century Germany, a history that should include not only living rooms but also closets and the political struggles that allowed gay men and lesbians to emerge from them.

Conclusion:
"What Should Our Future Research Questions Be?"

The editors ask contributors to consider what our future research questions should be, and my recommendation is that our study of the family should take us not only into the apartments and houses of German women, men, and children, but also into the streets, department stores, churches, doctors' offices, advertising agencies, sex shops, movie theaters, and halls of parliament. We should view the family, as Judith Stacey puts it, as "a locus not of residence but of meaning and relationships."[60]

Part of the agenda for future research is further exploration of the themes outlined here. It's not *all* in the family, but families are in many places. In addition to the keywords I have offered, however, there are other spaces where families lurk that warrant more systematic study. Let me outline five thematic clusters of which family histories should be a part and which, in turn, the history of the family could illuminate:

First, historical studies of the family have contained few *men* and paid little attention to *masculinity*. We seem to have written a fatherless history of the family. How does fatherhood figure as more than part of a symbolic patriarchal order? The slate is not completely blank, and historians have paid some attention to the historical dimensions of the "crisis of masculinity" in the wake of the two World Wars, but this work only suggests the outlines of a much broader research agenda that should extend to include a systematic look at fatherhood and the ways in which families are a place where masculinity is taught and learned.[61]

Second, many of the topics that were on the 1970s agenda of social historians of the early modern period and the early nineteenth century—a big cluster that would include class formation, aging, childhood, and kinship networks—are no less relevant to our study of twentieth-century families. How was class formed and reformed in the wake of wars; as new technologies changed the workplace and married women entered the wage labor force in ever greater numbers; and as the "proletarian habitus" of subsistence and life on the margins gave way to economic security, bolstered by an expanded welfare state? How was class learned and transmitted from one generation to the next within families in gender-specific ways? Under what circumstances have "family values" provided an alternative to class as a basis from which to demand rights?[62] How have intergenerational relationships and kinship networks served to fill the gaps left by the welfare state in areas like child and elder care and care for the disabled?[63] What of the history of adoption and foster care in the twentieth century and the families that emerge from nurture, not nature? To be sure, returning to these topics does not mean a simple application of the methodologies of a no longer so new "new social history," an approach in which socioeconomic causality took pride of place. Rather, we can begin to examine them with methodologies that draw on "the history of daily life" (*Alltagsgeschichte*), oral history, and "cultural studies" in ways that take seriously the analysis of language and allow us to analyze how experience is mediated through laws, institutional structures like the welfare state, and a range of forms of representation—from daily newspapers and illustrated magazines to radio broadcasts, song, and film.[64]

Third, for a century so characterized by violence, we know remarkably little about the violence that took place in families. How has violence within families articulated and reinforced power relations between women and men, parents and children? How has German society's tolerance for violence within families changed over time? What is the relationship between gendered, socially sanctioned expressions of violence outside the family—in the workplace, on the battlefield, and at a soccer stadium and violence within families—at the dinner table, in the living room, in the bedroom?[65]

Fourth, perhaps precisely because "each unhappy family is unhappy in its own way"—and even happy ones, pace Tolstoy, do not all look alike—family dramas provide narratives that shape forms of cultural expression. Culture reflects and shapes popular conceptions of how families are supposed to be in ways historians have barely begun to explore. From nineteenth-century novels and illustrated magazines to *Heimatfilme*, Edgar Reitz's *Heimat*, and the TV and radio shows that filled German airwaves, there are many family stories that are markers of social attitudes. In still other cases—for example, the novels of many feminist authors in the German Democratic Republic—culture defined the realm in which an explicit critique of oppressive family relationships was possible.[66] And as Karin Hausen's analyses of the "invention of mother's day" in the Weimar Republic suggest, we should also expand our study of culture to include commercial culture and the ways in which families and the emotions they are thought to contain become vehicles for advertising and sales campaigns.[67]

Fifth, families are places where memories are produced and passed on from one generation to the next. Memory is mediated by ceremonies of public commemoration, museums, the writing of history, movies, literature, religious practice, interest groups, monuments, and political rhetoric, but we should also consider carefully how it is shaped within and across generations in families.[68]

The family I've outlined here is not the family we left behind in the 1980s. It does far more than determine who works where, what's for dinner, who marries whom, and when babies come into the world. It still can significantly constrain women's options, but it also can provide the basis from which women can make political demands and engage in collective action. Never a private space, it intersects with many institutional structures—from the neighborhood and the parish pump to the nation and the world. And made up of two genders and multiple generations, as metaphor, fantasy, utopia, and site of experience, its study can tell us much about the historical meanings of masculinity and femininity, growing up and getting old. This thematic review of spaces where the family resides and possibilities of where else we might look for it suggest that in the twentieth century, no more than the state has it withered away. And like the state, it's high time we acknowledged its significance and brought it back in, in the titles of our books, our subject headings, our keywords, and as a central focus of any history of gender in twentieth-century Germany.

Notes

1. Louise A. Tilly and Joan W. Scott, *Women, Work, and Family* (New York, 1987). The book was first published in 1978. Because of space constraints, I have attempted to keep references to a minimum throughout.

2. See for example Richard J. Evans and W. R. Lee, eds., *The German Family: Essays on the Social History of the Family in Nineteenth- and Twentieth-Century Germany* (London, 1981); and Karin Hausen, "Familie als Gegenstand historischer Sozialwissenschaft: Bemerkungen zu einer Forschungsstrategie," *Geschichte und Gesellschaft* 1 (1975): 171–209.

3. Tim Mason, "Women in Germany, 1925–1940: Family, Welfare and Work," in *Nazism, Fascism and the Working Class*, ed. Jane Caplan (Cambridge, 1995), 131–211; and Jill Stephenson, *Women in Nazi Society* (New York, 1975).

4. Claudia Koonz, *Mothers in the Fatherland: Women, the Family, and Nazi Politics* (New York, 1987), 414; and Gisela Bock, *Zwangssterilisation im Nationalsozialismus: Studien zur Rassenpolitik und Frauenpolitik* (Opladen, 1986).

5. Ralph M. Leck, "Conservative Empowerment and the Gender of Nazism: Paradigms of Power and Complicity in German Women's History," *Journal of Women's History* 12, no. 2 (2000): 147–169.

6. Kathleen Canning, *Languages of Labor and Gender: Female Factory Work in Germany, 1850–1914* (Ithaca, 1996), 170–171, 189, 210.

7. Young-Sun Hong, "The Contradictions of Modernization in the German Welfare State: Gender and the Politics of Welfare Reform in First World War Germany," *Social History* 17, no. 2 (1992): 251–70; Belinda Davis, *Home Fires Burning: Food, Politics, and Everyday Life in World War I Berlin* (Chapel Hill, 2000); Ute Daniel, *The War From Within: German Working-Class Women in the First World War,* trans. Margaret Ries (Oxford, 1997); Birthe Kundrus, *Kriegerfrauen: Familienpolitik und Geschlechterverhältnisse im Ersten und Zweiten Weltkrieg* (Hamburg, 1995); Atina Grossmann, *Reforming Sex: The German Movement for Birth Control and Abortion Reform, 1920–1950* (New York, 1995); Karen Hagemann, *Frauenalltag und Männerpolitik: Alltagsleben und gesellschaftliches Handeln von Arbeiterfrauen in der Weimarer Republik* (Bonn, 1990); Young-Sun Hong, *Welfare, Modernity, and the Weimar State, 1919–1933* (Princeton, 1998); and Cornelie Usborne, *The Politics of the Body in Weimar Germany: Women's Reproductive Rights and Duties* (Houndmills, 1992); also Kathleen Canning, "Feminist History after the Linguistic Turn: Historicizing Discourse and Experience," *Signs* 19, no. 2 (1994): 368–404.

8. Grossmann, *Reforming Sex*. See also Lisa Pine, *Nazi Family Policy, 1933–1945* (Oxford, 1997); and Gabriele Czarnowski, *Das kontrollierte Paar: Ehe- und Sexualpolitik im Nationalsozialismus* (Weinheim, 1991).

9. Lutz Niethammer, "Privat-Wirtschaft: Erinnerungsfragmente einer anderen Umerziehung," in *"Hinterher merkt man dass es richtig war, dass es schiefgegangen ist": Nachkriegs-Erfahrungen im Ruhrgebiet*, ed. Lutz Niethammer (Bonn, 1983), 46–48, 54, 93–94; Robert G. Moeller, *Protecting Motherhood: Women and the Family in the Politics of Postwar West Germany* (Berkeley, 1993).

10. Merith Niehuss, *Familie, Frau und Gesellschaft: Studien zur Strukturgeschichte der Familie in Westdeutschland 1945–1960* (Göttingen, 2001); Sibylle Buske, "Die Debatte über 'Unehelichkeit,'" in *Wandlungsprozesse in Westdeutschland: Belastung, Integration, Liberalisierung 1945–1980*, ed. Ulrich Herbert (Göttingen, 2002), 315–347.

11. Elizabeth Heineman, *What Difference Does a Husband Make? Women and Marital Status in Nazi and Postwar Germany* (Chapel Hill, 1999); Christine von Oertzen, *Teilzeitarbeit und die Lust am Zuverdienen: Geschlechterpolitik und gesellschaftlicher Wandel in Westdeutschland 1948–1969* (Göttingen, 1999); Carola Sachse, *Der Hausarbeitstag: Gerechtigkeit und Gleichberechtigung in Ost und West 1939–1994* (Göttingen, 2002); and Donna Harsch, "Society, the State, and Abortion in East Germany, 1950–1972," *American Historical Review* 102 (1997): 53–84; also Harsch, "Squaring the Circle: The Dilemmas and Evolution of Women's Policy," in *The Workers' and Peasants' State: Communism and Society in East Germany under Ulbricht, 1945–71*, ed. Patrick Major and Jonathan Osmond (Manchester, 2002), 151–170, quotation, 160.

12. Uta G. Poiger, *Jazz, Rock, and Rebels: Cold War Politics and American Culture in a Divided Germany* (Berkeley, 2000); and Dorothee Wierling, *Geboren im Jahr Eins: Der Jahrgang 1949 in der DDR: Versuch einer Kollektivbiographie* (Berlin, 2002).

13. On divorce, see Lothar Mertens, *Wider die sozialistische Familiennorm: Ehescheidungen in der DDR 1950–1989* (Opladen, 1998); and in general, for example, Gisela Helwig and Hildegard Maria Nickel, eds., *Frauen in Deutschland 1945–1992* (Berlin, 1993); Johannes Huinink et al., *Kollektiv und Eigensinn: Lebensverläufe in der DDR und danach* (Berlin, 1995), 145–188; and Mike Dennis, "Family Policy and Family Function in the German Democratic Republic," in *Social Transformation and the Family in Post-Communist Germany*, ed. Eva Kolinsky (New York, 1998), 37–56.

14. See Josef Mooser, *Arbeiterleben in Deutschland 1900–1970: Klassenlagen, Kultur und Politik* (Frankfurt/M., 1984).

15. The data are cited in Johannes Huinink and Michael Wagner, "Partnerschaft, Ehe und Familie in der DDR," in *Kollektiv und Eigensinn: Lebensverläufe in der DDR und Danach*, ed. Johannes Huinink, et al., (Berlin, 1995): 145–188.

16. Dieter Mühlberg, "'Leben in der DDR': Warum untersuchen und wie darstellen?" in *Befremdlich anders: Leben in der DDR*, ed. Evemarie Badstübner (Berlin, 2000), 682.

17. Nancy R. Reagin, *A German Women's Movement: Class and Gender in Hanover, 1880–1933* (Chapel Hill, 1995); and Renate Bridenthal, "'Professional' Housewives: Stepsisters of the Women's Movement," in *When Biology Became Destiny: Women in Weimar and Nazi Germany*, ed. Renate Bridenthal et al. (New York, 1984), 153–173.

18. Irene Stoehr, "Phalanx der Frauen? Wiederaufrüstung und Weiblichkeit in Westdeutschland 1950–1957," in *SozialeKonstruktionen: Militär und Geschlechterverhältnis*, ed. Christine Eifle and Ruth Seifert (Münster, 1999), 187–204.

19. From 1957, quoted in Gunilla-Friederike Budde, "Heldinnen der Arbeit: Öffentliche Fremd- und Selbstdarstellungen von Arbeiterinnen in der DDR der 50er und 60er Jahre," in *Arbeiter in der SBZ-DDR*, ed. Peter Hübner and Klaus Tenfelde (Essen, 1999), 859.

20. Marion Kaplan, *Between Dignity and Despair: Jewish Life in Nazi Germany* (New York, 1998); also idem, *The Making of the Jewish Middle Class: Women, Family, and Identity in Imperial Germany* (New York, 1991), 76–83; and Atina Grossmann, "Trauma, Memory, and Motherhood: Germans and Jewish Displaced Persons in Post-Nazi Germany, 1945–1949," in *Life after Death: Approaches to a Cultural and Social History of Europe During the 1940s and 1950s*, ed. Richard Bessel and Dirk Schumann (Cambridge, 2003), 93–128.

21. Belinda Davis, "Reconsidering Habermas, Gender, and the Public Sphere: The Case of Wilhelmine Germany," in *Society, Culture, and the State in Germany, 1870–1930*, ed. Geoff Eley (Ann Arbor, 1996), 397—426.

22. Tim Mason, "The Legacy of 1918 for National Socialism," in *German Democracy and the Triumph of Hitler: Essays in Recent German History*, ed. Anthony Nicholls and Erich Matthias (London, 1971), 215–239.

23. See the suggestive discussion in Temma Kaplan, *Crazy for Democracy: Women in Grassroots Movements* (New York, 1997).

24. Katherine Pence, "'You as a Woman Will Understand': Consumption, Gender and the Relationship between State and Citizenry in the GDR's Crisis of 17 June 1953," *German History* 19 (2001): 218–252.

25. See Günter Gaus, *Wo Deutschland liegt: Eine Ortsbestimmung* (Hamburg, 1983).

26. Quoted in Harold Marcuse, *Legacies of Dachau: The Uses and Abuses of a Concentration Camp, 1933–2001* (New York, 2001), 314.

27. Alan Rosenfeld, "Political Violence and an 'Excess' of Women's Liberation in West Germany, 1970–1977," unpublished paper, presented to the Conference of Europeanists, Chicago, March 2004, cited with permission of the author.

28. Wierling, *Geboren im Jahr eins.*

29. Claus Leggewie, "A Laboratory of Postindustrial Society: Reassessing the 1960s in Germany," in *1968: The World Transformed*, ed. Carole Fink et al. (Cambridge, 1998), 277–294.

30. See also Lynne Haney and Lisa Pollard, "In a Family Way: Theorizing State and Familial Relations," in *Families of a New World: Gender, Politics, and State Development in a Global Context*, ed. Lynne Haney and Lisa Pollard (New York, 2003), 1–14.

31. See Geoff Eley, "Culture, Nation and Gender," in *Gendered Nations: Nationalisms and Gender Order in the Long Nineteenth Century*, ed. Ida Blom et al. (Oxford, 2000), 27–40. My thoughts on these subjects have been strongly influenced by Ulrike Strasser, *State of Virginity: Gender, Religion, and Politics in the Early Modern Catholic State* (Ann Arbor, 2004).

32. See for example Blom et al., *Gendered Nations*; and Karen Hagemann, *"Männlicher Muth und Teutsche Ehre": Nation, Militär und Geschlecht zur Zeit der Antinapoleonischen Kriege Preussens* (Paderborn, 2002).

33. Lora Wildenthal, *German Women for Empire, 1884–1945* (Durham, 2001).

34. Nancy Reagin, "The Imagined *Hausfrau*: National Identity, Domesticity, and Colonialism in Imperial Germany," *Journal of Modern History* 73 (2001): 54–86.

35. Robert G. Moeller, "Heimkehr ins Vaterland: Die Remaskulinisierung Westdeutschlands in den fünfziger Jahren," *Militärgeschichtliche Zeitschrift* 60 (2001): 403–436.

36. Thomas Lindenberger, "Everyday History: New Approaches to the History of the Post-War Germanies," in *The Divided Past: Rewriting Post-War German History*, ed. Christoph Klessmann (Oxford, 2001), 43–67, quotations, 60–61.

37. Harsch, "Society, the State and Abortion," 69.

38. Annegret Schüle, *"Die Spinne": Die Erfahrungsgeschichte weiblicher Industriearbeit im VEB Leipziger Baumwollspinnerei* (Leipzig, 2001), 232.

39. Maria Höhn, *GIs and Fräuleins: The German-American Encounter in 1950s West Germany* (Chapel Hill, 2002).

40. See Rachel Tobey Greenwald, "The German Nation is a Homogeneous Nation? Race, the Cold War, and German National Identity, 1970–1993," Ph.D. diss., University of California, Irvine, 2000.

41. Moeller, "Heimkehr ins Vaterland," 403–436.

42. Johannes R. Becher, *Walter Ulbricht: Ein deutscher Arbeitersohn* (Berlin, 1967).

43. Ina Merkel, "Sex and Gender in the Divided Germany: Approaches to History from a Cultural Point of View," in Klessmann, *The Divided Past*, 91–104.

44. Petra Goedde, *GIs and Germans: Culture, Gender, and Foreign Relations, 1945–1949* (New Haven, 2003), 44.

45. Suggestive is Lynn Hunt, *The Family Romance of the French Revolution* (Berkeley, 1992).

46. Konrad H. Jarausch and Michael Geyer, *Shattered Past: Reconstructing German Histories* (Princeton, 2003), 273–274.

47. Erica Carter, *How German Is She? Postwar West German Reconstruction and the Consuming Woman* (Ann Arbor, 1997), 7.

48. Quotations in Moeller, *Protecting Motherhood*, 140.

49. Jennifer A. Loehlin, *From Rugs to Riches: Housework, Consumption and Modernity in Germany* (Oxford, 1999); and Michael Wildt, *Am Beginn der "Konsumgesellschaft": Mangelerfahrung, Lebenshaltung, Wohlstandshoffnung in Westdeutschland in den fünfziger Jahren* (Hamburg, 1994).

50. Paul Betts, "The *Nierentisch* Nemesis: Organic Design as West German Pop Culture," *German History* 19 (2001): 185–217.

51. See Wildt, *Am Beginn der "Konsumgesellschaft,"* 220; also Loehlin, *From Rugs to Riches*, 49.

52. Oertzen, *Teilzeitarbeit*, 263.

53. Rudy Koshar, *German Travel Cultures* (Oxford, 2000), 174–175; also Ina Merkel, *Utopie und Bedürfnis: Die Geschichte der Konsumkultur in der DDR* (Cologne, 1999), 321–324.

54. Victoria de Grazia, ed., *The Sex of Things: Gender and Consumption in Historical Perspective* (Berkeley, 1996). See also David F. Crew, ed., *Consuming Germany in the Cold War* (Oxford, 2003).

55. Merkel, *Utopie und Bedürfnis;* and Katherine Pence, "Labours of Consumption: Gendered Consumers in Post-war East and West German Reconstruction," in *Gender Relations in German History: Power, Agency and Experience from the Sixteenth to the Twentieth Century,* ed. Lynn Abrams and Elizabeth Harvey (London, 1996), 211–238.

56. Annette Kaminsky, *Wohlstand, Schönheit, Glück: Kleine Konsumgeschichte der DDR* (Munich, 2001), 78.

57. See for example Dagmar Herzog, *Sex after Fascism: Memory and Morality in Twentieth-Century Germany* (Princeton, 2005).

58. The literature on the history of homosexuality has focused on the Third Reich. See for example Burkhard Jellonnek and Rüdiger Lautmann, eds., *Nationalsozialistischer Terror gegen Homosexuelle: Verdrängt und ungesühnt* (Paderborn, 2002). On the postwar period, see Robert G. Moeller, "'The Homosexual Man is a 'Man,' the Homosexual Woman is a 'Woman': Sex, Society, and the Law in Postwar West Germany," *Journal of the History of Sexuality* 4 (1994): 395–429; Herzog, *Sex after Fascism;* and Jennifer V. Evans, "*Bahnhof* Boys: Policing Male Prostitution in Post-Nazi Berlin," *Journal of the History of Sexuality* 12, no. 4 (2003): 605–636.

59. BverfG, 1 BvF 1/01 vom 17.7.2002. Absatz-Nr. 1, retrieved 14 May 2004 from http://www.bverfg.de/entscheidungen/frames/ls20020717_1bvf000101; and Johanna Krauskopf, "Lebenspartnerschaftsgesetz: Karlsruhe hat entschieden," retrieved 14 May 2004 from http://www.br-online.de/politik-wirtschaft/mittagsmagazin/dynamisch/specials/Lebenspartnerschaftsgesetz/Lebenspartnerschaftsgesetz.htm

60. Judith Stacey, *Brave New Families: Stories of Domestic Upheaval in Late Twentieth Century America* (New York, 1990), 6.

61. See for example Paul Lerner, *Hysterical Men: War, Psychiatry, and the Politics of Trauma in Germany, 1890–1930* (Ithaca, 2003); Thomas Kühne, " . . . aus diesem Krieg werden nicht nur harte Männer heimkehren: Kriegkameradschaft und Männlichkeit im 20. Jahrhundert," in *Männergeschichte–Geschlechtergeschichte: Männlichkeit im Wandel der Moderne,* ed. Paul Lerner (Frankfurt, 1996), 174–192; Frank Biess, "Men of Reconstruction—The Reconstruction of Men: Returning POWs in East and West Germany, 1945–1955," in *Home/Front: The Military, War and Gender in Twentieth-Century Germany,* ed. Karen Hagemann and Stefanie Schüler-Springorum (Oxford, 2002), 335–358; Frank Biess, "'Pioneers of a New Germany': Returning POWs from the Soviet Union and the Making of East German Citizens, 1945–1950," *Central European History* 32, no. 2 (1999): 143–180; Heide Fehrenbach, "Rehabilitating Fatherland: Race and Remasculinzation," *Signs* 24, no. 1 (1998): 107–27; idem, *Cinema in Democratizing Germany: Reconstructing National Identity After Hitler* (Chapel Hill, 1995), 92–118; and Uta G. Poiger, "Krise der Männlichkeit: Remaskulinisierung in beiden deutschen Nachkriegsgesellschaften," in *Nachkrieg in Deutschland,* ed. Klaus Naumann (Hamburg, 2001), 227–266.

62. In general, Mooser, *Arbeiterleben in Deutschland;* and Gabriele Sonnenschein, "Der lange Abschied von der Lohntüte: 'Familienernährer' in den 60er Jahren," *WerkstattGeschichte* 6 (1993): 61–71.

63. See for example Vera Neumann, *Nicht der Rede wert: Die Privatisierung der Kriegsfolgen in der frühen Bundesrepublik* (Münster, 1999).

64. See Geoff Eley and Keith Nield, "Farewell to the Working Class?" *International Labor and Working-Class History* 57 (2000): 1–30, and the discussion that follows, 31–87; also Kathleen

Canning, "Gender and the Languages of Labor History: An Overview," *Traverse* 7, no. 2 (2000): 33–46. For superb models, see Kaplan, *The Making of the Jewish Middle Class;* and Ellen Ross, *Love and Toil: Motherhood in Outcast London, 1870–1918* (New York, 1993). For an excellent model for a study of adoption, see Barbara Melosh, *Strangers and Kind: The American Way of Adoption* (Cambridge, Mass., 2002).

65. Exemplary is Linda Gordon, *Heroes of Their Own Lives: The Politics and History of Family Violence—Boston, 1880–1960* (Urbana, 2002; first published in 1988). The few examples I could find of research that begins to ask these questions in the German case are articles by Eva Brückner, "'Und ich bin heil da 'rausgekommen': Gewalt und Sexualität in einer Berliner Arbeiternachbarschaft zwischen 1916/17 und 1958," in *Physische Gewalt: Studien zur Geschichte der Neuzeit*, ed. Thomas Lindenberger and Alf Lüdtke (Frankfurt/M., 1995), 337–65; and Vandana Joshi, *Gender and Power in the Third Reich: Female Denouncers and the Gestapo (1933–45)* (Houndmills, 2003).

66. See Patrice Petro, *Joyless Streets: Women and Melodramatic Representation in Weimar Germany* (Princeton, 1989); Carter, *How German Is She?* 171–202; Lynne Frame, "Gretchen, Girl, Garçonne? Weimar Science and Popular Culture in Search of the Ideal New Woman," in *Women in the Metropolis: Gender and Modernity in Weimar Culture*, ed. Katharina von Ankum (Berkeley, 1997), 12–34; Lu Seegers, *Hör zu! Eduard Rhein und die Rundfunkprogrammzeitschriften (1931–1965)* (Berlin, 2001); Vibeke Rützou Petersen, ed., *Women and Modernity in Weimar Germany: Reality and Representation in Popular Fiction* (New York, 2001); Sabine Hake, *Popular Cinema in the Third Reich* (Austin, 2001), 188–209; Judith Beile, *Frauen und Familien im Fernsehen der Bundesrepublik: Eine Untersuchung zu fiktionalen Serien von 1954 bis 1976* (Frankfurt/M., 1994); Fehrenbach, *Cinema in Democratizing Germany;* Johannes von Moltke, "Trapped in America: The Americanization of the Trapp-Family, or 'Papa's Kino' Revisited," *German Studies Review* 19, no. 3 (1996): 455–478; Robert G. Moeller, *War Stories: The Search for a Usable Past in the Federal Republic of Germany* (Berkeley, 2001), 128–165; and Barbara Einhorn, *Cinderella Goes to Market: Citizenship, Gender and Women's Movements in East Central Europe* (London, 1993), 52–53.

67. Karin Hausen, "Mothers, Sons, and the Sale of Symbols and Goods: The 'German Mother's Day,' 1923–33," in *Interest and Emotion: Essays on the Study of Family and Kinship*, ed. Hans Medick and David Warren Sabean (Cambridge, 1984), 371–413.

68. See the interesting work of Harald Welzer et al., eds, *"Opa war kein Nazi": Nationalsozialismus und Holocaust im Familiengedächtnis* (Frankfurt/M., 2002); Harald Welzer et al., *"'Was wir für böse Menschen sind!': Der Nationalsozialismus im Gespräch zwischen den Generationen* (Tübingen, 1997); and Karoline Tschuggnall and Harald Welzer, "Rewriting Memories: Family Recollections of the National Socialist Past in Germany," *Culture & Psychology* 8, no. 1 (2002): 130–145; also Wierling, *Geboren in Jahr Eins*.

SELECTED BIBLIOGRAPHY

Karen Hagemann and Jean Quataert

The choice of literature has been limited to the most important English and German publications on gender in modern German history. It is intended to provide general orientation and makes no claims to be exhaustive. Essays from collections are listed in the bibliography only if the volume in which they appeared is not included.[1]

The Selected Bibliography is organized as follows:

1. Bibliographies and Research Reports

2. Women's and Gender Studies as Practice

3. Gendering (German) History—Theories and Methods

4. Gender in German History—Introductions, Overviews, and Long-Term Analysis

5. Gender in Long Nineteenth Century Germany

6. Gender History of the Period of the First World War and the Weimar Republic

7. Gendering the History of the Third Reich, the Second World War, and the Holocaust

8. Gender in Postwar German History

1. Bibliographies and Research Reports

Allen, Ann Taylor, "The Holocaust and the Modernization of Gender: A Historiographical Essay," *Central European History* 30 (1997): 349–364.
———. "Review: The Genealogy of German Feminism," *History of European Ideas* 8 (1987): 615–619.
Bergen, Doris L., "Pandora's Box: Gender and the Complicating of Modern German History," *Journal of Women's History* 9, no. 2 (1997): 164–174.

Canning, Kathleen, "Class vs. Citizenship: Keywords in German Gender History," *Central European History* 37, no. 2 (2004): 225–244.

Cole, Helena, Hanna Schissler, and Jane Caplan, *The History of Women in Germany from Medieval Times to the Present: Bibliography of English-Language Publications* (Washington, 1990).

Conrad, Sebastian, "Schlägt das Empire zurück? Postkoloniale Ansätze in der deutschen Geschichtsschreibung," *WerkstattGeschichte* 30 (2001): 73–83.

Erhardt, Walter, "'Das zweite Geschlecht; ,Männlichkeit,' interdisziplinär. Ein Forschungsbericht," *Internationales Archiv für die Sozialgeschichte der deutschen Literatur*, 30, no. 3 (2005): 156–232.

Feist, Dagmar, "Zeitschriften zur historischen Frauenforschung: Ein internationaler Vergleich," *Geschichte und Gesellschaft* 22 (1996): 97–117.

Frevert, Ute, "Bewegung und Disziplin in der Frauengeschichte—Ein Forschungsbericht," *Geschichte und Gesellschaft* 14, no. 2 (1988): 240–262.

Gause, Ute, Barbara Heller, and Jochen-Christoph Kaiser, eds., *Starke fromme Frauen? Eine Zwischenbilanz konfessioneller Frauenforschung heute* (Hofgeismar, 2000).

Grossmann, Atina, "Feminist Debates about Women and National Socialism," *Gender & History* 3, no. 3 (1991): 350–358.

Hagemann, Karen, "Von Männern, Frauen und der Militärgeschichte," *L'Homme* 12 (2001): 144–154.

———. "Venus und Mars: Reflexionen zu einer Geschlechtergeschichte von Militär und Krieg," in *Landsknechte, Soldatenfrauen und Nationalkrieger: Militär, Krieg und Geschlechterordnung im historischen Wandel*, ed. Karen Hagemann and Ralf Pröve, (Frankfurt/M., 1998), 13–48.

Hämmerle, Christa, "Von den Geschlechtern der Kriege und des Militärs: Forschungseinblicke und Bemerkungen zu einer neuen Debatte," in *Was ist Militärgeschichte?* ed. Thomas Kühne and Benjamin Ziemann, (Paderborn, 2000), 229–262.

Hertz, Deborah, Jane Arnold, and Julie H. Rubin, "Jewish Women in Europe, 1750–1932: A Bibliographic Guide," *Jewish History* 7, no. 2 (1993): 127–153.

Herzog, Dagmar, "New Developments in German Women's History," *Journal of Women's History* 4, no. 3 (1993): 180–189.

Hoff, Joan, "Introduction: An Overview of Women's History in the United States," in *Journal of Women's History Guide to Periodical Literature*, comp. Gayle V. Fischer, (Bloomington, 1992), 9–37.

Kühne, Thomas, "Der nationalsozialistische Vernichtungskrieg im kulturellen Kontinuum des 20. Jahrhunderts: Forschungsprobleme und Forschungstendenzen der Gesellschaftsgeschichte des Zweiten Weltkriegs; Zweiter Teil," *Archiv für Sozialgeschichte* 40 (2000): 440–486.

———. "Der nationalsozialistische Vernichtungskrieg und die 'ganz normalen' Deutschen: Forschungsprobleme und Forschungstendenzen der Gesellschaftsgeschichte des Zweiten Weltkriegs; Erster Teil," *Archiv für Sozialgeschichte* 39 (1999): 580–662.

———. "Staatspolitik, Frauenpolitik, Männerpolitik: Politikgeschichte als Geschlechtergeschichte," in *Geschlechtergeschichte und allgemeine Geschichte: Herausforderungen und Perspektiven*, ed. Hans Medick and Anne-Charlott Trepp (Göttingen, 1998), 171–231.

Kundrus, Birthe, "Widerstreitende Geschichte: Ein Literaturbericht zur Geschlechtergeschichte des Nationalsozialismus," *Neue Politische Literatur* 45, no. 2 (2000): 67–92.

———. "Nur die halbe Geschichte: Frauen im Umfeld der Wehrmacht zwischen 1939 und 1945—Ein Forschungsbericht," in *Die Wehrmacht: Mythos und Realität*, ed. Rolf-Dieter Müller and Hans-Erich Volkmann (Munich, 1999) 719–735.

———. "Frauen und Nationalsozialismus: Überlegungen zum Stand der Forschung," *Archiv für Sozialgeschichte* 36 (1996): 481–499.

Lanzinger, Margareth, "Mediale und kommunikative Orte der Frauen- und Geschlechtergeschichte: Zeitschriften, Websites, Tagungen," in *Frauen- und Geschlechtergeschichte: Positionen/ Perspektiven*, ed. Johanna Gehmacher and Maria Mesner (Innsbruck, 2003) 53–70.

Leek, Ralph M., "Conservative Empowerment and the Gender of Nazism: Paradigms of Power and Complicity in German Women's History," *Journal of Women's History* 12, no. 2 (2000): 147–169.

Planert, Ute, "Vater Staat und Mutter Germania: Zur Politisierung des weiblichen Geschlechts im 19. und 20. Jahrhundert," in *Nation, Politik und Geschlecht: Frauenbewegungen und Nationalismus in der Moderne*, ed. Ute Planert, (Frankfurt/M., 2000), 15–65.

Reagin, Nancy R., "Recent Work on German National Identity: Regional? Imperial? Gendered? Imaginary?" *Central European History* 37 (2004): 273–289.

Reese, Dagmar, and Carola Sachse, "Frauenforschung und Nationalsozialismus: Eine Bilanz," in *Töchter-Fragen: NS-Frauen-Geschichte*, ed. Lerke Gravenhorst and Carmen Tatschmurat, (Freiburg i. Br., 1990), 73–106.

Ringelheim, Joan, "Women and the Holocaust: A Reconsideration of Research," *Signs* 10, no. 4 (1985): 74–161.

Rosenberg, Dorothy, "Women's Issues, Women's Politics, and Women's Studies in the Former German Democratic Republic," *Radical History Review* 54 (1992): 110–126.

Sachse, Carola, "Frauenforschung zum Nationalsozialismus," *Mittelweg 36* 6 (April–May 1997): 24–42.

Smith, Roger W., "Women and Genocide: Notes on an Unwritten History," *Holocaust and Genocide Studies* 8, no. 3 (1994): 315–334.

Sperber, Jonathan, "Kirchengeschichte or the Social and Cultural History of Religion?" *Neue politische Literatur* 43 (1995): 13–35.

von Saldern, Adelheid, "'Schwere Geburten': Neue Forschungsrichtungen in der bundesrepublikanischen Geschichtswissenschaft (1960–2000)," *Werkstatt Geschichte* 40, no. 2 (2005): 5–30.

———. "Victims or Perpetrators? Controversies about the Role of Women in the Nazi State," in *Nazism and German Society, 1933–1945*, ed. David F. Crew (London, 1994), 141–165.

———. "Opfer oder Mit-Täterinnen? Kontroversen über die Rolle der Frauen im NS-Staat," *Sozialwissenschaftliche Informationen* 20, no. 2 (1991): 97–103.

Wildenthal, Lora, "The Places of Colonialism in the Writing and Teaching of Modern German History," *European Studies Journal* 16, no. 2 (1999): 9–23.

2. Women's and Gender Studies as Practice

Allen, Ann Taylor, "The March through the Institutions: Women's Studies in the United States and West and East Germany, 1980–1995," *Signs* 22, no. 1 (1996): 152–180.

———. "Women's Studies as Cultural Movement and Academic Discipline in the United States and West Germany: The Early Phase," *Women in German Yearbook*, 9, no. 1 (1993): 1–25.

Beck-Rosenthal, Erika, ed., *Frauenförderung in der Praxis: Frauenbeauftragte berichten* (Frankfurt/M., 1990).

Beiträge zur feministischen Theorie und Praxis 5, "Dokumentation des 3. Historikerinnentreffens in Bielefeld, April 1981," in *Beiträge zur feministschen Theorie und Praxis* (1981).

Beiträge zur feministischen Theorie und Praxis 7, "Dokumentation der Tagung Weibliche Biograhien in Bielefeld, Oktober 1981," in *Beiträge zur feministschen Theorie und Praxis* (1982).

Beiträge zur feministischen Theorie und Praxis 11, "Frauenforschung oder feministische Forschung?" in *Beiträge zur feministschen Theorie und Praxis* (1984).

Biester, Elke, et al., eds., *Gleichstellungspolitik—Totem und Tabus: Eine feministische Revision* (Frankfurt/M., 1994).

Dölling, Irene, "Situation und Perspektive von Frauenforschung in der DDR," *ZIF Bulletin* 1, no. 1 (1990): 1–23.

Frauenmacht in der Geschichte: Beiträge des Historikerinnentreffens 1985 zur Frauengeschichtsforschung (Düsseldorf, 1986).

Hagemann, Karen, "Der Arbeitskreis historische Frauenforschung," *Metis* 2, no. 1 (1993): 87–92.

Hagemann, Karen, and María Teresa Fernández-Aceves, "Gendering Trans/national Historiographies: Similarities and Differences in Comparison," History Practice Section of the *Journal of Women's History* 18, no. (2007).

Hausen, Karin, and Helga Nowotny, eds., *Wie männlich ist die Wissenschaft?* (Frankfurt/M., 1986).

Hensel, Nancy E., *Realizing Gender Equality in Higher Education: The Need to Integrate Work and Family Issues* (Washington, DC, 1991).

Hirsch, Marianne, and Evelyn Fox Keller, eds., *Conflicts in Feminsim* (New York, 1990).

"History Practice: Conditions of Work for Women Historian in the Twenty-first Century," *Journal of Women's History* 18, no. 1 (2006): 121–180.

Joeres, Ruth-Ellen Boetcher, "Vom Frauenstudium zur Frauenforschung: Neure Trends im akademischen Feminismus in den USA," *Feministische Studien* 6 (November 1988): 129–135.

Johansson, Sheila Ryan, "'Herstory' as History: A New Field or Another Fad?," in *Liberating Women's History: Theoretical and Critical Essays*, ed. Berenice A. Carroll (Urbana, 1976), 400–430.

Marx Feree, Myra, "Equality and Autonomy: Feminist Politics in the U.S. and West Germany," in *The Women's Movement of the United States and Western Europe: Conciousness, Political Opportunity and Public Policy*, ed. Mary Faid Katzenstein and Carol McClure Miller (Philadelphia, 1987), 172–195.

Messer-Davidow, Ellen, *Disciplining Feminism: From Social Activism to Academic Discourse* (Durham, 2002).

Nienhaus, Ursula, "Wir fordern Beides: Autonomie und Geld," in *Autonomie oder Institution: Über die Leidenschaft und Macht von Frauen*, ed. Dokumentationsgruppe der Sommeruniversität der Frauen (Berlin, 1981), 118–124.

Schoepf-Schilling, Hanne-Beate, "Frauenstudien, Frauenforschung und Frauenforschungszentren in den USA: Neuere Entwicklungen," *Neue Sammlung* (1978): 156–173.

Die ungeschriebene Geschichte: Historische Frauenforschung; Dokumentation 5. Historikerinnentreffen Wien 16.–18. April 1984, ed. Wiener Historikerinnen (Vienna, 1985).

Wobbe, Theresa, "Zwischen Verlautbarung und Verwaltung: Überlegungen zum institutionellen Kontext von Frauenforschung," *Feministische Studien* 6 (November 1988): 124–128.

3. Gendering (German) History—Theories and Methods

Abrams, Lynn, and Elizabeth Harvey, "Introduction: Gender and Gender Relations in German History," in *Gender Relations in German History: Power, Agency and Experience from the Sixteenth to the Twentieth Century*, ed. Lynn Abrams and Elizabeth Harvey (Durham, 1997), 1–38.

Ahmed, Sara, *Differences That Matter: Feminist Theory and Postmodernism* (New York, 1998).

Alexander, M. Jacqui, and Chantra Talpade Mohanty, eds., *Feminist Genealogies, Colonial Legacies, Democratic Futures* (New York, 1997).

Alexander, Sally, "Women, Class and Sexual Differences in the 1830s and 1840s: Some Reflections on the Writing of a Feminist History," *History Workshop* 17 (1984): 125–154.

Allen, Ann Taylor, "Maternalism in German Feminist Movements," *Journal of Women's History* 5, no. 2 (1993): 99–103.

Beemyn, Brett, and Mickey Eliason, eds., *Queer Studies: A Lesbian, Gay, Bisexual, and Transgender Anthology* (New York, 1996).

Bell, Diane, and Renate Klein, eds., *Radically Speaking: Feminism Reclaimed* (N. Melbourne, 1996).

Benhabib, Seyla, Drucilla Cornell, and Nancy Fraser, eds., *Feminism as Critique: Essays on the Politics of Gender in Late-Capitalist Societies* (New York, 1987).

Benhabib, Seyla, Judith Butler, Drucilla Cornell, and Nancy Fraser, *Feminist Contentions: A Philosophical Exchange* (New York, 1995).

Bennett, Judith, "Feminism and History," *Gender & History* 1, no. 3 (1989): 251–272.

Bennett, Judith, *History Matters: Patriarchy and the Challenge of Feminism* (Philadelphia, 2006).

Berlanstein, Lenard R., ed., *Rethinking Labor History: Essays on Discourse and Class Analysis* (Urbana, 1993).

Bock, Gisela, "Equality and Difference in National Socialist Racism," in *Beyond Equality and Differences: Citizenship, Politics, and the Female Subjectivity*, ed. Gisela Bock and Susan James (London, 1992). Reprinted in *Feminism & History*, ed. Joan W. Scott (Oxford, 1996), 267–292.

———. "Women's History and Gender History: Aspects of an International Debate," *Gender & History* 1 (1989): 7–30.

———. "Geschichte, Frauengeschichte, Geschlechtergeschichte," *Geschichte und Gesellschaft* 14 (1988): 364–391.

———. "Historische Fragen nach Frauen: Historische Frauenforschung; Fragestellungen und Perspektiven," in *Frauen suchen ihre Geschichte: Historische Studien zum 19. und 20. Jahrhundert*, ed. Karin Hausen (Munich, 1982), 22–61.

Brod, Harry, and Michael Kaufman, eds., *Theorizing Masculinities* (Thousand Oaks, Calif., 1994).

Brown, Elsa Barkley, "'What Has Happened Here': The Politics of Difference in Women's History and Feminist Politics," *Feminist Studies* 18, no. 2 (1992): 295–312.

"African-American Women's Quilting," "Polyrhythms and Improvization," and "'What Has Happened Here': The Politics of Difference in Women's History and Feminist Politics," *Feminist Studies* 18, no. 2 (1992): 295–312.

Budde, Gunilla-Friederike, "Das Geschlecht der Geschichte," in *Geschichte zwischen Kultur und Gesellschaft*, ed. Thomas Mergel and Thomas Welskopp (Munich, 1997), 125–150.

Burton, Antoinette, "'History' is Now: Feminist Theory and the Production of Historical Feminisms," *Women's History Review* 1, no. 1 (1992): 25–38.

Butler, Judith, *Undoing Gender* (London, 2004).

———. *Bodies That Matter: On the Discursive Limits of "Sex"* (London, 1993).

———. *Gender Trouble: Feminism and the Subversion of Identity* (New York, 1990).

Butler, Judith, and Joan W. Scott, eds., *Feminists Theorize the Political* (New York, 1992).

Canning, Kathleen, *Gender History in Practice; Historical Perspectives on Bodies, Class, and Citizenship* (Ithaca, 2006).

———. "The Body as Method? Reflections on the Place of the Body in Gender History," *Gender & History* 11, no. 3 (1999): 499–513.

———. "Feminist History after the Linguistic Turn: Historicizing Discourse and Experience," *Signs* 19, no. 2 (1994): 368–404.

———. "German Particularities in Women's History/Gender History," *Journal of Women's History* 5 (1993): 102–114.

———. "Gender and the Politics of Class Formation: Rethinking German Labor History," *American Historical Review* 97, no. 3 (1992): 736–768.

Canning, Kathleen, and Sonya O. Rose, "Introduction: Gender, Citizenship and Subjectivity: Some Historical and Theoretical Considerations," *Gender & History* 13, no. 3 (2001): 427–443.

Caplan, Jane, "Postmodernism, Poststructuralism and Deconstruction: Notes for Historians," *Central European History* 22, no. 3/4 (1989): 119–137.

Connell, Robert W., *Masculinities* (St. Leonards, Vic., 1995).

———. *Gender and Power: Society, the Person and Sexual Politics* (Stanford, 1987).

Conrad, Franziska, and Hartmann Wunderer, *Geschlechtergeschichte: Historische Probleme und moderne Konzepte* (Braunschweig, 2005).

Conrad, Sebastian, and Shalini Randeria, eds., *Jenseits des Eurozentrismus: Postkoloniale Perspektiven in den Geschichts- und Kulturwissenschaften* (Frankfurt/M., 2002).

Cott, Nancy F., "On Men's History and Women's History," in *Meanings for Manhood: Constructions of Masculinity in Victorian America*, ed. Mark C. Carnes and Clyde Griffen (Chicago, 1990), 205–211.

———. "What's in a Name? The Limits of 'Social Feminism': Or, Expanding the Vocabulary of Women's History," *Journal of American History* 76, no. 3 (1989): 809–829.

Cranny-Francis, Anne, et al., eds., *Gender Studies: Terms and Debates* (Houndsmill, NY, 2003).

Davidoff, Leonore, Keith McClelland, and Eleni Varikas, eds., *Gender & History: Retrospect and Prospect* (Oxford, 2000).

Davis, Natalie Zemon, "'Women's History' in Transition: The European Case," *Feminist Studies* 3 (1976): 83–103.

———. *Frauen und Gesellschaft am Beginn der Neuzeit: Studien, über Familie, Religion und die Wandlungsfähigkeit des sozialen Körpers* (Berlin, 1986).

Donaldson, Mike. "What is Hegemonic Masculinity?" *Theory and Society*, 22, no 5 (1993): 643–657.

Editors' Forum: "Women's History in the New Millenium: Rethinking Public and Private," *Journal of Women's History* 15, no. 1 (2003): 11–69.

Eifert, Christiane, et al., eds., *Was sind Frauen? Was sind Männer? Geschlechterkonstruktionen im historischen Wandel* (Frankfurt/M., 1996).

Epple, Angelika, *Empfindsame Geschichtsschreibung: Eine Geschlechtergeschichte der Historiographie zwischen Aufklärung und Historismus* (Cologne, 2003).

Evans, Richard J., "The Concept of Feminism: Notes for Practicing Historians," in *German Women in the Eighteenth and Nineteenth Centuries: A Social and Literary History*, ed. Ruth-Ellen B. Joeres and Mary Jo Maynes (Bloomington, 1986), 247–258.

———. "Modernization Theory and Women's History," *Archiv für Sozialgeschichte* 20 (1980): 492–514.

———. "Feminism and Female Emancipation in Germany, 1879–1945: Sources, Methods and Problems of Research," *Central European History* 9 (1976): 323–351.

Farge, Arlette, "Praxis und Wirkung der Frauengeschichtschreibung," in *Geschlecht und Geschichte: Ist eine weibliche Geschichtschreibung möglich?*, ed. Michelle Perrot (Frankfurt/M., 1989), 29–45.

Faulstich-Wieland, Hannelore, *Einführung in Genderstudie* (Opladen, 2003).

Frader, Laura L., "Labor History after the Gender Turn: Transatlantic Cross Currents and Research Agendas," *International Labor and Working Class History* 63 (2003): 21–31

Fraser, Nancy, *Unruly Practices: Power, Discourse, and Gender in Contemporary Social Theory* (Minneapolis, 1989).

Frevert, Ute, "Frauengeschichte—Männergeschichte—Geschlechtergeschichte," in *Feministische Perspektiven in der Wissenschaft*, ed. Lynn Blattmann (Zurich, 1993), 23–40.

———. "Geschichte als Geschlechtergeschichte? Zur Bedeutung des 'weiblichen Blicks' für die Wahrnehmung von Geschichte," *Saeculum* 43, no. 1 (1992): 108–123.

———. "Männergeschichte," in *Was ist Gesellschaftsgeschichte? Positionen, Themen, Analysen*, ed. Manfred Hettling, Paul Nolte, and Hans-Walter Schmuhl (Munich, 1991), 31–43.

Gallagher, Ann-Marie, Cathy Lubelska, and Louise Ryan, eds., *Re-presenting the Past: Women and History* (Harlow, 2001).

Gayle, Rubin, "Thinking Sex: Notes for a Radical Theory of the Politics of Sexuality," in *Pleasure and Danger: Exploring Female Sexuality*, ed. Carole Vanced (New York, 1984), 267–319.

Gehmacher, Johanna and Maria Mesner, eds., *Frauen- und Geschlechtergeschichte: Positionen/Perspektiven* (Innsbruck, 2003).

Gordon, Linda, "On 'Difference,'" *Genders* 10 (Spring 1991): 91–111.

———. "What's New in Women's History," in *Feminist Studies, Critical Studies*, ed. Teresa de Lauretis (Bloomington, 1986), 20–30.

———. "What Should Women's Historians Do: Politics, Social Theory, and Women's History," *Marxist Perspectives* 1 (1978): 128–136.

Gosh, Durba, "Gender and Colonialism: Expansion or Marginalization?" *The Historical Journal* 47, no. 3 (2004): 737–755.

Grewal, Inderpal, and Caren Kaplan, eds., *Scattered Hegemonies: Postmodernity and Transnational Feminist Practices* (Minneapolis, 1994).

Grosz, Elizabeth, *Volatile Bodies: Toward a Corporeal Feminism* (Bloomington, 1994).

Habermas, Rebekka, "Geschlechtergeschichte und 'Anthropology of Gender': Geschichte einer Begegnung," *Historische Anthropologie* 2, no. 1 (1993): 463–487.

Harding, Sandra, ed., *Feminism and Methodology: Social Science Issues* (Bloomington, 1987).

Hartsock, Nancy, *The Feminist Standpoint Revisited and Other Essays* (Boulder, 1998).

Harvey, Karen, "The History of Masculinity, circa 1650–1800," *Journal of British Studies* 44, no. 2 (2005): 296–311.

Hausen, Karin, "Die Nicht-Einheit der Geschichte als historiographische Herausforderung: Zur historischen Relevanz und Anstößigkeit der Geschlechtergeschichte," in *Geschlechtergeschichte und allgemeine Geschichte: Herausforderungen und Perspektiven*, ed. Hans Medick and Anne-Charlotte Trepp (Göttingen, 1998), 15–55.

———. "Geschichte als patrilineale Konstruktion und historiographisches Identifikationsangebot: Ein Kommentar zu Lothar Gall, Das Bürgertum in Deutschland, Berlin 1989," *L'Homme* 8, no. 1 (1997): 109–131.

Hausen, Karin, and Heide Wunder, eds., *Frauengeschichte—Geschlechtergeschichte* (Frankfurt/M., 1992).

Higginbotham, Elizabeth Brooks, "Designing an Inclusive Curriculum: Bringing All Women into the Core, " *Women's Studies Quaterly* 8, no. 1–2 (1990), 1–2

———. "African-American Women's Histroy and the Metalanguage of Race," *Signs* 117, no. 2 (1992): 251–274.

Hoff, Joan, "Gender as a Postmodern Category of Paralysis," *Women's History Review* 3, no. 2 (1994): 149–168.

Hommen, Tanja, "Körperdefinition und Körpererfahrung," *Geschichte und Gesellschaft* 26, no. 4 (2000): 577–601.

Honegger, Claudia, and Caroline Arni, eds., *Gender—die Tücken einer Kategorie: Joan W. Scott, Geschichte und Politik* (Zurich, 2001).

Hooks, Bell, *Yearning: Race, Gender, and Cultural Politics* (Boston, 1990).

Hull, Isabel V., "Feminist and Gender History through the Literary Looking Glass: German Historiography in Postmodern Times," *Central European History* 22 (1989): 279–300.

Hunt, Lynn, "The Challenge of Gender: Deconstruction of Categories and Reconstruction of Narratives in Gender History," *Geschlechtergeschichte und Allgemeine Geschichte. Herausforderungen und Perspektiven*, ed. Hands Medick and Anne-Charlott Trepp (Göttingen, 1998), 57–98.

Kauffman, Linda, ed., *Gender and Theory: Dialogues on Feminist Criticism* (Oxford, 1989).

Kelly, Joan, "The Social Relations of the Sexes: Methodological Implications of Women's History," *Signs* 1, no. 4 (1976): 809–823.

Kelly, Joan, *Women, History, and Theory: The Essays of Joan Kelly* (Chicago, 1984).

Kerber, Linda K., "Separate Spheres, Female Worlds, Women's Place: The Rhetoric of Women's History," *Journal of American History* 75, no. 1 (1988): 9–39.

Kessel, Martina and Gabriela Signor, "Geschichtswissenschaft," in *Gender-Studien: Eine Einfüh-rung*, ed. Christina von Braun and Inge Stephan (Stuttgart, 2000), 119–129.

Kessler-Harris, Alice, "Gender and Work: Possibilities for a Global, Historical Overview," in *Women's History in Global Perspective*, vol. 1., ed. Bonnie G. Smith (Urbana, 2004), 229–275.

Kimmel, Michael S., Jeff Hearn and R. W. Connell, eds., *Handbook of Studies on Men and Masculinities* (London and New York, 2005).

Kuhn, Annette, "Feminismus, Frauengeschichte und historische Friedensforschung," in *Perspektiven der Friedensforschung*, ed. Bernhard Moltmann (Baden-Baden, 1988), 175–188.

Kühne, Thomas, "Männergeschichte als Geschlechtergeschichte," in *Männergeschichte—Geschlechtergeschichte: Männlichkeit im Wandel der Moderne*, ed. Thomas Kühne (Frankfurt/M., 1996), 7–30.

Landes, Joan, ed., *Feminism: The Public and the Private* (New York, 1998).

Laslett, Barbara, et al., eds., *History and Theory: Feminist Research, Debates, Contestations* (Chicago, 1997).

Leck, Ralph M., "Concervative Empowerment and the Gender of Nazism: Paradims of Power and Complicity in German Women's History," *Journal of Women's History* 12 (2002): 147–169.

Lerner, Gerda, "Placing Women in History: Definitions and Challenges," *Feminist Studies* 3 (Fall 1975): 5–14.

———. *The Majority Finds Its Past: Placing Women in History* (Chapel Hill, 2005; first published in 1979).

———. *Women and History*, 2 vols.; vol. 1: *The Creation of Patriarchy*; vol. 2: *The Creation of Feminist Consciousness: From the Middle Ages to Eighteen-seventy* (New York, 1986/1993). Printed in German in 1991/1993.

———. "Reconceptualizing Differences among Woman," *Journal of Women's History* 1, no. 3 (1990): 106–122.

Lister, Ruth, *Citizenship: Feminist Perspectives* (New York, 1997).

Littler, Margaret, ed., *Gendering German Studies: New Perspectives on German Literature and Culture* (Oxford, 1997).

Magnus, Shulamith, "'Out of the Ghetto': Integrating the Study of Jewish Women into the Study of the 'The Jews,'" *Judaism* 39, no. 1 (1990): 28–36.

Mansfield, Nick, *Subjectivity: Theories of the Self from Freud to Haraway* (New York, 2000).

Medick, Hans and Anne-Charlotte Trepp, eds., *Geschlechtergeschichte und allgemeine Geschichte: Herausforderungen und Perspektiven* (Göttingen, 1998).

Mohanty, Chandra Talpade, Ann Russo, and Lourdes Torres, eds., *Third World Women and the Politics of Feminism* (Bloomington, 1991).

Newton, Judith L., Mary P. Ryan, and Judith R. Walkowitz, eds., *Sex and Class in Women's History* (London, 1983).

Nicholson, Linda J., ed., *Feminism/Postmodernism* (New York, 1990).

Offen, Karen, "Defining Feminism: A Comparative Historical Approach," *Signs* 14 (1988): 119–157.

Offen, Karen, Ruth Roach Pierson, and Jane Rendall, eds., *Writing Women's History: International Perspectives* (Bloomington, 1991).

Okin, Susan Moller, "Gender, the Public, and the Private," in *Feminism and Politics*, ed. Anne Phillips (Oxford, 1998), 116–141.

Opitz, Claudia, *Um-Ordnungen der Geschlechter. Einführung in die Geschlechtergeschichte* (Tübingen, 2005).

Ortner, Sherry B., *Making Gender: The Politics and Erotics of Culture* (Boston, 1996).

Pateman, Carole, *The Sexual Contract* (Stanford, 1988).

———. *The Disorder of Women: Democracy, Feminism and Political Theory* (Stanford, 1989).

Penn, Donna, "Queer: Theorizing Politics and History," *Radical History Review* 62 (Spring 1995): 24–42.

Phelan, Shane, ed., *Playing with Fire: Queer Politics, Queer Theories* (New York, 1997).

Planert, Ute, "Der dreifache Körper des Volkes: Sexualität, Biopolitik und die Wissenschaften vom Leben," *Geschichte und Gesellschaft* 26, no. 4 (2000): 539–576.

Poovey, Mary, "Feminism and Deconstruction," *Feminist Studies* 15, no. 1 (1988): 51–65.

Reese, Dagmar, "Homo homini lupus—Frauen als Täterinnen," *Internationale wissenschaftliche Korrespondenz zur Geschichte der deutschen Arbeiterbewegung* 27 (1991): 25–34.

Riley, Denise, *"Am I That Name?" Feminism and the Category of "Women" in History* (Minneapolis, 1988).

Rogers, Rebecca, "Crossing Boundaries: Writing Women's History Internationally," *Journal of Women's History* 5, no. 1 (1993): 136–142.

Rose, Sonya E., et al., "Women's History/Gender History: Is Feminist History Losing Its Critical Edge?" *Journal of Women's History* 5, no. 1 (1993): 89–128.

Rupp, Leila, ed., "Women's History in the New Millennium: Rethinking Public and Private," special issue, *Journal of Women's History* 15, no. 1 (2003).

Schissler, Hanna, "Hält die Geschlechtergeschichte, was sie versprochen hat? Feministische Geschichtswissenschaft und 'Meistererzählungen,'" in *Die historische Meistererzählung: Deutungslinien der deutschen Nationalgeschichte nach 1945*, ed. Konrad H. Jarausch and Martin Sabrow (Göttingen, 2002), 194–213.

———. ed., *Geschlechterverhältnisse im historischen Wandel* (Frankfurt/M., 1993).

Scott, Joan W. "Gender: A Useful Category of Historical Analysis," in *American Historical Review* 98 (December 1986): 1053–1075.

———. "Deconstructing Equality-Versus-Difference: Or, the Uses of Poststructuralist Theory for Feminism," *Feminist Studies* 14, no. 1 (Spring 1988): 33–65.

———. "History and Differences," in *Learning about Women: Gender, Politics and Power*, Jill K. Conway, Susan C. Bourque and Joan W. Scott (Ann Arbor, 1989), 93–118.

———. "'Experiences,'" in *Feminists Theorize the Political*, ed. Judith Butler and Joan W. Scott (New York, 1992), 22–40.

———. ed., *Feminism and History* (Oxford, 1996).

———. *Gender and the Politics of History*, (New York, 1999).

———. "Millenial Fantasies: The Future of 'Gender' in the 21st Century," in *Gender—die Tücken einer Kategorie: Joan W. Scott, Geschichte und Politik*, ed. Claudia Honegger and Caroline Arni (Zurich, 2001), 19–37.

Sedgwick, Eve Kosofsky, *Epistemology of the Closet*, (Berkeley, 1990).

Sinah, Mrinalini, "Gender and Nation," in *Women's History in Global Perspective*, vol. 1., ed. Bonnie G. Smith (Urbana, 2004), 229–275.

Smith, Bonnie G., ed., *Women's History in Global Perspective*, vols. 1–3 (Urbana, 2004–2005).

———. *The Gender of History: Men, Women, and Historical Practice* (Cambridge, 1998).

Smith-Rosenberg, Carroll, "The New Woman and the New History," *Feminist Studies* 3 (Fall 1975): 185–198.

Spender, Dale, ed., *Men's Studies Modified: The Impact of Feminism on the Academic Disciplines* (Oxford, 1981).

Spongberg, Mary, *Writing Women's History since the Renaissance* (Houndsmill, NY, 2002).

Strobel, Margaret, and Majorie Bingham, "The Theory and Practice of Women's History and Gender History in Global Perspective," in *Women's History in Global Perspective*, ed. Bonnie G. Smith, vol. 1. (Urbana, 2004), 9–47.

Thurner, Manuela, "Subject to Change: Theories and Paradigms of U.S. Feminist History," *Journal of Women's History* 9, no. 2 (1997): 122–146.

Tosh, John, "Hegemonic, Masculinity and the History of Gender," in *Masculinities in Politics and War: Gendering Modern History*, ed. Stefan Dudink, Josh Tosh, and Karen Hagemann (Manchester, 2004), 41–60.

———. "What Should Historians Do with Masculinity? Reflections on Nineteenth-Century Britain," in John Tosh, *Manliness and Masculinities in Nineteenth-Century Britain: Essays on Gender, Family, and Empire* (Harlow, 2004), 29–60

Wierling, Dorothee, "Alltagsgeschichte und Geschichte der Geschlechterbeziehungen: Über historische und historiographische Verhältnisse," in *Alltagsgeschichte: Zur Rekonstruktion historischer Erfahrungen und Lebensweisen*, ed. Alf Lüdtke (Frankfurt/M., 1989), 169–190. Printed in English in 1995.

———. "Keine Frauengeschichte nach dem Jahr 2000!" in *Geschichtswissenschaft vor 2000: Perspektiven der Historiographiegeschichte, Geschichtstheorie, Sozial- und Kulturgeschichte; Festschrift für Georg G. Iggers zum 65. Geburtstag*, ed. Konrad H. Jarausch, Jörn Rüsen, and Hans Schleier (Hagen, 1991), 440–456.

4. Gender in German History— Introductions, Overviews, and Long-Term Analysis

Abrams, Lynn, *The Making of Modern Woman: Europe 1789–1918* (London, 2002).

Abrams, Lynn, and Elizabeth Harvey, eds., *Gender Relations in German History: Power, Agency, and Experience from the Sixteenth to the Twentieth Century* (Durham, 1997).

Anselm, Sigrun, and Barbara Beck, eds., *Triumph und Scheitern in der Metropole: Zur Rolle der Weiblichkeit in der Geschichte Berlins* (Berlin, 1987).

Appelt, Erna, *Geschlecht, Staatsbürgerschaft, Nation: Politische Konstruktionen des Geschlechterverhältnisses in Europa* (Frankfurt/M., 1999).

Bauer, Ingrid, Christa Hämmerle, and Gabriella Hauch, eds., *Liebe und Widerstand. Ambivalenzen historischer Geschlechterbeziehungen* (Vienna, 2005).

Benninghaus, Christina, and Kerstin Kohtz, eds., *"Sag mir, wo die Mädchen sind . . .": Beiträge zur Geschlechtergeschichte der Jugend* (Cologne, 1999).

Bergmann, Anna, *Die verhütete Sexualität: Die Anfänge der modernen Geburtenkontrolle* (Hamburg, 1992).

Blom, Ida, Karen Hagemann, and Catherine Hall, eds., *Gendered Nations: Nationalism and Gender Order in the Long Nineteenth Century* (Oxford, 2000).

Bock, Gisela, *Frauen in der europäischen Geschichte: Vom Mittelalter bis zur Gegenwart* (Munich, 2000). Printed in English in 2002.

Boukrif, Gabriele, et al., eds., *Geschlechtergeschichte des Politischen: Entwürfe von Geschlecht und Gemeinschaft im 19. und 20. Jahrhundert* (Münster, 2002).

Caine, Barbara, and Glenda Sluga, *Gendering European History, 1780–1920* (London, 2000).

Canning, Kathleen, *Languages of Labor and Gender: Female Factory Work in Germany, 1850–1914* (Ithaca, 1996).

Davy, Jennifer, Karen Hagemann und Ute Kätzel, eds., *Frieden-Gewalt-Geschlecht: Friedens-und Konfliktforschung als Geschlechterforschung* (Essen, 2006).

Duby, Georges, and Michelle Perrot, eds., *A History of Women in the West*, 5 vols. (Cambridge, 1992–1994), vol. 4: *Emerging Feminism from Revolution to World War*, ed. Geneviève Fraisse and Michelle Perrot; vol. 5: *Toward a Cultural Identity in the Twentieth Century*, ed. Françoise Thébaud.

Evans, Richard J., *Comrades and Sisters: Feminism, Socialism and Pacifism in Europe, 1870–1945* (Brighton, 1987).

————. *The Feminist Movement in Germany, 1894–1933* (London, 1976).

Evans, Richard J., and W. Robert Lee, eds., *The German Family: Essays on the Social History of the Family in Nineteenth- and Twentieth-Century Germany* (London, 1981).

Frevert, Ute, *Die kasernierte Nation: Militärdienst und Zivilgesellschaft in Deutschland* (Munich, 2001). Printed in English in 2004.

————. *"Mann und Weib und Weib und Mann": Geschlechter-Differenzen in der Moderne* (Munich, 1995).

————. *Ehrenmänner: Das Duell in der bürgerlichen Gesellschaft* (Munich, 1991).

————. *Frauen-Geschichte: Zwischen bürgerlicher Verbesserung und neuer Weiblichkeit* (Frankfurt/ M., 1986). Printed in English in 1989.

Frieden, Sandra, Vibeke R. Petersen, and Richard W. McCormick, eds., *Gender and German Cinema: Feminist Interventions*, 2 vols. (Providence, 1993).

Friedrichsmeyer, Sara, Sara Lennox, and Susanne Zantopp, eds., *The Imperialist Imagination: German Colonialism and its Legacy* (Ann Arbor, 1998).

Gerhard, Ute, *Atempause: Feminismus als demokratisches Projekt* (Frankfurt/M., 1999).

————. *Unerhört: Die Geschichte der deutschen Frauenbewegung* (Reinbek, 1990).

Gilman, Sander, *Freud, Race, and Gender* (Princeton, 1993). Printed in German in 1994.

Greven-Aschoff, Barbara, *Die bürgerliche Frauenbewegung in Deutschland 1894–1933* (Göttingen, 1981).

Hagemann, Karen, ed., "Nach—Kriegs—Helden: Kulturelle und politische DeMobilmachung in deutschen Nachkriegsgeschichten," special issue, *Militärgeschichtlichen Zeitschrift* 60, no. 2 (2001).

Hagemann, Karen, and Molly Ladd-Taylor, eds., "Gender and Rationalization in Comparative Historical Perspective—Germany and the United States," special issue, *Social Politics* 4, no. 1 (1997).

Hagemann, Karen, and Ralf Pröve, eds., *Landsknechte, Soldaten und Nationalkrieger: Militär, Krieg und Geschlechterordnung im historischen Wandel* (Frankfurt/M., 1998).

Hagemann, Karen, and Stefanie Schüler-Springorum, eds., *Heimat-Front: Militär- und Geschlechterverhältnisse im Zeitalter der Weltkriege* (Frankfurt/M., 2002). Printed in English in 2002.

Hausen, Karin, ed., *Geschlechterhierarchie und Arbeitsteilung: Zur Geschichte ungleicher Erwerbschancen von Männern und Frauen* (Göttingen, 1993).

————. , ed., *Frauen suchen ihre Geschichte: Historische Studien zum 19. und 20. Jahrhundert* (Munich, 1983).

Herlitzius, Anette, *Frauenbefreiung und Rassenideologie: Rassenhygiene und Eugenik im politischen Programm der "Radikalen Frauenbewegung" (1900–1933)* (Wiesbaden, 1995).

Herminghouse, Patricia, and Magda Mueller, eds., *Gender and Germanness: Cultural Productions of Nation* (Providence, 1997).

Joeres, Ruth-Ellen B., and Mary Jo Maynes, eds., *German Women in the Eighteenth and Nineteenth Centuries: A Social and Literary History* (Bloomington, 1986).

Kaplan, Marion, *The Jewish Feminist Movement in Germany: The Campaigns of the Jüdischer Frauenbund 1904–1938* (Westport, Conn., 1979).

————. "German-Jewish Feminism in the Twentieth Century," *Jewish Social Studies* 38, no. 1 (1976): 39–53.

Kaufmann, Doris, *Frauen zwischen Aufbruch und Reaktion: Protestantische Frauenbewegung in der ersten Hälfte des 20. Jahrhunderts* (Zurich, 1988).

Kessel, Martina, *Kunst, Geschlecht, Politik: Geschlechterentwürfe in der Kunst des Kaiserreichs und der Weimarer Republik* (Frankfurt/M., 2005).

Kratz-Ritter, Bettina, *Für "fromme Zionstöchter" und "gebildete Frauenzimmer": Andachtsliteratur für deutsch-jüdische Frauen im 19. und frühen 20. Jahrhundert* (Hildesheim, 1995).

Kühne, Thomas, ed., *Männergeschichte—Geschlechtergeschichte: Männlichkeit im Wandel der Moderne* (Frankfurt/M., 1996).

Kundrus, Birthe, *Kriegerfrauen: Familienpolitik und Geschlechterverhältnisse im Ersten und Zweiten Weltkrieg* (Hamburg, 1995).

Künzel, Christine, *Unzucht—Notzucht—Vergewaltigung: Definitionen und Deutungen sexueller Gewalt von der Aufklärung bis heute* (Frankfurt/M., 2003).

Kurth, Alexandra, *Männer—Bünde—Rituale: Studentenverbindungen seit 1800* (Frankfurt/M., 2004).

Labouvie, Eva, *Andere Umstände: Eine Kulturgeschichte der Geburt* (Cologne, 1998).

Losseff-Tillmanns, Gisela, *Frauenemanzipation und Gewerkschaften* (Wuppertal, 1978).

Malleier, Elisabeth, *Jüdische Frauen in Wien, 1816–1938: Wohlfahrt—Mädchenbildung—Frauenarbeit* (Vienna, 2003).

Mazón, Patricia M., *Gender and the Modern Research University: The Admission of Women to German Higher Education, 1865–1914* (Stanford, 2003).

Mazón, Patricia M., and Reinhild Steingröver, eds., *Not So Plain as Black and White: Afro-German Culture and History, 1890–2000* (Rochester, 2005).

Mosse, George L., *The Image of Man: The Creation of Modern Masculinity* (New York, 1996). Printed in German in 1997.

———. *Fallen Soldiers: Reshaping the Memory of the World Wars* (New York, 1990). Printed in German in 1993.

———. *Nationalism and Sexuality: Respectability and Abnormal Sexuality in Modern Europe* (New York, 1985). Printed in German in 1985.

Muschiol, Gisela, ed., *Katholikinnen und Moderne: Katholische Frauenbewegung zwischen Tradition und Emanzipation* (Münster, 2003).

Nienhaus, Ursula, *Vater Staat und seine Gehilfinnen: Die Politik mit der Frauenarbeit bei der deutschen Post (1864–1945)* (Frankfurt/M., 1995).

Offen, Karen, *European Feminisms 1700–1950: A Political History* (Stanford, 2000).

Planert, Ute, ed., *Nation, Politik und Geschlecht: Frauenbewegungen und Nationalismus in der Moderne* (Frankfurt/M., 2000).

Quataert, Jean, "Socialisms, Feminisms, and Agency: A Long View," *Journal of Modern History* 73, no. 3 (2001): 603–616.

Reagin, Nancy R., ., *Sweeping the German Nation: Domesticity and National Identity in Germany, 1870–1945* (Cambridge, 2007).

———. *A German Women's Movement: Class and Gender in Hanover, 1880–1933* (Chapel Hill, 1995).

Reese, Dagmar, Eve Rosenhaft, Carola Sachse, and Tilla Siegel, eds., *Rationale Beziehungen? Geschlechterverhältnisse im Rationalisierungsprozess* (Frankfurt/M., 1993).

Reulecke, Jürgen, *"Ich möchte einer werden so wie die . . ." Männerbünde im 20. Jahrhundert* (Frankfurt/M., 2001).

Sachße, Christoph, *Mütterlichkeit als Beruf: Sozialarbeit, Sozialreform und Frauenbewegung, 1871–1929* (Frankfurt/M., 1986).

Schaser, Angelika, *Frauenbewegung in Deutschland, 1848–1933* (Darmstadt, 2006).

Schilling, René, *"Kriegshelden": Deutungsmuster heroischer Männlichkeit in Deutschland 1813–1945* (Paderborn, 2002).

Schöck-Quinteros, Eva, and Christiane Streubel, eds., *"Ihrem Volk verantwortlich": Frauen der politischen Rechten 1890–1937; Organisationen—Agitationen—Ideologien* (Berlin, 2004).

Schulte, Regina, *Die verkehrte Welt des Krieges: Studien zu Geschlecht, Religion und Tod* (Frankfurt/M., 1998).

Smith, Bonnie G., *Changing Lives: Women in European History since 1700* (Lexington, 1989).

Süchting-Hänger, Andrea, *Das "Gewissen der Nation": Nationales Engagement und politisches Handeln konservativer Frauenorganisationen 1900 bis 1937* (Düsseldorf, 2002).

Sy-Quia, Hilary Collier, and Susanne Baackmann, eds., *Conquering Women: Women and War in the German Cultural Imagination* (Berkeley, 2000).

Thönnessen, Werner, *Die Frauenemanzipation in Politik und Literatur der deutschen Sozialdemokratie (1863–1933)* (Frankfurt/M., 1958). Printed in English in 1973.

von Olenhusen, Irmtraud Götz, ed., *Wunderbare Erscheinungen: Frauen und katholische Frömmigkeit im 19. und 20. Jahrhundert* (Paderborn, 1995).

Wecker, Regina, "Regulierung und Deregulierung des 'kleinen Unterschieds': Nachtarbeitsverbot und Konstruktion von Geschlecht, 1864–1930," *L'Homme* 11, no. 1 (2000): 37–48.

Weyrather, Irmgard, *Die Frau am Fließband: Das Bild der Fabrikarbeiterin in der Sozialforschung 1870–1985* (Frankfurt/M., 2003).

Wildenthal, Lora, *German Women for Empire, 1884–1945* (Durham, N.C., 2001).

Woycke, James, *Birth Control in Germany 1871–1933* (London, 1988).

zur Nieden, Susanne, ed., *Homosexualität und Staatsräson: Männlichkeit, Homophobie und Politik in Deutschland 1900–1945* (Frankfurt/M., 2005).

5. Gender in Long Nineteenth Century Germany

Aaslestad, Katherine B., "Material Identities: Tradition, Gender, and Consumption in Early Nineteenth Century Hamburg," in *Consortium on Revolutionary Europe 1750–1850: Selected Papers*, ed. Donald D. Horward, et. al. (Tallahassee, Fla., 1998): 599–607.

Adams, Carole E., *Women Clerks in Wilhelmine Germany: Issues of Class and Gender* (Cambridge, 1988).

Allen, Ann Taylor, *Feminism and Motherhood in Germany, 1800–1914* (New Brunswick, 1991). Printed in German in 2000.

———. "Feminism, Social Science, and the Meanings of Modernity: The Debate on the Origin of the Family in Europe and the United States, 1860–1914," *American Historical Review* 104, no. 4 (1999): 1085–1113.

———. "Feminism, Venereal Diseases, and the State in Germany, 1890–1918," *Journal of the History of Sexuality* 4, no. 1 (1993): 27–50.

———. "German Radical Feminism and Eugenics, 1900–1918," *German Studies Review* 11 (1988): 31–56.

———. "'Let Us Live with Our Children': Kindergarten Movements in Germany and the United States, 1840–1914," *History of Education Quarterly* 28, no. 1 (1988): 23–48.

———. "Gardens of Children, Gardens of God: Kindergartens and Day-Care Centers in Nineteenth-Century Germany," *Journal of Social History* 19, no. 3 (1986): 433–450.

———. "Mothers of the New Generation: Adele Schreiber, Helene Stöcker and the Evolution of a German Idea of Motherhood, 1900–1914," *Signs* 10 (1985): 418–438.

Baader, Benjamin M., *Gender, Judaism, and Bourgeois Culture in Germany, 1800–1870* (Bloomington, 2006).

———. "When Judaism Turned Bourgeois: Gender in Jewish Associational Life and in the Synagogue, 1750–1850," *Leo Baeck Institute Yearbook* 46 (2001): 113–123.

Bajohr, Stefan, "Illegitimacy and Working Class: Illegitimate Mothers in Brunswick, 1900–1933," in *The German Working Class, 1888–1933: The Politics of Everyday Life*, ed. Richard J. Evans (London, 1982), 142–173.

Baumann, Ulla, "Emancipation, and Politics in the Confessional Women's Movement in Germany, 1900–1933," in *Borderlines: Gender and Identities in War and Peace 1870–1930*, ed. Billie Melman (New York, 1998), 285–306.

Baumann, Ursula, *Protestantismus und Frauenemanzipation in Deutschland 1850 bis 1920* (Frankfurt/M., 1992).

Berneike, Christiane, *Die Frauenfrage ist Rechtsfrage: Die Juristinnen der deutschen Frauenbewegung und das Bürgerliche Gesetzbuch* (Baden-Baden, 1995).

Blackbourn, David, *Marpingen: Apparitions of the Virgin Mary in Nineteenth-Century Germany* (New York, 1994). Printed in German in 1997.

Bleker, Johanna, and Sabine Schleiermacher, *Ärztinnen aus dem Kaiserreich: Lebensläufe einer Generation* (Weinheim, 2000).

Brändli, Sabina, "Von 'schneidigen Offiziere' und 'Militärcrinolinen': Aspekte symbolischer Männlichkeit am Beispiel preußischer und schweizerischer Uniformen des 19. Jahrhunderts," in *Militär und Gesellschaft im 19. und 20. Jahrhundert*, ed. Ute Frevert (Stuttgart, 1997), 201–228.

Brentzel, Marianne, *Anna O.—Bertha Pappenheim: Biographie* (Göttingen, 2002).

Breuer, Gisela, *Frauenbewegung im Katholizismus: Der Katholische Frauenbund 1903–1918* (Frankfurt/M., 1998).

Budde, Gunilla-Friederike, *Auf dem Weg ins Bürgerleben: Kindheit und Erziehung in deutschen und englischen Bürgerfamilien 1840–1914* (Göttingen, 1994).

Buse, Dieter K., "Finding the Nation in Bremen. The Lower Class and Women after the Napoleonic Occupation," *Canadian Journal of History*, 40 (2005): 1–22.

Bussemer, Herrad-Ulrike, *Frauenemanzipation und Bildungsbürgertum: Sozialgeschichte der Frauenbewegung in der Reichsgründungszeit* (Weinheim, 1985).

Canning, Kathleen, *Languages of Labor and Gender: Female Factory Work in Germany, 1850–1914* (Ithaca, 1996).

———. "'The Man Transformed into a Maiden'? Languages of Grievance and the Politics of Class in Germany, 1850–1914," *International Labor and Working-Class History* 49 (1996): 47–72.

Chickering, Roger, "'Casting their Gaze More Broadly': Women's Patriotic Activism in Imperial Germany," *Past & Present* 118 (1988): 156–185.

Clemens, Bärbel, "*Menschenrechte haben kein Geschlecht!" Zum Politikverständnis der bürgerlichen Frauenbewegung* (Pfaffenweiler, 1988).

Cremer, Douglas J., "The Limits of Maternalism: Gender Ideology and the South German Catholic Workingwomen's Associations, 1904–1918," *Catholic Historical Review* 87, no. 3 (2001): 428–452.

Czelk, Andrea, *'Privilegierung' und Vorurteil. Positionen der Bürgerlichen Frauenbewegung zum Unehelichenrecht und zur Kindstötung im Kaiserreich* (Cologne, 2005).

Daniel, Ute, "Die Vaterländischen Frauenvereine in Westfalen," *Westfälische Forschungen* 39 (1989): 158–179.

Davy, Jennifer Anne, "Wege aus dem Militarismus: Die feministische und antimilitaristische Militarismuskritik der deutsche Pazifistinnen Anita Augspurg und Lida Gustava Heymann," in *Militarismus in Deutschland 1871 bis 1945: Zeitgenössische Analysen und Kritik*, ed. Wolfram Wette (Hamburg, 1999), 190–218.

Dawson, Ruth P., *The Contested Quill: Literature by Women in Germany, 1770–1800* (Newark, 2002).

Dickinson, Edward Ross, "Sex, Masculinity, and the 'Yellow Peril': Christian von Ehrenfels' Program for a Revision of the European Sexual Order, 1902–1910," *German Studies Review* 25, no. 2 (2002): 255–284.

Dünnebier, Anna, and Ursula Scheu, *Die Rebellion ist eine Frau: Anita Augspurg und Lida G. Heymann; Das schillerndste Paar der Frauenbewegung* (Kreuzlingen, 2002).

Eifert, Christiane, *Paternalismus und Politik: Preußische Landräte im 19. Jahrhundert* (Münster, 2003).

Ellerkamp, Marlene, *Industriearbeit, Krankheit und Geschlecht: Zu den sozialen Kosten der Industrialisierung; Bremer Textilarbeiterinnen 1870–1914* (Göttingen, 1991).

Evans, Richard J., "German Social Democracy and Women's Suffrage, 1891–1918," *Journal of Contemporary History* 15 (1990): 533–557.

Fassmann, Irmgard Maya, *Jüdinnen in der deutschen Frauenbewegung 1865–1919* (Hildesheim, 1996).

Fout, John C., "Sexual Politics in Wilhelmine Germany: The Male Gender Crisis, Moral Purity, and Homophobia," *Journal of the History of Sexuality* 2, no. 3 (1992): 388–421.

———. , ed., *German Women in the Nineteenth Century: A Social History* (New York, 1984).

Franzoi, Barbara, *At the Very Least She Pays the Rent: Women and German Industrialization, 1871–1914* (Westport, Conn., 1985).

Freidenreich, Harriet Pass, *Female, Jewish, and Educated: The Lives of Central European University Women* (Bloomington, 2002).

Frevert, Ute, "Citoyenneté, identités de genre et service militaire en Allemagne (XIXe–XXc siècle)," *Clio: Histoire, Femmes et Sociétés* 20 (2004): 71–96.

———. "Das Militär als 'Schule der Männlichkeit': Erwartungen, Angebote, Erfahrungen im 19. Jahrhundert," in *Militär und Gesellschaft im 19. und 20. Jahrhundert*, ed. Ute Frevert (Stuttgart, 1997), 145–173.

———. "Ehre—männlich/weiblich: Zu einem Identitätsbegriff des 19. Jahrhunderts," *Tel Aviver Jahrbuch für Deutsche Geschichte* 21 (1992): 21–68.

———. "Women Workers, Workers' Wives and Social Democracy in Imperial Germany," in *Bernstein to Brandt: A Short History of German Social Democracy*, ed. Roger Fletcher (London, 1987), 34–44.

———. "'Fürsorgliche Belagerung': Hygienebewegung und Arbeiterfrauen im 19. und frühen 20. Jahrhundert," *Geschichte und Gesellschaft* 11, no. 4 (1985): 420–446.

Gerstenberger, Katharina, *Truth to Tell: German Women's Autobiographies and Turn-of-the-Century Culture* (Ann Arbor, 2000).

Gleixner, Ulrike and Marion W. Gray, eds., *Gender in Transition: Discourses and Practices in German Speaking Europe, 1750–1830* (Ann Arbor, 2006).

Goltermann, Svenja, *Körper der Nation: Habitusformierung und die Politik des Turnens 1860–1890* (Göttingen, 1998).

Götsch, Silke, "'Der Soldat, der Soldat ist der erste Mann im Staat . . . ' Männerbilder in volkstümlichen Soldatenliedern 1855–1875," in *MannBilder: Ein Lese- und Quellenbuch zur historischen Männerforschung*, ed. Wolfgang Schmale (Berlin, 1998), 131–154.

Gray, Marion W., *Productive Men, Reproductive Women: The Agrarian Household and the Emergence of Separate Spheres in the German Enlightenment* (New York, 2000).

———. "Men as Citizen and Women as Wives: The Enlightenment Codification of Law and the Establishment of Separated Spheres," in *Reich oder Nation? Mitteleuropa 1780–1815*, ed. Heinz Duchhardt and Andreas Kunz (Mainz, 1998), 279–298.

———. "Prescriptions for Productive Female Domesticity in a Transitional Era: Germany's Hausmutter-Literatur, 1780–1840," in "Women in European Culture and Society," ed. Karen Offen, special issue, *History of European Ideas* 8 (1987): 413–426.

Grosse, Pascal, *Kolonialismus, Eugenik und bürgerliche Gesellschaft in Deutschland 1850–1918* (Frankfurt/M., 2000).

Habermas, Rebekka, *Frauen und Männer des Bürgertums: Eine Familiengeschichte (1750–1850)* (Göttingen, 2000).

———. "Weibliche Religiosität—oder: Von der Fragilität bürgerlicher Identitäten," in *Wege zur Geschichte des Bürgertums: Vierzehn Beiträge*, ed. Klaus Tenfelde and Hans-Ulrich Wehler (Göttingen, 1994), 125–148.

Hackett, Amy K., *The Politics of Feminism in Wilhelmine Germany, 1890–1918*, Ph.D. diss., Columbia University, 1976.

Hagemann, Karen, "Gendered Images of the German Nation: The Romantic Painter Friedrich Kersting and the Patriotic-National Discourse during the Wars of Liberation," *Nation and Nationalism* 12, no. 4, (2006): 653–679.

———. 'Be Proud and Firm, Citizens of Austria!' Patriotism and Masculinity in Texts of the 'Political Romantics' Written During Austria's Anti-Napoleonic Wars," *German Studies Review* 2, no. 1 (2006): 41–62.

———. "Die Perthes im Krieg: Kriegserfahrungen und -erinnerungen einer Hamburger Bürgerfamilie in der 'Franzosenzeit,'" in *Eliten im Wandel: Gesellschaftliche Führungsschichten im 19. und 20. Jahrhundert*, ed. Karl Christian Führer, Karen Hagemann, and Birthe Kundrus (Münster, 2004), 72–101.

———. "Female Patriots: Women, War and the Nation in the Period of the Prussian-German Anti-Napoleonic Wars," *Gender & History* 16, no. 3 (2004): 396–424.

———. *"Mannlicher Muth und Teutsche Ehre": Nation, Militär und Geschlecht zur Zeit der Antinapoleonischen Kriege Preußens* (Paderborn, 2002).

———. "A Valorous *Volk* Family: The Nation, the Military, and the Gender Order in Prussia in the Time of the Anti-Napoleonic Wars, 1806–15," in *Gendered Nations: Nationalisms and Gender Order in the Long Nineteenth Century*, ed. Ida Blom, Karen Hagemann, and Catherine Hall (Oxford, 2000), 179–205.

———. "Heldenmütter, Kriegerbräute und Amazonen: Entwürfe 'patriotischer' Weiblichkeit zur Zeit der Freiheitskriege," in *Militär und Gesellschaft im 19. und 20. Jahrhundert*, ed. Ute Frevert (Stuttgart, 1997), 174–200.

———. "Of 'Manly Valor' and 'German Honor': Nation, War and Masculinity in the Age of the Prussian Uprising against Napoleon," *Central European History* 30 (1997): 187–220.

———. "Nation, Krieg und Geschlechterordnung: Zum kulturellen und politischen Diskurs in der Zeit der antinapoleonischen Erhebung Preußens 1806–1815," *Geschichte und Gesellschaft* 22 (1996): 562–591.

Hauch, Gabriella, "Women's Spaces in the Men's Revolution of 1848," *in Europe in 1848. Revolution and Reform*, ed. Dieter Dowe, Heinz-Gerhard Haupt, Dieter Langewiesche, and Jonathan Sperber (New York, 2001), 639–693. Printed in Germany in 1998.

Hausen, Karin, "Technical Progress and Women's Labor in the Nineteenth Century: The Social History of the Sewing Machine," in *The Social History of Politics: Critical Perspectives in West German Historical Writing since 1945*, ed. Georg G. Iggers (Leamington Spa, 1985), 259–281.

———. "Family and Role Division: The Polarization of Sexual Stereotype in the Nineteenth Century—An Aspect of the Dissociation of Work and Family," in *The German Family: Essays on the Social History of the Family in Nineteenth- and Twentieth-Century Germany*, ed. Richard J. Evans and W. Robert Lee (London, 1981), 51–83. Printed in German in 1976.

Heineman, Elizabeth, "Gender Identity in the Wandervogel Movement," *German Studies Review* 12 (1989): 249–270.

Henke, Christiane, *Anita Augspurg* (Reinbek, 2000).

Hertz, Deborah, "The Lives, Loves, and Novels of August and Fanny Lewald, the Converted Cousins from Königsberg," *Leo Baeck Institute Yearbook* 46 (2001): 95–112.

———. "Why Did the Christian Gentleman Assault the *Jüdischer Elegant?* Four Conversion Stories from Berlin, 1816–1825," *Leo Baeck Institute Year Book* 40 (1995): 85–106.

———. "Leaving Judaism for a Man: Female Conversion and Intermarriage in Germany 1812–1819," in *Zur Geschichte der jüdischen Frau in Deutschland*, ed. Julius Carlebach (Berlin, 1993), 97–112.

———. "Emancipation through Intermarriage? Wealthy Jewish Salon Women in Old Berlin," in *Jewish Women in Historical Perspective*, ed. Judith R. Baskin (Detroit, 1991), 193–207.

———. *Jewish High Society in Old Regime Berlin* (New Haven, 1988). Printed in German in 1991.

———. "Intermarriage in the Berlin Salons," *Central European History* 16, no. 4 (1983): 303–346.

Herzog, Dagmar, *Intimacy and Exclusion: Religious Politics in Pre-Revolutionary Baden* (Princeton, 1996).

————. "Masculinity on Trial in Nineteenth-Century Germany," *The Consortium on Revolutionary Europe, 1750–1850: Proceedings* 23 (1994): 174–180.

Hommen, Tanja, *Sittlichkeitsverbrechen: Sexuelle Gewalt im Kaiserreich* (Frankfurt/M., 1999).

Honeycutt, Karen, "Socialism and Feminism in Imperial Germany," *Signs* 5 (1979): 30–41.

————. "Clara Zetkin: A Left-Wing Socialist and Feminist in Wilhelmian Germany," Ph.D. diss., Columbia University, 1975.

Huber-Sperl, Rita, "Organized Women and the Strong State: The Beginnings of Female Associational Activity in Germany, 1810–1840," *Journal of Women's History* 13, no. 4 (2002): 81–105.

————., ed., *Organisiert und engagiert: Vereinskultur bürgerlicher Frauen im 19. Jahrhundert in Westeuropa und den USA* (Königstein i.T., 2002).

Hüchtker, Dietlind, "Der 'Schmutz der Juden' und die 'Unsittlichkeit der Weiber': Ein Vergleich der Repräsentationen von Armut in Stadt- und Reisebeschreibungen von Galizien und Berlin (Ende des 18./Mitte des 19. Jahrhunderts)," in *Zeitschrift für Ostmitteleuropa-Forschung* 51, no. 3 (2002): 351–369.

————. *"Elende Mütter" und "liederliche Weibspersonen": Geschlechterverhältnisse und Armenpolitik in Berlin (1770–1850)* (Münster, 1999).

Hull, Isabel V., *Sexuality, State, and Civil Society in Germany, 1700–1815* (Ithaca, 1996).

Joeres, Ruth-Ellen B., *Respectability and Deviance: Nineteenth-Century German Women Writers and the Ambiguity of Representation* (Chicago, 1998).

————. "Louise Otto and her Journals: A Chapter in Nineteenth Century German Feminism," *Archiv für Sozialgeschichte der deutschen Literatur* 4 (1979): 100–129.

Joeres, Ruth-Ellen B., and Mary Jo Maynes, eds., *German Women in the Eighteenth and Nineteenth Centuries: A Social and Literary History* (Bloomington, 1986).

Kaplan, Marion A., *"Unter uns:* Jews Socialising with Other Jews in Imperial Germany," *Leo Baeck Institute Year Book* 48 (2003): 41–65.

————. "Friendship on the Margins: Jewish Social Relations in Imperial Germany," *Central European History* 34, no. 4 (2001): 471–501.

————. "Priestess and *Hausfrau:* Women and Tradition in the German-Jewish Family," in *The Jewish Family: Myths and Reality,* ed. Steven M. Cohen and Paula Hyman (New York, 1986), 62–81.

————. "For Love or Money: Marriage Strategies of Jews in Imperial Germany," *Leo Baeck Institute Yearbook* 28 (1983): 263–300.

————. "Tradition and Transition: The Acculturation, Assimilation and Integration of the Jews in Imperial Germany—A Gender Analysis," *Leo Baeck Institute Yearbook* 27 (1982): 3–35.

————. "Prostitution, Morality, Crusades and Feminism: German-Jewish Feminists and the Campaign against White Slavery," *Women's Studies International Forum* 5/6 (1982): 619–627.

————. "Bertha Pappenheim: Founder of German-Jewish Feminism," in *The Jewish Woman: New Perspectives,* ed. Elizabeth Koltun (New York, 1976), 149–163.

————. "German Jewish Feminism in the Twentieth Century," *Jewish Social Studies* 38 (1976): 38–53.

Kätzel, Ute, "A Radical Women's Rights and Peace Activist: Margarethe Lenore Selenka, Initiator of the First Worldwide Women's Peace Demonstration in 1899," *Journal of Women's History* 13, no. 3 (2001): 46–69.

————. "Militarismuskritik sozialdemokratischer Politikerinnen in der Zeit des Wilhelminischen Kaiserreiches—Möglichkeiten, Grenzen und inhaltliche Positionen," in *Militarismus in Deutschland 1871–1945: Zeitgenössische Analysen und Kritik,* ed. Wolfram Wette (Hamburg, 1999), 165–189.

Kerchner, Brigitte, *Beruf und Geschlecht: Frauenberufsverbände in Deutschland 1848–1908* (Göttingen, 1992).

Kessel, Martina, "The 'Whole Man': The Longing for a Masculine World in Nineteenth-Century Germany," *Gender & History* 15 (2003): 1–31.

Klausmann, Christina, *Politik und Kultur der Frauenbewegung in Kaiserreich: Das Beispiel Frankfurt am Main* (Frankfurt/M., 1997).

Kontje, Todd, *Women, the Novel, and the German Nation, 1771–1871: Domestic Fiction in the Fatherland* (Cambridge, 1998).

Kuhn, Bärbel, *Familienstand: Ledig: Ehelose Frauen und Männer im Bürgertum (1850–1914)* (Cologne, 2000).

Kulawik, Teresa, *Wohlfahrtsstaat und Mutterschaft: Schweden und Deutschland 1870–1912* (Frankfurt/M., 1999).

Kundrus, Birthe, *Moderne Imperialisten: Das Kaiserreich im Spiegel seiner Kolonien* (Cologne, 2003).

Labouvie, Eva, *Beistand in Kindsnöten: Hebammen und weibliche Kultur auf dem Land (1550–1910)* (Frankfurt/M., 1999).

Linton, Derek S., "Between School and Marriage, Workshops and Household: Young Working Women as Social Problem in Late Imperial Germany," *European History Quarterly* 18 (1988): 387–408.

Lipp, Carola, ed., *Schimpfende Weiber und patriotische Jungfrauen: Frauen im Vormärz und in der Revolution 1848/49* (Moos, 1986).

Lischke, Ute, *Lily Braun, 1865–1916: German Writer, Feminist, Socialist* (Rochester, NY, 2000).

Lopes, Anne and Gary Roth, *Men's Feminism: August Bebel and the German Socialist Movement* (Amherst, NY, 2000).

Mass, Sandra, "Das Trauma des weißen Mannes: Afrikanische Kolonialsoldaten in propagandistischen Texten, 1914–1923," *L'Homme* 12, no. 1 (2001): 11–33.

Maynes, Mary Jo, *Taking the Hard Road: Life Course in French and German Workers' Autobiographies in the Era of Industrialization* (Chapel Hill, 1995).

Meiwes, Relinde, *"Arbeiterinnen des Herrn": Katholische Frauenkongregationen im 19. Jahrhundert* (Frankfurt/M., 2000).

Meyer-Renschhausen, Elisabeth, *Weibliche Kultur und soziale Arbeit: Eine Geschichte der Frauenbewegung am Beispiel Bremens 1810–1927* (Cologne, 1989).

Möhle, Sylvia, *Ehekonflikte und sozialer Wandel: Göttingen 1740–1840* (Frankfurt/M., 1997).

Nagel, Christine: *"In der Seele das Ringen nach Freiheit"- Louise Dittmar. Emanzipation und Sittlichkeit im Vormärz und in der Revolution1848/49* (Königstein im Taunus, 2005).

Noyes, John, *Colonial Space: Spatiality in the Discourse of German South West Africa 1884–1915* (Chur, 1992).

O'Donnell, Krista, "Poisonous Women: Sexual Danger, Illicit Violence, and Domestic Work in German Southern Africa, 1904–1915," *Journal of Women's History* 11, no. 3 (1999): 31–54.

Omran, Susanne, *Frauenbewegung und "Judenfrage": Diskurse um Rasse und Geschlecht nach 1900* (Frankfurt/M., 2000).

Ortlepp, Anke, *„Auf denn, Ihr Schwestern!": Deutschamerikanische Frauenvereine in Milwaukee, Wisconsin, 1844–1914* (Stuttgart, 2004).

Paletschek, Sylvia, *Frauen und Dissens: Frauen im Deutschkatholizismus und in den freien Gemeinden 1841–1852* (Göttingen, 1990).

Peters, Dietlinde, *Mütterlichkeit im Kaiserreich: Die bürgerliche Frauenbewegung und der soziale Beruf der Frau* (Bielefeld, 1984).

Planert, Ute, *Antifeminismus im Kaiserreich: Diskurs, soziale Formation und politische Mentalität* (Göttingen, 1998).

Pore, Renate, *A Conflict of Interest: Women in German Social Democracy, 1919–1933* (Westport, Conn., 1981).

Prelinger, Catherine M., *Charity, Challenge, and Change: Religious Dimensions of the Mid-Nineteenth-Century Women's Movement in Germany* (New York, 1987).

Quataert, Jean H., *Staging Philanthropy: Patriotic Women and the National Imagination in Dynastic Germany, 1813–1916* (Ann Arbor, 2001).

———. "Women's Wartime Service under the Cross: Patriotic Communities in Germany, 1912–1918," in *Great War, Total War: Combat and Mobilization on the Western Front, 1914–1918*, ed. Roger Chickering and Stig Förster (Cambridge, 2000), 453–484.

———. "German Patriotic Women's Work in War and Peace Time, 1864–90," in *On the Road to Total War: The American Civil War and the German Wars of Unification, 1861–1871*, ed. Stig Förster and Jörg Nagler (Cambridge, 1997), 448–477.

———. "The Politics of Rural Industrialization: Class, Gender, and Collective Protest in the Saxon Oberlausitz of the Late Nineteenth Century," *Central European History* 20, no. 2 (1987): 91–124.

———. "Combining Agrarian and Industrial Livelihood: Rural Households in the Saxon Oberlausitz in the Nineteenth Century," *Journal of Family History* 10, no. 2 (1985): 145–162.

———. "The Shaping of Women's Work in Manufacturing: Guilds, Households, and the State in Central Europe, 1648–1870," *American Historical Review* 90, no. 5 (1985): 1122–1148.

———. "A Source Analysis in German Women's History: Factory Inspectors' Reports and the Shaping of Working-Class Lives, 1878–1914," *Central European History* 16, no. 2 (1983): 99–121.

———. *Reluctant Feminists in German Social Democracy, 1885–1917* (Princeton, 1979).

———. "Unequal Partners in an Uneasy Alliance: Women and the Working Class in Imperial Germany," in *Socialist Women: European Socialist Feminism in the Nineteenth and Early Twentieth Centuries*, ed. Marilyn J. Boxer and Jean H. Quataert (New York, 1978), 112–145.

Reagin, Nancy Ruth, "'A True Woman Can Take Care of Herself': The Debate over Prostitution in Hanover, 1906," *Central European History* 24, no. 4 (1991): 347–380.

———. "The Imagined *Hausfrau*: National Identitiy, Domesticity, and Colonialism in Imperial Germany," *The Journal of Modern History* 73 (March 2001): 54–86.

Reder, Dirk Alexander, *Frauenbewegung und Nation: Patriotische Frauenvereine in Deutschland im frühen 19. Jahrhundert (1813–1830)* (Cologne, 1998).

Schaser, Angelika, *Helene Lange und Gertrud Bäumer: Eine politische Lebensgemeinschaft* (Cologne, 2000).

———. "Women in the Nation of Men: The Politics of the Leagues of Germans's Women Associations (BDF) in Imperial Germany, 1894–1914," in *Gendered Nations: Nationalisms and Gender Order in the Long Nineteenth Century*, ed. Ida Blom, Karen Hagemann, and Catherine Hall (Oxford, 2000), 249–270.

Schmitt, Sabine, *Der Arbeiterinnenschutz im deutschen Kaiserreich: Zur Konstruktion der schutzbedürftigen Arbeiterin* (Stuttgart, 1995).

Schöck-Quinteros, Eva, "Heimarbeiterschutz für 'die Mütter des arbeitenden Volkes' 1896–1914 in Deutschland," *L'Homme* 9, no. 2 (1998): 183–215.

Schröder, Iris, *Arbeiten für eine bessere Welt: Frauenbewegung und Sozialreform 1890–1914* (Frankfurt/M., 2001).

Spalding, Almut, *Elise Reimarus (1735–1805): The Muse of Hamburg, A Woman of the Enlightenment* (Würzburg, 2005).

Stoehr, Irene, *Emanzipation zum Staat? Der Allgemeine Deutsche Frauenverein—Deutscher Staatsbürgerinnenverband (1893–1933)* (Pfaffenweiler, 1990).

Strain, Jacqueline, "Feminism and Political Radicalism in the German Social Democratic Movement, 1890–1914," Ph.D. diss., University of California, Berkeley, 1964.

Tate, Laura, "The Culture of Literary *Bildung* in the Bourgeois Women's Movement in Imperial Germany," *German Studies Review* 24, no. 2 (2001): 267–281.

Timoschenko, Tatjana, *Die Verkäuferin im Wilhelminischen Kaiserreich. Etablierung und Aufwertung eines Frauenberufes um 1900* (Bern and Frankfurt/M., 2005).

Trepp, Anne-Charlott, *Sanfte Männlichkeit und selbständige Weiblichkeit: Frauen und Männer im Hamburger Bürgertum zwischen 1770 und 1840* (Göttingen, 1996).

————. "The Private Lives of Men in Eighteenth-Century Central Europe: The Emotional Side of Men in Late Eighteenth-Century Germany (Theory and Example)," *Central European History* 27 (1994): 127–152.

van Rahden, Till, "Intermarriages, the 'New Woman,' and the Situational Ethnicity of Breslau Jews from the 1870s to the 1920s," *Leo Baeck Institute Year Book* 46 (2001): 125–150.

Vanchena, Lorie A., *Political Poetry in Periodicals and the Shaping of German National Consciousness in Nineteenth Century* (New York, 2000).

Vogel, Jakob, "Gardisten, temperamentvolle Tiralleurs und anmutige Damen: Geschlechter-bilder im deutschen und französischen Kult der 'Nation in Waffen,'" in *Militär und Gesellschaft im 19. und 20. Jahrhundert*, ed. Ute Frevert (Stuttgart, 1997), 245–264.

Walgenbach, Katharina, *Die weisse Frau als Trägerin deutscher Kultur: Koloniale Diskurse über Geschlecht, Rasse und Klasse im Kaiserreich* (Frankfurt/M., 2006).

Walther, Daniel J., "Gender Construction and Settler Colonialism in German Southwest Africa, 1894–1914," *Historian* 66, no. 1 (2004): 1–18.

Weckel, Ulrike, "A Lost Paradise of a Female Culture? Some Critical Questions Regarding the Scholarship on Late Eighteenth- and Early Nineteenth-Century German Salons," *German History* 18, no. 3 (2000): 310–336.

Wegener, Inke, *Zwischen Mut und Demut: Die weibliche Diakonie am Beispiel Elise Averdiecks* (Göttingen, 2004).

Wickert, Christl, *Helene Stöcker, 1869–1943: Frauenrechtlerin, Sexualreformerin und Pazifistin; Eine Biographie* (Bonn, 1991).

Wierling, Dorothee, *Mädchen für Alles: Arbeitsalltag und Lebensgeschichte städtischer Dienstmädchen um die Jahrhundertwende* (Berlin, 1987).

Wildenthal, Lora J., "Race, Gender, and Citizenship in the German Colonial Empire," in *Tensions of Empire: Colonial Cultures in a Bourgeois World*, ed. Frederick Cooper and Ann L. Stoler (Berkeley, 1997).

Wobbe, Theresa, *Gleichheit und Differenz: Politische Strategien von Frauenrechtlerinnen um die Jahrhundertwende* (Frankfurt/M., 1989).

Zantop, Susanne M., *Colonial Fantasies: Conquest, Family, and Nation in Precolonial Germany, 1770–1870* (Durham, 1997).

Zettelbauer, Heidrun, *Die "Liebe sei Euer Heldentum": Geschlecht und Nation in völkischen Vereinen der Habsburgermonarchie* (Frankfurt/M., 2005).

6. Gender History of the Period of the First World War and the Weimar Republic

Allen, Ann Taylor, "Feminism and Eugenics in Germany and Britain, 1900–1940: A Comparative Perspective," *German Studies Review* 23, no. 3 (2000): 477–505.

Baumhoff, Anja, *The Gendered World of the Bauhaus: The Politics of Power at the Weimar Republic's Premier Art Institute, 1919–1932* (Frankfurt/M., 2001).

Benninghaus, Christina, "Mothers' Toil and Daughters' Leisure: Working-class Girls and Time in 1920s Germany," *History Workshop Journal* 50, 2000: 45–72.

————. *Die anderen Jugendlichen: Arbeitermädchen in der Weimarer Republik* (Frankfurt/M., 1999).

Bessel, Richard, "Unemployment and Demobilisation in Germany after the First World War," in *The German Unemployed: Experiences and Consequences of Mass Unemployment from the Weimar Republic to the Third Reich*, ed. Richard J. Evans and Dick Geary (New York, 1987), 23–43.

Boak, Helen L., "Our Last Hope: Women's Votes for Hitler—A Reappraisal," *German Studies Review* 12 (1989): 289–310.

Braker, Regina, "Helene Stöcker's Pacifism in the Weimar Republic: Between Ideal and Reality," *Journal of Women's History* 13, no. 3 (2001): 70–97.

———. "Bertha von Suttner's Spiritual Daughters: The Feminist Pacifism of Anita Augspurg, Lida Gustava Heymann, and Helene Stöcker at the International Congress of Women at the Hague, 1915," *Women's Studies International Forum* 18 (1995): 103–111.

Bridenthal, Renate, "Beyond Kinder, Küche, Kirche: Weimar Women at Work," *Central European History* 6 (1973): 148–66.

Bridenthal, Renate, et al., eds., *When Biology became Destiny: Women in Weimar and Nazi Germany* (New York, 1984).

Daniel, Ute, *The War from Within: German Working-Class Women in the First World War* (Oxford, 1997).

———. "Women's Work in Industry and Family: Germany, 1914–1918," in *The Upheaval of War: Family, Work and Welfare in Europe, 1914–1918*, ed. Richard Wall and Jay Winter (Cambridge, 1988), 267–296.

———. "The Politics of Rationing versus the Politics of Subsistence: Working Class Women in Germany, 1914–1918," in *Bernstein to Brandt: A Short History of German Social Democracy*, ed. Roger Fletcher (London, 1987), 89–95.

Dasey, Robyn, "Women's Work and the Family: Women Garment Workers in Berlin and Hamburg before the First World War," in *German Family: Essays on the Social History of the Family in Nineteenth- and Twentieth-Century Germany*, ed. Richard C. Evans and W. Robert Lee (London, 1981), 221–255.

Davis, Belinda J., "Monuments, Memory, and the Future of the Past in Modern Urban Germany," *Journal of Urban History* 30, no. 4 (2004): 583–593.

———. "Experience, Identity, and Memory: The Legacy of World War I," *Journal of Modern History* 75, no. 1 (2003): 111–131.

———. *Home Fires Burning: Food, Politics, and Everyday Life in World War I Berlin* (Chapel Hill, 2000).

———. "Geschlecht und Konsum: Rolle und Bild der Konsumentin in den Verbraucherprotesten des Ersten Weltkrieges," *Archiv für Sozialgeschichte* 38 (1998): 119–139.

Davy, Jennifer A., "German Women's Peace Activism and the Politics of Motherhood: A Gendered Perspective of Historical Peace Research," in *Perspektiven der Historischen Friedensforschung*, ed. Benjamin Ziemann (Essen, 2002), 110–132.

Davy, Jennifer A., "'Manly' and 'Feminine' Antimilitarism: Perceptions of Gender in the Antimilitarist Wing of the Weimar Peace Movement," in *Frieden-Gewalt-Geschlecht: und Konfliktforschung als Geschelechterforschung*, ed. Jennifer Davy et. al. (Essen, 2006), 147–168.

———. "Pacifist Thought and Gender Ideology in the Political Biographies of Women Peace Activists in Germany, 1899–1970," *Journal of Women's History* 13, no. 3 (2001): 34–45.

Domansky, Elisabeth, "Militarization and Reproduction in World War I Germany," in *Society, Culture, and the State in Germany, 1870–1930*, ed. Geoff Eley (Ann Arbor, 1996), 426–454.

———. "Der Erste Weltkrieg," in *Bürgerliche Gesellschaft in Deutschland: Historische Einblicke, Fragen, Perspektiven*, ed. Lutz Niethammer (Frankfurt/M., 1990), 285–319.

Eifert, Christiane, "Coming to Terms with the State: Maternalist Politics and the Development of the Welfare State in Weimar Germany," *Central European History* 30, no. 1 (1997): 25–47.

———. *Frauenpolitik und Wohlfahrtspflege: Zur Geschichte der sozialdemokratischen "Arbeiterwohlfahrt"* (Frankfurt/M., 1993).

Eley, Geoff and Atina Grossmann, "Maternalism and Citizenship in Weimar Germany: The Gendered Politics of Welfare," *Central European History* 30, no. 1 (1997): 67–75.

Evans, Richard J., "German Women and the Triumph of Hitler," *Journal of Modern History* 48, no. 1 (1976): 123–175.

Gelblum, Amira, "Feminism and Pacifism: The Case of Anita Augspurg and Lida Gustava Heymann," *Tel Aviver Jahrbuch für deutsche Geschichte* 21 (1992): 207–225.

Gillerman, Sharon, "Samson in Vienna: The Theatrics of Jewish Masculinity," *Jewish Social Studies* 9, no. 2 (2003): 65–98.

———. "The Crisis of the Jewish Family in Weimar Germany: Social Conditions and Cultural Representations," in *In Search of Jewish Community: Jewish Identities in Germany and Austria, 1918–1933*, ed. Michael Brenner and Derek J. Penslar (Bloomington, 1998), 176–199.

Grossmann, Atina, *Reforming Sex: The German Movement for Birth Control and Abortion Reform, 1920–1950* (New York, 1995).

———. "Girlkultur or Thoroughly Rationalized Female: A New Woman in Weimar Germany?" in *Women in Culture and Politics: A Century of Change*, ed. Judith Friedlander et al. (Bloomington, 1986), 62–80.

———. "The New Woman and the Rationalization of Sexuality in Weimar Germany," in *Powers of Desire: The Politics of Sexuality*, ed. Ann Snitow, Christine Stansell, and Sharon Thompson (New York, 1983), 153–171. Printed in German in 1985.

———. "Satisfaction is Domestic Happiness: Mass Working-Class Sex Reform Organizations in the Weimar Republic," in *Towards the Holocaust: The Social and Economic Collapse of the Weimar Republic*, ed. Michael N. Dobkowski and Isidor Walliman (Westport, Conn., 1983), 243–264.

Hagemann, Karen, "Rationalizing Family Work: Municipal Family Welfare and Urban Working-Class Mothers in Germany," *Social Politics* 4, no. 1 (1997): 19–48.

———. "Of 'Old' and 'New' Housewives: Everyday Housework and the Limits of Household Rationalization in the Urban Working-Class Milieu of the Weimar Republic," *International Review of Social History* 41, no. 3 (1996): 305–330.

———. "Men's Demonstrations and Women's Protest: Gender in Collective Action in the Urban Working-Class Milieu during the Weimar Republic," *Gender & History* 5 (1993): 101–119.

———. *Frauenalltag und Männerpolitik: Alltagsleben und gesellschaftliches Handeln von Arbeiterfrauen in der Weimarer Republik* (Bonn, 1990).

———. "Equal but Not the Same: The Social Democratic Women's Movement in the Weimar Republic," in *Bernstein to Brandt: A Short History of German Social Democracy*, ed. Roger Fletcher (London, 1987), 133–143.

Hämmerle, Christa, "' . . . wirf ihnen alles hin und schau, daß du fort kommst.' Die Feldpost eines Paares in der Geschlechter(un)ordnung des Ersten Weltkriegs," *Historische Anthropologie* 6 (1998): 431–458.

———. "'Habt Dank, Ihr Wiener Mägdelein . . . ' Soldaten und weibliche Liebesgaben im Ersten Weltkrieg," *L'Homme* 8 (1997): 132–154.

———. "'Wir strickten und nähten Wäsche für Soldaten . . . ' Von der Militarisierung des Handarbeitens im Ersten Weltkrieg," *L'Homme* 3 (1992): 88–128.

Harvey, Elizabeth, "Pilgrimages to the 'Bleed.ing Border': Gender and Rituals of Nationalist Protest in Germany, 1919–39," *Women's History Review* 9, no. 2 (2000): 201–229.

———. "The Failure of Feminism? Young Women and the Bourgeois Feminist Movement in Weimar Germany, 1918–1933," *Central European History* 28, no. 1 (1995): 1–28.

———. "Youth Employment and the State: Public Policies towards Unemployed Youth in Hamburg during the World Economic Crisis," in *The German Unemployed: Experiences and Consequences of Mass Unemployment from the Weimar Republic to the Third Reich*, ed. Richard J. Evans and Dick Geary (New York, 1987), 142–171.

Hausen, Karin, "Die Sorge der Nation für ihre 'Kriegsopfer': Ein Bereich der Geschelecterpolitik während der Weimarer Republik," in *Von der Arbeiterbewegung zum modernen Sozialstaat*, ed. Jürgen Kock et. al. (Munich, 1994), 719–739.

———. "The German Nation's Obligations to the Heroe's Widows of World War I," in *Behind the Lines: Gender and the Two World Wars*, ed. Margaret Randolph Higonnet et al. (New Haven, 1987), 126–140.

———. "Unemployment Also Hits Women: The New and the Old Woman on the Dark Side of the Golden Twenties in Germany," in *Unemployment and the Great Depression in Weimar Germany*, ed. Peter D. Stachura (New York, 1986), 131–152.

———. "Mothers, Sons and the Sale of Symbols and Goods: The German 'Mother's Day,' 1923–1933," in *Interest and Emotion: Essays on the Study of Family and Kinship*, ed. Hans Medick and David Warren Sabean (London, 1984), 371–413. Printed in German in 1984.

Healy, Maureen, *Vienna and the Fall of the Habsburg Empire: Total War and Everyday Life in World War I* (Cambridge, 2004).

Heinemann, Rebecca, *Familie zwischen Tradition und Emanzipation: Katholische und sozialdemokratische Familienkonzeptionen in der Weimarer Republik* (Munich, 2004).

Hessler, Martina, "Educating Men How to Develop Technology: The Role of Professional Housewives in the Diffusion of Electrical Domestic Appliances in the Interwar-Period in Germany," *Icon: Journal of the International Committee for the History of Technology* 7 (2001): 95–105.

Hong, Young-Sun, *Welfare, Modernity, and the Weimar State, 1919–1933* (Princeton, 1998).

———. "Gender, Citizenship and the Welfare State: Social Work and the Politics of Femininity in the Weimar Republic," *Central European History* 30, no. 1 (1997): 1–24.

Jones, Elizabeth Bright, "A New Stage of Life? Young Farm Women's Changing Expectations and Aspirations about Work in Weimar Saxony," *German History* 19, no. 4 (2001): 549–570.

Kaplan, Marion A., *The Jewish Feminist Movement in Germany: The Campaigns of the Jüdischer Frauenbund, 1904–1938* (Westport, Conn., 1979). Printed in German in 1981.

———. "German Jewish Feminism in the Twentieth Century," *Jewish Social Studies* 38 (1976): 38–53.

Kienitz, Sabine, *Beschädigte Helden: kriegsinvalide Körper in der Kultur. Deutschland 1914–1923* (Paderborn, 2006).

———. "'Fleischgewordenes Elend': Kriegsinvalidität und Körperbilder als Teil einer Erfahrungsgeschichte des Ersten Weltkrieges," in *Die Erfahrung des Krieges: Erfahrungsgeschichtliche Perspektiven von der Französischen Revolution bis zum Zweiten Weltkrieg*, ed. Nikolaus Buschmann and Horst Carl (Paderborn, 2001), 215–238.

———. "Die Kastrierten des Krieges: Körperbilder und Männlichkeitskonstruktionen im und nach dem Ersten Weltkrieg," *Zeitschrift für Volkskunde* 95 (1999): 63–82.

Kontos, Silvia, *Die Partei kämpft wie ein Mann: Frauenpolitik der KPD in der Weimarer Republik* (Frankfurt/M., 1979).

Koonz, Claudia, "Conflicting Allegiances: Political Ideology and Women Legislators in Weimar Germany," *Signs* 1 (1976): 663–683.

Kotowski, Elke-Vera, and Julius H. Schoeps, eds., *Der Sexualreformer Magnus Hirschfeld: Ein Leben im Spannungsfeld von Wissenschaft, Politik und Gesellschaft* (Berlin, 2004).

Lacey, Kate, *Feminine Frequencies: Gender, German Radio, and the Public Sphere, 1923–1945* (Ann Arbor, 1996).

Lauterer, Heide-Marie, *Parlamentarierinnen in Deutschland 1918/19–1949* (Königstein i.T., 2002).

Lerner, Paul, *Hysterical Men: War, Psychiatry, and the Politics of Trauma in Germany, 1890–1930* (Ithaca, 2003).

———. "Hysterical Cures: Hypnosis, Gender and Performance in World War I and Weimar Germany," *History Workshop Journal* 45 (1998): 79–101.

Makela, Maria, "The Rise and Fall of the Flapper Dress: Nationalism and Anti-Semitism in Early-Twentieth-Century Discourses on German Fashion," *Journal of Popular Culture* 34, no. 3 (2000): 183–208.

Malleier, Elisabeth, "Formen männlicher Hysterie: Die Kriegsneurosen im Ersten Weltkrieg," in *Körper—Geschlecht—Geschichte: Historische und aktuelle Debatten in der Medizin*, ed. Elisabeth Mixa et al. (Innsbruck, 1996), 147–163.

Mason, Tim, "Women in Germany, 1925–1940: Family, Welfare and Work," 2 parts, in *History Workshop Journal*, Part I: 1 (1976): 74–113; Part II: 2 (1976): 5–32.

Mass, Sandra, *Weiße Helden, schwarze Krieger: Zur Geschichte kolonialer Männlichkeit in Deutschland 1918–1964* (Cologne, 2006).

———. "Von der 'schwarzen Schmach' zur 'deutschen Heimat': Die Rheinische Frauenliga im Kampf gegen die Rheinlandbesetzung 1920–1929," *WerkstattGeschichte* 32 (2002): 44–57.

McCormick, Richard W., *Gender and Sexuality in Weimar Modernity: Film, Literature, and "New Objectivity,"* (New York, 2001).

Petersen, Vibeke R., *Women and Modernity in Weimar Germany: Reality and its Representation in Popular Fiction* (New York, 2001).

Peterson, Brian, "The Politics of Working-Class Women in the Weimar Republic," *Central European History* 10 (1977): 87–111.

Petro, Patrice, *Joyless Streets: Women and Melodramatic Representation in Weimar Germany* (Princeton, 1989).

Pore, Renate, *A Conflict of Interest: Women in German Social Democracy, 1919–1933* (Westport, Conn., 1981).

Quataert, Jean, "Women's Wartime Service under the Cross: Patriotic Communities in Germany, 1912–1918," in *Great War, Total War: Combat and Mobilization on the Western Front, 1914–1918*, ed. Roger Chickering and Stig Förster (Cambridge, 2000), 453–484.

Rouette, Susanne, "Frauenarbeit, Geschlechterverhältnisse und staatliche Politik," in *Eine Welt von Feinden: Der große Krieg 1914–1918*, ed. Wolfgang Kruse (Frankfurt/M., 1997), 92–126.

———. "Mothers and Citizens: Gender and Social Policy in Germany after the First World War," *Central European History* 30, no. 1 (1997): 48–66.

———. *Sozialpolitik als Geschlechterpolitik: Die Regulierung der Frauenarbeit nach dem Ersten Weltkrieg* (Frankfurt/M., 1993).

———. "Zurück zur 'normalen' Hierarchie der Geschlechter," in *Geschlechterhierarchie und Arbeitsteilung: Zur Geschichte ungleicher Erwerbschancen von Männern und Frauen*, ed. Karin Hausen (Göttingen, 1993), 167–190.

Schaser, Angelika, "Bürgerliche Frauen auf dem Weg in die linksliberalen Parteien (1908–1933)," *Historische Zeitschrift* 263, no. 3 (1996): 641–680.

Scheck, Raffael, *Mothers of the Nation: Right-Wing Women in Weimar Germany* (Oxford, 2004).

———. "Women against Versailles: Materialism and Nationalism of Female Bourgeois Politicians in the Early Weimar Republic," *German Studies Review* 22, no. 1 (1999): 21–42.

———. "German Conservatism and Female Political Activism in Early Weimar Republic," *German History* 15, no. 1 (1997): 34–55.

Rowe, Dorothy, *Representing Berlin: Sexuality and the City in Imperial and Weimar Germany* (Burlington, 2003).

Schubert-Weller, Christoph, *"Kein schönrer Tod . . . " Die Militarisierung der männlichen Jugend und ihr Einsatz im Ersten Weltkrieg 1890–1918* (Weinheim, 1998).

Schulte, Regina, "Käthe Kollwitz's Sacrifice," *History Workshop Journal* 41 (1996): 193–221.

Seiffert, Anja, "Männer—Soldaten—Krieger: Zur Männlichkeitskonstruktion im Frühwerk Ernst Jüngers," *Widersprüche* 15 (1995): 129–143.

Sneeringer, Julia, *Winning Women's Votes: Propaganda and Politics in Weimar Germany* (Chapel Hill, 2002).

Stibbe, Matthew, "Anti-feminism, Nationalism and the German Right, 1914–1920: A Reappraisal," *German History* 20, no. 2 (2002): 185–210.

Stoehr, Irene, "Housework and Motherhood: Debates and Policies in the Women's Movement in Imperial Germany and the Weimar Republic," in *Maternity and Gender Policies: Women and the Rise of the European Welfare States, 1880s–1950s*, ed. Gisela Bock and Pat Thane (London, 1991), 213–232.

Tatar, Maria, *Lustmord: Sexual Murder in Weimar Germany* (Princeton, 1995).

Theweleit, Klaus, *Männerphantasien*, 2 vols. (Reinbek, 1980). Printed in English in 1987 and 1989.

Usborne, Cornelie, "The New Woman and Generation Conflict: Perceptions of Young Women's Sexual Mores in the Weimar Republic," in *Generations in Conflict: Youth Revolt and Generation Formation in Germany, 1770–1968*, ed. Mark Roseman (Cambridge, 1995), 137–163.

———. *The Politics of the Body in Weimar Germany: Women's Reproductive Rights and Duties* (Ann Arbor, 1992). Printed in German in 1994.

———. "The Christian Churches and the Regulations of Sexuality in Weimar Germany," in *Disciplines of Faith: Studies in Religion, Politics and Patriarchy*, ed. Jim Obelkevich, Lyndal Roper, and Raphael Samuel (London, 1987), 99–112.

von Ankum, Katharina, ed., *Women in the Metropolis: Gender and Modernity in Weimar Culture* (Berkeley, 1997). Printed in German in 1999.

Wickert, Christl, *Unsere Erwählten: Sozialdemokratische Frauen im Deutschen Reichstag und im Preußischen Landtag 1919 bis 1933*, 2 vols. (Göttingen, 1986).

Woodfin, Carol, "Reluctant Democrats: The Protestant Women's Auxiliary and the German National Assembly Elections of 1919," *Journal of the Historical Society* 4, no. 1 (2004): 71–112.

7. Gendering the History of the Third Reich, the Second World War, and the Holocaust

Amesberger, Helga, Katrin Auer, and Brigitte Halbmayr, *Sexualisierte Gewalt: Weibliche Erfahrungen in NS-Konzentrationslagern* (Vienna, 2004).

Apel, Linde, *Jüdische Frauen im Konzentrationslager Ravensbrück 1939–1945* (Berlin, 2003).

Ascheid, Antje, *Hitler's Heroines: Stardom and Womanhood in Nazi Cinema* (Philadelphia, 2003).

Baer, Elizabeth R., and Myrna Goldenberg, *Experience and Expression: Women, the Nazis, and the Holocaust* (Detroit, 2003).

Baumel, Judith Tydor, "Women's Agency and Survival Strategies during the Holocaust," *Women's Studies International Forum* 22, no. 3 (1999): 329–347.

———. *Double Jeopardy: Gender and the Holocaust* (London, 1998).

———. "Social Interaction among Jewish Women in Crisis during the Holocaust," *Gender & History* 7, no. 1 (1995): 64–84.

Beck, Birgit, *Wehrmacht und sexuelle Gewalt: Sexualverbrechen vor deutschen Militärgerichten 1939–1945* (Paderborn , 2004).

———. "Sexuelle Gewalt und Krieg: Geschlecht, Rasse und der nationalsozialistische Vernichtungsfeldzug gegen die Sowjetunion, 1941–1945," in *Geschlecht hat Methode: Ansätze und Perspektiven in der Frauen- und Geschlechtergeschichte; Beiträge der 9. Schweizerischen Historikerinnentagung 1998*, ed. Veronika Aegerter et al. (Zurich, 1999), 223–234.

Bergen, Doris L., *Twisted Cross: The German Christian Movement in the Third Reich* (Chapel Hill, 1996).

Bock, Gisela, ed., *Genozid und Geschlecht: Jüdische Frauen im nationalsozialistischen Lagersystem* (Frankfurt/M., 2005).

———. "Die Frauen und der Nationalsozialismus," *Geschichte und Gesellschaft* 15 (1989): 563–579.

———. "No Children at Any Cost: Perspectives on Compulsory Sterilization, Sexism and Racism in Nazi Germany," in *Women in Culture and Politics: A Century of Change*, ed. Judith Friedlander et al. (Bloomington, 1986), 286–298.

———. *Zwangssterilisation im Nationalsozialismus: Studien zur Rassenpolitik und Frauenpolitik* (Opladen, 1986).

Bremer, Sigrid, *Muckefuck und Kameradschaft: Mädchenzeit im Dritten Reich: Von der Kinderlandverschickung 1940 bis zum Studium 1946* (Frankfurt/M., 1988).

Brown, Daniel Patrick, *The Camp Women: The Female Auxiliaries Who Assisted the SS in Running the Nazi Concentration Camp System* (Atglen, Pa., 2002).

Brysac, Shareen Blair, *Resisting Hitler: Mildred Harnack and the Red Orchestra* (Oxford, 2000). Printed in German in 2003.

Campbell, D'Ann, "Women in Combat: The World War II Experience in the United States, Great Britain, Germany, and the Soviet Union," *Journal of Military History* 57 (1993): 301–323.

Campt, Tina, *Other Germans: Black Germans and the Politics of Race, Gender, and Memory in the Third Reich*, Ann Arbor, 2004.

Cosner, Shaaron, and Victoria Cosner, *Women under the Third Reich: A Biographical Dictionary* (Westport, Conn., 1998).

Crane, Cynthia, *Divided Lives: The Untold Stories of Jewish-Christian Women in Nazi Germany* (New York, 2000).

Czarnowski, Gabriele, *Das kontrollierte Paar: Ehe- und Sexualpolitik im Nationalsozialismus* (Weinheim, 1991).

Dickinson, Edward Ross, "Biopolitics, Fascism, Democracy: Some Reflections on Our Discourse about 'Modernity,'" *Central European History* 37, no. 1 (2004): 1–48.

Distel, Barbara, ed., *Frauen im Holocaust* (Gerlingen, 2001).

Drolshagen, Ebba D., "Das Schweigen: Das Schicksal der Frauen in besetzten Ländern, die Wehrmachtssoldaten liebten," *Metis* 8, no. 15 (1999): 28–47.

———. *Nicht ungeschoren davongekommen: Das Schicksal der Frauen in den besetzten Ländern, die Wehrmachtssoldaten liebten* (Hamburg, 1998).

Ebbinghaus, Angelika, ed., *Opfer und Täterinnen: Frauenbiographien des Nationalsozialilsmus* (Nördlingen, 1987).

Eschebach, Insa, Sigrid Jacobeit and Silke Wenk, eds., *Gedächtnis und Geschlecht: Deutungsmuster in Darstellungen des nationalsozialistischen Genozids* (Frankfurt/M., 2002).

Fritsche, Maria, *Entziehungen: Österreichische Deserteure und Selbstverstümmler in der Deutschen Wehrmacht* (Vienna, 2004).

Füllberg-Stolberg, Claus, ed., *Frauen in Konzentrationslagern: Bergen-Belsen, Ravensbrück* (Bremen, 1994).

Gehmacher, Johanna, "Zukunft, die nicht vergehen will: Jugenderfahrungen in NS-Organisationen und Lebensentwürfe österreichischer Frauen," in *"Sag' mir, wo die Mädchen sind . . ." Beiträge zur Geschlechtergeschichte der Jugend*, ed. Christina Benninghaus and Kerstin Kohtz (Cologne, 1999), 261–274.

———. *"Völkische Frauenbewegung": Deutschnationale und nationalsozialistische Geschlechterpolitik in Österreich* (Vienna, 1998).

Gelber, Mark H., *Melancholy Pride: Nation, Race, and Gender in the German Literature of Cultural Zionism* (Tübingen, 2000).

Gellately, Robert, and Nathan Stoltzfus, eds., *Social Outsiders in Nazi Germany* (Princeton, 2001).

Gerber, Pia, *Erwerbsbeteiligung von deutschen und ausländischen Frauen 1933–1945 in Deutschland: Entwicklungslinien und Aspekte politischer Steuerung der Frauenerwerbstätigkeit im Nationalsozialismus* (Frankfurt/M., 1996).

Goldenberg, Myrna, "'From a World Beyond': Women in the Holocaust," *Feminist Studies* 22, no. 3 (1996): 667–687.

———. "Testimony, Narrative, and Nightmare: The Experiences of Jewish Women in the Holocaust," in *Active Voices: Women in Jewish Culture*, ed. Maurie Sacks (Urbana, 1995), 94–106.

———. "Different Horrors, Same Hell: Women Remembering the Holocaust," in *Thinking the Unthinkable: Meanings of the Holocaust*, ed. Roger S. Gottlieb (New York, 1990), 150–166.

Gravenhorst, Lerke, and Carmen Tatschmurat, eds., *Töchter-Fragen: NS-Frauen-Geschichte* (Freiburg i. Br., 1990).

Grossmann, Atina, "Women and the Holocaust: Four Recent Titles," *Holocaust and Genocide Studies* 16, no. 1 (2002): 94–108.

Guenther, Irene, *Nazi Chic? Fashioning Women in the Third Reich* (Oxford, 2004).

Hachtmann, Rüdiger, "Industriearbeiterinnen in der deutschen Kriegswirtschaft 1936–1944/45," *Geschichte und Gesellschaft* 19 (1993): 332–366.

Hagemann, Karen, "'Jede Kraft wird gebraucht': Militäreinsatz von Frauen im Ersten und Zweiten Weltkrieg," in *Erster Weltkrieg—Zweiter Weltkrieg: Ein Vergleich; Krieg, Kriegserlebnis, Kriegserfahrung in Deutschland*, ed. Bruno Thoß and Hans-Erich Volkmann (Paderborn, 2002), 79–106.

Harvey, Elizabeth, *Women and the Nazi East: Agents and Witnesses of Germanization* (New Haven, 2003).

———. "'Man muss bloß einen unerschütterlichen Willen haben': Deutsche Kindergärtnerinnen und der nationalsozialistische 'Volkstumskampf' im 'Distrikt Galizien' 1941–1944," *L'Homme* 12, no. 1 (2001): 98–123.

———. "'We Forgot All the Jews and Poles': German Women and the 'Ethnic Struggle' in Nazi-Occupied Poland," *Contemporary European History* 10, no. 3 (2001): 447–461.

———. "'Die deutsche Frau im Osten': 'Rasse,' Geschlecht und öffentlicher Raum im besetzten Polen 1940–1944, *Archiv für Sozialgeschichte* 38 (1998): 191–214.

Heineman, Elizabeth D., "Sexuality and Nazism: The Doubly Unspeakable?" *Journal of the History of Sexuality* 11, no. 1/2 (2002): 22–66.

———. , "Whose Mothers? Generational Difference, War, and the Nazi Cult of Motherhood," *Journal of Women's History* 12, no. 4 (2001): 138–163.

Heinsohn, Kirsten, Barbara Vogel, and Ulrike Weckel, eds., *Zwischen Karriere und Verfolgung: Handlungsräume von Frauen im nationalsozialistischen Deutschland* (Frankfurt/M., 1997).

Herbermann, Nanda, *Der gesegnete Abgrund: Schutzhäftling Nr 6582 im Frauenkonzentrationslager Ravensbrück* (Nürnberg, 1946). Printed in English in 2000.

Herbert, Ulrich, "Forced Laborers in the Third Reich: An Overview," *International Labor and Working-Class History* 58 (2000): 192–218.

Hering, Sabine, and Kurt Schilde, *Das BDM-Werk "Glaube und Schönheit": Die Organisation junger Frauen im Nationalsozialismus* (Berlin, 2000).

Herzog, Dagmar, ed., *Sexuality and German Fascism* (New York, 2005).

———. "Hubris and Hypocrisy, Incitement and Disavowal: Sexuality and German Fascism," *Journal of the History of Sexuality* 11, no. 1/2 (2002): 3–21.

Horowitz, Sara R., "Memory and Testimony of Women Survivors of Nazi Genocide," in *Women of the Word: Jewish Women and Jewish Writing*, ed. Judith R. Baskin (Detroit, 1994), 258–282.

Jellonnek, Burkhard, and Rüdiger Lautmann, eds., *Nationalsozialistischer Terror gegen Homosexuelle: Verdrängt und ungesühnt* (Paderborn, 2002).

Joshi, Vandana, *Gender and Power in the Third Reich: Female Denouncers and the Gestapo (1933–45)* (Basingstoke, 2003).

———. "Changing Perspectives on the Role of Women in Nazi Germany: The Case of Women Denouncers," *Studies in History* 18, no. 2 (2002): 209–230.

———. "The 'Private' Became 'Public': Wives as Denouncers in the Third Reich," *Journal of Contemporary History* 37, no. 3 (2002): 419–435.

Jureit, Ulrike, "Zwischen Ehe und Männerbund: Emotionale und sexuelle Beziehungsmuster im Zweiten Weltkrieg," *WerkstattGeschichte* 22 (1999): 61–73.

Kaltenecker, Siegfried, "Weil aber die vergessenste Fremde unser Körper ist: Über Männer-Körper-Repräsentationen und Faschismus," in *The Body of Gender: Körper, Geschlechter, Identitäten*, ed. Marie-Luise Angerer (Vienna, 1995), 91–109.

Kaplan, Marion A., "Macht Glück glücklich? Jüdische Frauen im Untergrund 1942–1945," *L'Homme* 10, no. 2 (1999): 214–236.

———. *Between Dignity and Despair: Jewish Life in Nazi Germany* (New York, 1998). Printed in German in 2001.

———. "Jewish Women in Nazi Germany: Daily Life, Daily Struggles, 1933–1939," *Feminist Studies* 16, no. 3 (1990): 579–606.

Köhler, Heike, *Deutsch—Evangelisch—Frau: Meta Eyl—eine Theologin im Spannungsfeld zwischen nationalsozialistischer Reichskirche und evangelischer Frauenbewegung* (Neukirchen-Vluyn, 2003).

Koonz, Claudia, *The Nazi Conscience* (Cambridge, Mass., 2003).

———. *Mothers in the Fatherland: Women, the Family and Nazi Politics* (London, 1986). Printed in German in 1991.

———. "Nazi Women before 1933: Rebels against Emancipation," *Social Science Quarterly* 56 (1976): 553–563.

Kühne, Thomas, Kameradschaft: *Die Soldaten des nationalsozialistischen Krieges und das 20. Jahrhundert* (Göttingen, 2006).

———. "Gruppenkohäsion und Kameradschaftsmythos in der Wehrmacht," in *Die Wehrmacht: Mythos und Realität*, ed. Rolf-Dieter Müller and Hans-Erich Volkmann (Munich, 1999), 534–549.

———. "Zwischen Männerbund und Volksgemeinschaft: Hitlers Soldaten und der Mythos der Kameradschaft," *Archiv für Sozialgeschichte* 38 (1998): 165–189.

———. "Kameradschaft—'das Beste im Leben des Mannes': Die deutschen Soldaten des Zweiten Weltkrieges in erfahrungs- und geschlechtergeschichtlicher Perspektive," *Geschichte und Gesellschaft* 22 (1996): 504–529.

Kundrus, Birthe, "Forbidden Company: Romantic Relationships between Germans and Foreigners, 1939–1945," *Journal of the History of Sexuality* 11, no. 1/2 (2002): 201–222.

———. "Loyal, weil satt: Die innere Front im Zweiten Weltkrieg," *Mittelweg 36* 6, no. 5 (1997): 80–93.

Linden, R. Ruth, *Making Stories, Making Selves: Feminist Reflections on the Holocaust* (Columbus, 1993).

Livi, Massimiliano, *Gertrud Scholtz-Klink. Die Reichsfrauenführerin. Politische Handlungsräume und Identitätsprobleme der Frauen im Nationalsozialismus am Beispiel der Führerin aller deutschen Frauen* (Münster, 2005).

Maierhof, Gudrun, *Selbstbehauptung im Chaos: Frauen in der jüdischen Selbsthilfe 1933–1943* (Frankfurt/M., 2002).

Meinen, Insa, *Wehrmacht und Prostitution im besetzen Frankreich* (Bremen, 2002).

———, "Wehrmacht und Prostitution—Zur Reglementierung der Geschlechterbeziehungen durch die deutsche Militärverwaltung im besetzten Frankreich 1940–1944," *1999. Zeitschrift für Sozialgeschichte des 20. und 21. Jahrhunderts* 14, no. 2 (1999): 35–55.

Moeller, Robert G., "What Did You Do in the War, Mutti? Courageous Women, Compassionate Commanders, and Stories of the Second World War," *German History* 22 (2004): 563–594.

Morrison, Jack G., *Ravensbrück: Everyday Life in a Women's Concentration Camp 1935–45* (Princeton, 2000). Printed in German in 2000.

Mushaben, Joyce Marie, "Memory and the Holocaust: Processing the Past through a Gendered Lens," *History of the Human Sciences* 17, no. 2/3 (2004): 147–185.

Neary, Brigitte U., Holle Schneider-Ricks, eds., *Voices of Loss and Courage: German Women Recount Their Expulsion from East Central Europe, 1944–1950* (Rockport, Maine, 2002).

Niethammer, Ortrun, ed., *Frauen und Nationalsozialismus: Historische und kulturgeschichtliche Positionen* (Osnabrück, 1996).

Nolan, Mary, "Air Wars," *Central European History* 38, no. 1 (2005): 7–40.

Ofer, Dalia, and Lenore J. Weitzman, eds., *Women and the Holocaust* (New Haven, 1998).

Owings, Alison, *Frauen: Germany Women Recall the Third Reich* (New Brunswick, 1993). Printed in German in 1999.

Paul, Christa, *Zwangsprostitution: Staatlich errichtete Bordelle im Nationalsozialismus* (Berlin, 1994).

Pine, Lisa, *Nazi Family Policy, 1933–1945* (Oxford, 1997).

Quack, Sibylle, ed., *Between Sorrow and Strength: Women Refugees of the Nazi Period* (Cambridge, 1995).

———. *Zuflucht Amerika: Zur Sozialgeschichte der Emigration deutsch-jüdischer Frauen in die USA 1933–1945* (Bonn, 1995).

Reagin, Nancy R., "Marktordnung and Autarkic Housekeeping: Housewives and Private Consumption under the Four-Year Plan, 1936–1939," *German History* 19, no. 2 (2001): 162–184.

Reese, Dagmar, *Straff, aber nicht stramm—herb, aber nicht derb: Zur Vergesellschaftung von Mädchen durch den Bund Deutscher Mädel im sozialkulturellen Vergleich zweier Milieus* (Weinheim, 1989).

Remmler, Karen, "Gender Identities and the Remembrance of the Holocaust," *Women in German Yearbook* 10 (1994): 167–187.

Richter, Isabel, *Hochverratsprozesse als Herrschaftspraxis im Nationalsozialismus: Frauen und Männer von dem Volksgerichtshof, 1934–1939* (Münster, 2001).

———. "Das Abseits als unsicherer Ort: Gnadengesuche politischer Gefangener im Nationalsozialismus als autobiographische Texte," *Österreichische Zeitschrift für Geschichtswissenschaften* 13, no. 2 (2002): 57–83.

———. "Entwürfe des Widerstehens: Männer und Frauen aus dem linken Widerstand in Verhören der Gestapo 1934–1939," *WerkstattGeschichte*, 26 (2000): 47–70.

Ringelheim, Joan Miriam, "Women and the Holocaust: A Reconsideration of Research," *Signs* 10 (1985): 741–761.

———. "The Unethical and the Unspeakable: Women and the Holocaust," *Simon Wiesenthal Center Annual* 1 (1984): 69–87.

Rittner, Carol, and John K. Roth, eds., *Different Voices: Women and the Holocaust* (New York, 1993).

Roseman, Mark, *A Past in Hiding: Memory and Survival in Nazi Germany* (New York, 2001).

Ross, Chad, *Naked Germany: Health, Race, and the Nation* (New York, 2005).

Rüdiger, Jutta, ed., *Zur Problematik von Soldatinnen: Der Kampfeinsatz von Flakhelferinnen im 2. Weltkrieg; Berichte und Dokumentationen* (Lindhorst, 1987).

Rupp, Leila J., "'I Don't Call that Volksgemeinschaft': Women, Class and War in Nazi Germany," in *Women, War, and Revolution*, ed. Carol R. Berkin and Clara M. Lovett (New York, 1980), 37–53.

———. "Mothers of the Volk: The Images of Women in Nazi Germany," *Signs* 3 (1979): 362–379.

———. *Mobilizing Women for War: Germany and American Propaganda, 1939–1945* (Princeton, 1978).

Sachse, Carola, *Siemens, der Nationalsozialismus und die moderne Familie: Eine Untersuchung zur sozialen Rationalisierung in Deutschland im 20. Jahrhundert* (Hamburg, 1990).

Saidel, Rochelle G., *The Jewish Women of Ravensbrück Concentration Camp* (Madison, 2004).

———. "Women's Experiences during the Holocaust: New Books in Print," *Yad Vashem Studies* 28 (2000): 363–378.

Scheck, *Raffael, Hitler's African Victims: The German Army Massacres of 1940* (Cambridge, 2006).

Schikorra, Christa, *Kontinuitäten der Ausgrenzung: "Asoziale" Häftlinge im Frauen-Konzentration-slager Ravensbrück* (Berlin, 2001).

Schoppmann, Claudia, *Verbotene Verhältnisse: Frauenliebe 1938–1945* (Berlin, 1999).

———. *Zeit der Maskierung: Lebensgeschichten lesbischer Frauen im "Dritten Reich,"* (Berlin, 1993). Printed in English in 1996.

Schupetta, Ingrid, *Frauen- und Ausländererwerbstätigkeit in Deutschland von 1939 bis 1945* (Cologne, 1983).

Schwarz, Gudrun, *Eine Frau an seiner Seite: Ehefrauen in der "SS-Sippengemeinschaft,"* (Hamburg, 1997).

Schwarze, Gisela, *Kinder, die nicht zählten: Ostarbeiterinnen und ihre Kinder im Zweiten Weltkrieg* (Essen, 1997).

Schwertfeger, Ruth, *Women of Theresienstadt: Voices from a Concentration Camp* (Oxford, 1989).

Stephenson, Jill, *Women in Nazi Germany* (Harlow, 2001).

———. "Propaganda, Autarky and the German Housewife," in *Nazi Propaganda: The Power and the Limitations*, ed. David Welch (London, 1983), 117–142.

———. "Middle-Class Women and Nationalist Socialist 'Service,'" *History* 67 (1982): 32–44.

———. "Women's Labor Service in Nazi Germany," *Central European History* 15 (1982): 241–265.

———. *The Nazi Organisation of Women* (London, 1981).

———. "Reichsbund der Kinderreichen: The League of Large Families in the Population Policy of Nazi Germany," *European Studies Review* 9 (1979): 350–374.

———. *Women in Nazi Society* (London, 1975).

Stibbe, Matthew, *Women in the Third Reich* (London, 2003).

Stoltzfus, Nathan, *Resistance of the Heart: Intermarriage and the Rosenstrasse Protest in Nazi Germany* (New York, 1996). Printed in German in 1999.

Tec, Nechama, *Resilience and Courage: Women, Men and the Holocaust* (New Haven, 2003).

———. "Sex Distinctions and Passing as Christians during the Holocaust," *East European Quarterly* 18, no. 1 (1984): 113–123.

Wickert, Christl, ed., *Frauen gegen die Diktatur: Widerstand und Verfolgung im nationalsozialistischen Deutschland* (Berlin, 1995).

Wildmann, Daniel, *Begehrte Körper: Konstruktion und Inszenierung des "arischen" Männerkörpers im "Dritten Reich,"* (Würzburg, 1998).

Willmot Louise, "Women in the Third Reich: The Auxiliary Military Service Law of 1944," *German History* 2 (1985): 10–20.

Winkler, Dörte, *Frauenarbeit im "Dritten Reich,"* (Hamburg, 1977).

Wobbe, Theresa, ed., *Nach Osten: Verdeckte Spuren nationalsozialistischer Verbrechen* (Frankfurt/M., 1992).

8. Gender in Postwar German History

Barnouw, Dagmar, *The War in the Empty Air: Victims, Perpetrators, and Postwar Germans* (Bloomington, 2005).

Germany 1945: Views of War and Violence (Bloomington, 1996).

Bauer, Ingrid, "Die 'Ami-Braut'—Platzhalterin für das Abgespaltene? Zur (De)Konstruktion eines Stereotyps der österreichischen Nachkriegsgeschichte 1945–1955," *L'Homme* 7 (1996): 107–121.

Biddiscombe, Perry, "Dangerous Liaisons: The Anti-fraternization Movement in the U.S. Occupation Zones of Germany and Austria, 1945–1948," *Journal of Social History* 34, no. 3 (2001): 611–647.

Biess, Frank, *Homecomings: Returning POWs and the Legacies of Defeat in Postwar Germany* (Princeton, 2005).

———. "'Pioneers of a New Germany?' Returning POWs from the Soviet Union and the Making of East German Citizens, 1945–1950," *Central European History* 32 (1999): 143–180.

Böttger, Barbara, *Das Recht auf Gleichheit und Differenz: Elisabeth Selbert und der Kampf der Frauen um Art. 3.2 Grundgesetz* (Münster, 1990).

Brauerhoch, Annette, *Fräuleins und GI's* (Frankfurt/M., 2006).

Bridge, Helen, *Women's Writing and Historiography in the GDR* (Oxford, 2002).

Brückner, Hannah, *Gender Inequality in the Life Course: Social Change and Stability in West Germany, 1975–1995* (Hawthorne, NY, 2004).

Budde, Gunilla-Friedcrike, "Der Körper der 'sozialistischen Frauenpersönlichkeit': Weiblichkeits-Vorstellungen in der SBZ und der frühen DDR," *Geschichte und Gesellschaft* 26, no. 4 (2000): 602–628.

———. *Frauen der Intelligenz: Akademikerinnen in der DDR, 1945–1975* (Göttingen, 2003).

Carpenter, K. M. N., "'For Mothers Only': Mothers' Convalescent Homes and Modernizing Maternal Ideology in 1950s West Germany," *Journal of Social History* 34, no. 4 (2001): 863–893.

Carter, Erica, *How German Is She? Postwar West German Reconstruction and the Consuming Woman* (Ann Arbor, 1997).

Davis, Belinda J., "'Women's Strength against Their Crazy Male Power': Gendered Language in the West German Peace Movement of the 1980s," in *Frieden-Gewalt-Geschlecht: Friedens- und Konfliktforschung als Geschlechterforschung*, ed. Jennifer Anne Davy et. al. (Essen, 2005), 250–272.

———. "The Gender of War and Peace: Rhetoric in the West German Peace Movement of the Early 1980s," *Mitteilungsblatt des Instituts für soziale Bewegungen* 32 (2004): 83–114.

———. "Activism from Starbuck to Starbucks, or Terror: What's in a Name?," *Radical History Review* 85 (2003): 37–57.

Domansky, Elisabeth, and Jutta de Jong, *Der lange Schatten des Krieges: Deutsche Lebens-Geschichten nach 1945* (Münster, 2000).

Domentat, Tamara, *"Hallo Fräulein": Deutsche Frauen und amerikanische Soldaten* (Berlin, 1998).

Eifler, Christine, "Bewaffneter Frieden: Zum Konzept der Friedenssicherung in der DDR und seinen geschlechterpolitischen Implikationen," in *Frieden-Gewalt-Geschlecht: Friedens- und Konfliktforschung als Geschlechterforschung*, ed. Jennifer A. Davy et. al. (Essen, 2005), 210–226.

———. "'Ewig unreif': Geschlechtsrollenklischees in der Armeerundschau," in *Zwischen"Mosaik" und "Einheit": Zeitschriften in der DDR*, ed. Simone Barck, Martina Langermann, and Siegfried Lokatis (Berlin, 1999), 180–188.

Esser, Raingard, "'Language no Obstacle': War Brides in the German Press, 1945–49," *Women's History Review* 12, no. 4 (2003): 577–603.

Fehrenbach, Heide, *Race After Hitler: Black Occupation Children in Postwar Germany and America* (Princeton, 2005).

———. "Rehabilitating Fatherland: Race and German Remasculinization," *Signs* 24, no. 1 (1998): 107–127.

———. *Cinema in Democratizing Germany: Reconstructing National Identity after Hitler* (Chapel Hill, 1995).

Ferree, Myra Marx, "'The Time of Chaos Was the Best': Feminist Moblization and Demobilization in East Germany," *Gender & Society* 8, no. 4 (1994): 597–623.

Gerhard, Ute, "Westdeutsche Frauenbewegung: Zwischen Autonomie und dem Recht auf Gleichheit," *Feministische Studien* 10, no. 2 (1992): 35–55.

Goedde, Petra, *GIs and Germans: Culture, Gender, and Foreign Relations, 1945–1949* (New Haven, 2003).

Goltermann, Svenja, "Die Beherrschung der Männlichkeit: Zur Deutung psychischer Leiden bei den Heimkehrern des Zweiten Weltkrieges 1945–1956," *Feministische Studien* 18, no. 2 (2000): 7–19.

———. "Verletzte Körper oder 'Building National Bodies': Kriegsheimkehrer, 'Krankheit' und Psychiatrie in der westdeutschen Nachkriegsgesellschaft, 1945–1955," *WerkstattGeschichte* 24 (1999): 83–98.

Gravenhorst, Lerke, *Moral und Geschlecht: Die Aneignung der NS-Erbschaft; Ein soziologischer Beitrag zu Selbstverständigungen vor allem in Deutschland* (Freiburg i.Br., 1997).

Grossmann, Atina, "Victims, Villains, and Survivors: Gendered Perceptions and Self-Perceptions of Jewish Displaced Persons in Occupied Postwar Germany," *Journal of the History of Sexuality* 11, no 1, 2 (2002): 291–318.

———. "Trauma, Memory, and Motherhood: Germans and Jewish Displaced Persons in Post-Nazi Germany, 1945–1949," *Archiv für Sozialgeschichte* 38 (1998): 215–239.

———. "A Question of Silence: The Rape of German Women by Occupation Soldiers," in *West Germany under Construction: Politics, Society, and Culture in the Adenauer Era*, ed. Robert G. Moeller (Ann Arbor, 1997), 33–52.

Hagemann, Karen, "Between Ideology and Economy: The "Time Politics" of Child Care and Public Education in the Two Germanies," *Social Politics*, 13, no. 1 (2006): 217–260.

Harsch, Donna, "Approach/Avoidance: Communists and Women in East Germany, 1945–9," *Social History* 25, no. 2 (2000): 156–182.

Heineman, Elizabeth D., "Gender, Sexuality, and Coming to Terms with the Nazi Past," *Central European History* 38, no. 1 (2005): 41–74.

———. "Single Motherhood and Maternal Employment in Diveded Germany: Ideology, Policy, and Social Pressures in the 1950s," *Journal of Women's History* 12, no. 3 (2000): 146–172.

———. *What Difference Does a Husband Make? Women and Marital Status in Nazi and Postwar Germany* (Berkeley, 1999).

———. "Complete Families, Half Families, No Families at All: Female-Headed Households and the Reconstruction of the Family in the Early Federal Republic," *Central European History* 29, no. 1 (1996): 19–60.

———. "The Hour of the Woman: Memories of Germany's 'Crisis Years' and West German National Identity," *American Historical Review* 101, no. 2 (1996): 354–395.

Helwig, Gisela, and Hildegard Maria Nickel, eds., *Frauen in Deutschland 1945–1992* (Berlin, 1993).

Herzog, Dagmar, *Sex after Fascism: Memory and Morality in Twentieth-Century Germany* (Princeton, 2005).

———. "'Pleasure, Sex, and Politics Belong Together': Post-Holocaust Memory and the Sexual Revolution in West Germany," *Critical Inquiry* 24, no. 2 (1998): 393–444.

Höhn, Maria, *GIs and Fräuleins: The German-American Encounter in 1950s West Germany* (Chapel Hill, 2002).

Holland-Cunz, Barbara, *Die alte neue Frauenfrage* (Frankfurt/M., 2003).

Hornung, Ela, "'Penelope und Odysseus': Zur Paarstruktur von Heimkehrer und wartender Frau in der Nachkriegszeit," in *Eiszeit der Erinnerung: Vom Vergessen der eigenen Schuld*, ed. Ulf Brunnbauer (Vienna, 1999), 65–83.

Jerome, Roy, ed., *Conceptions of Postwar German Masculinity* (Albany, NY, 2001).

Kätzel, Ute, *Die 68erinnen: Porträt einer rebellischen Frauengeneration* (Berlin, 2002).

Kolbe, Wiebke, *Elternschaft im Wohlfahrtsstaat: Schweden und die Bundesrepublik im Vergleich 1945–2000* (Frankfurt/M., 2002).

Kreutzer, Susanne, *Vom "Liebesdienst" zum modernen Frauenberuf: Die Reform der Krankenpflege nach 1945* (Frankfurt/M., 2005).

Kucera, David, *Gender, Growth, and Trade: The Miracle Economies of the Postwar Years* (London, 2001).

Merkel, Ina, *Utopie und Bedürfnis: Die Geschichte der Konsumkultur in der DDR* (Cologne, 1999).

Mertens, Lothar, *Wider die sozialistische Familiennorm: Ehescheidungen in der DDR 1950–1989* (Opladen, 1998).

Meyer, Kathrin, *Entnazifizierung von Frauen: Die Internierungslager der US-Zone 1945–1952* (Berlin, 2004).

Miethe, Ingrid, *Frauen in der DDR-Opposition: Lebens- und kollektivgeschichtliche Verläufe in einer Frauenfriedensgruppe* (Opladen, 1999).

———. "From 'Mothers of the Revolution' to 'Fathers of Unification': Concepts of Politics among Women Activists following German Unification," *Social Politics* 6, no. 1 (1999): 1–22.

Möding, Nori, "Die Stunde der Frauen? Frauen und Frauenorganisationen des bürgerlichen Lagers," in *Von Stalingrad zur Währungsreform: Zur Sozialgeschichte des Umbruchs in Deutschland*, ed. Martin Broszat, Klaus-Dietmar Henke, and Hans Woller (Munich, 1988), 619–647.

Moeller, Robert G., „Heimkehr ins Vaterland: Die Remaskulinisierung Westdeutschlands in den fünfziger Jahren," *Militärgeschichtliche Zeitschrift* 60, no. 2 (2001): 403–436.

———. "'The Last Soldiers of the Great War' and Tales of Family Reunions in the Federal Republic of Germany," *Signs* 24, no. 1 (1998): 129–145.

———. "The 'Remasculinization' of Germany in the 1950s: Introduction," *Signs* 24, no. 1 (1998): 101–106.

———. ed., *West Germany under Construction: Politics, Society, and Culture in the Adenauer Era* (Ann Arbor, 1997).

———. *Protecting Motherhood: Women and the Family in the Politics of Postwar West Germany* (Berkeley, 1993). Printed in German in 1997.

———. "War Stories: The Search for a Usable Past in the Federal Republic of Germany," *American Historical Review* 101 (1996): 1008–1048.

———. "'The Homosexual Man is a 'Man,' the Homosexual Woman is a 'Woman'": Sex, Society, and the Law in Postwar West Germany," *Journal of the History of Sexuality* 4, no. 3 (1994): 395–429.

———. "The State of Women's Welfare in European Welfare States," *Social History* 19, no. 3 (1994): 384–393.

———. "Protecting Mother's Work: From Production to Reproduction in Postwar West Germany," *Journal of Social History* 22, no. 3 (1989): 413–437.

———. "Reconstructing the Family in Reconstruction Germany: Women and Social Policy in the Federal Republic, 1949–1955," *Feminist Studies* 15, no. 1 (1989): 137–169.

Mühlhäuser, Regina, "Massenvergewaltigungen in Berlin 1945 im Gedächtnis betroffener Frauen: Zur Verwobenheit von nationalistischen, rassistischen und geschlechtsspezifischen Diskursen," in *Geschlecht hat Methode: Ansätze und Perspektiven in der Frauen- und Geschlechtergeschichte. Beiträge der 9. Schweizerischen Historikerinnentagung 1998*, ed. Veronika Aegerter et al. (Zurich, 1999), 235–246.

Neumann, Vera, *Nicht der Rede wert: Die Privatisierung der Kriegsfolgen in der frühen Bundesrepublik: Lebensgeschichtliche Erinnerungen* (Münster, 1999).

Niehuss, Merith, *Familie, Frau und Gesellschaft: Studien zur Strukturgeschichte der Familie in Westdeutschland 1945–1960* (Göttingen, 2001).

Notz, Gisela, *Frauen in der Mannschaft: Sozialdemokratinnen im Parlamentarischen Rat und im Deutschen Bundestag, 1948/49–1957* (Bonn, 2003).

———. "Klara Marie Fassbinder and Women's Peace Activities in the 1950s and 1960s," *Journal of Women's History* 13, no. 3 (2001): 98–123.

Pence, Katherine, "'You as a Woman Will Understand': Consumption, Gender and the Relationship between State and Citizenry in the GDR's Crises of 17 June 1953," *German History* 19, no. 2 (2001): 218–252.

Petö, Andrea, "Stimmen des Schweigens: Erinnerungen an Vergewaltigungen in den Hauptstädten des 'ersten Opfers' (Wien) und 'letzten Verbündeten' Hitlers (Budapest) 1945," *Zeitschrift für Geschichtswissenschaft* 47 (1999): 892–913.

Poiger, Uta G., *Jazz, Rock and Rebels: Cold War Politics and American Culture in a Divided Germany* (Berkeley, 2000).

———. "A New, 'Western' Hero? Reconstructing German Masculinity in the 1950s," *Signs* 24, no. 1 (1998): 147–162.

Poudrus, Kirsten, "Ein fixiertes Trauma—Massenvergewaltigungen bei Kriegsende in Berlin," *Feministische Studien* 13, no. 2 (1995): 120–129.

Remmler, Karen, "Gender Identities and the Remembrance of the Holocaust," *Women in German Yearbook* 10 (1994): 167–187.

Rupieper, Hermann-Josef, "Bringing Democracy to the Frauleins: Frauen als Zielgruppe der amerikanischen Demokratisierungspolitik in Deutschland 1945–1952," *Geschichte und Gesellschaft* 17, no. 1 (1991): 61–91.

Sachse, Carola, *Der Hausarbeitstag: Gerechtigkeit und Gleichberechtigung in Ost und West 1939–1994* (Göttingen, 2002).

———. "Normalarbeitstag und Hausarbeitstag: (Ost)deutsche Variationen einer Mesalliance, 1943–1991," *L'Homme* 11, no. 1 (2000): 49–64.

Sander, Helke, and Barbara Johr, eds., *BeFreier und Befreite: Krieg, Vergewaltigungen, Kinder* (Munich, 1992).

Schaser, Angelika, ed., *Erinnerungskartelle: Zur Konstruktion von Autobiographien nach 1945* (Bochum, 2003).

Schissler, Hanna, ed., *The Miracle Years: A Cultural History of West Germany, 1949–1968* (Princeton, 2001).

Schüle, Annegret, *"Die Spinne": Die Erfahrungsgeschichte weiblicher Industriearbeit im VEB Leipziger Baumwollspinnerei* (Leipzig, 2001).

Schüller, Elke, *Wer stimmt bestimmt? Elisabeth Selbert und die Frauenpolitik der Nachkriegszeit* (Wiesbaden, 1996).

Schulz, Kristina, *Der lange Atem der Provokation: Die Frauenbewegung in der Bundesrepublik und in Frankreich 1968–1976* (Frankfurt/M., 2002).

Schwarz, Uta, *Wochenschau, westdeutsche Identität und Geschlecht in den fünfziger Jahren* (Frankfurt/M., 2002).

Spicka, Mark E., "Gender, Political Discourse, and the CDU/CSU Vision of the Economic Miracle, 1949–1957," *German Studies Review* 25, no. 2 (2002): 305–332.

Stoehr, Irene, "Kalter Krieg und Geschlecht: Überlegungen zu einer friedenshistorischen Forschungslücke," in *Perspektiven der historischen Friedensforschung*, ed. Benjamin Ziemann (Essen, 2002), 133–145.

———. "Phalanx der Frauen? Wiederaufrüstung und Weiblichkeit in Westdeutschland 1950–1957," in *Soziale Konstruktionen—Militär und Geschlechterverhältnis*, ed. Christine Eifler and Ruth Seifert (Münster, 1999), 187–204.

———. "'Feministischer Antikommunismus' und weibliche Staatsbürgerschaft in der Gründungsdekade der Bundesrepublik Deutschland," *Feministische Studien* 16, no. 1 (1998): 86–94.

———. "Der Mütterkongreß fand nicht statt: Frauenbewegung, Staatsmänner und Kalter Krieg 1950," *WerkstattGeschichte* 17 (1997): 66–82.

Tröger, Annemarie, "'Between Rape and Prostitution': Survival Strategies and Chances of Emancipation for Berlin Women after World War II," in *Women in Culture and Politics: A Century of Change*, ed. Judith Friedlander et al. (Bloomington, 1986), 97–117.

von Oertzen, Christine, *Teilzeitarbeit und die Lust am Zuverdienen: Geschlechterpolitik und gesell-schaftlicher Wandel in Westdeutschland 1948–1969* (Göttingen, 1999). Printed in English in 2005.

———. "Abschied vom Normalarbeitstag: Die rechtliche Einbürgerung der Teilzeitarbeit in Westdeutschland, 1955–1969," *L'Homme* 11, no. 1 (2000): 65–82.

Weckel, Ulrike, and Edgar Wolfrum, eds., *"Bestien" und "Befehlsempfänger": Frauen und Männer in NS-Prozessen nach 1945* (Göttingen, 2003).

Wiggershaus, Renate, *Geschichte der Frauen und der Frauenbewegung in der Bundesrepublik Deutsch-land und in der Deutschen Demokratischen Republik nach 1945* (Wuppertal, 1979).

Zachmann, Karin, *Mobilisierung der Frauen: Technik, Geschlecht und Kalter Krieg in der DDR* (Frankfurt/M., 2004).

———. "A Socialist Consumption Junction: Debating the Mechanization of Housework in East Germany, 1956–1957," *Technology and Culture* 43, no. 1 (2002): 73–99.

Notes

1. The editors would like to thank all authors for their cooperation in creating this selection.

CONTRIBUTING AUTHORS

Ann Taylor Allen is Professor of History at the University of Louisville, Kentucky. Her publications include *Satire and Society in Wilhelmine Germany: Simplicissimus and Kladderadatsch, 1890–1914* (1984), and *Feminism and Motherhood in Germany, 1800–1914* (1991); the latter appeared in a German translation in 2001. In addition, she has published many articles on the history of German women's movements, some of which have a comparative focus. Her new book *Feminism and Motherhood in Western Europe, 1890–1970: The Maternal Dilemma* was published by Palgrave-Macmillan in 2005.

Benjamin Maria Baader is Assistant Professor of European History and Jewish History at the University of Manitoba, Canada. He holds a doctorate in Jewish history from Columbia University, has taught at Indiana University, Bloomington, and the University of Toronto, and was the recipient of the postdoctoral fellowship of the American Academy for Jewish Research as well as of the Killam Postdoctoral Fellowship at Dalhousie University. He has published several articles on Jewish gender history in Germany and America, and his book, *Gender, Judaism, and Bourgeois Culture in Germany, 1800–1870* (2006) won the Koret Foundation Jewish Studies Publication Award.

Kathleen Canning is Arthur F. Thurnau Professor of History, Women's Studies, and German and Director of the Eisenberg Institute of Historical Studies at the University of Michigan. She was North American co-editor of *Gender & History* from 1998 through 2002. Her first book *Languages of Labor and Gender: Female Factory Work in Germany, 1850–1914* (1996) was published by Cornell University Press in 1996 and reissued in paperback by the University of Michigan Press in 2002. She is co-editor with Sonya Rose of the volume, *Gender, Citizenships and Subjectivities* (2002). Her recent publications have examined themes such as gender and citizenship during the First World War and Weimar Republic, the category of experience, and the history of the body. Her book of essays, *Gender History in Practice: Historical Perspectives on Bodies, Class, and Citizenship*, appeared with Cornell University Press in 2006.

She is currently at work on a book project entitled *Embodied Citizenships: The Aftermath of War and Revolution in Germany*.

Belinda Davis is Associate Professor of History at Rutgers University. Her work on gender, protest, and movements, spanning the twentieth century, has focused particularly on the World War I era and on the 1960s and 1970s. Her recent book is entitled *Home Fires Burning: Food, Politics, and Everyday Life in World War I Berlin* (Chapel Hill, 2000). She is currently a co-investigator of a multiyear Volkswagen Stiftung grant, *Das Fremde im Eigenen: Interkultureller Austausch und kollektive Identitäten in der Revolte der 1960er Jahre*.

Atina Grossmann is Professor of History in the Faculty of Humanities of the Cooper Union for the Advancement of Science and Art in New York City. Her publications include *When Biology Became Destiny: Women in Weimar and Nazi Germany* (ed. with Renate Bridenthal and Marion Kaplan, 1984); *Reforming Sex: The German Movement for Birth Control and Abortion Reform, 1920–1950* (1995), and *Crimes of War: Guilt and Denial in the Twentieth Century* (ed. with Omar Bartov and Mary Nolan, 2001). Her book *Jews, Germans and Allies: Close Encounters in Occupied Germany* will be published by Princeton University Press in 2007.

Karen Hagemann is James G. Kenan Distinguished Professor of History at the University of North Carolina at Chapel Hill. She has published on the history of welfare states, labor culture, and women's movements, as well as the history of the nation, the military, and war. Her books include: *Frauenalltag und Männerpolitik: Alltagsleben und gesellschaftliches Handeln von Arbeiterfrauen in der Weimarer Republik* (1990); *Gendered Nations: Nationalisms and Gender Order in the Long Nineteenth Century* (ed. with Ida Blom and Catherine Hall, 2000); *Home/Front: Military and Gender in 20th Century Germany* (ed. with Stefanie Schüler-Springorum, 2002; in German, 2002); *"Mannlicher Mut und Teutsche Ehre." Nation, Militär und Geschlecht zur Zeit der Antinapoleonischen Kriege Preussens* (2002); *Masculinities in Politics and War: Gendering Modern History* (ed. with Stefan Dudink and John Tosh, 2004). *Frieden-Gewalt-Geschlecht: Friedens-und Konfliktforschung als Geschlechterforschung* (ed. with Jennifer Davy and Ute Kätzel, 2005).

Claudia A. Koonz is Professor of History at the History Department of Duke University. Her major books are: *Becoming Visible: Women in European History* (ed. with Renate Bridenthal and Susan M. Stuard, revised ed., 1987); *Mothers in the Fatherland: Women, the Family, and Politics in Nazi Germany* (1987; revised German edition, *Mütter im Vaterland* and French, Japanese, Italian, and Dutch translations); *The Nazi Conscience* (2003).

Birthe Kundrus is Senior Researcher at the Hamburg Institute for Social Research and teaches Modern German and European History, Gender History and Colonial History at the University of Oldenburg. Currently she holds the Maria-Goeppert-Mayer Visiting professorship for international Women and Gender Studies at the University of Hannover. Her most recent books are: *Kriegerfrauen. Familienpolitik und Geschlechterverhältnisse im Ersten und Zweiten Weltkrieg* (1995); *„Phantasiereiche."* Zur Kulturgeschichte des deutschen Kolonialismus (ed., 2003); *Moderne Imperialisten. Das Kaiserreich im Spiegel seiner Kolonien* (2003).

Robert Moeller is Professor for German and European History at the University of California, Irvine where he also directs a teacher professional development project for middle and high school history teachers. He has written about the social and political history of twentieth-century Germany, and his books include: *Protecting Motherhood: Women and the Family in the Politics of Postwar West Germany* (1993); and *War Stories: The Search for a Usable Past in the Federal Republic of Germany* (2001).

Jean H. Quataert is Professor of History and Women's Studies at Binghamton University, State University of New York. Her most recent book is entitled *Staging Philanthropy: Patriotic Women and the National Imagination in Dynastic Germany, 1813–1916* (2001). From this gendered study of the politics of charity and relief, she has turned to related questions of rights and international law. Quataert received a German Marshall Fund Research grant, 2001–2002, to begin a new archival project on women and humanitarianism, tracing the early international rights communities in Europe and North America from 1864 to 1919. She has just published an essay-pamphlet for the American Historical Association's project on global and comparative history entitled *The Gendering of Human Rights in the International Systems of Law in the Twentieth Century* (2006). She also is finishing a book on *Advocating Dignity: Historical Perspectives on Human Rights Struggles in Global Politics, 1945–2005*, which currently is under consideration.

Angelika Schaser is Professor for Modern History at the University of Hamburg. Her recent publications include studies of Transylvanian social and economic history from the sixteenth to the eighteenth century, minorities, collective memory, and nation and gender in the German history of the nineteenth and twentieth centuries. Her most recent books are *Helene Lange und Gertrud Bäumer. Eine Politische Lebensgemeinschaft* (2000); *Zur Aktualität einer Klassikerin: Käte Hamburger* Querelles. Jahrbuch für Frauenforschung, vol. 8, ed. with Johanna Bossinade, (2003); *Erinnerungskartelle. Zur Konstruktion von Autobiographien nach 1945* (ed., 2003), and *Frauenbewegung in Deutschland 1848 bis 1933* (2006).

Index of Names

Subject Index

Breinigsville, PA USA
02 September 2010
244742BV00004B/14/P